MW00412862

IN SEARCH OF OLD PEKING

Ming Emperor Yung Lo

IN SEARCH
OF
OLD PEKING

L. C. ARLINGTON AND
WILLIAM LEWISOHN

With an Introduction by Geremie Barmé

HONG KONG
OXFORD UNIVERSITY PRESS
OXFORD NEW YORK

Oxford University Press

Oxford New York Toronto
Petaling Jaya Singapore Hong Kong Tokyo
Delhi Bombay Calcutta Madras Karachi
Nairobi Dar es Salaam Cape Town
Melbourne Auckland

and associated companies in
Berlin Ibadan

First published by Henri Vetch, Peking 1935
© L.C. Arlington and William Lewisohn 1935
Introduction © Oxford University Press 1987

This edition reprinted, by arrangement with Kelly and Walsh, Limited,
and with the addition of an Introduction,
by Oxford University Press 1987
Reissued in Oxford Paperbacks 1991
Second impression 1991
Published in the United States
by Oxford University Press Inc., New York

ISBN 0 19 585395 4

British Library Cataloguing in Publication Data
Arlington, L. C. (Lewis Charles) b. 1859
In search of Old Peking.
1. China. Peking. Description & travel 1927-1949
I. Title   II. Lewisohn, William
915.11 560442
ISBN 0-19-585395-4

Library of Congress Catalog Card Number
87-28218

Printed in Hong Kong
Published by Oxford University Press, Warwick House, Hong Kong

INTRODUCTION

IN 1933, even as this enthralling book was being written, the
Nationalist government ordered the removal of the vast treasures of
the Imperial Palace in Peking (Beijing) to the south for 'safe-keeping';
much of it was to be sold illicitly while the prizes of the collection were
shipped to Taiwan. The authors saw this as the culmination of a process
of neglect and vandalism that had been eroding the imperial city since
the end of the Manchu dynasty in 1911. 'That the Chinese people, formerly
so attached to their own culture and customs, should have acquiesced in
this wanton destruction of their ancient works of art, . . . is not only
surprising, but is of serious ill-omen for the artistic and cultural future
of the country as a whole.' (See Foreword, p. vi.)[1]

Little more than ten years earlier Juliet Bredon, in her tender account
of Peking, had been more confident. 'The history of Peking is the history
of China in miniature. The town, like the country, has shown the same
power of taking fresh masters and absorbing them.'[2] This was certainly
true of the city left by the Ming emperors, conquered, and then endlessly
embellished by the Manchu rulers to become one of the most extraordinary
monuments to any civilization in the classical world. In the late nineteenth
and early twentieth centuries, the avarice and folly of both foreign aggressors
and local thugs threatened to destroy the city, yet Peking survived their
depredations relatively unscathed. Even the Nationalist revolutionaries
and the northern warlords who variously fought over and abandoned the
city after 1911 simply satisfied their cupidity by plundering the accumulated
riches of temples and palaces, allowing the celestial geometry of the city's
design to remain substantially unchanged. The invading Japanese treated
Peking no less kindly, leaving little outward mark of their decade-long
occupation behind them, although memories of the city's grace were to
haunt Japanese intellectuals and writers years later, giving birth to a lyrical
literature of nostalgia.

Then, in 1949, Mao Tse-tung (Mao Zedong) and his peasant insurgents swelled into the city from their guerilla bases. For a time it appeared as though Peking would work its magic once more and seduce these latest conquerers. Plans were mooted to construct a home for the burgeoning new central bureaucracy outside the precincts of old Peking, a sweeping range of renovations would begin, and the imposing city walls were to be converted into a sylvan garden promenade for the public. But the charm that had protected the city for seven centuries was broken. Mao and his cotton-clad mandarins were determined to refashion Peking to fit the image of their New China. A strategy for the obliteration of a city now despised as a testimony to a retrogressive feudal order, the heart of China's imperial world, was carefully formulated and painstakingly realized over the next four decades, and as a result, Peking today boasts all the ills of an overcrowded, polluted, and inefficient Third World metropolis. All that reminds one of those wondrous walls are a handful of disembodied names and two gates, a select number of the few remaining temples that have not been turned into street factories have been restored to make a meagre living off the tourist trade, and the princely mansions that once dotted the city have either been demolished or sequestered by the lumpen communist gentry. The idea for a garden promenade was recently revived, however, although it has been grafted on to the plans for the preservation of Sian (Xi'an), the ancient capital of the T'ang (Tang) dynasty and the sole example of China's unique traditional city planning permitted to make its contribution to 'modernization' as a massive and lucrative museum display. Thus it is a cruel irony that has proved Bredon's observation true: the history of Peking *is* the history of China in miniature. And in the ugly fate of a once grand city we see the shadow of a bane that has visited itself upon every corner of the country.

Although a detailed chronicle of the despoliation of Peking has yet to appear, the 'death by a thousand cuts' that the city has suffered has been witnessed and admirably recorded by a number of passionate observers. Of these Simon Leys has given us the most moving and unsettling literary tribute to the city under socialism in *Chinese Shadows*, a volume which stands as an indictment of Maoism and its pervasive legacy. Another is a bitter essay by the Italian reporter Tiziano Terzani written just ten years after Leys' powerful *cri de coeur*; once published, it became the object of extreme official displeasure in China.[3] In fact, both writers have been banned from the country, victimized for their love of a refined civilization which has allowed itself to be brutalized by a cynical and grey totalitarianism, a civilization that found its quintessential expression in the city of old Peking.

The readers who approach this book to find a guide to help in their own search for old Peking will invariably be disappointed. To be sure, no major city in the world is the same as it was half a century ago, yet the usefulness of Arlington and Lewisohn's carefully researched record of Peking, like Nagel's still popular traveller's companion, has been rendered little more than academic. Indeed, the city has been so greatly transformed that rather than using it as a guide book to some physical reality it may serve better as an adjunct to a parlour game of pinning the tail on the donkey — one in which the traveller, rendered sightless with a blindfold engineered by the people's urban planners, tries vainly to identify the contours of a capital of the celestial empire in a tawdry cityscape of cement blockhouses and smog.

The true magic of Peking, the city as monument to the past, is lost to us forever. Yet it is in this loss that one can perhaps find some reason for the callous disregard with which the citizens of the city witnessed the glories of the capital pass away. In fact, to regard the physical remains of the past with indifference seems to be a characteristic of Chinese culture. For it is in a literature redolent with allusions and literary references, rather than in the ephemeral works of man, that China immortalized her past.[4] Literary and historical references are like a weave through the very texture of Chinese culture. They are a decoction of individual as well as collective experience; freezing both in an ancient ideographic language and accumulated over the centuries in volumes of poetry and prose like so many strata of culture in an archaeological dig, forever waiting to be revived and lived anew.

The city of Peking has been no exception to this form of literary preservation, and just as each new dynasty, every new emperor, would remodel and add to the city, so its literary legacy was constantly being enhanced and refined. Even now as the government obliterates the scarce remnants of old Peking, a wealth of written material about the city in the form of fiction, poetry, and popular tales is being published for an eager local audience. These readers are not simply being caught up in a faddish wave of nostalgia, for they are collaborating in the conservation of their city in the most time-honoured of methods, by perpetuating the written word. What remains of Peking is then not merely the ruins of dynasties past, but the names of those ruins, names embellished by multilayered poetic and literary associations constantly evoked and endlessly bewitching. In a sense it is as part of this written legacy that the present work belongs.

None the less, the battered stones of Peking themselves may speak to us yet, albeit in muffled tones. Here too *In Search of Old Peking* can come to our aid. In fact, a comparison of the map at the end of this book with any of the recent maps of the city will reveal to the careful observer a tale of pathos, tragedy, and farce with which no amount of well-written history could compare. It is a story of parallels and felicitous coincidences, an old plot with new characters, only the most scant outlines of which I can give here.

The Central and Southern Seas (Chung Nan Hai, Zhongnanhai) was formerly an imperial pleasance, the Empress Dowager Tz'ŭ Hsi's (Cixi) favourite residence in the city. It was there that she also imprisoned the rebellious Emperor Kuang Hsü (Guangxu) on an island in the southern lake (see p. 94). Since 1949, it has been the seat of the Communist Party government and home to most of China's leaders including Mao Tse-tung. Within this massive compound stands the 'Throne Hall of Purple Effulgence', or the Tzǔ Kuang Ko (Ziguangge), used first by the Emperor Ch'ien Lung (Qianlong) to receive the envoys of tributary states in 1761. It is here, in 1873, that the Emperor T'ung Chih (Tongzhi) first met with foreign diplomats, thereby sparing the Forbidden City the inauspicious presence of barbarians (p. 101). The hall is still in regular use for it is where Party leaders often choose to greet foreign dignitaries. Nearby, on the south-east corner of the Pei Hai Park (Beihai Park), stands the Ta Kao Tien (Dagaodian), an impressive old hall used for centuries to worship the Taoist (Daoist) deities (p. 132). Nowadays it is still kept in good order and under constant military guard, for it houses a major recreation club for high-level cadres working in the central government.

The Forbidden City itself remains largely unchanged, although considerable areas not open to the public have fallen into decay, while the east and west flanks of the palace, guarded by the Tung Hua Mên (Donghuamen) and Hsi Hua Mên (Xihuamen) Gates respectively, are now the preserve of the People's Liberation Army. The western side of the palace has, however, seen new development for in the early 1970s it was discovered that a canny sniper would be able to shoot straight into Party headquarters from the top of the new wing of the Peking Hotel, then the tallest building in the city. Not satisfied with demolishing the top storey of the new hotel, government leaders ordered a row of offices constructed on the western side of the palace grounds to block off the treacherous view-corridor entirely. The resulting structure is a ham-fisted attempt at high-rise palace architecture, but as it is closed to the public there is little chance of inspecting the damage at close range. The buildings house the State Archives, a closet veritably bursting with skeletons, and it is only fitting that Chang Yü-fêng (Zhang Yufeng), amanuensis and concubine to Mao Tse-tung in his years of decline, should hold the keys.

Similarly, the former T'ai Miao (Tai Miao) or Ancestral Temple used for the worship of deceased emperors is now the Cultural Palace in the Workers' Park to the right of the entrance to the Forbidden City (pp. 62–76). The main hall of the temple complex is sometimes used to display the remains of government leaders during state funerals. After lying in state for a number of days, the corpses are transferred to the Revolutionary Columbarium at Pa Pao shan (Babaoshan), to the west of the city, which according to a presumably defunct tradition is the first step on the way to the Western Paradise of the Buddhists. The area around Pa Pao Shan also happens to be the site of many of Peking's oldest non-dynastic cemeteries, in particular those of the imperial concubines and eunuchs (p. 309).

To the east, on the other side of the city, one finds that the former site of the Examination Halls, scene of the examinations that selected China's literati rulers (p. 152), now accommodates a bland, brown multi-storey building, the Chinese Academy of Social Sciences, one of the main centres of conflict between orthodox and dissenting intellectual opinion in the country. The North Hostel (Pei Kuan, Beiguan), a large area in the north-eastern corner of the old city, evinces a similarly eerie sense of continuity. It was originally used to accommodate the Albzin Cossack prisoners brought to the capital in 1685, and later given to the Russian Orthodox Church in 1858 (p. 177). It is now the site of the Soviet Embassy compound.

On the road to the Western Hills there is a hill commanded by a number of pagodas. This is the imperial retreat and park at the Jade Spring Fountain (Yü Ch'üan Shan, Yuquanshan) (p. 293), one of the Eight Famous Sights of Peking. Now it is under the control of the Chinese airforce, and is used by high-level military leaders as a summer residence. It is also the subject of an intriguing Chinese urban myth, for according to Yao Mingle's tale of Lin Piao's (Lin Biao) demise, it is here that Mao Tse-tung is said to have had his close comrade-in-arms liquidated with rocket launchers.[5] On the road back to the city at a spot just behind the Summer Palace, is a large, walled compound that houses the Institute of International Relations. This seemingly innocuous academy is run by the not so innocent Ministry of National Security, China's KGB. Secreted in a maze of prefab dormitories within the enclosure stand the doleful remnants of a grand residence, formerly that of Tz'ŭ Hsi's favourite eunuch, the powerful and sly Li Lien-ying (Li Lianying).

Our comparison of maps and written records of the city reveals a disturbing new feature of Peking as well, one which, in consideration of the present nature of Chinese society, I choose to call the topographical memory hole. 'Memory holes' are a phenomenon peculiar to communist societies. They are the hand-maidens, so to speak, of the political purge; for whenever a Party leader or historical event is found to be wanting ideologically, the State, through its control of the media, publishing houses, and libraries, opens up a memory hole and consigns the suspect object to oblivion. The never-ending battle to cover up the tracks of non-persons and non-events results in such things as retouched photographs, rewritten history texts, banned films, pulped books, and so on. In George Orwell's *1984* the Ministry of Truth employed Winston Smith to make memory holes.

Examining the maps produced by the Chinese authorities today, one discovers large unnamed areas scattered over the landscape where once stood princely palaces, temples, or simply a tangle of lanes. In most cases, the places that have been engorged by these cartographical memory holes are classified as state secrets. They include such mundane non-things as gaols as well as the headquarters of police and security organizations. The latter, in fact, occupy a massive area behind the Museum of History on the eastern side of T'ien An Mên (Tian'anmen) Square, housed in the grandiose buildings of the British and Russian legations and barracks (pp. 15 and 17 respectively). They also contain more exotic places such as secret clubs, and stores for cadres, as well as the sprawling residential areas of the members of China's new imperial clans, the homes of Central Committee members and their labyrinthine families which, due to the inexorable mechanism of historical coincidence, tend to occupy the grounds of the former Imperial City encircling the Forbidden City and Coal Hill Park (pp. 118–38).

Occasionally, due to a quirk of political in-fighting or death, the identity of one of these memory holes is revealed. Following the demise of Madame Soong Ch'ing-ling (Song Qingling), China's State President, in 1981, a palace suddenly reappeared as if out of nowhere. After 1949, the stately residence on the northern shore of the Shih Ch'a Hai (Shichahai, Ten Temples of the Sea) had secretly been divided between the Ministry of Hygiene and Soong, and now, out of a politic respect for the memory of Sun Yat-sen's widow and Mother of the Nation, Soong's quarters have been refurbished as a shrine and opened to the public. It is, in fact, Prince Ch'un's (Chun) Palace, birthplace of the Emperor Hsüan T'ung (Xuantong), Henry P'u Yi (Puyi), the last incumbent of the imperial throne (pp. 198–200). The same is true of the residence of the the writer-cum-revolutionary Kuo Mo-jo (Guo Moruo) — Mao's favourite literary toady and a sometime archaeologist — which is situated to the south of the Shih Ch'a Hai (p. 206). Although it had been occupied for many years by the Catholic University, after Liberation the eastern courtyards and stables of what had been the Palace of Prince Ch'ing (Qing) were given over to Kuo. Some years after his death, the stables were converted once more, this time into a memorial for the man lauded by the country's officialdom as a model for China's intellectuals. Placing scholastic achievements aside, Kuo's real talent lay in an unalloyed acumen for pre-empting every political campaign by making an abject self-denunciation. There seems to be some poetic justice in the fact that the place is rarely open to the public.

The residence of K'ang Shêng (Kang Sheng), the architect of China's spy system and a man who combined a passion for purges with a talent for ink painting, has not enjoyed such a happy fate. K'ang Shêng has been posthumously disgraced for his bloody part in Mao's capricious rule, and his serene courtyard dwelling, formerly a temple situated to the north-west of the Bell Tower (pp. 174–5), has suffered a modern two-storey extension and been converted into the Bamboo Garden restaurant-hotel complete with a Western-style cocktail bar for hard-currency customers.

Thus, it is only through natural attrition or political misfortune that we may ever be able to fill in other memory holes and wrest the last secrets of this great city from the grip of her government. But perhaps it is for the best that we do not know the fate of the buildings and parks hidden behind the walls of the memory holes, for as Juliet Bredon mused upon being frustrated in her attempts to see the section of the Forbidden City reserved for the dethroned emperor in the 1920s: 'The charm of the forbidden that leads to so much devouring of unripe apples in early youth still holds good for later years. And to the end of time the sight we may not see will probably be the sight that haunts our dreams.'[6]

GEREMIE BARMÉ

NOTES

1. All page references are to *In Search of Old Peking*.

2. Juliet Bredon, *Peking: A Historical and Intimate Description of its Chief Places of Interest* (Shanghai, Kelly and Walsh, 1919; reprinted by Oxford University Press in Hong Kong, 1982), p. 2.

3. See Simon Leys (Pierre Ryckmans), *Chinese Shadows* (New York, The Viking Press, 1977), pp. 53–64; and Tiziano Terzani, *The Forbidden Door* (Hong Kong, Asia 2000, 1985), pp. 22–59.

4. See Pierre Ryckmans, *The Chinese Attitude Towards the Past,* The 47th George Ernest Morrison Lecture in Ethnology 1986 (Canberra, The Australian National University, 1986), pp. 5 and 18–19.

5. Yao Ming-le, *The Conspiracy and Murder of Mao's Heir* (London, Collins, 1983), pp. 160–3.

6. Bredon (1982), see note 2 above, p. 128.

IN SEARCH OF
OLD PEKING

BY

L. C. ARLINGTON

AND

WILLIAM LEWISOHN

With Maps, Plans and Illustrations

HENRI VETCH
THE FRENCH BOOKSTORE
PEKING   MCMXXXV

FOREWORD

WHAT would one naturally wish to see first in Peking? This book, it is hoped, will tell you, not only what to "See First," but "WHAT TO SEE" worth the telling from A to Z. But, as it is about "Old Peking," it describes not only buildings that are to be seen to-day, but also those that have disappeared completely.

Readers may be led to believe that the authors have sometimes mixed up the two, when during their rambles round Peking they are unable to find monuments or buildings that are mentioned in the book as still existing. This, unfortunately, is not the fault of the authors—they would be only too glad if it was—but is due to the indifference of the Chinese themselves, more especially of their authorities, towards the historical monuments in which Peking is so rich. The loss by vandalism and utter neglect has been proceeding at such a rate that, on repeated occasions, buildings and historical monuments have actually disappeared while the authors were still writing about them.

One might, perhaps, pass over minor acts of vandalism, such as converting historic palaces into modern restaurants and tea-houses; famous temples into barracks and police-stations; cutting down ancient cypresses to sell for firewood; defacing age-old walls and tablets with political slogans, and so forth. But in many instances historical buildings and monuments have actually been destroyed by official orders. The work of destruction culminated in 1933 with the removal of the entire priceless collection of Palace Treasures to the South, where they are stored in the vaults of banks, the beautiful paintings doomed to be eaten by moths, or destroyed by the damp.

And not only is this spoliation going on within the city, but without as well. Once beautiful temples have been left to go to wrack and ruin. Wonderful groves of cedar and pine—Peking's silver pines renowned the world over—have been ruthlessly cut down and sold for timber.

Between the outer walls of Peking and the Western Hills and beyond—a stretch of some twenty miles—what were at one time exquisite beauty spots, are now a wilderness of weeds and ruins.

That the Chinese people, formerly so attached to their own culture and customs, should have acquiesced in this wanton destruction of their ancient works of art, derived from a civilization going back for thousands of years, is not only surprising, but is of serious ill-omen for the artistic and cultural future of the country as a whole. This is not written in a carping spirit or the narrow view of a foreigner: many Chinese think the same, and say so quite freely.

To all of us who have lived long in Peking and love it, this neglect is closely related to tragedy. Nothing can be more painful than to be the unwilling witness of the slow, but sure death, of a place one has learned to love for its quiet beauty and for the wonderful tradition that it holds.

ACKNOWLEDGMENTS

THE acknowledgments and thanks of the authors are due to Mr. V. Petersen for valuable suggestions, and the loan of several of the illustrations ; to Mrs. D. Hope Danby for reading the original MSS and her criticisms thereon; as well as to the Palace Museum authorities for allowing them to visit sections of the Forbidden City not otherwise open to the public.

As regards the illustrations, those showing some of the Altars, Examination Halls, Hanlin, Ploughing Ceremony, etc., were taken from the Chinese books entitled *Ta Ch'ing Hui Tien*, *Ch'ên Yüan Chih Lüeh*, and the *Kuo Ch'ao Shêng Tien*, all of the K'ang Hsi period.

THE AUTHORS.

PEIPING (Peking),
DECEMBER, 1934.

CONTENTS

CONTENTS

PART II

ILLUSTRATIONS

MAPS AND PLANS

MAPS AND PLANS

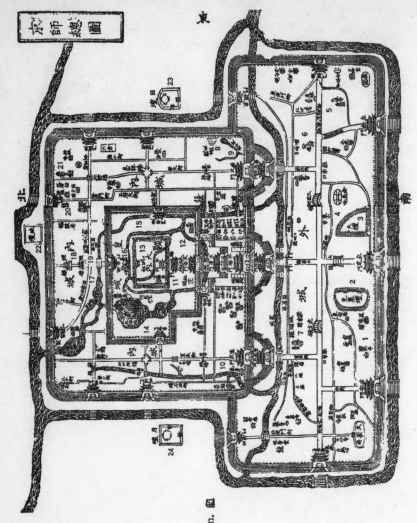

2. OLD CHINESE MAP OF PEKING

1 T'ao Jan T'ing.
2 Altar of Agriculture.
3 Altar of Heaven.
4 Gold-Fish Ponds.
5 Fa T'a Ssŭ.
6 Temple of God of Fire.
7 Liu Li Ch'ang.
8 Observatory.
9 P'ao Tzŭ Ho.
10 Elephant Stables.
11 Altar of Land and Grain.
12 T'ai Miao.
13 Forbidden City.
14 The Three Lakes.
15 Imperial City.
16 Coal Hill.
17 Shih Ch'a Hai.
18 Bell Tower.
19 Drum Tower.
20 Temple of Confucius.
21 Lama Temple.
22 Altar of Earth.
23 Altar of the Sun.
24 Altar of the Moon.

INTRODUCTION

THE magic of Peking, the world-wide fame and charm of this city of enchantment, spring from an enduring source. For nearly three centuries it was the capital of a mighty empire, the seat of some of the ablest, most cultured, and most artistic monarchs who have ever sat on a throne. On its embellishment they lavished continual care and attention and expended vast sums of money.

History was made here, not only that of China, but of the whole Far East, and within its walls many a dramatic incident has taken place. There is scarcely a building of any age in this great city that cannot make its contribution towards the history of the country. Many have been the changes and devastations that Peking has undergone, but even to-day, when shorn of all her glory she is but a city of the past, she remains the city of romantic legend, the Mecca of lovers of art from all over the world, and to tourists the chief attraction in China, if not in the whole of the East.

The city of Peking—or Peiping (Northern Peace) as it is now called—lies in a plain with the beautiful Western Hills, twenty miles away, forming a splendid background. It is a walled and moated city, with an area of about twenty-five square miles, of a peculiar shape : a square imposed upon a parallelogram. The former, the Tartar or Inner City, lies to the north and has a circuit of 23.72 kilometres or about $14\frac{3}{4}$ English miles. The latter, the Chinese or Outer City, adjoining the other on the south, measures five miles by two. The south wall of the Tartar City forms the main portion of the north wall of the Chinese city.

The walls of both cities are of earth and concrete, faced with brick. Those of the Tartar City are forty feet high, sixty-two feet thick at the base and thirty-four feet at the top, access thereto from within being by stone-paved ramps. The walls are strengthened at intervals of sixty yards by huge buttresses that project outwards fifty feet. The parapets of both wall and buttresses are crenellated. The walls of the Chinese City are only thirty feet high and twenty-five feet thick at the base.

The whole circumvallation is pierced by sixteen gates, nine of which are in the Tartar City, and seven in the Chinese City. Of the former, three (excluding the modern gate, the Ho P'ing Mên) are in the south wall communicating with the Chinese City, and two in each of the other three sides. Of the latter, three are in the south wall, one in the east, one in the west, and one each, opening towards the north, in the two portions of the wall which project east and west from the common wall of the two cities. Each gate is protected by a demilune or enceinte and is surmounted by a lofty three-storeyed tower, covered with green glazed tiles.

The Tartar City is literally a nest of cities. In its centre lies the Forbidden City containing the Imperial Palaces, with a crenellated wall and moat. Around the Forbidden City, again, lies the Imperial City with its own high brick wall, coloured red, with a circumference of over six miles. Both these inner cities have (or had) their own separate gates, four in number. There is one other separate city that must be mentioned, a foreign excrescence. This is the Legation Quarter, lying in the southeast part of the Tartar City; it has its own wall and gates, and is entirely cut off, and different, from the rest of Peking.

The gates of Peking have given the city the general outlines of its streets, which run roughly between them, at right angles to one another. Parallel to these main streets run many lesser streets, so that, when looked at on a small scale map, the city has a very regular appearance. But in between, and connecting up, the larger thoroughfares there is a perfect network of narrow lanes which wind about in every possible direction. These are the famous *Hutungs* of Peking in which dwell the greater part of the inhabitants.

Though the compounds of the private citizens of Peking, with their numerous courtyards, secluded gardens, and covered-in verandahs, have a special charm and fascination of their own, and often make very comfortable homes, architecturally they have little of interest to offer, as they are one-storeyed buildings, all constructed on the same plan and in the same

style.* It is to the temples and palaces that we must turn, in
order to study and observe the ancient architecture of China.

Chinese classical architecture differs greatly from that of
other countries in that there is no essential distinction between
sacred and secular buildings. The farther we go back into
antiquity, the more clear does it appear that the palace was a
temple, and the temple a palace. In the construction of the
ancient palaces of the Chinese Emperors three objects were
kept in view: religious ceremonies, feudal audiences and
conferences, and private apartments for the sovereign. Feudal
compacts had to be confirmed by a religious rite, the Emperor
being the chief worshipper. In China there was never any
notion of local sanctity attached to buildings; a palace was
reverenced as the dwelling-place of the sovereign and his
ancestors. The arrangement of the buildings in Peking at
the present time is therefore in principle based on the ancient
classical system, which combines the three ideas of temple, hall
of audience, and private residence.

The origins of Peking go back far into antiquity. Close
to the spot where Peking lies to-day, there stood in the 12th
century B.C. the City of Chi. In a pavilion of yellow tiles in
the hamlet of *Huang T'ing-tzŭ* (Yellow Pavilion), about a
mile north-west of the present city, there is a tablet with an
inscription by the Emperor Ch'ien Lung known as the *Chi
Mên Yen Shu* (The Density of the Trees Surrounding the
Gate of Chi), so-named because if one stands by the tablet
and looks in any direction, groves of trees may be seen in
the distance. It is, incidentally, one of the " Eight Views of
Peking."* From 723 to 221 B.C. this city of Chi, according
to Chinese records, was the capital of the kingdom of Yen.
It was taken and completely destroyed by Ch'in Shih Huang
Ti in 221 B.C.

In the time of the T'ang dynasty A.D. 618-906, a town
called Yu-chou, the seat of a Governor-General, was built
around and outside of the south-west corner of the present
Tartar City. In 986 this was destroyed by the Liaos who
built their capital on the same site, calling it *Nan-ching* (Southern
Capital) to distinguish it from their Northern Capital in Manchuria. This name was changed to Yen-ching in 1013. In

*See " Notes " at end.

1135 the Chins overthrew the Liaos and enlarged the old city, giving it the name of Chung-tu. After the overthrow of the Chins by the Mongols, Kublai Khan erected in 1264 a new city farther north, calling it *Ta Tu* (Great Capital), or as its Mongol equivalent was, Cambaluc. In 1368 the Chinese dynasty of the Mings drove out the Mongols, Peking becoming merely a district, under the name of Pei-p'ing (as at present) until 1421 when Yung Lo made it his permanent capital, from which time on it was called *Pei Ching* (Northern Capital).

The Manchus took over Peking from the Mings in 1644, and it remained within the same limits until the present.

In 1928, when the Nationalist Government removed the capital to Nanking, Peking once more became merely a provincial town under the name Pei-p'ing, as in the first Ming period. (See also Appendix A)

There has been much talk in recent years of making this ancient city a centre of attraction for sightseers, in the same way as has been done with Kyoto in Japan. The sooner this is done the better, so that the innumerable relics of Peking may be preserved to the world before it is too late. Many of them, however, have already disappeared, and the more famous ones therefore, we have attempted to reconstruct for our readers in their " Search for Old Peking."

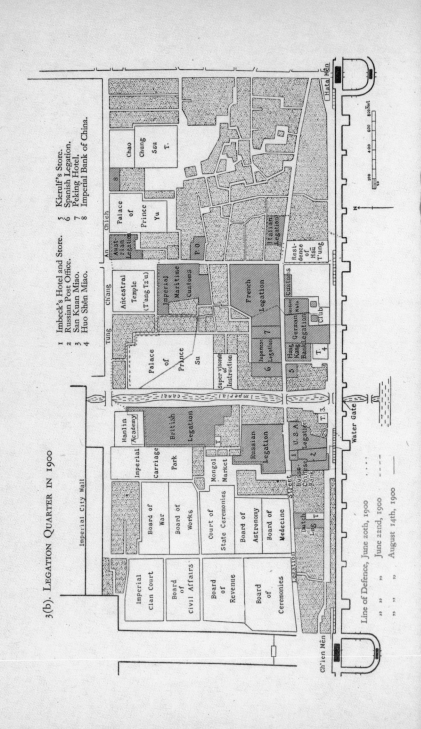

3(b). LEGATION QUARTER IN 1900

1 Imbeck's Hotel and Store.
2 Russian Post Office.
3 San Kuan Miao.
4 Huo Shên Miao.

5 Kierulf's Store.
6 Spanish Legation.
7 Peking Hotel.
8 Imperial Bank of China.

Imperial City Wall

Ch'ien Mên

Board of Ceremonies
Board of Revenue
Board of Civil Affairs
Imperial Clan Court

Board of Medicine
Board of Astronomy
Court of State Ceremonies
Board of Works
Board of War

Legation Street

Dutch Leg. T.

Mongol Market
Imperial Carriage Park
Hanlin Academy

British Legation

Russian Legation
U.S.A Legation
Belgian Council Build.

T. 3.
Water Gate

Imperial Canal

Supervisorat of Instruction
Palace of Prince Su

Japanese Legation
7
6
5
Hong Kong Bank
T. 4
Custom's
German Legation
Custom's
Club

Ancestral Temple (T'ang Tz'u)
Imperial Maritime Customs

French Legation

Austrian Legation
P.O.
Italian Legation
Residence of Hsü Tung

Palace of Prince Yü
8
Chao Chung Ssu T.

Tung   Chiang   An   Chieh

Hata Mên

N

Line of Defence, June 20th, 1900 · · · · ·
" " " June 22nd, 1900 - - - -
" " " August 14th, 1900 ————

100 200 300 400 600 800 Feet
10

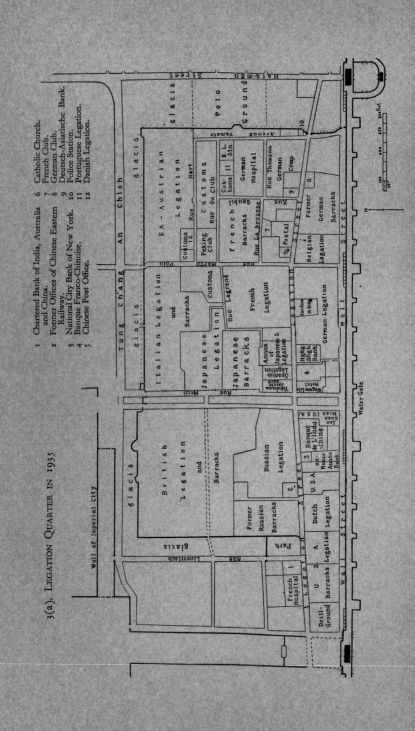

3(a). LEGATION QUARTER IN 1935

1 Chartered Bank of India, Australia and China.
2 Former Offices of Chinese Eastern Railway.
3 National City Bank of New York.
4 Banque Franco-Chinoise.
5 Chinese Post Office.
6 Catholic Church.
7 French Club.
8 German Club.
9 Deutsch-Asiatische Bank.
10 Police Station.
11 Portuguese Legation.
12 Danish Legation.

CHAPTER I.

THE LEGATION QUARTER

WE start out on our search for "Old Peking" with the Legation Quarter, which is a miniature city lying within its own walls and with its own administration, a city quite apart and entirely different from the rest of Peking. The Quarter, as it exists to-day, is comparatively modern, less than thirty-five years old. Prior to 1900, the "Boxer Year," the Legations lay scattered, though fairly close to each other, in this section of the city, interspersed amongst a veritable rabbit-warren of Chinese houses, with unpaved and unlighted streets.

After 1900, by the terms of the Peace Treaty, the so-called Protocol of 1901, a definite area was fixed within which all Chinese public buildings and the few still remaining private houses were razed to the ground, and the land divided up amongst the various foreign governments and a small number of foreign firms. That the Legation Quarter is situated where it is to-day, in the south-west section of, and right inside, the city was not due to any carelessness on the part of the first diplomatic representatives, nor—having regard to the events of 1900—to any far-sighted treacherous plans of the Chinese, but was the result of what may be called ironical historical circumstances.

Prior to Treaty days the only embassies in Peking were those of the vassal kingdoms of Annam, Burma, Korea, and Mongolia, which came annually to Peking bringing tribute to the Throne. These embassies were housed in the Public Hostel for Tributary Nations (*Ssŭ I Kuan*—Four Barbarians' Hostel) situated about where the Banque de l'Indo-Chine is to-day. Here they were kept under very strict surveillance, even to being followed by guards whenever they went about the city. When by the Treaty of Kiachta in 1727 Russia was

allowed to keep a permanent ecclesiastical mission in Peking, a
site opposite this Hostel was allotted to it—the present Russian
Legation—in order to emphasize the claim of the Manchu
dynasty that Russia, too, was a tributary nation.

In 1860, the British and French having wrested from the
reluctant Chinese the right to keep permanent diplomatic
representatives in Peking, the Chinese government, in a vain
last effort to keep them outside the city, offered them first the
grounds of the Yüan Ming Yüan (the old Summer Palace)
which had been destroyed by their armies, and then a site
outside the west wall, where the British cemetery now is. But
the British and French envoys were determined to have their
Legations *inside* the city.

Having in the course of their negotiations with the Chinese
made great use of the services of the Russian Mission, their
attention was naturally drawn to this quarter of Peking. All the
more so, as only a short distance away, at the west end of the
street, lay the chief government offices, the Six Boards, in one
of which they naturally assumed the Foreign Office would be
established. Herein, however, they reckoned without their
hosts, for as we shall see, when describing the Tsung Li Yamên
(Chapter XI), the Chinese put the Foreign Office right away in
the East City.

The main street running east and west through the Quarter,
known to foreigners as LEGATION STREET, is the eastern portion
of one long street that is cut in two by the approach to the
Forbidden City ; the two sections have the same name, except
for the addition of east (*tung*) and west (*hsi*) respectively. In
the days of the Mongol dynasty, when there was a Custom-office
in this street to check the imports of rice and other commodities
from the South, the Chinese name for Legation Street was *Tung
Chiang Mi Hsiang* (East Riverine Rice Lane).

When the Ming Emperor Yung Lo moved the city walls
further south, the Custom-office was moved to outside the Ha
Ta Mên (gate). The name was changed later to *Tung Chiao
Min Hsiang* (East Intercourse of the People's Lane), which
is the name the Pekingese use at the present day, not only for
Legation Street itself, but for the whole Quarter. This name
probably referred to the fact that the Chinese of the South traded
with those of the North along this street.

Starting from the west end of Legation Street we have on our right the LEGATION OF THE UNITED STATES OF AMERICA and the barracks of the guard. These date only from 1901, when they were erected on the ruins of Chinese buildings destroyed during the Siege.

On either side of the road that runs north directly from the main gate of the American Legation there stood until 1900 various government offices. Of these the BOARD OF CERE-MONIES, lay on Legation Street, occupying the whole block as far as the west end of the street. In olden times, when public ceremonies figured so largely in the functions of government, this was one of the most important of the Boards. Here was signed, amidst much pomp and ceremony—at least on the foreign side—the treaty of peace, on October 24, 1860, between China represented by Prince Kung on the one hand, and England represented by Lord Elgin and France by Baron Gros, on the other.

To the east of the American Legation lies the DUTCH LEGATION, occupying practically the same site as did the old Legation which was completely destroyed in 1900.

On the north side of the street are the old Russian Barracks and Legation. The former dates only from 1900. The RUSSIAN LEGATION, however, goes back to the eighteenth century. As we have already said, this site, called *Nan Kuan* (South Hostel), was allotted to Russia after the Treaty of Kiachta, by which she was allowed to send a trade caravan to Peking every three years and to keep an ecclesiastical mission permanently in Peking, consisting of four Russian priests and six language students. Here the mission remained, the Archimandrite carrying out the duties of a diplomatic agent, until 1858, when new treaties were made and a proper minister appointed. The ecclesiastical mission then joined up with the Albazin mission at the *Pei Kuan* (North Hostel) in the north-east quarter of the city (Chapter XIII). The ancient buildings of the days of Timkowski, the envoy who visited Peking in 1727, were pulled down and modern ones erected, with the exception of the small chapel, which is therefore the oldest foreign building in Peking.

Continuing east we come to the Banque de l'Indo-Chine, on the south side. This was the site of the AMERICAN LEGATION from its start in 1860 right up to 1900. In former times the Hostel of the Tributary Nations, which we mentioned above, was situated here. For that reason, the street at the back, running under the wall, was in those days lined with shops selling the famous ginseng, regarded by the Chinese as a great medicinal tonic; it was brought to Peking each year by the Korean embassy.

During the Siege the buildings of the American Legation were so badly damaged that, whilst waiting for the erection of the new Legation on the present site, the staff found accommodation in the adjoining Chinese houses which run south from the corner of Legation Street to the wall, facing the Wagons-Lits Hotel. This whole complex of buildings is known to this day as the *San Kuan Miao* (Three Officials Temple), though the actual temple itself lay at the south-east corner, close to the wall, where the American Military Attaché's office now is. (For the name " Three Officials," see Chapter XIII). This property belongs to the U.S.A. and is still occupied by residences of the Legation staff and offices.

The WAGONS-LITS HOTEL, the large modern building across the road, is called in Chinese *Liu Kuo Fan Tien*. This name is not, as has been stated, derived from the story in Chinese classical history of the six states contending against the powerful Ch'in state, but refers to the *Liu Kuan* (Six Regions): Heaven, Earth, North, South, East, and West; that is to say the Universe.

The garden walk running down the centre along the whole length of this street is a recent creation. In former days an evil-smelling canal, almost dry except in the rainy season, in which was dumped the refuse from the adjoining houses, ran from the Imperial City and out under the Tartar City wall into the south moat, which to-day still offers a good picture of what this canal was once like. As it was supposed to carry off the waters of the " Three Seas " it went by the somewhat exaggerated name of *Yü Ho* (Imperial Canal—not Jade Canal, as it is called on some maps). It was spanned by three stone bridges : one immediately under the Tartar City wall, one at the crossing of Legation Street, and one to the north, just outside the Quarter. Some years after 1900 the banks were lined with brick, but it was not till about 1925 that it was completely covered in.

VIEW OF LEGATION QUARTER BEFORE 1900

(*Looking north from city wall*)

THE LEGATION QUARTER AFTER 1900

The canal passed under the wall of the Tartar City through an archway which was closed by a kind of wooden sluice-gate, called WATER GATE (*Shui Kuan*). It was through this Water Gate that on August 14, 1900, the British forces of the Relief Column entered the city, on the information of Mr. Squiers, First Secretary of the American Legation, thus being the first to enter the Legations, whilst the other armies were still fighting their way in by the city gates. After 1900 a proper gateway was built in the wall, still called the Water Gate, which now forms the direct approach from the Legation Quarter to the railway station.

We have now reached the central portion of the Quarter. Most of the sites in this section are still held by the same occupants, as in 1900, though in some cases considerably enlarged. The red door in an old-style Chinese gateway, on the north side of the street, is the entrance to the SPANISH LEGATION, on its original site. It was here that the peace negotiations took place and the Protocol was signed in 1901. Adjoining it on the east, some tall modern buildings, residences belonging to the Japanese Legation, mark the site of that Legation up to 1900. Further east, where the Chinese Post Office now is, stood the first Peking Hotel, which being in those days one of the few two-storeyed foreign buildings suffered very badly from the Chinese bombardment. Here a large proportion of the combatants were supplied with meals during the whole period of the Siege by the manager, Monsieur Chamot, a Swiss, who together with his wife made a name for himself by his energy and courage during those troublous times.

From the Post Office to the next corner (Rue Marco Polo) stretches the FRENCH LEGATION with its imposing entrance on the main street. It was originally the palace of a Duke Ch'in, famous for its beautiful gardens; but as it was unoccupied in 1860, the family having fallen on evil days, it was rented by the French from the Chinese government. The site is practically the same as it was in 1900, but the buildings are all new, as it was almost entirely destroyed during the Siege. The two stone lions together with the stone posts and chains at the main entrance are probably all that remain of the old Legation. This was the scene of some of the fiercest fighting of the Siege. The Chinese sprang several mines in the grounds, repeatedly forcing the defenders back, step by step, until at the end of the Siege only the south-west corner still remained in French hands.

Of the buildings on the south side of the street there is nothing special to be said, all of them, with two exceptions, occupy the original sites.   On part of the frontage between the Wagons-Lits Hotel and the Hongkong and Shanghai Bank used to stand KIERULF's famous store, the first foreign shop to be opened in Peking.   The Chinese strongly opposed its opening in the early 'nineties on the ground that Peking was not a Treaty Port and therefore foreign trade forbidden, but finally gave way to the argument that the members of the Legations required a shop where they could buy the necessities of life.   We might add in passing, that even at the present day Peking is not a Treaty Port, though foreigners have actually traded here for over forty years.   Why this anomalous situation, which has provided the dispatch writers on both sides with unlimited opportunities of displaying their talents, was not regularized by the foreign Powers in 1901, when they had the opportunity is another of those mysteries in which the foreign relations of China abound.   As a matter of fact, it was not the Diplomatic Body (known, by the way, as D.B.) that made the fortune of Kierulf's store, but the Manchu and Mongol princes, who right up to the time of the 1911 Revolution could be seen almost any day wandering through the shop, accompanied by a bevy of concubines and their retainers, selecting every and any kind of foreign toy that happened to strike their fancy.

The other site where there has been a complete change of ownership is that of the BELGIAN LEGATION, at the corner facing Rue Marco Polo.   Up to 1900 this Legation was the only one that was situated outside the Quarter, far away from all the other legations, off Hatamen Street on the second turning north of Eternal Peace Street (*Ch'ang An Chieh*).   Owing to its isolated position, it had to be abandoned at the very outbreak of the trouble and was completely destroyed.

The present site of the BELGIAN LEGATION is of considerable historic interest as here stood in 1900 the residence of Hsü T'ung, a Chinese Bannerman who had been tutor to the Emperor T'ung Chih, rising to be Grand Secretary in the late 'nineties. He was notorious for his violently anti-foreign sentiments which he displayed both in word and deed. The former by repeatedly and loudly expressing the hope that it would one day be granted to him to cover his sedan-chair with the skins of the foreign devils ; and the latter by always using the side-gate of his residence and going along the back street under the wall, rather than set foot on the macadamized road of the hated foreigner. By the irony of Fate, his house being in the vicinity of the Legations, he was caught inside the defence lines, when the trouble first started. Through the carelessness of a member of the French Legation—to call it nothing worse—he was given a safe-conduct with which he passed out through the main barricade held by French marines. But when he came to an outpost of volunteers he was stopped and unceremoniously dragged out of his sedan-chair. Unfortunately, whilst they were debating what to do with him, another member of the Diplomatic Body came along and persuaded them to let him go.

This dramatic incident, though only mentioned in one or two of the numerous accounts of the Siege, was a fatal mistake, typical of the general lack of plan and order in the defence ; for Hsü T'ung was not only a high official, but above all a special favourite of the Empress-Dowager and one of the leaders of the reactionaries, and would therefore have been an invaluable hostage. Needless to say, he showed his gratitude for his escape by inciting the Boxers and their supporters to ever greater acts of violence. However, for himself it was only a temporary respite, for after the failure of the rising, Hsü T'ung with his whole family committed suicide on the day that the Allied armies entered the city, thus anticipating the punishment which the foreign powers would certainly have demanded. His home has become the site of a foreign legation.

The eastern section of Legation Street presents nothing of interest, all the buildings, including the Church, dating from after 1900. This whole section lay outside the area of the defence. The Italian Legation, which stood in those days about where the Postal Commissioner's house is, was the easternmost of the foreign residences along this street. In a moment of panic it was abandoned in the early days of the Siege and was promptly set on fire by the Chinese.

We now turn north up Rue Marco Polo which is merely a continuation of *Wang Fu Ching Ta Chieh* (Morrison Street)

(Chapter XI).   Under the Mings this portion of the street was called *T'ai Chi Ch'ang* (Firewood Terrace Enclosure), because there was a high stone terrace here on which the firewood for the neighbouring princely palaces was laid out to dry.   The Manchus retained the sound of this name, but changed the first two characters to read *T'ai-chi* (a rank of Manchu nobility), by which name the street is still known to the Pekingese.

On the right we pass Rue Labrousse leading to the French Barracks and to the FRENCH CLUB opposite.   The latter stands on the site of the *An Chün Wang Fu* (Palace of Prince An), a Manchu prince who was degraded for corrupt practices under Yung Chêng and restored to favour in 1778 under Ch'ien Lung. Labrousse, by the way, was a French captain of Marines who had the double misfortune to be caught in the troubles whilst on a holiday, and then to be killed only two days before the Siege was raised, after having taken part as a volunteer through all the fiercest fighting in the French Legation.

Further along, on the right, is the PEKING CLUB, erected in 1902.   Prior to that date it occupied a building, now included in the grounds of the German Legation, behind the present Jardine Matheson site.

Across the road, on the west side, lies the CUSTOMS compound where the famous Inspector-General of Customs, Sir Robert Hart, and his successors had their residence from about 1870 up to 1927, when the Inspectorate-General of Customs was removed to the foreign settlement of Shanghai.   This building was also evacuated at the beginning of the Siege, in a moment of panic, and burnt to the ground by the Chinese, Sir Robert Hart losing all his belongings and only escaping with the clothes in which he stood.   His precious diary, however, was saved by mere luck by one of his assistants.

In 1900 the AUSTRIAN LEGATION included only the west end of the present ex-Austrian Legation together with the glacis as far as the main road.   Although it thus occupied a very important position in the defence line, commanding as it did both the Ch'ang An Chieh and Morrison Street to the north, it too was abandoned in a sudden panic, thus greatly weakening the line of defence.

Immediately opposite the Austrian Legation, on what is now the north-east corner of the Italian Legation and the adjoining part of the glacis, lay the *T'ang Tzŭ* (Ancestral Hall). This was a most important temple, as it was the family shrine of the Manchu dynasty, whose emperors used to worship there on the 8th day of the 4th Moon. It was one of the few buildings in this part of the town that suffered little damage during the Siege, the Boxers and Chinese soldiery probably sparing it, because of its close connection with the Imperial House. But after the Siege, despite all the efforts of the Chinese plenipotentiaries to save it, the Powers insisted on its being razed to the ground, as it lay within the area mapped out for the new Quarter. The Ancestral Hall was therefore transferred to a new site in the south-east corner of the Imperial City where it now stands. (For other details of this temple see Chapter IX.)

On the west side of Marco Polo Street is Rue Lagrené, a short lane leading by a narrow passage-way to the back of the Japanese Legation. Prior to 1900 this whole section between Marco Polo Street and the east wall of the *Su Wang Fu* (Prince Su's Palace) was a maze of narrow alleyways. The grounds of this palace are now included in the JAPANESE AND ITALIAN LEGATIONS. This Prince Su was a descendant of one of the eight " iron-capped " princes who helped to conquer China. When after the burning of the South Church by the Boxers and the massacres of Christian converts there, several thousand native Christians were brought into the Legations, the question of finding accommodation for them became acute. Dr. Morrison, " The Times " correspondent, and Professor James of the Imperial University—who was shortly afterwards captured and executed by Prince Tuan—on their own initiative called on Prince Su and asked him to allow the native Christians to take shelter in his grounds, hinting pretty broadly that it would be done, whether he liked it or not. The Prince, although by no means anti-foreign, but aware that in those stormy days the slightest appearance of conciliation to foreigners might cost him his head, replied that he could not give this permission. At the same time, however, he let it be privately known that, if they took forcible possession, he would offer no opposition. This being done, he quietly withdrew with his family to another of his palaces in a less dangerous part of the city.

The " Fu," as it is called in all the accounts of the Siege, became one of the most important sectors of the Defence. It was defended with the greatest gallantry by a handful of Japanese marines under the Military Attaché, Colonel Shiba. Some very fierce fighting took place there, in the course of which the whole surrounding rabbit-warren of Chinese houses was completely destroyed.

We might remark here that in those days the Christian converts, as also any other Chinese who worked for a foreigner, were dubbed *Erh Maotzŭ* (Second Hairs i.e. Second-class Hairy Ones); and there were even third-class ones, *San Maotzŭ*, those who bought, sold, or used foreign articles; foreigners themselves were simply *Maotzŭ*. This term first came into use at the time of the great rebellion of the T'ai P'ings, who wore their hair long and dishevelled, not plaited into queues like the Manchus and their adherents. Those who joined the rebels in the later stages were called " Second Hairs, " which name originated with the Tientsin populace, though also used to a lesser extent by the Pekingese. It is seldom, if ever, heard in the South. The Chinese used the expression as applying to those who did not " talk reason " and sought to override all argument by violence ; in other words, foreigners were savages, like the rebels, who would not submit to the civilizing influence of the Middle Kingdom.

Whilst on this subject, we might add that when foreigners, the British especially, first came to reside in Peking after 1860, the inhabitants used to shout out after them in the streets the peculiar word *Wei-lo*. It had no meaning at all, and was a corruption of the Cantonese word *Hui-lo* (to go or get out) originated by the British soldiers in the first Chinese War, and thus associated in the minds of the Chinese with the English, as a word they heard them constantly using. That, at least, is the explanation of the sinologues of those days.

Emerging by the main entrance of the Japanese Legation and crossing the garden walk we find ourselves at the main gate of the BRITISH LEGATION. A little to the north of the gate is a plain stone obelisk to commemorate the Siege, but only inscribed with the official date : 6th June—August 14th. At the north end of the street, facing the gate of the Quarter, a small portion of the original wall can still be seen, pitted with bullet marks, and with the words " LEST WE FORGET " painted across it.

The British Legation or *Liang Kung Fu* (Palace of Duke Liang) was originally an Imperial property given by the Emperor K'ang Hsi to one of his thirty-three sons whose descendants were known as Dukes Liang. In 1860 the bearer of this title held a command on the Great Wall and, having become impoverished, did not live in the palace which was falling into ruins. He therefore agreed to rent it to the British Government in perpetuity for an annual rental of Taels 1,500 (about £500). Up to 1900 this rent was taken in silver bullion regularly every Chinese New Year to the *Tsung Li Yamên* (Foreign Office) by the senior language student, for whose use, in order that he might appear respectably attired, a special top-hat was kept. After 1900 the ground became Crown property. It was first occupied on May 26, 1861, by Sir Frederick Bruce, brother of Lord Elgin and first British Minister to China.

The south-east portion of the present Legation, from about the southern edge of the lawn at the entrance to the south wall, did not, however, belong to the original Liang Kung Fu, but was taken in afterwards. This piece of ground was first occupied in 1861 by a Prussian Diplomatic Mission which soon departed again. The British Government then purchased the site for $5,000 and rented it to the Lockhart Mission Hospital which was removed a few years later to its present location on Hatamên Street. The Prussians, who returned again in 1866, occupied it for another short period, until they moved to the present German Legation, when the piece of ground was finally included in the British Legation compound.

The original palace was considerably altered, and adapted to modern requirements, but the Legation remained substantially the same for the next forty years, until 1900, when it was enlarged by taking in the site of the Hanlin, the Carriage Park, and some of the lesser Boards. As it is one of the few Legations that suffered comparatively lightly during the Siege, most of the buildings that stand to-day on the old site are still the same as they were seventy odd years ago.

Part of the Minister's house which lies to the north of the two large open pavilions is the original main building of Duke Liang's palace. His garden was noted for its numerous ornamental kiosks, one of which has become famous in history as the " Bell Tower " and is still standing to-day. This was the central point of the Defence during the Siege. Here were held the Councils of War, whilst in the evening those not on duty used to forgather here to discuss the rumours of the day, the optimists fixing the date of relief, and the pessimists that on which the Chinese were going to break in. The bell was used to sound the alarm ; and on the four pillars were posted up bulletins and the duty rosters.

Turning north past the bell tower we come to the garden behind the Minister's house, in which is a tombstone to David Oliphant, a member of the British Legation, who was shot on this spot while cutting down a tree.

This garden and the glacis to the north was occupied by the famous *Han Lin Yüan* (College of Literature), which consisted of from twenty to twenty-five separate halls. It was first formed under the T'ang dynasty in A.D. 740 and combined the functions of an Academy of Letters with those of a College of Heralds. The members were selected from the highest graduates in the Triennial Examinations (Chapter XI). Their duties were manifold ; to name only a few of the more important : super-intending all literary productions, expounding the classics before the Emperor in the Wên Hua Tien (Chapter II), compos-ing prayers for ceremonial occasions, preparing honorary titles for Imperial wives and concubines, drawing up patents of nobil-ity, and proposing posthumous titles for deceased Emperors. The Academy also contained a valuable library, especially the Great Encyclopædia of Yung Lo of nearly twenty-three thousand volumes.

On the 23rd of June, 1900, it was set on fire by the Moham-medan soldiery of Tung Fu-hsiang, in the hope that the flames would spread to the adjoining British Legation. About as clear a case of cutting off one's nose to spite one's face, as could well be imagined. Luckily for the defenders, the wind veered round, and the Legation remained unharmed, whilst the Han Lin Yüan was completely destroyed together with its marvellous library, many of the priceless volumes of the encyclopædia being actually used by both sides to strengthen their barricades. As showing the peculiar mentality of the diplomats during the Siege, it is an incredible, but undisputed fact, that on the following day Sir

THE HANLIN ACADEMY

Claude Macdonald, the British Minister, sent a dispatch through the lines to the Chinese Foreign Office, informing them of the steps he had taken to try and save the library and requesting them to come and collect what remained. Needless to say, the Chinese Government having at that moment quite other fish to fry—to use a very suitable phrase—ignored his note. A few volumes of Yung Lo's encyclopædia found their way subsequently into the Oriental libraries at Cambridge and the British Museum.

On the north face of the present Consulate (the two-storeyed building to the west of, and at right angles to, the present Chancery) can still be seen the cement patches covering the bullet marks of the Siege. As this building, at that time the Students' Mess, lay close to the north-west corner of the Legation, it was particularly exposed to Chinese fire from the wall of the Imperial City, about two hundred yards to the north.

The low piece of wall with a grass mound, on the east side of the path running immediately behind the Consulate, is the remains of the wall that divided the Legation from the IMPERIAL CARRIAGE PARK (*Luan I Wei*). It was a long, narrow site covering the ground between the glacis and the main road through the Legation ; and the path to the west of the park where the radio masts are, was in those days a lane that ran outside its west wall. As the name indicates, the Carriage Park contained all the paraphernalia used in Court ceremonies and processions, such as carriages, sedan-chairs, flags, decorations, the liveries for the sedan-chair coolies and so forth. The buildings were unusually high with very thick walls, and with roofs of yellow tiles, some of which are still to be seen lining the drains in this part of the grounds.

For some reason or other, in spite of the fighting that took place in the Park, the buildings escaped serious injury and were used by the British troops of occupation as barracks until they were pulled down to make room for the extension of the Legation. Just east of the present Students' Quarters there used to be a large and deep hole, a mine that the Chinese had dug, but failed to explode ; it was fenced in for several years, but later on filled in.

South-west, where the tennis courts are to-day, and on part of the adjoining ex-Russian barracks, was an open space, called the MONGOL MARKET where the Mongols held a fair every winter. It was in a sortie at this spot that Captain Halliday, of the British Marines, gained his Victoria Cross.

The ground covered by the barracks of the British Legation Guard occupies roughly the sites of the old Board of War (*Ping Pu*), Board of Works (*Kung Pu*), and the Court of State Ceremonies (*Hung Lu Ssŭ*), the present Officers' Mess being about the centre of the latter place. Here the unskilled, such as Korean ambassadors and other "Barbarians," had to come to be instructed in the necessary ceremonial procedure, before being allowed to have their audience with the Emperor.

We might here include a building which, though not strictly belonging to the Legation Quarter—as it stood beyond the glacis, opposite the north-west corner of the British Legation —was of dramatic interest in the history of the Manchu dynasty. This was the *Tsung Jên Fu* (Imperial Clan Court) which looked after the affairs of the Imperial family and where in special cases, by orders of the Throne, courts were held to try the crimes of its members. At the back, was a row of buildings, the famous "Empty Chamber," in which condemned princes and others were imprisoned, or, on occasions, provided with a scarf of red silk—a special sign of Imperial clemency—with which to commit suicide.

It is impossible, within the scope of this book, to give a detailed account of the famous Siege of the Legations which was the direct cause for the creation of the present Legation Quarter, and we must confine ourselves to a few general facts and explanatory comments.

A list of books dealing with the Siege will be found under Appendix G. Of these, "Indiscreet Letters from Peking," by Putnam Weale, is probably the most picturesque and romantic, whilst the accounts of the Rev. Arthur Smith and R. Allen would appear to be the most objective and accurate. Owing to the fact, that so many different nationalities were concerned, a completely impartial account has never yet been written.

The Siege lasted for fifty-five days, from June 20 to August 14, 1900. Cooped up in an area of less than half a square mile were about 900 foreigners of eleven different nationalities together with about 3,000 Chinese Christians. The line of defence which was held by about 525 combatants (450 Legation Guards and 75 Volunteers) is shown in red on the accompanying map and ran amidst a veritable warren of Chinese houses and narrow lanes, the only clear line being the massive wall of the Tartar City covering the south front. Moreover, the 470 odd civilian population of whom 228 were women and children, were crowded into the British Legation which, as can be seen from the maps, was at that time less than a third of its present size. The besieged never ran any risk of actual starvation : several large grain shops in Legation Street had been commandeered at the beginning of the Siege and there were a large number of ponies in all the Legations ; also there were numerous sweet-water wells. Nor do the non-combatants seem to have been in any great danger from the bombardment ; only one woman was hit the whole time, and she, after the relief had marched in. The hardships of the Siege were caused by the crowded and insanitary conditions, the tremendous heat, the continual noise of firing and above all by the uncertainty which hung over their heads— they were completely cut off from the outside world for the greater part of the time. The total losses of the combatants in killed amounted to sixty-seven, the French suffering the heaviest. The actual heavy fighting took place at the beginning, for about one month, from June 20 to July 18, and for a few days at the end. Between that time there was a kind of armed truce during which some of the most ridiculous diplomatic correspondence took place that has ever enlivened this world, the Tsung Li Yamên even sending the condolences of the Chinese Government at the death of certain high persons in countries whose representatives they were bombarding.

Much conjecture has been expended on the question of how it was that the Legations were not wiped out. A consideration of all the happenings, from a perusal of the considerable literature on the subject and from talks with witnesses on both sides, would seem rather to evoke surprise that the Chinese managed to keep it up as long and violently, as they did. In the first place, already in those days, although the defenders failed to realize it at the time, the local conditions were all in their favour. Five hundred determined men armed with modern rifles and fighting in narrow alleys and under cover of buildings and barricades presented a most formidable military problem which nullified the numerical superiority of the attackers, and to tackle which successfully, quite different powers of generalship were required than the Chinese ever possessed.

Indeed, had the besieged had a single person in authority, of courage and determination, whose personality could have overcome the violent international jealousies, who could have co-ordinated the defence under his sole command and by a few determined sorties at the beginning could have assured a sound defence line, it seems doubtful, whether the Chinese would ever have pressed their attacks at all. Unfortunately for the Legations, the only possible person of that description, the German Minister, Baron von Ketteler, was killed before the Siege started. After that all was confusion and recrimination, each nationality suspecting the other of trying to let it down, with the result that there were a number of quite unnecessary panics in which vital points in the defence were abandoned without a shot (as for instance the Austrian and Italian Legations, and, at one time, even the Tartar City wall). The Chinese seeing the foreigners on the run naturally became emboldened to press their attacks.

Book titles such as " China against the World " or " China and the Allies " have tended to put the Siege in a false perspective, by creating the impression of this handful of foreigners besieged by the million odd population of Peking. In actual fact, not more than a few thousand Chinese ever seem to have taken part in the fighting, whilst the great mass of the population remained entirely passive and at heart very much alarmed about the whole business. Already at the very outbreak of the trouble, hundreds of thousands of Chinese left the city, foreseeing very well that, whichever side came out on top in the struggle, it was they who would have to pay the score—as in fact happened in the end.

And if confusion reigned in the defenders' lines, conditions on the Chinese side can only be described as complete chaos. Amongst the leaders there were not only divided counsels, but the most bitter and deadly antagonisms, whilst their polyglot forces, composed of three different races, and with entirely conflicting loyalties, were just as heartily, or if anything, more heartily, engaged in fighting with one another over loot, than in attacking the Legations. Of all this mob, the only forces that took a serious hand in the business were the Kansu Moham-

medans of Tung Fu-hsiang, and some of the Banner troops
belonging to the so-called Boxer Princes, probably at the outside five to six thousand men at any time. The much over-
rated Boxers—as they have been absurdly named—who were
only armed with swords and spears, took scarcely any part in the
attack on the Legations after the first few days when they
suffered very heavy losses, but confined themselves to the safer
task of looting and massacring their own countrymen under the
pretext of searching for Christian converts.

The Chinese attacks were entirely lacking in co-ordination
or plan, none of the fire-eating princes ever going anywhere
near the firing-line. The ex-brigand, Tung Fu-hsiang, who
was supposed to be in command, like some of his prototypes
of the Great War, was constantly inventing fresh excuses for
his failure to take the Legations, his chief one being the lack of
modern artillery. Almost all the writers on the Siege have
agreed with him in ascribing their salvation to the refusal of
Jung Lu to hand over the Krupp guns in his possession. There
is, however, no reason to think that, even had the latter been
foolish enough to hand them over—which he was not likely
to do, seeing that that they would probably have been turned
on himself first—these guns would really have turned the scale.
In the first place the half dozen guns that were already being used
against the Legations did remarkably little damage, seeing the
number of shots they fired—sometimes as many as 300 a day.
All accounts agree that they fired much too high, most of the
shots going over into the unfortunate Chinese city. Nor is this
surprising, when one remembers that they were mounted a
few hundred yards from the Legations on special ramps erected
behind high walls. In the second place there were no trained
artillerymen to serve the guns anyhow, as they were all down
at Tientsin helping to stem the invasion of the Allied forces.

As to the question of responsibility for the attacks on the
Legations, it is now generally assumed, as a result of the publication of Ching Shan's famous diary in that fascinating book,
" China under the Empress-Dowager, " that this remarkable old
lady was entirely responsible for the whole business. But this
would appear to be a much too facile explanation which ignores
several vital factors. To take only one instance : it should be
noted that Ching Shan was no longer on the active list, but was

an elderly retired official of over seventy, and so deaf at that, that he could not hear a gun firing a few hundred yards away from his house (Chapter IX). He was never himself present at any of the War Councils or other audiences that he describes so dramatically. The mixture of gossip and High Politics that he noted down in his diary was obtained mostly from second, or even third, hand, by persons anxious to make out a good case for themselves.

The more correct view of the case, which we can only state here in outline, would appear to be that at that moment the Empress-Dowager had lost control of the situation which was in the hands of the reactionaries under Prince Tuan who were actually attempting a Palace revolution, to seize supreme power and restore the throne to the elder branch of the Manchu House. As they knew that several of the foreign Powers were in favour of the Emperor Kuang Hsü, and had on a previous occasion intervened to save him, they thought that by stirring up trouble for the Legations they would be able to occupy their attention, whilst the revolution was being carried through. Their plans miscarried owing to the refusal of the ministers to leave Peking, to Jung Lu's loyalty to the Empress-Dowager, to the neutrality of Prince Ch'ing and, last but not least, to the indiscipline of their own followers. That the Empress-Dowager had lost control in those days is sufficiently established by the remarkable fact that certain moderate Manchus, such as Lien Yüan and Li Shan, who were favourites of hers, but personal enemies of Prince Tuan, were publicly executed without her even knowing about it.

The Siege remains one of the most extraordinary and interesting events of modern times, in which tragedy and comedy were closely interwoven, and in which all the workings of human nature, both good and bad, can be seen at close quarters. Its chief dramatic appeal, however, lies in the strong contrast between the futility and vacillation of the leaders on both sides and the dogged courage of some of the more humble participants.

The following description of Peking by the Rev. Arthur Smith, a few days after the Relief, will form a fitting ending to this chapter :

" It is impossible to say exactly how great an area has been destroyed by fire, but the places are numerous and some of the tracts very large. From the Russian and the American Legations west to the Ch'ien Mên for a width of many hundred yards and over a quarter of a mile in length there is now a stretch without a single building intact. A similar devastation is seen to the north of the northern gate of the Imperial City, and on a smaller scale in multitudes of other places as well. When it was possible for foreigners again to traverse the streets of Peking, the desolation which met the eye was appalling. Dead bodies of soldiers lay in heaps, or singly, in some instances covered with a torn old mat, but always a prey to the now well-fed dogs. Dead dogs and horses poisoned the air of every region. Huge pools of stagnant water were reeking with rotting corpses of man and beast; lean cats staring wildly at passers-by; gutted shops boasting such signs as ' Perpetual Abundance,' ' Springs of Plenty,' and so forth. Over the door of a place thrice looted and lying in utter ruin one might see the cheerful motto ' Peace and Tranquillity.' For miles upon miles of the busiest streets of the Northern and Southern Cities not a single shop was open for business, and scarcely a dozen persons were anywhere to be seen."

CHAPTER II.

THE SOUTH AND CENTRAL SECTIONS OF
THE FORBIDDEN CITY

EMERGING from the fortress-like gate at the west end of the Legation Quarter, you see immediately before you the first example of Chinese architecture, an ornamental wooden arch that spans the street. As according to the best canons of Chinese art everything must always be in pairs, on the other side of the open space, where the street continues again, is a similar one. These arches—other examples of which we shall repeatedly come across during our tour of the city—are called *P'ai Lou* (Memorial Arches) and were generally granted to loyal statesmen, virtuous widows, and similar exceptional people. Those in Peking, however, are mostly merely decorative. Their names are often used by the Pekingese when referring to a certain district, as for instance, *Tung Tan P'ai Lou* (East Single Arch) or *Hsi Ssŭ P'ai Lou* (West Four Arches), much as people in London say: " I want to go to Marble Arch."

The stone-flagged square across the road is called *Ch'i P'an Chieh* (Chess Board Street), referring to the Chinese game called *Wei Ch'i*, played with black and white counters on 324 squares. It was a favourite game of the scholars of ancient China. When the Ming Emperor Yung Lo, the real founder of modern Peking, removed the capital to this city from Nanking in 1421, he constructed this square in the form of a chess-board, enclosing it with a stone palisade with gates at the north and south entrances. Amongst the common people the enclosed square was formerly known as *Chu Chüan* (Pig Sty), a misnomer that originated from the illiterate confusing the family name of the Mings, *Chu* (Pearl) with *Chu* (Pig). After the fall of the Mings the " Pig Sty " was perpetuated in a popular saying :—" *Chüan tsai, chu pu tsai ; chüan tsai, chu hai lai*" (The pen is here, but not the pig ; so long as the pen is here, the pig will come back).

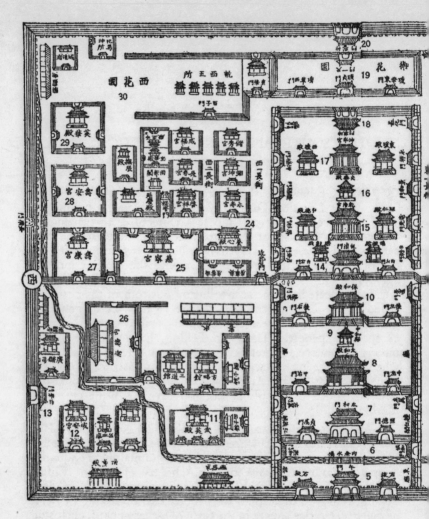

4. OLD CHINESE MAP OF THE

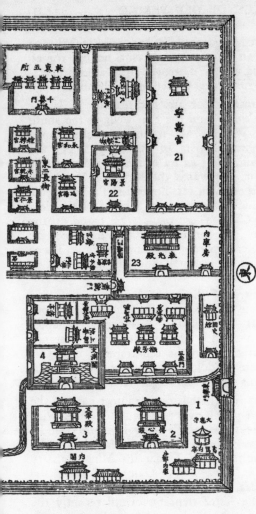

11 *Wu Ying Tien* (Hall of Military Prowess)

12 *Hsien An Kung* (Palace of Perfect Peace)

13 *Hsi Hua Mên* (West Flowery Gate)

14 *Ch'ien Ch'ing Mên* (Gate of Heavenly Purity)

15 *Ch'ien Ch'ing Kung* (Palace of Heavenly Purity)

16 *Chiao T'ai Tien* (Hall of Vigorous Fertility)

17 *K'un Ning Kung* (Palace of Earthly Tranquillity)

18 *K'un Ning Mên* (Gate of Earthly Tranquillity)

19 *Yu Hua Yüan* (Imperial Flower Garden)

20 *Shên Wu Mên* (Gate of Divine Military Genius)

21 *Ning Shou Kung* (Palace of Peaceful Old Age)

22 *Ching Yang Kung* (Palace of Southern View)

23 *Fêng Hsien Tien* (Hall of Worshipping Ancestors)

24 *Yang Hsin Tien* (Hall of the Culture of the Mind)

25 *Tz'ǔ Ning Kung* (Palace of Peace and Tranquillity)

26 *Nei Wu Fu* (Board of Household Affairs)

27 *Shou K'ang Kung* (Palace of Vigorous Old Age)

28 *Shou An Tien* (Hall of Longevity and Peace)

29 *Ying Hua Tien* (Hall of Heroic Splendour)

30 *Hsi Hua Yüan* (Western Flower Garden)

FORBIDDEN CITY

7 *T'ai Ho Mên* (Gate of Supreme Harmony)

8 *T'ai Ho Tien* (Hall of Supreem Harmony)

9 *Chung Ho Tien* (Hall of Middle Harmony)

10 *Pao Ho Tien* (Hall of Protecting Harmony)

The inference was that the Mings would be restored to the throne one day. The Republican government having no use for an emperor of any kind, has utterly destroyed the famous chess-board, part of which has now been turned into a shrubbery.

This square is interesting for another reason. It is the nose of the " Man of Peking," and the two wells at the south corners are his eyes. We do not mean the Peking man recently dug up by anthropologists in these parts, but the symbolic figure for Peking, *No Cha* by name. Tradition tells us that when Prince Yen, afterwards the Emperor Yung Lo, first arrived in Peking, an eminent astrologer Liu Po-wên, gave him a sealed package which contained the lay-out of the new capital, to be called *No Cha*. These plans were based on the most approved principles of geomancy and allotted a certain building or open space to each part of the human body. (Those who are interested in this subject will find further details in Appendix B.)

Standing in the centre of the stone-flagged square and looking south, there looms up before us the *Ch'ien Mên* (Front Gate), the central south gate of the Tartar city (Chapter XV), through which you can nowadays see in the far distance the gate of the Southern city. In the old Imperial days this was not possible as the outer middle gate was kept closed except when the Emperor paid his state visits to the Altar of Heaven.

Turning north we approach the southernmost gate of the Imperial City. The blue panel over the central tunnel with gilt Chinese characters gives the name : *Chung Hua Mên* (Middle Flowery Gate) which it has borne since the establishment of the Middle Flowery Republic in 1911. Under the Ming Dynasty it was called *Ta Ming Mên* (Great Bright Gate), and under the Manchus, *Ta Ch'ing Mên*, *Ta Ch'ing* (Great Purity) being the Chinese name for the latter dynasty. Until recently the old panel with the name *Ta Ch'ing Mên* in large bronze characters, over two feet in length, was still to be seen amongst the treasures of the Palace Museum.

Before leaving this gate we might examine three of its ornamental features that are common to most of the other public gates and buildings and which we shall therefore be constantly meeting with again. The first is the pair of stone lions in front of the gate. The one on your right is the male, playing with a ball, and that on the left the female, fondling a cub*. These lions are to be found outside all imperial and princely palaces.

Then there are the rows of gilt studs that adorn the gate panels. According to tradition these were invented by Lu Pan, the God of carpenters and masons. Happening to touch a conch shell one day, he noticed that the occupant at once retired inside closing the entrance tightly, and thus conceived the idea of putting a conch shell on all doors as a symbol of tightness and security. (This Lu Pan, as we shall have repeated occasion to hear, seems to have had quite a lot to do with the architectural problems of Peking). The official and correct name for these knobs is *Chin Ou Fu Ting* (Gilt Floating Bubble Nails), because they were supposed to resemble water bubbles, when studded over a flat surface in this way. But the popular names, if less elaborate, would appear to be more striking, as for instance: *Man T'ou Ting*, from the shape of the Chinese bread rolls (*Man T'ou*); or *Mo Ku Ting* (mushroom nails), or *Yü Yen* (fish eyes) and several others.

The other features are the various curious creatures perched in single file on the angles of the roof, each one cast in a single piece with the tile on which it is resting. The origin of these figures is as follows :—

In the year 283 B.C. the cruel tyrant, Prince Min, of the State of Ch'i, after being defeated by a combination of other states, was strung up to the end of a roof ridge and left hanging there without food or water, exposed to the burning rays of the sun until he died. In order to stigmatize his evil deeds the people of the State of Ch'i placed his effigy, riding a hen, on the roof of their houses. With the weight of the prince on its back, the hen could not fly down to the ground, and in order to prevent it escaping over the roof, a *ch'ih wên*, a kind of dragon, was placed at the other end of the ridge. This is the fierce beast you see, with horns and bushy tail and its mouth wide open, as if to swallow Prince Min and the hen, if they venture near him. It was not until the time of the Ming Emperor Yung Lo that the other figures were added. A correct set was put together in the following order : hen, dragon, phœnix, lion, unicorn, celestial horse, *ch'ih wên*. If more were required, any of the figures could be repeated, with the

* See " Notes " at end.

exception of the hen and the *ch'ih wên*, but always so as to form an odd number up to eleven. The reason for this was that odd numbers come under the influence of *Yang** or Male Principle. However, in later times both the principle of odd numbers and the conventional arrangement of the set were departed from. In most cases the only figures that were used, between the hen and the *ch'ih wên*, were those that foreigners call dogs, but which are really lions. Moreover, since the latter days of the Republic, even the hen with Prince Min was removed from the roofs of public buildings, so as to prevent, it is said, any possible unpleasant political comparisons.

Passing through the gate and proceeding north along a stone-flagged path, the old *Yü Lu* (Imperial Way), now lined with flowering shrubs on either side, but formerly with quarters for the Imperial Guard, we come to the open space in front of the imposing *T'ien An Mên* (Gate of Heavenly Peace). At the end of this avenue, inside a rickety wooden fence, lies a stone slab which bears an inscription stating that beneath this spot is buried a brass picture of Sun Yat-sen. This, it would appear, is to indicate that he is the founder of a new state, if not exactly a dynasty.

The two pillars standing south of the marble bridge beautifully carved with dragons winding round them, and with two ornaments at the top looking like wings, but meant to represent clouds, are called *Hua Piao* (Flowery Sign-posts) and are of the Ming period. They were intended as reminders to the emperors to walk in the path of virtue, and are traditionally explained as survivals of the Boards of Criticism and Detraction instituted by the Emperors of the Golden Age outside the palace gates, where criticisms of the acts of the ruler and suggestions for reforms could be handed in. There are two pairs of these *Hua Piao* : this pair outside and another inside the gate. The figure of a lion is superimposed at the top of each column. The lions on the south side *face* south, with wide *open* mouths, signifying that it is their duty to report to the Sovereign any malpractices amongst the Court officials during his Majesty's absence. Those on the north *face* north, with *closed* mouths, indicating that when the Emperor has left the palace incognito, silence regarding this is to be strictly observed.

See " Notes " at end.

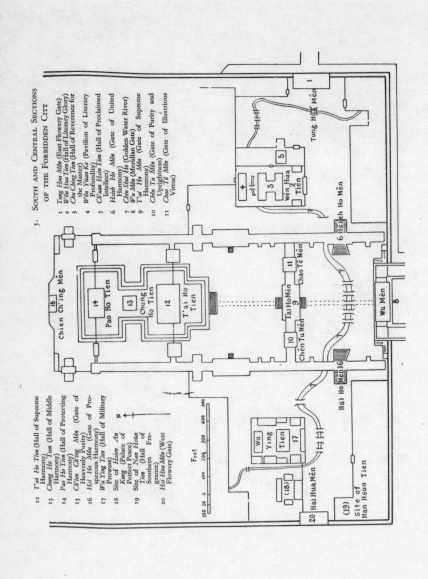

5. SOUTH AND CENTRAL SECTIONS OF THE FORBIDDEN CITY

1 *Tung Hua Mên* (East Flowery Gate)
2 *Wên Hua Tien* (Hall of Literary Glory)
3 *Chu Ching Tien* (Hall of Reverence for the Master)
4 *Wên Yüan Ko* (Pavilion of Literary Profundity)
5 *Ch'uan Hsin Tien* (Hall of Proclaimed Intellect)
6 *Hsieh Ho Mên* (Gate of United Harmony)
7 *Chin Shui Ho* (Golden Water River)
8 *Wu Mên* (Meridian Gate)
9 *T'ai Ho Mên* (Gate of Supreme Harmony)
10 *Chên Tu Mên* (Gate of Purity and Uprightness)
11 *Chao Tê Mên* (Gate of Illustrious Virtue)

12 *T'ai Ho Tien* (Hall of Supreme Harmony)
13 *Chung Ho Tien* (Hall of Middle Harmony)
14 *Pao Ho Tien* (Hall of Protecting Harmony)
15 *Ch'ien Ch'ing Mên* (Gate of Heavenly Purity)
16 *Hsi Ho Mên* (Gate of Prosperous Harmony)
17 *Wu Ying Tien* (Hall of Military Prowess)
18 Site of *Hsien An Kung* (Palace of Perfect Peace)
19 Site of *Nan Hsün Tien* (Hall of Southern Fragrance)
20 *Hsi Hua Mên* (West Flowery Gate)

The pair of large stone lions close to the *Hua Piao* south of the gate are of the Ming period. There is a popular legend connected with them. When Li Tzŭ-ch'êng, the brigand chief who captured Peking from the Mings in 1644 was riding towards this gate to enter the Forbidden City, two huge lions suddenly sprang up in front of him barring the way. Li drew his bow and discharged a couple of arrows at them, when they disappeared. He pursued them, but could only find these two stone lions sitting in front of the gate. Those who care to, can verify this story by feeling the belly of the lion on the left (west), when they will find the hole caused by Li Tzŭ-ch'êng's arrow, from which wound, according to popular belief, moisture is still dripping !

This gate is associated with another deed of the same Li Tzŭ-ch'êng. Just below the gilt character *T'ien* 天 (Heaven) on the blue panel, that hangs under the centre of the upper roof of the gate-tower, there is a small hole. The story goes that, as Li Tzŭ-ch'êng was entering the gate, he stopped and aimed an arrow at the top character, "Heaven," in the belief that, if he hit it, it would mean that Heaven was favourable to his ascending the Imperial throne. As can be seen, he missed his mark, and his retinue took this as a sign that Heaven had rejected him, which later proved to be the case, when he was overthrown by the Manchus.

Imperial decrees were publicly read outside this gate. From the top of the gate Yüan Shih-k'ai held a grand review on the occasion of his inauguration as First President of the Chinese Republic. The stone coping in the centre was removed on that occasion and has never been replaced. At a much later date the portrait of Sun Yat-sen painted in blue and white, the Kuomintang colours, adorned the space just over the central tunnel, and was only removed quite recently, prior to the visit of the Lytton Commission in 1932.* Since the establishment of the Republic the square in front of the gate has repeatedly been used for political meetings that have often led to minor riots rather belying the name of "Heavenly Peace." The radical and democratic speeches made on such occasions would have sounded very strange to the ears of the great Ming and Manchu Emperors of the past !

* See "Notes" at end.

PROCESSION ENTERING THE WU MÊN

Passing under the tunnel of the *T'ien An Mên* and along a stone road under shady trees with guard-houses on either side, in which are some old cannon placed there in recent times and having nothing to do with the palace, we go through the *Tuan Mên* (Gate of Correct Deportment). Before us towers the mighty *Wu Mên* (Meridian Gate), the main gate of the "Forbidden City" (*Tzŭ Chin Ch'êng*). It should be noted that this name has often been wrongly translated as "Purple (or Violet) Forbidden City." The character *Tzŭ* is used in this connection for *Tzŭ Wei* (The Pole Star), referring to the Emperor as the pole around which everything revolves. It is the largest of all the Palace gates and is crowned with five towers, known as the "Five Phœnix Towers." Right and left of the gate are a stone sun-dial and a pint measure, symbols of Time and Quantity. When the Emperor passed through the gate a bell in the tower above was struck ; and a drum was beaten, while sacrifice was being performed at the Temple of Ancestors. The essential parts of this whole elaborate gateway were built at the beginning of the Manchu dynasty, in the middle of the 17th century. The rooms over the wings of this gate were used as government offices to which the officials concerned had access through the two side gates. In recent times they have been turned into a Museum for the Palace treasures.

For some mysterious reason the public is not allowed further access from this side*—excepting on certain holidays. We must therefore go right round to the eastern entrance of the Forbidden City, the *Tung Hua Mên* (East Flowery Gate).

On entering we have a group of buildings on our right. The first, from the south, is the *Wên Hua Tien* (Hall of Literary Glory) where the "Feast of Classics" was celebrated in the Second Moon of each year, when noted scholars expounded the Classics before the Emperor. The central building is the *Ch'ung Ching Tien* (Hall for the Reverence of the Master) which was used for lectures on Confucianism. The building at the back is the *Wên Yüan Ko* (Pavilion of Literary Profundity), a famous library built by Ch'ien Lung. The books are in manuscript and form a unique collection of Chinese literary treasures ;

*Since writing the above it is now possible to enter here.

they are now in the National Library of Peiping. This library was also called *Ssŭ K'u* because it was compiled under four main divisions : Classics, History, Philosophy, and Literature. It was one of four similar sets, the other three being at the Imperial residences : Yüan Ming Yüan (the old Summer Palace), Jehol (the summer residence of the Court), and Mukden (the home of the dynasty). Adjoining the compound on the east is the *Ch'uan Hsin Tien* (Hall of Proclaimed Intellect) where sacrifices were offered up to Imperial tutors and other learned men. It is now the residence of some of the Palace watchmen, and one cannot enter.

Until recently these buildings, as also those at the West entrance, were used as a museum for the Palace treasures. These were removed from Peking, despite the protests of the Pekingese, by the Central Government in 1933, on the pretext that they might fall into the hands of the Japanese, if the latter occupied the city. What could be worse than ruthlessly tearing these marvellous works of art from their incomparable setting amidst the beautiful old palaces, and scattering them in various places quite unsuited for their safe accommodation? This unique display is now lost to the world, as it may be safely predicted that the majority of the pieces will never see the light of day again, at least not all together in a public collection.

Continuing westwards we come to the *Hsieh Ho Mên* (Gate of United Harmony). If you look behind the right (south) wing of the doorway you will see attached to one of the pillars a short length of chain which is always just stirring slightly, even if there is no breeze at all. According to tradition this chain was used to tether a small black donkey that the Emperor K'ang Hsi used to ride, when he made his excursions incognito into the city.

We have now reached the great courtyard in front of the *T'ai Ho Mên* (Gate of Supreme Harmony). Through it runs a moat called *Chin Shui Ho* (Golden Water River), forming a wide curve shaped like a bow, and spanned by five marble bridges symbolical of the Five Virtues. Of this moat a Peking rhyme sings :—

" One piece bow	*I chang kung,*
Five pieces arrows	*Wu chih chien,*
Ten lengths of beam	*Shih chia t'o*
Can't be seen."	*K'an pu chien.*

In front of this gate stand two enormous bronze lions and two carved marble ornaments, the one representing the box in which petitions to the Emperor used to be placed, and the other the box in which the Imperial seals were preserved. As with all the other gates, the central gateway was used by the Emperor only. The officials who awaited him in front of this gate passed through the two gates at the side, the civil officers on the east, and the military on the west. The sloping floor between the two staircases, decorated with dragons and other symbolical animals, was the path over which the Emperor's sedan-chair was carried, whilst his retinue used the 28 steps on each side. The T'ai Ho Mên is of the Ming period, but was repaired during the reign of the Emperor Kuang Hsü between 1887 and 1890.

Between this gate and the *T'ai Ho Tien* (Hall of Supreme Harmony) is another large court about 200 yards long, which appears to be even vaster than it really is, because of its complete emptiness and the low buildings on either side. On high ceremonial occasions at the T'ai Ho Tien, it was packed to overflowing with a large assemblage of officials of all ranks. At the last public ceremony that took place in this court, the Armistice celebration in 1918, even though the whole of the Allied garrisons in Peking together with a large contingent of Chinese troops paraded here, they still appeared almost lost in its vastness.

The *T'ai Ho Tien* is the first of the three great halls of ceremony (*San Ta Tien*) erected on the three-storeyed marble terrace called "Dragon Pavement" which is laid out in the form of a double cross without a head. The eighteen three-legged bronze urns standing on the triple staircase ascending to the hall are symbolic of sovereignty and represent the Eighteen Provinces of Manchu times; they are said to be imitations of the Nine Tripods of the Chou Dynasty. The two large bronze cranes and two tortoises* standing on the terrace itself are symbolical of Longevity and Strength. The tortoises have dragons' heads and are a primitive form of dragon, called *Hao Hêng*, which was supposed to exercise a restraining influence on official greed and oppression. According to a curious custom, the successful candidate who headed the list in the Triennial Examinations had the right to stand on the head of one of these tortoises after his interview with the Emperor. In the words

---

*See " Notes " at end.

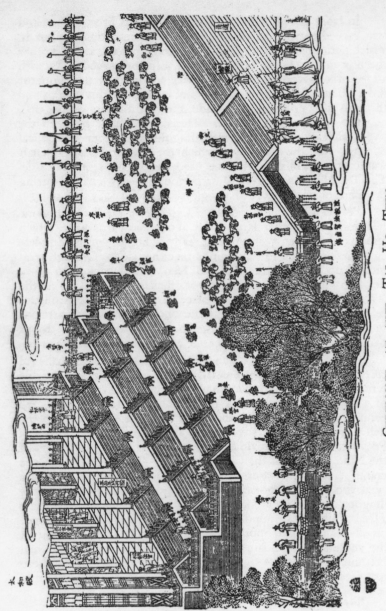

Ceremony at the Tai Ho Tien

of the famous poet Hung Liang-chi (1746-1809), he was " occupying alone the leviathan's head," i.e. the first place. On the terrace are also a marble sun-dial and a marble bushel, and four enormous bowls of gilt bronze which are said to have been filled with oil and used as lamps with floating wicks. The large iron pots arranged round the courtyard were used for keeping water in case of fire. Altogether there were in the whole Palace seventy-two iron and eight gilt-bronze pots, corresponding to the seventy-two Earth (evil) spirits and the Eight Good Buddhas.

To the T'ai Ho Tien the Emperors came to receive the congratulations of the Court on New Year's day, the Winter Solstice, Imperial birthdays, announcement of victories, and other grand ceremonial occasions. The Emperor sat on his high throne in the centre of the vast and gloomy hall, shrouded still further from the gaze of the profane by clouds of incense. Around the throne stood fifty Manchu attendants of high rank ; on the steps leading to the hall the princes of first and second degree had first place followed by the lower grades of the nobility. In the great courtyard below stood the other officials of the nine grades, dressed in their splendid ceremonial robes, and standing in eighteen double rows according to rank and precedent, the civil officials on the east and the military on the west. Two diagonal lines of square paving-stones which were used to mark the positions can still be seen running across the courtyard. Over these stones were placed bronze covers, shaped like inverted shells, on which were embossed the official rank in Chinese and Manchu. Till recently they were still on view in the hall itself. As soon as the Emperor had taken his seat on the throne, an order was called out and the whole assemblage, as one man, performed the Nine Prostrations, the chief act of the whole ceremony.

Further north, on the same terrace, lies the *Chung Ho Tien* (Hall of Middle Harmony), a smaller, but if anything, even more beautiful pavilion than the last. In this hall the Emperor prepared the messages to be read at the Temple of Ancestors and used to wait before repairing to the *T'ai Ho Tien*.

It was here that the unfortunate Emperor Kuang Hsü was arrested in September 1898, and placed in confinement on the South Lake. At one time an arrow was still to be seen embedded in the roof of this Hall. It was said to have been

BANQUET TO MONGOL CHIEFS

除日保<ruby>和<rt>わ</rt></ruby><ruby>殿<rt>でん</rt></ruby><ruby>宴<rt>えん</rt></ruby><ruby>外<rt>ぐわい</rt></ruby><ruby>藩<rt>はん</rt></ruby><ruby>古<rt>こ</rt></ruby><ruby>知<rt>ち</rt></ruby><ruby>末<rt>まつ</rt></ruby><ruby>紫<rt>し</rt></ruby>

AT THE PAO HO TIEN

shot by Tao Kuang, when as Crown Prince in the 18th year of
the reign of his father Chia Ch'ing (1813) he opposed the
revolutionaries who had broken into the Palace in an attempt
to overthrow the Manchus. This revolution was very nearly
successful, as the guards were completely panic-stricken, and
the rebels actually gained access to the inner palaces. But
they seem to have been badly led, and without any clear plans,
so that Tao Kuang, who still possessed some of the virile
qualities of his forbears was able to collect a few followers
and hold the rebels up, until other troops arrived and drove
them out again. In the hall itself, an iron tablet erected in
1655 prohibiting eunuchs from interfering in public affairs is
worth noting, if only for the persistency with which this order
was ignored, especially in the latter days of the Manchu dynasty.

The third of the three Great Halls is the *Pao Ho Tien* (Hall of
Protecting Harmony) where the Emperor received the scholars
who had taken the highest degree in the Metropolitan Examinations and also the princes of vassal states. All three halls are
of the Ming period.

This is as far as we can go on this side of the Forbidden
City. Returning to the courtyard in front of the T'ai Ho Mên
and passing out through the west entrance, *Hsi Ho Mên* (Gate
of Prosperous Harmony) we come to the *Wu Ying Tien* (Hall of
Military Prowess) which in the old days was used as a printing-
office where the poetical and other literary works of the
Emperors were printed and carefully preserved. For no matter
how bad a poet an Emperor might be, his effusions were all
carefully recorded for the delight of future generations. Indeed,
it was one of the greatest honours an official could receive, if on
his birthday or other auspicious occasion, the Emperor sent him
a scroll, tablet, or piece of porcelain inscribed with a set of verses
or even only a single character written by the Imperial hand.
As a matter of fact, the Emperor Ch'ien Lung, according even
to modern republican views, wrote some quite good verses,
many of which have been preserved on stone tablets in various
places in and around Peking.

The printing-office was burnt down in 1869, and again in
1900, when a large part of the collection was destroyed ; it was
rebuilt in 1903. Adjoining it on the west was the *Hsien An
Kung* (Palace of Perfect Peace), a school where Tibetan and

Turkish were taught for use in the public service, which had become necessary as a result of Ch'ien Lung's conquests in those parts.   To the west of this is a small building reputed to be the bath-house that the Emperor Ch'ien Lung had specially built for K'o Fei, the " Concubine from Afar " (Chapter VII).

Across the way, in the south-west corner, stood the *Nan Hsün Tien* (Hall of Southern Fragrance) which contained the portraits of all the Emperors and their consorts from Fu Hsi downwards, together with those of eminent statesmen and scholars.

From here we emerge from the Forbidden City by the *Hsi Hua Mên* (West Flowery Gate).

CHAPTER III.

NORTH AND EASTERN SECTIONS OF
THE FORBIDDEN CITY

THIS part of the Forbidden City can only be visited from the north. The entrance is by the *Pei Shang Mên* (Northern Upper Gate) which faces the entrance to the Coal Hill. During Imperial times there was a wide open space between this gate and the *Huang Wa Mên* (Yellow Tiled Gate), which latter was the entrance to the Coal Hill. The two walls on the east and west sides of this open space have been pulled down and a highway constructed : thus dividing the Coal Hill from the Forbidden City. The Pei Shang Mên is now the entrance gate to the " Palace Museum " and the former Huang Wa Mên is now the Ching Shan Mên, the entrance to the Coal Hill.

Inside looms up the famous *Shên Wu Mên* (Gate of Divine Military Genius). This is the main north gate of the Forbidden City in a direct line with, and corresponding to, the Wu Mên on the south. It was through this gate that the Empress-Dowager and the Emperor Kuang Hsü fled in the early morning of August 15, 1900, before the approach of the Allied Armies. The ugly inscription in black characters on white stone which defaces the north face of this gate is quite modern, the Chinese name for " Palace Museum. "

Having taken a ticket at the office on the right, we pass in through the gate to an open courtyard, on the east side of which is a well, reputed to be the true centre of the city of Peking. In front of us is a smaller, double set of triple gateways ; that in front, is the *Shun Chên Mên* (Straight True Gate), and behind it is the *Ch'êng Kuang Mên* (Gate of Inherited Lustre). The latter used to have a wooden framework over it ; that is to say it was put in a cangue as punishment for having let the last Emperor of the Mings pass through to his death in 1644 (Chapter IX). We enter through the east side-gate to the Garden of the Imperial Palace (*Yü Hua Yüan*) and see immediately in front of us a high narrow rockery with a pavilion at the top, the *Yü Ching T'ing* (Pavilion of Imperial View). It is now closed on the score of being unsafe. The cave at the foot goes by the poetical name of " Grotto of the Fairies' Home " (*Hsien Chia Tung*). Passing in front of this along a path which, like all the paths in this garden, is artistically paved with multi-coloured pebbles and adorned with numerous specimens of quaint fossils, we come to a pavilion built over a pool called the *Fu Pi T'ing* (Jade-Green Floating Pavilion). The ordinary-looking building to the north of this used to be a library where the Emperor Ch'ien Lung kept his more valuable books. Immediately in front of the pavilion are two old cypresses which have grown together forming an arch, called " Joined-together Cypress." Continuing south we pass the *Wan Ch'un T'ing* (Pavilion of Ten Thousand Springs) standing on a terrace with marble balustrade and approached by four stairways, and come to the *Chiang Hsüeh Hsüan* (Porch of Red Snow) where Ch'ien Lung and his courtiers are said to have forgathered to compose many of the famous Imperial poems. Here, too, in modern times the last Emperor, Hsüan T'ung, used to entertain his foreign guests. In front of it is a raised flower-bed, faced with green and yellow tiles, where grows a flowering shrub called " Peace Flower " which was a favourite of the Empress-Dowager.

Leaving the garden by a small gate in the south-east corner we enter a section of the Forbidden City where there are seven minor residential palaces that were occupied by female members of the Imperial family. The broad stone-flagged passage-way between high red walls is typical of the palace communications and are actually called " streets " in Chinese. The first gate on our left brings us to the *Chung Sui Kung* (Palace of Pure Affection) and then, east across another " street, " to the *Ching Yang Kung* (Palace of Southern View). South of these lies the *Yung Ho Kung* (Palace of Eternal Harmony) which was occupied till her death by Chin Fei, a concubine of the Emperor Kuang Hsü. It now contains an interesting collection of old clocks of European manufacture.

We might add that most of these palaces contain collections of one kind or another, which are, however, no longer of any great interest, as all the best pieces were removed in 1933 to Shanghai, Nanking and other places.

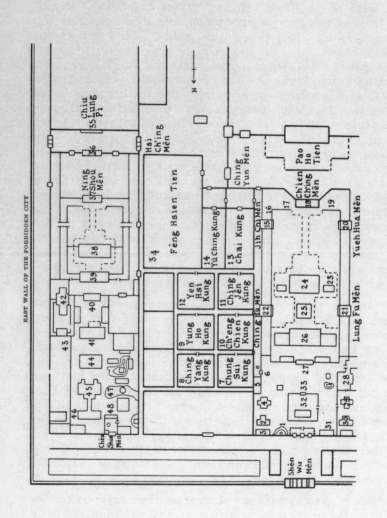

EAST WALL OF THE FORBIDDEN CITY

35 Chiu Lung Pi

36

37 Ning Shou Mên

Hsi Ch'ing Mên

38

39

42

40

43

41

44

45

46

47

48

Chia Shun Mên

34 Fêng Hsien Tien

Yü Ching Kung 14

13 Chai Kung

Ching Yun Mên

12 Yen Hsi Kung

11 Ching Jên Kung

9 Yung Ho Kung

10 Ch'eng Chien Kung

8 Ching Yang Kung

7 Chung Sui Kung

Ching Ho Mên

Jih Ch'i Mên

15 16

17

18 Chien Ch'ing Mên

Pao Ho Tien

19

20

24

25

23

21

22

26

27

5

6

4

3

2

1

32 33

35

31

28

29

30

Lung Fu Mên

Yüeh Hua Mên

Shên Wu Mên

N

6. North-Central and Eastern Section of the Forbidden City

1 *Yü Ching T'ing* (Pavilion of Imperial View)
2 *Fou Pi T'ing* (Jade-green Floating Pavilion)
3 *Li Tsao T'ang* (Hall of Pears and Pondweed)
4 *Wan Ch'un T'ing* (Pav. of Ten Thousand Springs)
5 *Chiang Hsüeh Hsüan* (Porch of Red Snow)
6 *Ch'iung Yüan Mên* (Beautiful Park Gate)
7 *Chung Sui Kung* (Palace of Pure Affection)
8 *Ching Yang Kung* (Palace of Southern View)
9 *Yung Ho Kung* (Palace of Eternal Harmony)
10 *Ch'êng Ch'ien Kung* (Palace of Heavenly Favour)
11 *Ching Jên Kung* (Palace of Benevolent Prospect)
12 *Yen Hsi Kung* (Palace of Prolonged Happiness)
13 *Chai Kung* (Palace of Refinement)
14 *Yü Ch'ing Kung* (Palace in Honour of Talent)
15 *Jih Chi Mên* (Gate of Sunbeams)
16 *Yü Yao Fang* (Imperial Drug Store)
17 *Shang Shu Fang* (Upper Library)
18 *Ch'ien Ch'ing Mên* (Gate of Heavenly Purity)
19 *Nan Shu Fang* (South Library)
20 *Yüeh Hua Mên* (Flowery Moon Gate)
21 *Lung Fu Mên* (Gate of Abundant Happiness)
22 *Ching Ho Mên* (Gate of Complete Harmony)
23 *Hung Tê Tien* (Hall of Vast Virtue)
24 *Ch'ien Ch'ing Kung* (Palace of Heavenly Purity)
25 *Chiao T'ai Tien* (Hall of Vigorous Fertility)
26 *K'un Ning Kung* (Palace of Earthly Tranquillity)
27 *K'un Ning Mên* (Gate of Earthly Tranquillity)
28 *Yang Hsing Chai* (Studio of Character Training)
29 *P'ing Ch'iu T'ing* (Pavilion of Equable Autumn)
30 *Ch'êng Jui T'ing* (Pavilion of Auspicious Clarity)
31 *Yen Hui Ko* (Pavilion of Prolonged Glory)
32 *Ch'in An Tien* (Hall of Imperial Peace)
33 *T'ien I Mên* (Heaven's First Gate)
34 *Fêng Hsien Tien* (Hall of Worshipping Ancestors)
35 *Chiu Lung Pi* (Nine Dragon Screen)
36 *Huang Chi Mên* (Gate of Imperial Supremacy)
37 *Ning Shou Mên* (Gate of Peaceful Old Age)
38 *Huang Chi Tien* (Hall of Imperial Supremacy)
39 *Ning Shou Kung* (Palace of Peaceful Old Age)
40 *Yang Hsing Mên* (Gate of the Culture of Character)
41 *Yang Hsing Tien* (Hall of the Culture of Character)
42 *Ch'ang Yin Ko* (Pavilion of Pleasant Sounds)
43 *Yüeh Shih Lou* (Tower of Inspection of Truth)
44 *Lo Shou T'ang* (Hall of Pleasure and Longevity)
45 *I Ho Hsüan* (Porch of Combined Harmony)
46 *Ching Ch'i Ko* (Pavilion of Great Happiness)
47 *Pi Lo T'ing* (Jade-gre en Porch Pavilion)
48 *Chên Fei Ching* (Well of teh Chên Concubine)

To the west of the Yung Ho Kung is the *Ch'êng Ch'ien Kung* (Palace of Heavenly Favour) which at the end of Manchu times was used as a kind of servants' quarters, where gold-fish and caged birds were housed during the winter months. To the south lie two more palaces ; on the west is the *Ching Jên Kung* (Palace of Benevolent Prospect) which was the residence of the unfortunate "Pearl Concubine" (*Chên Fei*), the favourite of Kuang Hsü. On the east is the *Yen Hsi Kung* (Palace of Prolonged Happiness), now closed. The last palace along the " street " is the *Chai Kung* (Palace of Refinement). East of the Chai Kung is the *Yü Ch'ing Kung* (Palace where congratulations are offered for the birth of a son). In this palace Ch'ien Lung crowned the Heir Apparent Chia Ch'ing, when he abdicated in the sixtieth year of his reign. It was used as a study by the Emperor Hsüan T'ung.

From the residential buildings in this section we now turn west through the *Jih Ching Mên* (Gate of Sun Beams) into the central courtyard. The room immediately south of this gate is the *Yü Yao Fang* (Imperial Drug Store) where there is a shrine to the God of Medicine, together with samples of medicines and medical instruments. Going round to the south terrace we pass some rooms called *Shang Shu Fang* (Upper Library) which were used as a school-room for the sons and grandsons of the Emperor. In the last days of the dynasty the Prince-Regent had his offices here. This brings us to the *Ch'ien Ch'ing Mên* (Gate of Heavenly Purity), the entrance to the Inner Court (*Nei Ch'ao*). Under this name is comprised the whole northern portion of the Forbidden City, especially the residential part, as distinguished from the great Ceremonial Halls. Up to the time of the Republic, the Inner Court was in direct communication with the southern portion. President Yüan Shih-k'ai had the walls east and west of the Ch'ien Ch'ing Mên extended, so as to close off the quarters of the deposed Emperor from the ceremonial halls which it was his intention to use.

The Imperial palaces were built by the Ming Emperor Yung Lo in 1417. The main buildings of this central courtyard were rebuilt and rearranged under the first Manchu Emperor, Shun Chih, in 1655. Though most of them have been repeatedly destroyed by fire and restored, the *Ch'ien Ch'ing Mên* itself is said to be practically untouched and is therefore one of the oldest buildings in the Forbidden City. The early Mings used to give audiences in the open air under this gateway.

On the west of the gate are some rooms called *Nan Shu Fang* (South Library) which were used by members of the Hanlin Academy when in attendance at court. A wooden board with this name, written by a famous scholar, Lu Shih-an, can be seen hanging on the wall facing the door. In a room on the west side of the courtyard, just north of the side gate, used to be exhibited the pictures of Castiglione, the Court painter of Ch'ien Lung. The adjoining room was the study of the Emperor K'ang Hsi. It contains an interesting panoramic view of the Forbidden City and the Lake Palaces painted in the time of Ch'ien Lung. The T'uan Ch'êng and Yü Ho Ch'iao (Chapter VI) can be clearly seen in the middle of the picture.

The raised causeway in the centre of the courtyard forms an impressive approach to the *Ch'ien Ch'ing Kung* (Palace of Heavenly Purity), a building full of historical associations, which the Chinese consider to be the most important of all the Imperial Palaces. In its construction it has undergone many vicissitudes; for since its original erection by Yung Lo it has been burnt down and rebuilt no less than three times, the last being in 1797 under Chia Ch'ing. In Ming times this palace, then called *Ch'ien Ming Kung* (Palace of Heavenly Brightness), was used as living quarters by the last four Emperors; under the Manchus it was converted into an audience-hall.

Two famous banquets were given here : one in 1711 by K'ang Hsi to a thousand old men over sixty, and the other in 1785 by Ch'ien Lung to two thousand old men, on which occasion those over ninety were waited on by the Emperor's sons. After 1900, in accordance with the terms of the Protocol, the foreign envoys were received here in audience. Since the Republic this palace served not only as audience-hall for the ex-Emperor, but also for all his Court ceremonies, the last ever to be held here being on the occasion of his marriage in December 1922.

In later times, two sets of rooms were partitioned off at either end of the main hall by thick red walls and occasionally used by certain Emperors as their private apartments. In one of these side-rooms the Emperor T'ung Chih died of small-pox

CAM-HY
Empereur de la Chine
et de la Tartarie orientale,
agé de 41 an et peint a l'âge
de 32.

THE EMPEROR K'ANG-HSI

in 1874 owing, it is said, to a relapse caused by a violent scene in his presence, when his mother assaulted the Empress Aleuté. The west room was used as an audience-chamber by Kuang Hsü where he saw his officials privately after the public audiences in the main hall. It was in this room that he met and discussed with K'ang Yü-wei his ill-fated reform programme of 1898. And it was in the adjoining main hall that he gave Yüan Shih-k'ai his final audience in the early hours of a September morning, after having taken every precaution that they should not be overheard.

The Emperor seated on his Dragon Throne in the gloomy hall—almost for the last time—gave Yüan Shih-k'ai, who knelt before him, his instructions : to arrest and put to death Jung Lu, the Viceroy of Chihli, the supporter of the Empress-Dowager, and then having taken his place to return with his modern-drilled troops and arrest the old lady. Yüan Shih-k'ai, however, went and betrayed the plan to Jung Lu, and it was the Emperor himself who was arrested and, for all practical purposes, deposed. Here we have a real turning-point, one of the dramatic moments, in Chinese history. For had Yüan Shih-k'ai remained loyal to his master, the whole history of modern China might have taken a different course, and China would at least have been spared the humiliations of the Boxer year.

The small building immediately to the west of the Hall is the *Hung Tê Tien* (Hall of Vast Virtue), once used as a bedroom by the Emperor Hsien Fêng.

Behind the Ch'ien Ch'ing Kung lies a very much smaller hall, the *Chiao T'ai Tien* (Hall of Vigorous Fertility), in the same way as in the " Three Great Ceremonial Halls " the small Chung Ho Tien lies behind the T'ai Ho Tien (Chapter II). This was considered to be the throne-room of the Empress. The Imperial seals (probably facsimiles) are kept here, of which there are twenty-five, looking like ghosts in their long yellow cowls. The oldest seal is said to have belonged to the Emperor, Ch'in Shih Huang (240 B.C.), the burner of the books and the builder of the Great Wall. The water-clock, on the east side, dates from the time of Ch'ien Lung.

Beyond this hall, at the north end of the terrace, stands another interesting palace, the *K'un Ning Kung* (Palace of Earthly

Tranquillity). In Ming times it was the residence of the Empresses. Under the Manchus it was reconstructed and divided into two unequal parts. The larger western part, to which one enters through a comparatively small door at one side, was used as a kind of chapel for the Shaman rites of the Manchus; the utensils and musical instruments used in these rites are still on view here. In the right-hand (north-east) corner is a large stove with huge cauldrons for boiling the sacrificial meats. On the terrace outside is a curious wooden pole, a Sacred Post (*Shên Chu*), on which were hung up bones and strips of meat from the sacrifices and around which the worshippers used to dance.

These Shaman rites were very secret; they took place in the early hours of the morning between 3 and 4 a.m., and none but Manchus were allowed to take part in them. They were held on the birthdays of Emperors or Empresses, as also on the 1st of the 1st Moon. The ceremony was opened by the " Guardian of the Nine Gates " giving the signal for a man to crack a long whip three times, when the huge drum in front of the T'ai Ho Tien was beaten three times, the music struck up, and the Emperor ascended his throne. Troops of men, from sixteen to thirty-two in number, arranged in two rows, then gave a kind of mimic performance. One such pantomime, called " Mi-hu-ma-hu," referred to a legend, that Nurhachu, the real founder of the Manchu dynasty (1559-1626), had in his youth destroyed tigers and bears that devoured children. Killing the tigers was called " mi-hu " and killing the bears " ma-hu." The performers, half of them dressed in black sheep-skins and half in bear-skins, were drawn up in two lines facing each other; each man wore a mask of the animal he was to represent, and a high hat with feathers. The leader of the troupe who took the part of Nurhachu, in a high helmet and fantastic costume, rode on a horse between the lines, firing arrows at the opposing " animals." One of these, supposed to be hit, then fell down, and the others ran off, as if terror-stricken.

Another display was that of *Yang Shang Shu* (Lamb up a Tree). This, too, originated with a story about Nurhachu who is said to have hung a lamb on a tree and waited for a tiger to come, when he shot him with an arrow thus saving the lamb. A third, curious play was that called *Kua Po Chi* (Scraping the Winnowing Fan), also taken from the life of Nurhachu who once met a tiger in a farmyard and, having no weapon to hand, picked up a winnowing-fan, scraped it with a stick and thus scared the beast away. Still another ceremony was that of riding on hobby-horses which were supposed to represent the Eight Banner Corps.* The riders each wore a different costume and a different-coloured flag stuck at the back of their necks, with stilts on their feet covered with small bells which set up a-jingling, as they pranced about on their hobby-horses and imitated the neighing of their steeds. During these ceremonies the band played martial airs, and at the end of each play, the performers made obeisance to the Emperor or Empress.

In the corner of the stove there is an altar to the Kitchen God (*Tsao Chün*), who is to be found in all Chinese households. On the 23rd of the 12th Moon he ascends to heaven to report on the behaviour of the family during the year. On this day all families burn incense to him and offer up honey and other sweetstuffs, the latter, as some say, in order that he might report only sweet things; according to others, in order that his mouth should become sticky so that he could not talk. Here the Emperor Ch'ien Lung used to sacrifice to the Kitchen God in person, beating a drum and singing a popular song called " The emperor in search of honest officials," with the Court drawn up in two rows, and ending with a discharge of crackers to speed the god on his way.

At the east end of the building, divided off by a wall, and with a separate entrance by a large red door, are two rooms which were used as bridal chambers for Imperial weddings. For that reason the interior is painted red entirely, and all the coverings and furniture are red, this being the "lucky" colour, whilst the character *Fu* (Happiness) is painted on the lacqueur screens and doors, as can be seen through the windows from outside.

Passing round to the north by a narrow passage-way, on either side, we come to the *K'un Ning Mên* (Gate of Earthly Tranquillity) through which we re-enter the Imperial Flower Garden.

Turning west we come to the *Yang Hsin Chai* (Studio of Character Training), a two-storeyed building somewhat hidden

*See " Notes " at end.

by an ugly modern scaffolding of painted woodwork for the
mat-shed awning. This was the place where the last Manchu
Emperor Hsüan T'ung's foreign teacher Mr. (now Sir) R. F.
Johnston lived for a time. To the north lie two pavilions,
exactly corresponding to those on the east side : the first is the
P'ing Ch'iu T'ing (Pavilion of Equable Autumn), and north of
it standing over a pool the *Ch'êng Jui T'ing* (Pavilion of
Auspicious Clarity) which contains an altar to the God of the
Pole-Star who is also the God of Literature. To the east,
against the wall, is another two-storeyed building, the *Yen
Hui Ko* (Pavilion of Prolonged Glory) which was used as a
place of refreshment when entertaining visitors.

Retracing our steps south we enter a small separate enclosure, the *Ch'in An Tien* (Hall of Imperial Peace), by the
south gate which bears the striking name *T'ien I Mên* (Heaven's
First Gate). It is flanked by two fierce-looking beasts
in gilt bronze, sitting on their haunches and with erect manes
and tails. They are called *Hao*. Inside the enclosure is a
small, but elaborately arranged, temple to Hsüan Wu Ti, which
is the literary name for the God of Fire. In the courtyard
is an exceptionally tall and thick painted flagstaff, said to be
of one piece.

Leaving the enclosure by the west gate and turning north
we emerge from the grounds by a side door opposite to the
one by which we entered.

Further to the east is another large complex of buildings
containing some of the most interesting palaces in the whole
Forbidden City. When open to visitors, you enter by the Ching
Yün Mên, the gate south-east of the Ch'ien Ch'ing Mên, and
cross an open space to the *Hsi Ch'ing Mên* (Gate of the
Bestowal of Rewards). The enclosure on the north of this
open space contains the memorial hall *Fêng Hsien Tien* (Hall for
Worshipping Ancestors) which is dedicated to the ancestors of
the Imperial family.

Inside the Hsi Ch'ing Mên, on the south wall, is a " Nine
Dragon Screen " (*Chiu Lung Pi*) of coloured glazed tiling,
which is considered by many an even finer specimen of this kind
of work than the one in the North Lake (Chapter VI). Turning
north through the *Huang Chi Mên* (Gate of Imperial Sovereignty)
and then through the *Ning Shou Mên* (Gate of Peaceful Old

Age) we enter the main enclosure containing the buildings of the same name.

It will be noticed that the names of the two gates are arranged in the same order as the two buildings, and it should be observed that the whole enclosure is known by the name of the *Ning Shou Kung* (Palace of Peaceful Old Age). The design, with marble terrace and causeway, is a replica on a minor scale, of the northern central set of halls. This Palace was built by the Emperor Ch'ien Lung in the 37th year of his reign (1773), when he was 62 years of age, and intended for his use, when he retired from the cares of state. It took four years to build. And he actually did retire here in 1795 after a reign of sixty years, abdicating in favour of his son Chia Ch'ing, on the grounds that it would be showing disrespect to exceed the length of reign of his grandfather, K'ang Hsi, who had reigned sixty-one years. Ch'ien Lung lived on here for another four years, not entirely without cares, as he watched the first signs of decay in the great empire which he himself had done so much to build up. After his death the buildings remained unoccupied for nearly one hundred years. When on the accession of the Emperor Küang Hsü in 1889 the Empress-Dowager Tz'ŭ Hsi retired nominally into private life, she took over the buildings for her own use.

The first building, at the end of the raised causeway, a smaller copy of the Ch'ien Ch'ing Kung, is the *Huang Chi Tien* (Hall of Imperial Supremacy). In her later years it was used by the Empress-Dowager as an audience-hall and reception-room. Here took place those final dramatic audiences in the summer days of 1900, when it had become clear that the great gamble had failed and Nemesis was close at hand. The last audience that the Empress-Dowager gave in this hall was late on the night of August 14, when only three ministers attended, everyone else having run away. But she who had still kept her head amidst the panic gave clear and precise instructions for her departure on the following day. It was in this hall too that her coffin was kept for nearly a year, whilst awaiting an auspicious date for burial.

The building behind is the Ning Shou Kung, an exact replica, not only in style, but also in purpose, of the K'un Ning

Kung. For it too was used as a kind of temple for the Shaman rites of the Manchus.

North of this enclosure is an imposing gate, the Yang Hsing Mên, flanked by two fine gilt lions and two large gilt pots, through which we come to a most interesting building, the *Yang Hsing Tien* (Hall of the Culture of Character)—to be distinguished from the *Yang Hsin Tien* (Hall of the Culture of the Mind) in the Western Section. It was the private apartments of both Ch'ien Lung who died here on February 17, 1799, and of the Empress-Dowager Tz'ŭ Hsi. Architecturally it is interesting, because it follows the old Manchu form of construction, differing from the usual regular Chinese type, in that the eastern portion of the front porch is entirely dispensed with. The internal decoration of the building is particularly striking. The palace is divided into three sections, that on the west contained the Empress-Dowager's bed-room, that on the east was used as an ante-chamber for the officials awaiting private audience. In the front courtyard stand two white pines and a sun-dial; in her day it was filled with flowers and rare plants in pots, of which she was so fond. The buildings to the left and right of the courtyard were used as waiting-rooms for the Court ladies in attendance. According to Princess Der Ling who was lady-in-waiting for some months, they left much to be desired, as they leaked badly in summer, and were very cold in winter. But that did not trouble the self-centred old lady. Prior to her flight in 1900 the Empress-Dowager buried her treasure either in this courtyard, or in a secret passage-way behind a hidden panel in her bed-room. Anyhow, wherever she did hide the treasure, she found it untouched on her return from exile. She continued to reside here until the Lake Palaces which had been desecrated by foreign occupation had been purified and repaired.

The "Old Buddha" as the Empress-Dowager was also called, never cared for the Forbidden City and only resided there for short periods, when the exigencies of state or special state ceremonies demanded the presence of the Emperor and herself. Otherwise she lived in a palace at the Chung Hai (Chapter VII) in winter and at the Summer Palace during the rest of the year. She lived in this palace during the stormy summer days of 1900, and a most dramatic scene took place in this courtyard. The Boxers under Prince Tuan broke into the palace one day with shouts of "Kill the *Secondary Hairy One*!", referring to the Emperor Kuang Hsü for whom they were searching and who was suspected of having leanings towards the "Foreign Devils." The Empress-Dowager who was taking her morning tea came out on to the porch in a great rage and soundly rated Prince Tuan and his Boxer braves who were rioting outside. The formidable old lady dominated the critical situation so completely that the whole rabble departed in utter confusion.

On the east is a separate enclosure in which stands an imposing three-storeyed building, the *Ch'ang Yin Ko* (Pavilion of Pleasant Sounds). It is a real theatre, fitted with a special apparatus for letting down the gods and goddesses from heaven by means of a windlass in the top storey. From the building opposite, the *Yüeh Shih Lou* (Tower of Inspection of Truth), the Imperial family used to watch the theatrical performances, while round the sides of the courtyard were boxes for the Court retinue.

To the west is another separate enclosure with a rock garden and numerous small buildings and pavilions.

Continuing north we come to the *Lo Shou T'ang* (Hall of Pleasure and Longevity) which was used by Ch'ien Lung as a library. The west front room was a resting-place for the Empress-Dowager, and several of her personal articles of daily use are still preserved there. There are also two huge blocks of beautifully carved greenish jade, one representing the Mountain of Longevity and one the Sea of Happiness, which for some reason or other have so far not been removed. The wood carving and internal decoration of this building are again worthy of note. The walls of the outside verandahs round the front and back courtyards are covered with stone tablets inscribed with the poems of the Emperor Ch'ien Lung. Behind this building is the *I Ho Hsüan* (Porch of Combined Harmony) which was also used by Ch'ien Lung and the Empress-Dowager. Connected with this is a two-storeyed building, the *Ching Ch'i Ko* (Pavilion of Great Happiness).

On the east side of these latter buildings are numerous rockeries with small kiosks planted on the top, and surrounded by a maze of small, and now dilapidated, buildings. This was a favourite resort of Ch'ien Lung in the last years of his life, especially the beautiful little pavilion perched high up on a rock, to the west of the I Ho Hsüan, called *Pi Lo T'ing* (Jade-green Conch Pavilion).

Finally we come to the *Chên Shun Mên* (True Straight Gate). (It will be noted that these are the same two characters, but reversed, as for the central north gate, mentioned above.) This was the gate used by the Empress-Dowager in her flight on the early morning of August 15, 1900. In the tiny compound, just inside the gate, took place one of the most poignant tragedies of the Forbidden City. For down the well—which can still be seen—was thrown the " Pearl Concubine " (*Chên Fei*),* a favourite of the Emperor Kuang Hsü. There are two versions of this tragedy. The one is as follows :—

Prior to leaving the palace, the Empress-Dowager summoned all the concubines before her and told them of her intended departure with the Emperor. Thereupon the " Pearl " Concubine—who had a will of her own—begged her to leave the Emperor behind, so that he could try and save the country from the wrath of the foreign powers. This interference in public affairs so irritated the old lady, who had anyhow no love for the " Pearl," that she gave orders to throw her down the well, which were carried out there and then in the presence of the Emperor.

The other version, as related by a eunuch who claimed to have been present, is somewhat different. The tragedy took place the day before departure, on the 14th. On that evening, immediately after the last audience of the Grand Council, at which the flight had been decided on, the Empress-Dowager came straight to this spot and sent for the " Pearl " Concubine, who was confined in disgrace in one of the buildings close-by, because at the time of the *coup d'état* she had dared to protest against the deposition of the Emperor. She then told the kneeling girl that she was to be left behind, and that to save her honour she should commit suicide at once by jumping into the well, to which she pointed. The girl rose to her feet protesting that she had committed

---

* See " Notes " at end.

no crime worthy of death, but was interrupted in her pleading by the attendant eunuchs shouting " Obey Her Majesty's commands ! " At a sign from the Empress-Dowager one of the eunuchs, a man called Ts'ui, seized the struggling girl round the waist, carried her over to the well, and thrust her in, the old lady sitting on the stone coping of the little house facing the gate and looking grimly on. The Emperor was not present.

There is also, of course, the Empress-Dowager's own version of this affair, as given in the Decree that she issued on her return from exile, conferring posthumous honours on the " Pearl " Concubine for " her virtuous conduct in committing suicide when unable to accompany the Court in its tour of inspection. This, however, was merely so much eye-wash for the edification of the foreign public. Whichever of the above versions may be the correct one, the cold-blooded murder of the unfortunate girl on this spot is an undoubted fact.

After the deaths of the Empress-Dowager and the Emperor Kuang Hsü the " Lustrous " Concubine, the sister of the murdered girl, erected in the small room to the right of the gate a tablet to her memory before which incense was burnt on the 1st and 15th of each Moon.

The Chinese who enjoy a *double entendre* of this kind say that her death on this spot was ordained by fate, because the name of the gate *Chên Shun* sounds similar to the words *Chên Hsün* (Chên's Death).

We turn west along the broad path outside this gate and arrive back at the main entrance at the Shên Wu Mên.

CHAPTER IV.

WEST SECTION OF THE FORBIDDEN CITY

THE entrance to this section is through a side door in the
north-west corner of the " Imperial Flower Garden "
(Chapter III). On the south side of the courtyard is a
small stage for theatricals, and opposite it is the *So Fang Chai*
(Studio of Pure Fragrance), the palace of Chin Fei, a concubine
of the Emperor T'ung Chih. Adjoining the compound on the
west, is the *Ch'ung Hua Kung* (Palace of Mighty Glory), where
Ch'ien Lung lived when he was a prince; afterwards it was used
by him as a banqueting-hall. The building south of it is the
Ch'ung Ching Tien (Hall of Honour), also intimately associated
with Ch'ien Lung.

We leave this enclosure by the south gate and turn west
through a gateway bearing the curious name of *Pai Tzŭ Mên*
(One Hundred Characters Gate). The first turning on our
right brings us to the *Hsien Fu Kung* (Palace of Complete Happiness). The original name was *Shou An Kung* (Palace of Longevity
and Peace) which was changed to the present name in the
14th year of Chia Ch'ing (1809). For many years it remained
unoccupied; under the Empress-Dowager Tz'ŭ Hsi it
served as a treasure-house; and at the present time it contains
a collection of the favourite personal articles used by Ch'ien
Lung. This palace was repaired in 1932 with the help of a
subscription from Sir Miles Lampson, British Minister to China
(1927-1933), in memory of his wife. In the building at the
back, the *T'ung Tao T'ang* (Hall of Common Principle), the
Emperor T'ung Chih was born.

Going out again by the main gate we turn west and then
north, and come to a group of buildings in a dilapidated
condition. The first is the *Fu Ch'ên Tien* (Hall of Controlling
Time) which was used as a place of retirement and meditation,
and then the *Chien Fu Kung* (Palace of Established Happiness),
a building with blue tiles which was repaired in the 5th year of
Ch'ien Lung (1740). These blue tiles, which distinguish it
from the other palace buildings, were intended to indicate that

it was a retreat for the members of the Imperial family who were in mourning for their parents. In the east room used to be kept the spirit-tablet of the Empress Tz'ŭ An, the Eastern Empress, the consort of the Emperor Hsien Fêng. North of this is a small open pavilion, with green and yellow tiles, called the *Hui Fêng T'ing* (Pavilion of Favourable Winds) which contains some large specimens of fossil wood.

From here we come out on to a large open space called the *Hsi Hua Yüan* (West Flower Garden) where stood several palaces that were all burnt down on the night of June 26, 1923. The dynastic treasures stored in these buildings are said to have all been lost in the fire. Officially the fire was ascribed to carelessness—though there were rumours at the time that it was caused on purpose, in order to hide the considerable pilfering that had been going on. It is certainly strange that the famous *Chung Chêng Tien* (Hall of Righteousness and Equipoise), a temple separated from the other buildings by the rockery that is still to be seen, should have caught fire at the same time and been also totally destroyed. After the fire the ruins were cleared away and the site was turned into a tennis-court and playground for the ex-Emperor Hsüan T'ung. In the north-east corner is a small modern shed containing a pair of huge shoes and a Chinese cap, the Emperor's winter playthings.

Leaving the playground by the way we entered and continuing south and then west, we come to an enclosure in which stands a very fine building of three storeys still in excellent repair. This is the *Yü Hua Ko* (Rain Flower Pavilion), a Lama temple, built in the Ming dynasty under the name of *Lung Tê Tien* (Hall of Abundant Virtue), repaired under Ch'ien Lung, and again in recent times. The brilliant colouring of the decoration and the ornamental carving is particularly fine; the large gilt wooden dragons projecting from under the eaves are a very striking form of decoration which is not to be found in any of the other buildings of the Forbidden City. In the top storey were five idols of "Joyful Buddhas" (*Huan Hsi Fo*); on the middle floor was a shrine to the Emperor K'ang Hsi with his spirit-tablet; and on the ground floor were numerous Tibetan idols, together with lamps of human skulls and boxes made of human bones. The two-storeyed building in the north-west corner is called *Fan Ts'ung Lou* (Tower of the

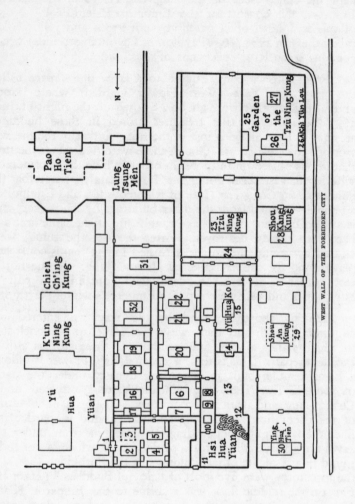

N

Pao
Ho
Tien

Lung
Tsung
Mên

Chien
Ch'ing
Kung

K'un
Ning
Kung

31

32

19

18

16

17

1

3

2

4

5

Yü
Hua
Yüan

Hua
Yüan

21 22

20

6

7

8 9

10

Hsi
Hua
Yüan

11

12

13

14

15 Yü Hua Ko

24

23
Tzŭ
Ning
Kung

28 Shou K'ang Kung

29 Shou An Kung

30 Ying Hua Tien

25
Garden
of
the

26

27 Tzŭ Ning Kung

26A Ch'êng Yün Lou

WEST WALL OF THE FORBIDDEN CITY

7. WESTERN SECTION OF THE FORBIDDEN CITY

1 Entrance from *Yü Hua Yüan* (Imperial Flower Garden)
2 *So Fang Chai* (Studio of Pure Fragrance)
3 Theatrical Stage
4 *Ch'ung Hua Kung* (Palace of Mighty Glory)
5 *Ch'ung Ching Tien* (Hall of Honour)
6 *Hsien Fu Kung* (Palace of Complete Happiness)
7 *T'ung Tao T'ang* (Hall of Common Principle)
8 *Fu Ch'ên Tien* (Hall of Controlling Time)
9 *Chien Fu Kung* (Palace of Established Happiness)
10 *Hui Fêng T'ing* (Pavilion of Favorable Winds)
11 *Hsi Hua Yüan* (West Flower Garden)
12 Rockery
13 Site of the *Chung Chêng Tien* (Hall of Righteousness and Equipoise)
14 *Pao Hua Tien* (Hall of Precious Splendour)
15 *Yü Hua Ko* (Rain Flower Pavilion)
16 *Chu Hsiu Kung* (Palace of Accumulated Elegance)
17 *Li Ching Hsüan* (Porch of Beautiful View)
18 *T'i Ho Tien* (Hall of Sympathetic Harmony)
19 *I K'un Kung* (Palace of Emperor's Assistant)
20 *Ch'ang Ch'un Kung* (Palace of Eternal Spring)
21 *T'i Yüan Tien* (Hall of the Basis of Propriety)
22 *T'ai Chi Tien* (Hall of the Most Exalted)
23 *Tz'ŭ Ning Kung* (Palace of Peace and Tranquillity)
24 *Ta Fo T'ang* (Large Buddha Hall)
25 Garden of the *Tz'ŭ Ning Kung*
26 *Hsin Jo Kuan* (Home of Public Welfare)
26A *Chi Yün Lou* (Tower of Auspicious Clouds)
27 *Lin Hsi T'ing* (Pavilion on the Brink of the Burn)
28 *Shou K'ang Kung* (Palace of Vigorous Old Age)
29 *Shou An Kung* (Palace of Longevity and Peace)
30 *Ying Hua Tien* (Hall of Heroic Splendour)
31 *Yang Hsin Tien* (Hall of the Culture of the Mind)
32 *Yung Shou Kung* (Palace of Eternal Longevity)

Ancestors of Brahma—*Fan Kuo* or Brahma's Country i.e. India). Here were kept the clothes of the Dalai Lama of Tibet, when he visited Peking. If one can obtain permission to enter the *Yü Hua Ko*, a very fine view over the Forbidden City can be had from the top gallery.

North of this, in a separate enclosure, is the *Pao Hua Tien* (Hall of Precious Splendour). Built originally under the Mings as a Taoist temple it was converted into a Buddhist temple under the Manchus.

From here we return north and then east by the way we came, and crossing the "street," enter the *Ch'u Hsiu Kung* (Palace of Accumulated Elegance). This was the residence of the ex-Emperor Hsüan T'ung's consort ; the room in the centre is the throne-room, her sleeping apartments were on the east, and reception-room on the west. The furniture is still as she left it. At the back is the *Li Ching Hsüan* (Porch of Beautiful View) ; south is the *T'i Ho Tien* (Hall of Sympathetic Harmony) ; the side building on the west was the Empress's study. The next building south is the *I K'un Kung* (Palace of Emperor's Assistance, i.e. the Empress), used as residence by various former Empresses. The Empress-Dowager Tz'ŭ Hsi lived here, when she first entered the palace ; some of the books she used are still to be seen. A famous piece of furniture was a large circular mirror, symbolical of conjugal happiness.

Leaving this compound by the main, south gate, and recrossing the street west we enter the *Ch'ang Ch'un Kung* (Palace of Eternal Spring). As its larger proportions indicate, this was one of the more important palaces. Li Fei, a concubine of the Ming Emperor T'ien Ch'i, lived here, as also many other well-known concubines ; and in recent times the secondary wife of Hsüan T'ung. But above all, it was in this palace that the Empress-Dowager Tz'ŭ Hsi lived during the reign of T'ung Chih. The wall paintings in the verandahs at the four corners of the courtyard, from the famous Chinese novel, *Hung Lou Mêng* (Dream of the Red Chamber), are very fine. The perspective is so realistic that, looking across the front of the main building in either direction, the pictures appear to be a prolongation of the verandah. To the south is the *T'i Yüan Tien* (Hall of the Basis of Propriety) which was the original site of the Ch'ang Ch'un Kung. T'ung Chih's principal concubine, Yü T'ai,

lived here till 1924. The last building in this enclosure is the
T'ai Chi Tien (Hall of the Most Exalted), also known as *Chi
Hsiang Kung* (Palace of Revealed Good Fortune). The Ming
Emperor Hung Chih (1487-1505) was born here. The scrolls
on the walls were written by the Empress-Dowager Tz'ŭ Hsi.

Emerging by the main gate we turn west and then south
down another " street," to the second gate on our right which
brings us to the *Tz'ŭ Ning Kung* (Palace of Peace and Tranquillity),
the largest and most important palace in the Western Section.
We enter through a triple gateway flanked by two gilt *chi lin*
(so-called unicorns). The palace was built about the year 1650.
Chien Lung's mother, the famous Empress-Dowager Niuluku,
lived here during the latter part of her life and died here well
over eighty. She was a lady of strong character and exercised
a very considerable influence over her celebrated son who was
greatly attached to her. It was also the residence of the Empress
Tz'ŭ An, the " Eastern Empress," the easy-going and more
respectable colleague of the Empress Tz'ŭ Hsi, the "Western Empress "; they were co-regents during the minority of T'ung Chih.

It was in this palace that Tz'ŭ An, who had been in perfect
health, suddenly fell ill one day in April 1881, and died in a few
hours. The numerous secret Court Memoirs of those times
are unanimous not only in placing her death at the door of Tz'ŭ
Hsi, but also in regard to the details. It is said that she
was taken ill immediately after partaking of some small cakes
of which she was particularly fond that had been sent round to
her by Tz'ŭ Hsi. The accounts differ, however, as to the reasons
for Tz'ŭ Hsi's wishing to do away with her. Some say it was
out of revenge, because Tz'ŭ An, together with Prince Kung,
was responsible for the execution of Tz'ŭ Hsi's favourite eunuch,
An Tê-hai ; others have it that Tz'ŭ An had caught her colleague
in flagrante delicto in one of her love affairs and had reproached
her ; while according to a third version, it was because Tz'ŭ An,
in a moment of expansiveness, had been incautious enough to
show Tz'ŭ Hsi a special edict that their husband, the Emperor
Hsien Fêng, had handed to her on his death-bed, empowering
her to put Tz'ŭ Hsi to death, if she misbehaved herself. How
much truth there is in all this, it is impossible to say ; nor is it
likely that the actual facts will ever be known. Our walk
between the high red walls and through this labyrinth of secluded

palaces will have enabled us to realize, how the darkest crimes
could have been committed here in comparative secrecy, except
for the whispered gossip passed on under bated breath by the
inhabitants of this " Forbidden " city. In any case there is
nothing in the character of the Empress Tz'ŭ Hsi, which should
lead us to regard such a deed on her part as entirely incredible.

At the back of the main hall of the Tz'ŭ Ning Kung is the
Ta Fo T'ang (Large Buddha Hall), an interesting temple the
contents of which appear up to now to have remained completely undisturbed. It is full of finely carved gilt wooden idols ;
at the two sides are the Eighteen Lohans*; in front are two fine
bronze nine-storeyed pagodas and some ancient cloisonné altar-
vessels. The walls are covered with small plaques of the Buddha,
and on the two front pillars hang two large boards inscribed
with characters written by the Emperor Ch'ien Lung.

South of this enclosure, across the way, is a large garden
belonging to the Tz'ŭ Ning Kung, known as " The Garden of
Fallen Favourites." In it stand several temples which used to
contain Tibetan idols of every kind. The central building is
the *Hsien Jo Kuan* (Home of Public Welfare), whilst further
south is a small pavilion over a pool—now dry—the *Lin Hsi
T'ing* (Pavilion on the Brink of the Burn). The building on the
west, the *Chi Yün Lou* (Tower of Auspicious Clouds), is said to
contain " Ten Thousand " Buddhas. And it is true that if you
peer in through the dust-covered windows, you can catch a
glimpse of thousands of plaques with the figure of Buddha
imprinted on them. They are said to be made of special earth
imported from Tibet. In the building along the north wall are
hundreds of small bronze Buddhas of every description, lying
about on the floor, ready for packing, no doubt.

A few more buildings are worth noting, though not
generally shown to visitors. Adjoining the Tz'ŭ Ning Kung
on the west is the *Shou K'ang Kung* (Palace of Vigorous Old Age)
which was the residence of various concubines and other female
members of the Court ; as also was another palace to the north-
east, the *Yung Shou Kung* (Palace of Eternal Longevity).

In an enclosure in the extreme north-west corner is a temple
called the *Ying Hua Tien* (Hall of Heroic Splendour) which has
been repaired in recent times. In front of it stand two
trees which put forth yellow blossoms in June, and bear seed

See " Notes " at end.

in autumn, not from the flowers but from the back of the leaves. These seeds are smooth and round and are called " Buddha's Pearls." · The trees were planted by the Empress-Dowager. In the centre of the courtyard is an open pavilion with a tablet erected by Ch'ien Lung in praise of the Yellow Sect of Lamaism.

Historically interesting is the palace lying close to the Tz'ŭ Ning Kung on the north-west, the *Yang Hsin Tien* (Hall of the Culture of the Mind). It was at various times the residence of the last three Emperors of the Manchu Dynasty. T'ung Chih lived here during his minority; Kuang Hsü too, during both the early and last years of his reign. In fact, it was in this palace that he expired on the afternoon of November 14, 1908.

The circumstances attending the last hours of this well-meaning and unfortunate monarch tend to show that, contrary to the stories of certain apologists of the Empress-Dowager, he had never really got over the degradation of his position nor had forgiven the true author of his downfall. Only a few hours before he became unconscious he wrote out with his own hand a message for his brother, the Prince-Regent, exhorting him to behead Yüan Shih-k'ai at the very first opportunity; while as if to stress the illegality of his position during the latter half of his reign, he obstinately refused to don the ceremonial robes in which, according to etiquette, the sovereign is supposed to expire.

The third and last ruler of the Manchu House to use this palace was the ex-Emperor Hsüan T'ung, also known as " Mr. Henry P'u Yi" who resided here from 1912 until 1924, when he was forcibly expelled for good and all from the Forbidden City into which his ancestors had entered in triumph some two hundred and eighty years before. This was the work of Marshal Fêng Yü-hsiang who to show the purity of his Republican principles, not only allowed his subordinates to loot the palaces, but even tried to have the ex-Emperor shot. The latter managed to escape to the Japanese Legation and later retired to live as a private person in the Japanese Concession in Tientsin. In this case, however, the wheel of Fortune has turned a complete circle. For at the time of writing Marshal Fêng Yü-hsiang is living in retirement and disgrace on the slopes of the sacred mountain, T'ai Shan, in Shantung, whilst P'u Yi has now become Emperor of Manchoukuo, in the original home of the Manchu Dynasty.

CHAPTER V.

THE T'AI MIAO AND THE CENTRAL PARK

THE *T'ai Miao* (Great Imperial Temple), the ancestral temple of the Emperors of China, lies immediately east of the T'ien An Mên, to the south-east of the Forbidden City, that is to say in the most auspicious and important quarter. Here were preserved the spirit-tablets of the Emperors and their Consorts during the Ming and Manchu dynasties. After the downfall of the former, the Manchus consigned the Ming spirit-tablets to the flames and installed their own instead.

The T'ai Miao was built in the 18th year of the Ming Emperor Yung Lo (1420), in exactly the same style as the original ancestral temple at Nanking. It was repaired in 1449, destroyed by fire in 1462 and rebuilt two years later, from which time the present buildings date, though they have been repeatedly repaired and redecorated since then.

The entrance to the east of the T'ien An Mên is of quite recent construction. After taking a ticket, we enter the grounds and see before us a fine grove of wonderful cedars most of which are hundreds of years old. The small bronze bell hanging in the kiosk immediately on our right dates from the 39th year of the Ming Emperor Chia Ching (1560). We follow the path leading north until we come to a broad avenue running east and west. This is called the " Spirit Path " (*Shên Lu*) and leads from a gate in the west wall of the grounds, by which the Emperor entered when coming from the palace. The tree at the corner, the " Spirit Tree " (*Shên Shu*), is said to have been planted by Yung Lo himself who during a visit to the park noticed that most of the trees were dying. No sooner had the new sapling, planted by Imperial hands, taken root than all the other trees recovered and have continued to thrive ever since. It is recorded that, whenever an Emperor passed along this avenue, he descended from his sedan-chair and made three bows to the tree.

From here we enter the temple enclosure itself through a triple gateway and crossing a short courtyard in which are dotted about marble blocks with holes in them for flagpoles, ascend a marble staircase to the *Tsai Mên* (Gate of Lances). On the right of the gateway is a dilapidated-looking kind of cage which according to a notice of the Museum authorities was used by the Emperors for disrobing. This statement, however, seems open to doubt, as a special tent was erected for the Emperor in front of the gate. Some racks for carrying spears and four large wooden frames for lanterns can still be seen in the porch of the gate. In the east side-gate there stands a wooden frame with carrying-poles : this was the conveyance used for carrying the spirit-tablets from their shrines in the rear hall to the main hall.

The oblong-shaped construction of glazed yellow tiles standing on the east side of the main courtyard dates from Ming times and was used for burning the paper and silk offerings connected with the sacrifices ; in the extreme south-west corner stands a similar stove of plain stone for burning the incense.

The rows of buildings on either side contain spirit-tablets. Thirteen on the east side are those of Associate Princes and Dukes, and the same number on the west of Associate Meritorious Ministers. They shared in the Imperial sacrifices, incense being burnt and three bows made before each tablet by Imperial princes specially deputed to perform this ceremony once every quarter. These tablets can still be seen in their places. In the east wing are two tablets of interest. The sixth one from the north end is that of the famous warrior Dorgun who conquered China for the Manchus and acted as regent during Shun Chih's minority. When he was posthumously disgraced, his tablet was removed from here, but was restored to its place by Ch'ien Lung. The other, the last but one from the south end, is that of Prince Kung who managed the affairs of the Empire, and especially its foreign relations, during the greater part of the reign of the Empress-Dowager Tz'ŭ Hsi. In the west wing the only tablet of interest to foreigners is that at the south end, that of the famous Mongol general, Prince Sêng Ko Lin Ch'in—" Sam Collinson " as the British soldier used to call him—who opposed the advance of the Anglo-French forces in 1860. In the two rooms at the north end of each wing were kept the musical instruments and other utensils used in the ceremonies, some of which can still be seen, completely dilapidated and covered with dust.

We now ascend the marble staircase to the first or principal hall called *Ch'ien Tien* (Front Hall), also *Hsiang Tien* (Hall of Joyful Sacrifice). The large tablet in gilt lettering above the entrance bears the two characters *T'ai Miao*, though this name applies to the whole enclosure. The elaborate gilt and green ceiling and the vast dimensions of this building are especially notable. The "Front Hall" is really a Throne Hall and contains the thrones of all the Manchu Emperors and their consorts arranged in the following order :—

NORTH

```
 _____
|     |    |    |    |    |    |    |    |          |
|     | 7  | 5  | 3  | 1  | 2  | 4  | 6  |          |
|     |____|____|____|____|____|____|____|          |
|                                                   |
|  9                                             8  |
|_____|
|                                                   |
|  11                                           10  |
```

1. T'ai Tsu and one Consort	7. Chia Ch'ing and two consorts
2. Tai Ts'ung and two Consorts	8. Tao Kuang „ four „
3. Shun Chih „ two „	9. Hsien Fêng „ three „
4. K'ang Hsi „ four „	10. T'ung Chih „ one consort
5. Yung Chêng „ two „	11. Kuang Hsü „ one „
6. Ch'ien Lung „ two „	

T'ai Tsu or T'ien Ming who is considered the founder of the dynasty reigned as king in Liaotung (Southern Manchuria) from 1616 to 1626. He was succeeded by T'ai Ts'ung or T'ien Ts'ung who took the title of Emperor in 1635.

The above list of names is in chronological order, so that it will be seen that the thrones are placed in alternating sequence to the left and right of the founder of the dynasty.

KEY

1 South Main Entrance	13 West Wing
2 Bell	14 East Wing
3 Spirit Tree (*Shên Shu*)	15 Front Hall (*Ch'ien Tien*)
4 Gate Emperor entered the Grounds by	16 Central Hall (*Chung Tien*)
5 Side Gate (*Shên Chu Mên*)	17 Rear Hall (*Tiao Tien*)
6 Outer Gate to Ancestral Halls	18 Back-gate
7 Kitchen for Sacrificial Offerings	19 Side Entrance to Grounds
8 Store-room for Sacrificial Utensils	20 "Elephant's Trunk" Tree
9 Gate of Lances (*Tsai Mên*)	21 Heronry
10 Side-gates	22 Slaughter-place for Sacrificial
11 and 12 Sacrificial Stoves	Victims

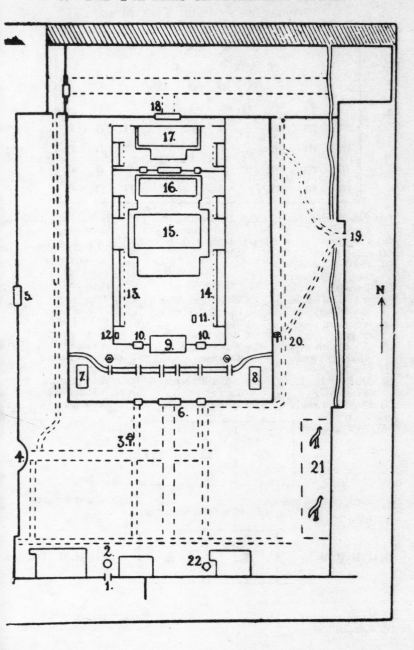

9. DIAGRAM SHOWING POSITION OF SACRIFICIAL OFFERINGS AT THE T'AI MIAO

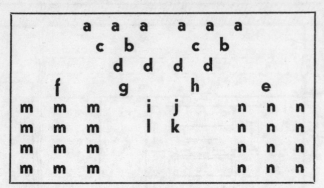

(a) Jade Wine-cups
(b) Lamps
(c) Cauldrons
(d) Soup basins
(e) Bamboo vessel with fruit (*pien*)
(f) Porcelain dish with dried grapes (*tou*)
(g) Vessel with boiled grain (*fu*)
(h) Round dish with parched grain (*kuei*)
(i) Dish with glutinous millet
(j) Dish with paddy

(k) Dish with panicled millet
(l) Dish with yellow millet
(m) Twelve dishes containing :—
  1 White flour cakes
  2 Hazel-nut kernels
  3 Meat cubes
  4 Black meal cakes
  5 Water-chestnuts
  6 Crayfish
  7 Parched grain
  8 Water-lily seeds
  9 Dates
  10 Bean-flour cakes

  11 Dried deer's meat
  12 Chestnuts

(n) Twelve dishes containing :—
  1 Leeks
  2 Celery
  3 Tripe
  4 Pickled meats
  5 Pickled rabbit
  6 Sucking pig
  7 A sauce
  8 Another sauce
  9 Biscuits
  10 A Meat sauce
  11 A Fish sauce
  12 Sea slugs

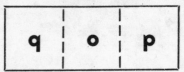

(o) Flesh of a red bullock   (p) Flesh of a white sheep
(q) Flesh of a black boar

u u u u u   s r s   u u u u u

t

(r) Incense burner   (t) Bamboo basket (*fei*)
(s) Candlesticks   (u) Bronze wine jars (*chi tsun*)

The throne of the Emperor is embroidered with a dragon, that of his Consorts with a phœnix; the throne-sets on the east side have the Emperor's throne on the left (of the spectator), on the west side on the right. On the seat of each throne can be seen a flat rectangular stand with a hole in the centre, on which the spirit-tablet was placed at the time of worship.

The various vessels on the tables in front of the thrones are mostly incomplete and modern imitations of the original sets used in the sacrificial ceremonies. The arrangement and details of these sacrifices offered to the ancestral spirits are shown in diagram No. 9.

The sacrificial animals were placed on a special table called *Tsu* in the following order: a red bullock in the centre, a black pig on the west, and a white sheep on the east. These sacrificial tables as can be seen were divided into three parts. After the ceremony the offerings were placed in a special bamboo basket and were distributed in definite and fixed proportions amongst the officials who had taken part in the ceremony. There was also another table on which were placed bundles of silk and satin of various colours which were cut to the right size for making a coat or jacket. After the ceremony was over the Emperor with his own hands presented a piece to each of the officials present. Both the sacrificial viands and these silks were supposed to bring good luck.

The sacrifices took place five times a year: on the 1st day of the 1st, 4th, 7th, and 10th Moons, and on the 29th of the 12th Moon. The spirit-tablets were brought to this hall from the central and rear halls, and elaborate ceremonies were performed called *Ho Chi* (United Sacrifices).

In the olden days, after a victorious campaign a kind of triumphal service was held here, when the prisoners taken in the war were marched in to be shown to the spirits of the departed Emperors who were believed to be looking on. On November 26, 1911, a ceremony of great historical significance took place in this temple, when the Prince-Regent and other Manchu princes, accompanied by the Premier, Yüan Shih-k'ai, performed the nine prostrations in front of the spirit-tablets of their ancestors and confirmed that they had abjured their autocratic rights and had accepted the nineteen articles of the New Constitution, thus transforming the Empire into a Constitutional Monarchy. The Manchu dynasty having lasted well over two and a half centuries, these ancestors must have been considerably surprised, when only a few months later the Constitutional Monarchy came to an end and China became a Republic, since when the ancestral sacrifices have ceased altogether.

Without descending from the terrace we go round to the back of this hall and come to the *Chung Tien* (Central Hall) where the actual spirit-tablets were kept (together with their miniature thrones), arranged in the same order as in the "Front Hall." In the background can be seen the shrines in which the tablets were ensconced, with wooden doors, curtains of yellow silk, and cushions of the same material on which reposed the spirit-tablets. These last were made of wood, as also their covers which were ornamented with rich gilt lacqueur and inscribed with the name and title in Chinese, Manchu and Mongol. Incense was burnt here before them on the 1st and 15th of each Moon by Imperial princes specially deputed by the Emperor. The folded umbrellas standing in front of each group were used to hold over the tablets in wet weather, when they were being taken to the front hall. The Imperial tablets have now been removed from here together with the other Palace treasures, and will doubtless one day fetch up in the "Chinese Room" of some foreign millionaire.

At the back of this second hall is a third one called *T'iao Tien*, the Ancestral Hall of those ancestors who were canonized as Emperor with posthumous honours. That is to say, they were originally merely Tartar chieftains, ancestors of the Manchu House, who were given Imperial rank after the Manchus had ascended the Dragon Throne. Starting from the left (west) they are : Ching Tsu Yi, Chao Tsu Yüan, Hsing Tsu Chih, and Hsien Tsu Hsüan; each with one consort. Incense was burnt before them on the 1st and 15th of each Moon.

At the back of the hall is a gate leading out to an avenue of cypresses overlooking the moat of the Forbidden City. This moat is attractive at all times. In summer it is covered with lotus, whilst in spring one gets the most beautiful effects from the reflection of the wall and of the graceful pavilion at the corner mirrored on its placid surface. We can return from here by going either east or west, and then south outside the temple enclosure. Taking the east route we pass through an opening in the wall and along an avenue of old trees. About half-way down, on the left, is a second entrance to the grounds, that from the Nan Ch'ih Tzŭ. The fourth tree from the south end, where a path joins from the left, has a board bearing the Chinese characters for " Elephant's Trunk Tree " ; an excrescence on the bole of the tree is supposed to resemble a trunk.

In the fenced-in thicket of ancient trees on the east is a heronry. The movements of these birds are said to be very regular. They arrive here on the " Feast of Excited Insects " (roughly early in March) and depart again after the 15th of the 7th Moon, the " Lantern Festival " (about the end of August). During the breeding-season the noise and excitement is great, as they fly to and fro bringing fish for their young from the " Three Sea " lakes.

The park of the T'ai Miao was also notable to the Pekingese in the old days as the nesting-place of vast flocks of crows. Every day at the break of dawn, no matter whether wet or fair, the crows used to assemble in flocks and after circling round several times flew off to the west with hoarse cries. So regular were they in their habits that the inhabitants of Old Peking used to fix the time by their movements and instead of saying " At dawn " used the expression " At the time the crows call. " There was, however, one exception. If the Emperor was going to worship at these dynastic shrines, the crows, it is said, took care to depart at an earlier hour than usual, so as not to meet him. But if a mere prince or other official was deputed to conduct the sacrifices, they did not alter the hour of their departure. The officials in charge of the T'ai Miao used to sacrifice to the crows, deeming them sacred birds. There is a story that, at the time when the Boxer movement was starting in Peking, Prince Ch'ing was deputed to perform the usual ceremony here on behalf of the Emperor. On this occasion, it was noted, that the crows, instead of flying off as usual, continued to circle round over-head for more than an hour uttering loud and harsh cries. Then, at last, they flew off to the west, not to return until the Court came back to Peking after its exile in Sianfu. " Is it not astonishing," remarks the Chinese chronicler, " that the feathered tribe should have a better knowledge of coming events than even the highest and most learned statesmen ? " It seems a pity to have to spoil this pleasant sarcasm, but the truth is, that the noise of the firing and the smoke of the burning buildings during the Boxer madness which had then started was probably quite enough to frighten the crows away from the city for the time being. And for many months afterwards, when the Allied troops were occupying the city, people had quite other things to think of than to notice whether the crows had returned or not. It is, however, an undoubted fact that in recent years the numbers of these crows have very greatly decreased, whether because, as loyal adherents of the dynasty, they disapprove of the Republic, or for what other reason, may be left to the reader to decide.

To the south of the heronry is a small pavilion where the sacrificial animals were slaughtered. A few steps to the west bring us back to the main entrance.*

On the opposite side of the T'ien An Mên, in a position exactly corresponding to that of the T'ai Miao, is the CENTRAL PARK. This is the site of the ALTAR OF LAND AND GRAIN (*Shê Chi T'an*) which dates back to the time of Yung Lo. Since the Republic, however, the Altar has been turned into a fine modern park called *Chung Shan Kung Yüan* (Central Mountain Public Park). Originally the name given to it was *Chung Yang Kung Yüan* (Public Park of the Central Zone); the Central Zone is supposed to be the abode of the Gods of the Soil and forms the centre of the Eight Palaces of Divination; it is sometimes used for " China." The more recent name, Chung Shan, is that adopted by Sun Yat-sen who married a Japanese lady of that name when he was in exile in Japan. Under this name he has since been deified ; and innumerable roads, parks, buildings and even the semi-European form of dress that he used to favour, has become Chung Shan this or that.

On entering the park, after taking a ticket at the office to the right of the entrance, the first thing that strikes the eye, is the marble *p'ai lou* inscribed with the characters *Kung Li Chan Shêng* (Right triumphs over Might). This is the so-called Ketteler Monument, which after the victory of the Allied

---

*In the summer of 1934 the T'ai Miao was used for holding a railway exhibition !

Powers over Germany was transferred to this park, the original inscription having been removed and replaced by the present one (See Chapter XI). Passing under the arch and proceeding north we come to two bronze statues standing on a high pedestal. These are Wang Chin-ming and Shih Ts'ung-yün, who were company commanders in the 20th Division, stationed at Lanchou in 1911. When the Revolution started they went over to the revolutionaries, but were caught and executed. The former " Christian " General Fêng Yü-hsiang did the same, but with his usual luck escaped and many years later, in 1928, when he had risen to power, erected this monument to the two officers who had been in the same battalion as himself, bestowing on them the posthumous titles of " Great Military Commander " and " Deputy Generalissimo."

Going west from here we see on our left (south) a beautiful pavilion the *Hsi Li T'ing* in which the Emperor used to practice the ceremonies to be performed at the Altar. Immediately in front of this, on the north side, is a pedestal erected to Sun Yat-sen by the Peking Labour Unions on May 26, 1929, when his mortal remains were laid to rest at Nanking.

To the north is a sun-dial and, a short distance from it, are a couple of large stone lions, one on each side of the massive red gate in the outer wall of the altar enclosure. Entering this gate we proceed along a broad path lined on both sides with fruit trees and with flower-beds of cement which, it is said, only the expert masons of Peking can construct. These flower-beds contain chiefly peonies, the national flower of China which blooms about the same time as the cherry blossom in Japan, towards the end of May. At that time these flowers are surrounded by admiring crowds from early morn till late at night.

At the end of the avenue we pass through one of the four arches in a low wall that is constructed with tiles of different colours: red on south, black on north, blue on east, and white on west. Inside the wall stands the Altar of Land and Grain, representing the integrity and independence of China. The floor of the square terrace of the Altar is covered with earth of five different colours: yellow in the centre, black on the north, green on the east, red on the south, and white on the west. That is to say: the four cardinal points of the compass with China, the Centre of the Universe, in the middle. The earth was sent as special tribute from four places in the province of Chihli, namely : Chochow, Pachow, Fang-shan Hsien, and Tung-an Hsien. It was forwarded direct to the Board of Rites, where, after a careful scrutiny to see that it was perfectly clean and contained no extraneous matter, it was stored until the date set for the ceremonies, when it was brought to the Altar and sprinkled over the old earth accumulated there.

The gods worshipped at this altar were *T'ai Shên* (God of the Soil) and *Shê Chi* (God of the Harvest), the latter being a divine personification of the energy of the Earth.

Sacrifices were offered here by the Emperor in person in spring on the first lucky day of the first ten days of the 2nd Moon, and thanks returned by him for the harvest in autumn on a corresponding day in the 8th Moon. This form of worship has come down from the practice of the Chou dynasty, nearly one thousand years before our era, when according to tradition the great sage Chou Kung, in choosing a site for a new city on the Lo River, offered up two bullocks to Heaven outside, and to the Spirit of the Land inside, the new city. Kou Lung, Minister of Works to the legendary Emperor Chuan Hsü, was transformed into a divinity representing the Land, and Hou Shih, ancestor of the Chou dynasty, was similarly turned into the God of Grain. Their tablets were placed on the Altar during the sacrifices, the former facing west and the latter east.

In the course of the ceremonies there was music and dancing by young lads between ten and fifteen years of age. Four men in official robes stood round the Altar waving long bamboo poles in the air to frighten away the birds, as it was believed that if anything came between the Altar and Heaven the offerings would fail to reach the gods for whom they were destined.

Some years ago two beautiful and massive urns stood here, which according to official records were cast during the reign of Yung Lo. They have since disappeared and been replaced by four made in the time of Ch'ien Lung.*

---

*Recently two of these have been replaced by two of Kuang Hsü date.

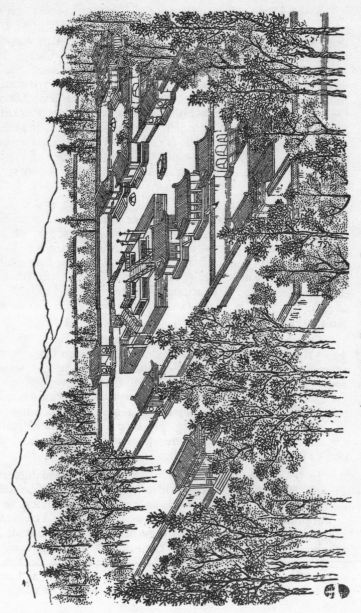

ALTAR OF LAND AND GRAIN

North of the Altar is the *Shê Chi Tien* (Hall of Sovereignty) where the ceremonial instruments were kept ; amongst them were seventy-two halberds, the arms of the bodyguard supposed to protect the Altar. This hall is now called Chung Shan T'ang, in honour of Sun Yat-sen whose portrait hangs on the wall. Behind it is the *Chü Fu Tien* in which the Emperor changed his robes for the sacrifice ; it is now called Chung Shan Library. On the east side of this building is a monument erected to President Harding in gratitude for his assistance to China during the Washington Conference (1922). On the west is another monument, to Ts'ai Kung-shih, the Commissioner of Foreign Affairs at Tsinanfu who was killed by the Japanese on May 23, 1928.

Passing out through the north gate of the enclosure we come to a stone pavilion erected since the Republic, with eight columns bearing classical quotations in large script, of such exemplary nature as :—" When civil officials are no longer intent on gain, and military officers no longer fear death," (peace will prevail). Or, (The Superior Man) " cherishes his old knowledge and is continually acquiring new." Or, " The root of the State is in the family ; the root of the family is in the individual," and so forth.

On the north the grounds are bounded (as at the *T'ai Miao*) by the moat of the Forbidden City. From here we may retrace our steps either east or west. Choosing the western route, i.e. left from the stone pavilion, we pass a " Wee Golf Course," a small park with a few deer, and a skating rink, and turn south along a path lined with tea-houses and restaurants in which large crowds of pleasure-seekers are refreshing themselves. At the end of this path is a verandah leading to one of the most interesting relics in the park.

In a glass-house in which are a few stuffed birds and animals, is a large stone slab with a picture of scenery carved on its north face. On the back is an inscription referring to the " Story of the Orchid Pavilion " (*Lan T'ing Hsü*). The famous calligraphist, Wang Hsi-chih, together with forty friends—all scholars—visited Lanchu, in the district of Shaohing in Chekiang, to celebrate the Festival of Purification on the 3rd of the Third Moon, A.D. 354. There is a small lake at Lanchu with a hilly islet in the middle on the summit of which stood the "Orchid Pavilion." It was in this pavilion that the ceremony took place, and of which Wang Hsi-chih narrated the story of the Purification (*Hsü*). On the north face of the stone tablet is engraved a general view of the place, and amongst the scenery can be seen the forty-one scholars, with the pavilion at the top. (It is a fascinating, but not easy, pastime to try and count these forty-one scholars). On the reverse side is an inscription by Ch'ien Lung in praise of Wang and his friends. In 1785 Ch'ien Lung erected a replica of this pavilion in the grounds of the Yüan Ming Yüan, the old Summer Palace—lake, islet and all. It was destroyed during the Boxer outbreak in 1900, but the stone tablet survived and was later brought here.

Continuing east along the closed-in verandah we reach a place with a number of tubs containing gold-fish. Many of these are of grotesque and even horrible shape, with dragon eyes, finless backs, and calico colours. The names given to gold-fish are peculiar and interesting. Thus we have the "Red Dragon Eye" (*Hung Lung Ching*), somewhat similar to the Japanese Shubunkin ; the "Celestial Telescope" (*Wang T'ien Yü*), with eyes on the top of its head, transparent scales, silver and gold colour; another variety is the "Blue Dragon Eye" (*Lan Lung Ching*). Then there is the "Five Colour Stripes" (*Wu Hua Wên*), distinguished by an extraordinary development of tail fin, which is very long and double, forming a beautiful drapery-like mass which falls into graceful folds sometimes covering the whole body. What is termed in America "The Comet" the Chinese call "Red Stripes" (*Hung Wên*), of which a number are to be seen in the tubs. A most curious-looking specimen is the "Toad Head" (*Ha Ma T'ou*), well-named as it greatly resembles that reptile. Another strange specimen is the "Tiger's Head" (*Hu T'ou*) which foreigners call "Oranda" and the Japanese "Dutch Lion Head." The Chinese claim that the "Tiger-Head" was imported into Korea from China and thence to Japan sometime during the 15th century, for which reason it is also known as the "Korean Gold-fish."

The exact date when gold-fish were first artificially reared in China is not known; but it is undoubtedly of considerable antiquity, going back to the 11th or 12th centuries

A.D. Gold-fish were first mentioned in China by one, Su Shun-ch'in (A.D. 1008-1048) who has left us the following verse: " I stand on the bridge spanning the river and enjoy watching the gold-fish swim by." He was probably referring to them in their wild state, but as China is the original home of gold-fish, where they are still to be found in a wild state, and as they were introduced into Korea in the 15th century, their cultivation in China must have been much earlier.

Leaving these gold-fish tubs and proceeding west along the gallery we cross a bridge spanning the lotus pond and come to a restaurant. Lotus pond, bridge, and restaurant have all been constructed since the Republic, part in 1925 and the remainder in 1928. On the north-west side of the pond is a small eating-house. In Manchu days this was a Temple of the God of War (*Lao Yeh Miao*) whose idol has been removed elsewhere, as he would probably object to the goings-on here at all hours of the day and night.

CHAPTER VI.

THE PEI HAI OR "NORTH SEA" LAKE

THE three lakes on which the Emperors of the various dynasties built their palaces and summer pleasances, are known under the general name of *T'ai I Ch'ih* (Pool of Great Fertilizing Spume), a term having symbolical reference to the female and male principles of nature (*Yin* and *Yang*). The northern lake according to tradition dates back to the Chin (Gold) or Nü-chên Tartars (12th century A.D.), when an Emperor had the waters from the springs in the hills near the present Summer Palace brought to the north of the then capital. Hence the stream which feeds the lake still goes by the name of *Chin Shui* (Golden Water). The lake and park were enlarged by the Mongol Emperor, Kublai Khan, who raised a hill on an island in the lake and planted it with rare trees, giving it the name *Wan Sui Shan* (Hill of Ten Thousand Years). It is the hill on which the white pagoda stands to-day and is described by Marco Polo in very glowing terms.

Yung Lo, when rebuilding Peking, had all three lakes dug out and added greatly to the number of palaces and gardens, as did his successors of the same dynasty and also the Manchus. The Pei Hai was the favourite resort of the Emperors K'ang Hsi and Ch'ien Lung, and especially of the Empress-Dowager Tz'ŭ Hsi, who did more than any of her predecessors towards its embellishment. Under the Manchus, winter carnivals were held on the ice, when displays of skating, skipping and jumping were given by picked men of the Eight Banners. In order to prepare a smooth surface, all bumps in the ice were flattened out with hot irons.

One gets the best view of the lakes from the famous marble bridge which separates the North and Middle Lakes, popularly known as *Yü Ho Ch'iao* (Imperial Canal Bridge). It has two other names : the original name which is sometimes still used, *Chin Hai Ch'iao* (Golden Sea Bridge) ; and the official name

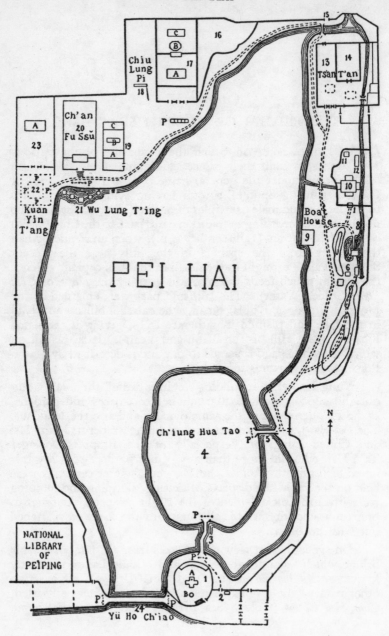

10. PEI HAI

KEY

1 *T'uan Ch'êng* (Circular City)
  A The " Jade Buddha "
  B The " Wine Bowl "
2 South Entrance to Park
3 *Wu Kung Ch'iao* (Centipede Bridge)
4 *Ch'iung Hua Tao* (Hortensia Island)
                See Separate Map No. 11
5 *Chih Chu Ch'iao* (Bridge of Perfect Wisdom)
6 *Yün Hsiu Han* (Cloudy Peak Cliff)
7 *Ch'ung Chiao Shih* (House for Viewing Plants)
8 *Hao P'u Chien* (Drain between Hills and Streams)
9 Boat House
10 *Ch'un Yü Lin T'ang* (Pool from which Plants derive Nourishment)
11 *Ao Kuang* (Inscrutable Mysteries of Heaven)
12 *Tê Hsing Hsüan* (Porch for Recovering Virtue)
13 *Ts'an T'an* (Altar of Silk-worms)
14 *Ch'in Ts'an Tien* (Hall of Imperial Silk-worms)
15 North Entrance to Park
16 *Ching Hsin Chai* (Place of Restful Mind)
17 *Hsiao Hsi Tien* (Small Western Heaven)
  A *Ta Tzŭ Chên Ju Tien* (Hall of the Great and Compassionate True Buddha)
  B *Shih Fo T'a* (Ten Buddha Pagoda)
  C *Ta Liu Li Pao Tien* (Glazed Tile Precious Hall)
18 *Chiu Lung Pi* (Nine Dragon Screen)
19 *Sung P'o T'u Shu Kuan* (Pine Hill Library)
  A *Ch'êng Kuan T'ang* (Hall of Crystal Waters)
  B *Yü Lan Hsüan* (Porch in which Orchids are washed)
  C *K'uai Hsüeh T'ang* (Hall of Joyful Snow)
20 *Ch'an Fu Ssŭ* (Temple of Happy Meditation)
21 *Wu Lung T'ing* (Five Dragon Pavilions)
22 *Kuan Yin T'ang* (Hall of Kuan Yin)
23 *Ta Hsi Tien* (Large Western Heaven)
  A *Ju Lai Fo Tien* (Hall of the Coming Buddha)
24 *Yü Ho Ch'iao* (Imperial Canal Bridge)
  P P P—*Pailous*

Chün Ao Yü Tung Ch'iao (Bridge of the Golden Sea-turtle and Jade Butterfly). These characters are inscribed on the ornamental archways that stand at either end of the bridge, *Chün Ao* on the western and *Yü Tung* on the eastern one. It is undoubtedly the most magnificent of all the bridges in Peking, both on account of its length—it has no less than nine arches—and its finely carved marble balustrades. Its beauties have been the constant theme of Chinese poets, the scholarly Emperor Ch'ien Lung himself having also written some verses which are inscribed on the pillars of the bridge.

Immediately to the east of the bridge is the *T'uan Ch'êng* (Circular City), a fortress-like structure built on what was originally an artifical mound and levelled off at the same height as the top of the walls by which it is surrounded. It dates from the Yüan dynasty when it was called *I T'ien Tien* (Hall of Virtuous Heaven), afterwards changed by Yung Lo to *Ch'êng Kuang Tien* (Hall of Inherited Lustre). There are several old cypresses in the enclosure, one of which called *Ma Sung Wei* (Horse-tail Pine) is said to have been planted under the Chins, before the place was built, a matter of some eight hundred years. There is also a fine solitary white pine just inside the entrance. Through the glass doors of the " Hall of Inherited Lustre " which are kept carefully locked and sealed you can catch a glimpse of the famous " Jade " Buddha seated on a raised platform in the background. The reason why you are not allowed to approach too close is probably that the so-called " Jade " Buddha is not jade at all, but some kind of stone brought from Tibet. Nevertheless it is a remarkable piece of carving, well worth inspection, if only for the beauty of its serene countenance. In the courtyard stands a small blue-tiled pavilion, built by Ch'ien Lung, containing a huge bowl, called " Black Jade Wine Bowl " (*Hei Yü Chiu Wêng*). It is most beautifully carved with mountain streams in which fishes and dragons are seen disporting themselves, whilst the interior is engraved in small script with a wine-song by the Emperor Ch'ien Lung. Verses singing its praises by famous scholars are inscribed on various parts of the pavilion. The bowl is said to be a relic of Mongol times and, according to one account, was lost when this dynasty came to an end, but discovered again under the early Manchus in a small temple where it was being used as a receptacle for pickling vegetables.

In this " Circular City " the British Minister, Mr. O'Connor, was received by the Emperor Kuang Hsü in 1893, when presenting his credentials, instead of in the usual hall, the Tzǔ Kuang Ko in the Middle Lake (Chapter VII). Of further historical interest is the fact that Ts'ao K'un, the last President of the Chinese Republic, who is said to have paid something like thirteen million silver dollars to get himself elected president, was confined in this " city " by General Fêng Yü-hsiang in October 1924, until released by Marshal Chang Tso-lin in 1926. One may suppose that his enforced residence in this historical spot did not cause Ts'ao K'un, who had risen from a very humble station, any illusions as to his having " inherited lustre," imperial or otherwise.

To the east of the T'uan Ch'êng is the entrance to the Pei Hai for which we take a ticket at the box-office. A short distance inside, we come to a pair of stone lions in front of an arch and crossing the marble bridge to a second arch and pair of lions. The characters on these arches read *Chi Tsui* (Accumulated Moisture of Heaven) and *Tui Yün* (Piled-up Clouds). The bridge leads to the island on which is the so-called "White Pagoda." During the Chin and Mongol dynasties it was called " Hortensia Island " (*Ch'iung Hua Tao*), from a plant that is supposed to confer immortality when partaken of. It was not until the 8th year of Shun Chih (1651) that, in commemoration of the first visit of a Dalai Lama of Tibet to Peking, the White Pagoda was built, when the name " Pai T'a Shan " was given to the hill. According to tradition some of the rocks on the hill were brought here from the province of Honan by the Chin Emperors, whence arose the popular legend that the whole hill had moved from there.

Immediately facing the bridge is a group of buildings called *Yung An Ssǔ* (Temple of Everlasting Peace) with a Bell and a Drum Tower in the courtyard and the " Hall of Law " at the back. The name is nowadays somewhat out-of-date, for a modern loud-speaker has been installed in the Drum Tower and certainly does not make for " everlasting peace." Ascending the broad stairway and passing under a *p'ai lou* bearing on its south face the characters *Lung Kuang* (Imperial Brightness), and on the north *Tzǔ Chao* (May a Lucky Star shine on you), we come to a couple of fine pavilions : on

the east is "Welcome Victory"; on the west "Purification of
the Heart." They contain stone tablets with inscriptions recording the history of the island by the Emperors Shun Chih and
Yung Chêng. Behind the eastern pavilion is a large piece of
rock carved with the characters *K'un Lun*, the name of a fabulous
mountain in Tibet with which the hill is supposed to be compared; it was erected by Ch'ien Lung in 1752. To the north-east
in a small separate enclosure are a couple of tablets inscribed with
Buddhist quotations in praise of the temple. Ascending the
next flight of steps we arrive on a terrace with another group of
buildings, the centre one of which is the "Hall of Spiritual
Perception." High above us, on either side, tower two more
pavilions. That on the west is "Far-Off Thoughts" and on the
east "Favourable Clouds"; they were erected by Ch'ien Lung
in 1773. Passing along the front of these buildings in a westerly
direction we come to a large compound containing some fine
trees, called after one of the buildings in it, the *Yüeh Hsin Tien*
(Hall of Joyful Heart). The largest and most prominent
building, however, is the two-storeyed *Ch'ing Hsiao Lou* (Tower
of Felicitous Skies), erected in the reign of Yung Chêng, where
according to tradition the Emperor Ch'ien Lung used to come
with his mother, the Empress-Dowager, on the 8th of the 12th
Moon, to attend the skating parties on the lake.

Following the edge of the terrace round to the east we come
to a broad stone-stepped path which ascends steeply to the
platform on which stands the WHITE PAGODA (*Pai T'a*). On its
southern face is a large yellow character, the mystic Tibetan
monogram: Nam-c'u-vau-dan (The All-Powerful Ten), written
in the form of the Indian character called Ranja or Lantsa.
Directly in front of the pagoda stands a small, high, square
building faced with plaques of Buddha in blue, green and yellow
glazed tiles. This is the *Shan Yin Ssŭ* (Temple for Cultivating
Good Deeds) in which is enshrined Yamantaka, a fierce-looking Lamaistic god, with 7 heads, 34 hands and 16 feet, and a
rosary of human skulls around his neck. In his left hand he
holds an alms bowl, and in the right a bell with which to rouse
the world. The Chinese say that only a horrible-looking god
like this can keep such wild people as the Mongols in order.
From the upper terrace of this temple one gets a very good
view of the city. Behind the White Pagoda stand five (now
only four) large masts that were used in Imperial times to hoist

signal-guns in case of some unusual occurrence such as a fire
or an uprising.

On the slopes of the hill, especially to the north and west, lie
several dozen kiosks, pavilions, and other small ornamental
buildings. They are scattered about in all directions, so that
it is impossible to visit them in any fixed order, and we shall
therefore deal with only a few of the more interesting places.
Those who wish to see all of them should consult the Map
No. 11 to which the numbers in the text also refer.

On the western side, just before reaching the camel-back
bridge, you will notice on your right a small pile of rocks.
These are called *I Fang Shan*, referring to the name of a peak on
which the Western Mother (*Hsi Wang Mu*)* is supposed to dwell
in Fang-shan Hsien in Hopei. On the other side of the bridge
and up the hill is a small building with the same name (15). To
the north of this you see a high square building called
" Source of Sweet Waters " (14) under which is a doorway
leading to a well, " Eye of the Sea " (*Hai Yen*), supposed to be
fathomless and in direct connection with the sea. Still further
north, at the foot of the hill, is the " Pavilion of Diffused Coolness " (48), the tower at the west end of the verandah that runs
round the north side of the island, and close to it a high semi-
circular building, the " Tower for Inspecting Ancient Script "
(19). This name refers to the collection of over 400 stone tablets,
of equal size, which line the walls and contain inscriptions by
three famous calligraphists who lived in the 2nd century A.D.
—Wang Hsi-chih, Wang Hsien-chih, and Wang Hsün. Ch'ien
Lung ordered the building of this " tower " and commanded
the Hanlin Academy to select the best specimens of the above
writings. On the hill-side immediately behind this building is a
curious small octagonal pavilion (20) with stone pillars covered
with inscriptions.

The long double-storeyed verandah, and the numerous
ornamental buildings through which it ran, were in olden days
one of the most beautiful sights in the whole park; they
have now been converted into restaurants. Entering through
any of these buildings and looking up at the hill-side one
gets a good idea of the number and distribution of the
pavilions on this north slope of the hill. Right above us,

---

*See "Notes" at end

KEY

1 *Yung An Ssŭ* (Temple of Everlasting Peace)
2 *Fa Lun Tien* (Hall of Buddha's Law)
3 *Ying Shêng T'ing* (Pavilion of Welcome Victory)
4 *Ti Ai T'ing* (Pavilion of Purification of the Heart)
5 Carved Stone
6 Two Stone Tablets
7 *Yün I T'ing* (Pavilion of Favorable Clouds)
8 *I Yüan T'ing* (Pavilion of Far-off Thoughts)
9 *Ch'êng Chüeh Tien* (Hall of Spiritual Perception)
10 *Pai T'a* (The White Pagoda)
11 *Shan Yin Ssŭ* (Temple for Cultivating Good Deeds)
12 *Yüeh Hsin Tien* (Hall of Joyful Heart)
12A *Ch'ing Hsiao Lou* Tower of Felicitous Skies)
13 *Chieh Hsiu T'ing* (Pavilion of Blossoming Beauty)
14 *Shui Ching Yü* (Source of Sweet Waters)
15 *I Fang Shan* (The Lone Hill)
16 *P'an Ching Shih* (Cottage embowered in Verdure)
17 *Lin Kuang Tien* (Hall of Glittering Gems)
18 *Kan Lu Tien* (Hall of Sweet Dew)
19 *Yüeh Ku Lou* (Tower for Inspecting Ancient Script)
20 Octagonal Kiosk
20A *Mu Chien Shih* (Office of the Overseer)
21 *Pao Ch'ung Shih* (House of Contented Mind)
22 *Yen Chia Ching Shê* (Home of Perpetual Beauty and Peace)
23 *Tê Hsiang Lou* (Tower of Recovering Senses)
24 *Ch'êng Lu P'an* (Receiving Dew Plate)
25 *Hsiao K'un Ch'iu T'ing* (Pavilion of the Small Hidden Mound)
26 *Yen Nan Hsün T'ing* (Pavilion of Perpetual Southern Melodies)
27 *I Hu T'ien Ti* (Pot containing Heaven and Earth—Isles of Bliss)
28 *Huan Pi Lou* (Tower of Pure Jade-green)
29 *Ch'ien Yen Shih* (Home of Steep Cliffs)
30 *P'an Lan Ching Shê* (Peaceful Cottage amidst Coiled Mists)
31 *Hsieh Miao Shih Shih* (Cottage with Beautiful Stone Inscriptions)
32 *Han Ku T'ang* (Hall of Merry-making)
33 *Lan Tsui Hsüan* (Porch of Olive-green Kingfishers)
34 *Chiao Ts'ui T'ing* (Pavilion Girt with Kingfisher Feathers)
35 *K'an Hua Lang* (Corridor for Viewing Pictures)
36 *Ku I T'ang* (Hall of Ancient Rites)
37 *Luan Yin T'ing* (Pavilion in the Shadow of the Peak)
38 *Chien Ch'un T'ing* (Pavilion for Watching the Spring)
39 *Pan Jo Hsiang T'ai* (Wisdom's Fragrant Terrace)
40 *Chên Fang T'ing* (Pavilion of Excited Fragrance)
41 *Hui Jih T'ing* (Pavilion of the Sun's Brightness)
42 Marble Tablet of Ch'ien Lung
43 *I Ch'ing Lou* (Tower at the Edge of Fine Waters)
44 *Yi Lan T'ang* (Hall of Rippling Waves)
45 *Tao Ning Chai* (Studio of Salubrious Peace)
46 *Yüan Fan Ko* (Distant Sails Pavilion)
47 *Pi Chao Lou* (Tower Reflecting the Blue of the Sky)
48 *Fên Liang Ko* (Pavilion of Diffused Coolness)

A A Bridges
B B P'ailous
D Gold-fish Tubs

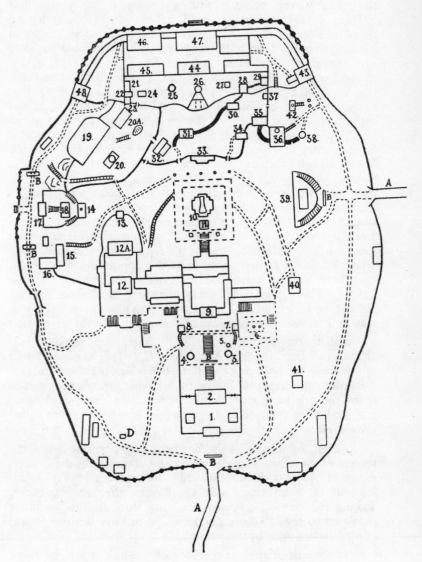

II. WHITE PAGODA ISLAND

standing on a small square terrace with a marble balustrade, towers a carved column with a bronze figure at the top holding a plate above its head, called "Plate for gathering dew" (*Ch'êng Lu P'an*) (24). This is the figure of an Immortal holding over his head with outstretched hands a brass basin to catch the dew. The Han Emperor Wu Ti (A.D. 25-57) is said to have used slaves to stand out in the open all night to catch the dew from Heaven, which His Majesty drank in the belief that it was the elixir of life. A little further down the hill, to the east of the "Dew Plate," is the small, round "Pavilion of the Small K'un Lun Mountain" (25) which recalls memories of a famous story in Chinese legend. It was at this place that Yü Po-ya, a high official of the State of Ch'u, and also noted as a famous lute-player, met a poor wood-cutter called Ch'ung Tzŭ-ch'i, who was even more skilled on that instrument than Yü himself. The latter therefore tried to persuade the wood-cutter to accompany him, but he refused on the plea that his parents were too old to be left alone. They therefore arranged to meet again the following year at the same place and date. But when Yü Po-ya turned up to keep this appointment, he learnt that the wood-cutter had died of grief at the parting the year before. Thereupon in his disappointment he dashed his lute against the rocks and took an oath never to play again. (Ch'ung Tzŭ-ch'i is now the name used for a connoisseur of music.)

Still further to the east, slightly higher up, stands a fan-shaped building, the *Yen Nan Hsün T'ing* (26), a name about which there has been much dispute, but which may be translated "Pavilion of Perpetual Southern Melodies," probably derived from the tradition that the Emperor Shun (2317-2208 B.C.) invented a five-stringed lute and composed a Southern air called *Nan Hsün*.

About the middle of the northern slope, not far below the terrace of the White Pagoda, is a small building with the curious name "Cottage with beautiful stone inscriptions" (31). Leading out of it on either side are tunnels through the rocks. Taking the one on the east you pass through various other pavilions to the "Tower on the Edge of Fine Weather" (42) at the east entrance of the verandah.

Just south of this, at the foot of the hill, is a large stone tablet with inscriptions on all four sides by the Emperor Ch'ien

Lung. On the front are four large characters reading " Hortensia Island Spring Warmth " ; the inscription at the back, dated autumn 1751, commends a certain Kên Yü of the Sung dynasty who " transported many rocks from the South and placed them here in fanciful positions to make them look like dragons' scales." The inscriptions on the sides record visits paid by the Emperor in fine weather and pay a tribute to the beauties of the park generally. In front of this tablet are two shallow basins, each with a carved stone dragon lying in it. According to popular belief both these basins are filled from some supernatural source, as, it is said they neither overflow in the wettest weather nor run dry in the driest.

Proceeding south along the shore we come to a beautiful archway standing in front of a high walled terrace with a curving staircase on either side (39). This is called "Wisdom's Fragrant Terrace" supposed to be the last stage of Nirvana. Facing it is the " Bridge of Perfect Wisdom." The road on the other side of the bridge leads north to the Altar of Silkworms. On the east side of this road we pass several further sets of pleasances, hidden behind high mounds. The first are some pavilions scattered over a rocky hillock which lead to a secluded pool with stone arches inscribed with felicitous phrases. North of this is a large walled enclosure with buildings surrounding another pool, out of which runs the *Hao P'u Chien* (Drain between Hills and Streams). It is occupied by various official bodies and closed to the public. On the bank, on the left, is a former Imperial boathouse, now fast falling into ruins.

Through the triple gateway immediately in front of us we enter the enclosure of the ALTAR OF SILKWORMS (*Ts'an T'an*) with two stone terraces standing in the midst of a beautiful grove of mulberry trees. That on the east is the Altar itself where sacrifices were offered to the God of Mulberries, whilst on the western one the mulberry leaves were examined before being given to the silkworms.   North of the eastern terrace is another enclosure, the *Ch'in Ts'an Tien* (Hall of Imperial Silkworms) in which sacrifices were offered up to the Goddess of Silkworms by the Empress or her deputies on a lucky (*chi*) day during the 3rd Moon of each year. Along the east wall of the main enclosure runs a row of dilapidated buildings, in which the silkworms were reared, and in front of them the Hao P'u Chien the water of which was used for washing the cocoons.

According to the Book of Poetry (*Shih Ching*) the cultivation of the mulberry tree and the manufacture of silk are said to have been invented by Hsi Ling, the wife of Huang Ti in 2602 B.C. But as Chinese history prior to the 8th century B.C. is doubtful, the statement that the cultivation of silkworms goes back to such or, as some Chinese assert, even remoter antiquity, must be accepted with reserve. There are, however, well-attested notices of the cultivation of the mulberry tree and the manufacture of silk as far back as 782 B.C.

Leaving by the north gate of the enclosure we cross the bridge under which run the waters that feed the Pei Hai. On our right (east) is the north entrance to the park. We proceed west past a walled enclosure called *Ching Hsin Chai* (Studio of Restful Mind)· which was a favourite resort of the Empress-Dowager Tz'ŭ Hsi. It contains numerous pools, bridges, arbours, pavilions, all with poetical names such as : " Rare Jade Pavilion," " Playing the Lute Studio," "House of Rare Paintings," " Saving Time Hall," " Pearl House," and so forth. This park is closed to visitors. Continuing south-west along the shore we come to a fine triple archway of green and yellow tiles. On the front (south) face are characters reading " Place of Preservation of the Sutra," and on the north face " Spring-Time in the Centre of the Buddhist World." The *p'ai lou* stands in front of the temple, *Hsiao Hsi T'ien* (Small Western Heaven) to which we enter through a triple gateway, " The Gate of Heavenly Kings." In the first courtyard are drum and bell towers in a state of decay and behind each of them a stone pagoda. In the main hall, the *Ta Tz'ŭ Chên Ju Tien* (Hall of the Great Compassionate and True Buddha), are three Buddhas, with four large models of pagodas in front of them (two of bronze and two of painted wood), and the Eighteen Lohans, nine on either side. In the next courtyard is a pavilion called *Shih Fo T'a* (Ten Buddha Pagoda) containing marble slabs engraved with pictures of the disciples of Buddha. Immediately behind it is the *Ta Liu Li Pao Tien* (Glazed Tile Precious Hall), a beautiful three-storeyed building faced with wonderful green and yellow tiles, the greater part of which bear the figure of Buddha. It was built during the reign of Ch'ien Lung.

Immediately west of the *Hsiao Hsi T'ien* is the famous
CURTAIN WALL OF THE NINE DRAGONS (*Chiu Lung Pi*). This
beautiful example of glazed tilework is famous for its colouring,
and it is worth visiting the park to see this alone. It was
originally erected to ward off evil influences from the *Wan Fo
T'ien* (Hall of Ten Thousand Buddhas), a temple that used to
stand where the athletic ground now is and that was completely
destroyed by fire.

Returning to the shore we come to another walled enclosure,
the PINE HILL LIBRARY (*Sung P'o T'u Shu Kuan*) erected by
Ch'ien Lung. In it are the *Ch'êng Kuan T'ang* (Hall of Crystal
waters), *Yü Lan Hsüan* (Porch where Orchids are Washed—as
was done at the Dragon Festival on the 5th of the 5th Moon),
and *K'uai Hsüeh T'ang* (Joyful Snow Hall). The last name is
taken from a poem by Wang Hsi-chih of the Chin Dynasty who,
while in the act of composing some verses about snow, was
overjoyed to see a snowstorm suddenly occur, thus giving zest
to his poetic inspiration. The stone tablet on which the poem
was inscribed was lost for many centuries, until it was unearthed
by a man named Huang and presented to Ch'ien Lung who had
it deposited in this hall. The "Pine Hill Library" has in
recent times been converted into a Memorial Library to Ts'ai
Ao, the revolutionary leader who, by starting a rebellion against
Yüan Shih-k'ai in 1916, upset the latter's plans to make himself
Emperor, thus preserving the republic for a grateful country.
As in the opinion of many Chinese Yüan Shih-k'ai had twice
betrayed the Manchu house, the establishment of this " Ts'ai Ao
Memorial Library " in one of Ch'ien Lung's favourite haunts,
will perhaps have been regarded with more composure by the
shades of that Emperor than might otherwise have been the case.

Continuing along the shore, we come to the famous
FIVE DRAGON PAVILIONS (*Wu Lung T'ing*) built out in the lake
and connected with the shore, and with each other, by a short
stone causeway. If you examine carefully the position of these
five pavilions, you will notice that they are built on tiny penin-
sulas forming curves to resemble a dragon's body. The dome
of the largest and central pavilion is decorated with many
beautifully carved dragons. In Chinese legend the Five Dragons
refer to the five sons of Kung Sha-mu, who lived at Chiaotung
in the province of Shantung in the 2nd century A.D. These

five sons all became famous in the Academy of Learning under
the name of the " Five Dragons of Learning." Each of the
pavilions has its special designation. Starting from the east, we
have " Fertilizing Fragrance," " Pure and Productive Waters,"
the central one " Dragon Marsh," " Bubbling Luck,"
" Floating Kingfisher Feathers." All these are simply felicitous
phrases in praise of the lake over which the pavilions are built.

Immediately north of these pavilions is a temple in complete ruin, called *Ch'an Fu Ssŭ* (Temple of Happy Meditation)
which contains an idol of *Ju Lai Fo* (The Coming Buddha),
and at the back a couple of stone tablets with inscriptions by
Ch'ien Lung in Chinese, Manchu, and Mongol.

Further west we come to the *Ta Hsi T'ien* (Great Western
Heaven), built in the reign of K'ang Hsi. The vast open
hall standing in front of the temple is of unusual construction
and is surrounded on four sides by beautiful archways of glazed
tiling with inscriptions from Buddhist texts. This hall has
several names : *Kuan Yin Tien* (Hall of Kuan Yin), *Wan Fo Lou*
(Tower of Ten Thousand Buddhas), and *Lo Han Shan* (Lohan
Mountain). It contains several hundred plaster figures supposed
to represent. the different stages of reincarnation. It was
possible a few years ago to climb the rickety stairs to the top
of the " Heavenly Mountain" ; but the gate leading to the
stairs has been sealed with heavy chains to prevent the public
from entering in order to avoid the structure from tumbling
down. In the front courtyard of the temple are a marble
bridge, some stone arches, and several buildings in a state of
complete dilapidation. At the back is a three-storeyed building,
the *Ju Lai Fo Tien* (Hall of the Coming Buddha). In front
stands a square stone tablet with Chinese, Manchu, Mongol,
and Tibetan script. It was erected by the order of Ch'ien
Lung in 1770 to commemorate the anniversary of K'ang Hsi's
sixtieth birthday, stating *inter alia* that all the nations of the
world sent congratulations in honour of the event. The
companion tablet on the east side has completely disappeared.
In the temple itself is an idol of the Ju Lai Fo and one of his
disciples ; the remainder—there were formerly thirteen all told—
are missing, as also every one of the small plaster Buddhas that
used to fill the niches in the woodwork which covers the walls.
At the back of this hall, in a small pavilion on the west side, is a

circular dagoba on which are engraved sixteen Lohans, with the name inscribed above each picture.

From the days of the Chins right down to recent times this "North Sea" was forbidden ground, unseen by the eye of ordinary mortals. In 1925 it was turned into a public park, in spite of the outcry raised by those still imbued with monarchist sympathies, and has remained so ever since. One might, therefore, have expected that the Chinese public would have insisted on keeping in good repair the beautiful historical buildings in these grounds, in which they themselves are able to roam at leisure, and that wealthy Chinese patrons of art would have subscribed freely for this purpose. But such has not been the case. A few of the larger buildings have been converted into modern tea-houses and restaurants, because they bring in a little money, and all the rest are left to go to wrack and ruin.

The best time to visit the parks is during the 6th and 7th Moons (July and August) when the lotus or water-lily (*Nelumbium speciosum*) is in blossom.*

We have now finished our tour of the "North Sea," and may return to the gate by which we entered, by taking a "Flower-boat" across to the island or, to save a longer walk, may leave by the north gate.

---

*See "Notes" at end

KEY

1 *Hsin Hua Mên* (New Flowery Gate)—South Entrance
2 *Ying T'ai* (Ocean Terrace)
3 *Hsiang Lûan Ko* (Pavilion of Soaring Phoenixes)
4 *Han Yûan Tien* (Hall of Cherishing the Constitution)
5 *Hsiang I Tien* (Hall of Fragrant Robes)
6 *Ying Hsün T'ing* (Pavilion of Welcome Fragrance)
7 *Ch'un Ming Lou* (Tower of Brightness of Spring)
8 *Chan Hsü Lou* (Tower of Tranquil Firmament)
9 *Jan Yü T'ing* (Pavilion of Darting Fish)
10 *Jên Tzǔ Liu* (Man Character Willow)
11 *Yün Hui Lou* (Tower Seeing through the Clouds)
12 *Jih Chih Ko* (Pavilion of Daily Increasing Knowledge)
13 *Pi Shu Lou* (Tower for Escaping the Heat)
14 *Fêng Tsê Yûan* (Fruitful Garden)
15 *Wan Tzǔ Lang* (Swastika Gallery)
16 *Chü Jên T'ang* (Hall of Exalted Aim)
17 *Huai Jên T'ang* (Palace Steeped in Compassion)
      (A) *Yen Ch'ing Lou* (Tower of Prolonged Prosperity)
      (B) *I Lûan Tien* (Hall of Ceremonial Phoenixes)
18 Swimming Pool
19 *Tzǔ Kuang Ko* (Throne Hall of Purple Effulgence)
20 *Shih Ying Kung* (Seasonable Palace)
21 *Fu Hua Mên* (Happy Flowery Gate)—North Entrance
22 *Wan Shan Tien* (Hall of Ten Thousand Virtues)
23 *Ta Pei Tien* (Hall of Sympathy and Sorrow)
24 *Shui Yün Hsieh* (Kiosk of Clouds reflected in the Waters)
25 Boat House
26 *Hsi Yûan Mên* (West Park Gate)—East Entrance

CHAPTER VII.

THE NAN HAI AND CHUNG HAI OR "SOUTH AND MIDDLE SEA" LAKES

DURING the Chin dynasty this whole chain of lakes was called *Hsi Hai Tzŭ* (Western Sea), also *Hsi Hua T'an* (West Flower Lake). Under the Liao dynasty it had already been dredged, the mud being used to construct the island in the South Sea. Many pavilions, palaces and arbours were erected, thousands of trees and shrubs planted, and it was used as a kind of Travelling Lodge (*Hsing Kung*). During the Yüan or Mongol dynasty the name was changed to *Ta Nei* (Imperial Palace Enclosure) and it was made their "Forbidden City." It was not until the Mings that the present "Forbidden City" was built, when the name Ta Nei was altered to *Hsi Yüan* (West Park), also *Chin Hai* (Golden Sea). The Ming Emperor Yung Lo improved the "Sea" and made it his pleasure resort. K'ang Hsi altered the Ming names to North, Central and South Seas, as we have them at present ; he and his successors also added to the beauties of the park.*

I. THE "SOUTH SEA" LAKE (NAN HAI)

We enter the South Sea Park by the *Hsin Hua Mên* (New Flowery Gate) which lies on the north side of the Hsi Ch'ang An Chieh. The present gate was originally not a gate at all, but a two-storeyed pavilion that the Emperor Ch'ien Lung had erected for the Mohammedan concubine of whom he was so fond, officially known as *Hsiang Fei* (Fragrant Concubine), but more commonly referred to as *K'o Fei* (Stranger Concubine). To this pavilion he gave the very appropriate name of *Wang Chia Lou* (Thoughts of Home Tower), for it was from here that the Fragrant Concubine used to gaze out on the

---

*Both the Nan Hai and the Chung Hai were thrown open to the public in 1928, but have been closed again since 1933.

Mohammedan quarter across the way (Chapter XII) which reminded her of her far-off home in Turkestan.

This Hsiang Fei was the wife of a Mohammedan chief, Ali Arslan. The fame of her beauty, and especially of the softness of her skin, which had spread all over her homeland, had come to the ears of the Emperor who ordered his generals to try and secure her for his Court. When her husband committed suicide after his defeat by the Chinese, she was brought to Peking where the Emperor at once succumbed to her beauty. He was, however, unable to bend her to his will, either by kindness or by intimidation, for she threatened to slay him first and then herself, rather than become his concubine. Nevertheless, the Emperor hoping against hope that time would weaken her resolution determined to wait patiently and in the meantime did everything to try and gain her goodwill. Nor would he listen to the advice of his mother, the Empress-Dowager, who strongly disapproved of her son's infatuation for the Fragrant Concubine and tried to persuade him to send her back to her home.

But on the Winter Solstice, when Ch'ien Lung had left the palace to go out to worship at the Altar of Heaven, she sent for the Fragrant Concubine and told her that she must either submit to the Emperor's wishes or commit suicide. The girl chose the latter alternative and was taken to an empty side building where she hanged herself.* When Ch'ien Lung was told by a confidential eunuch that his mother had summoned the Fragrant Concubine to her presence, he became very alarmed and, contrary to all precedent, left the Hall of Abstinence where he was awaiting the ceremony of the following day and hastened back to the palace, only to find that he was too late. Hsiang Fei was buried with all the honours of a concubine of the first rank. According to tradition her grave is said to lie west of the Altar of Agriculture (Chapter XV).

When Yüan Shih-k'ai as President of China adopted the South and Middle Seas for his place of residence, the "Thoughts of Home Tower" was made into a gate, and the name changed to its present form.

Skirting the lake in a westerly direction—we can also take a boat straight across the lake—we come to the plank bridge

*See "Notes" at end.

which leads to the island called *Ying T'ai* (Ocean Terrace).
The name of the island has undergone several changes. In
Chin and Liao times it was called *Yao T'ai* (Posturing Terrace)
where theatrical performances were held for the Emperors
and their Court. Under the Mings it was *Nan T'ai* (Southern
Terrace). The first Manchu Emperor, Shun Chih, changed
this to its present name. The island is supposed to be a replica
of the Isles of the Blest (*P'êng Lai*) which according to tradition
lie somewhere off the coast of Shantung.

It was on this island that the late Empress-Dowager confined the unfortunate Emperor Kuang Hsü in 1898, the very
spot, by the way, where the reformer K'ang Yu-wei, the
Emperor's confidant had suggested confining the lady herself.
The Emperor was not imprisoned in any particular palace, as
has sometimes been stated, but was allowed to roam about the
island at will. The planks of the bridge were simply withdrawn,
and no boats were allowed to approach the island. It is said,
however, that on one occasion, in winter when the lake was
frozen over, the Emperor actually did make an attempt to
escape across the ice. We might add that Kuang Hsü did not
die on the island, as is commonly reported, but in the
Yang Hsin Tien, in the Forbidden City (Chapter IV).

Mounting the steps that lead up from the bridge we have
before us a long gallery known as the *Hsiang Luan Ko* (Pavilion
of Soaring Phœnixes). Passing through this we come to the
Han Yüan Tien (Hall of Cherishing the Constitution) where the
monarchs used to rest after they had transacted public business.
Beyond it again is the *Hsiang I Tien* (Hall of Fragrant Robes)
where the Emperors changed their robes. This Hall—converted into a restaurant since the park was thrown open to
the public—is often referred to as the Ying T'ai itself. The
whole complex of buildings was used by the Emperor Kuang
Hsü and his retainers as living quarters.

Outside the Hsiang I Tien, on the south, is a petrified tree,
Mu Pien Shih, which the Chinese regard as a veritable " Nine
Days' Wonder." At the southernmost point of the island,
standing out in the water is the beautiful pavilion called *Ying
Hsün T'ing* (Pavilion of Welcome Fragrance). To the east
of it, on the edge of the lake, is a pretty little kiosk, the *Ch'un
Ming Lou* (Tower of Brightness of Spring) and to the west a

corresponding one, *Chan Hsü Lou* (Tower of Tranquil Firmament). Standing right out in the lake on the east side of the
island is a tiny pavilion with the appropriate name of *Jan Yü
T'ing* (Pavilion of Darting Fish). These are only a few of the
more striking of the numerous pavilions, caves, verandahs
and so forth that are dotted about the island.

On leaving the island by the bridge we see a little
way off on our right a large stone tablet with a willow tree on
either side. This is the *Jên Tzŭ Liu* (Man Character Willow)
so called because the two willows meeting in a fork over the
top of the tablet are supposed to form the Chinese character
for " man " (人). The tablet is inscribed on all four sides with
poems by Ch'ien Lung of which the following are short extracts.

That on the face fronting the lake (south), dated Spring
1752, reads :—" The Man-Character Willow derives its life-
giving influence from the Fertilizing Spume of the Lake (*T'ai
I Ch'ih*). Therefore it grows luxuriantly for ever. It is as
old as P'êng Tsu (a great grandson of the Emperor Chüan
Hsü, 2514, B.C. who is said to have been over eight hundred
years of age when he disappeared). No pine or cypress can
compare with it in length of years."

The verse at the back, dated 1753, reads : " The Man-
Character Willow having existed for several hundred years
was blown down this autumn by a storm. The official in
charge is hereby commanded to replace it without delay."

The inscription on the east face, dated Spring 1754, reads :
" The Man-Character Willow is a relic of ancient days. At
the approach of spring it once more puts forth tender shoots."

That on the west face, dated Winter 1767, reads : " In
the days of yore when dancing took place on the Posturing
Terrace the dancers faced towards the Man-Character Willow."

Here our route divides in opposite directions. Taking
the easterly one first, we come to a veritable maze of
rockeries, small gardens, pavilions and kiosks, of which we
will only mention the more important. Crossing a small bridge
we have before us the

T'ai Yüeh Hsüan (Porch for Awaiting the Moon) where the
    Emperor waited for the Empress or some favourite
    concubine whose beauty is likened to the moon.

Hai Shên Tz̆ŭ (Ancestral Hall of the Sea-Spirit).

Ching Kuang (Mirror of Brightness). A hexagonal pavilion.

Ch'ang Ch'un Shu Wu (Studio of Eternal Spring).

Ch'a Hu. A pair of natural curved stone pillars. The name refers to the ivory tablets (*Hu*) that in ancient times Ministers of State held in their hands when addressing the sovereign.

Pao Yüeh Lou (Precious Moonlight Tower), where the Emperor and his consort used to come on moonlight nights to think of Li T'ai-p'o, the famous poet, who wrote a sonnet to the moon and who is said to have been drowned when leaning out of a boat in a merry mood to embrace the reflection of the moon in the water.

From here we cross a second bridge and pass the

Ts'ui Hung T'ing (Suspended Rainbow Pavilion) standing at the top of a pile of rocks.

Shu Ch'ing Yüan (Park of Equable Temperature).

Pao Kuang Shih (Cottage of Congealed Brilliance), where the Emperors used to study.

Crossing a third bridge we have the

Yün Ku T'ang (Harmonious Bell Hall). It is recorded that in the 30th year of Ch'ien Lung (1765) the governor of Kiangsi presented a sweet-sounding bell to the Emperor who ordered it to be hung in this pavilion.

Liu Pei T'ing (Pavilion of the Flowing Bowl).

Ch'ien Ch'ih Hsüeh (Thousand Feet of Snow). A pool which is shaded from the sun most of the year by a pavilion of the same name that stands over it.

Jih Chih Ko (Pavilion of Daily Increasing Knowledge), where the Emperors came to sit in silent meditation.

P'in Chu Shih (Bamboo Guest Chamber).

Yün Hui Lou (Tower Seeing through Clouds). A large two-storeyed building standing at an angle of the shore.

Ch'ing Yin Ko (Sweet-Sounding Pavilion).

Ch'uan Wu (Boat-house). On the edge of the lake.

If we go west from the Jên Tzŭ Liu, we pass a hideous modern structure called *Pi Shu Lou* (Summer Resort) erected by Yüan Shih-k'ai for his numerous wives, and afterwards occupied for a short time by Marshal Chang Tso-lin. To the west of it lies the beautiful park called *Fêng Tsê Yüan* (Fruitful Park). Both K'ang Hsi and Ch'ien Lung took a personal interest in this park, frequently visiting it in order to supervise the planting and care of the mulberry trees growing therein. A large number of the ancient buildings that it contained have been destroyed to make room for new ones that were erected by the Empress-Dowager.

To mention only a few of them, we have the
Ch'ung Ya Tien (Hall of Noble Refinement).
Ching Chi Hsüan (Porch of Secret Repose).
Huai Yuan Chai (Studio of Thoughts of Far-off Days).
Ch'un I Chai (Studio of Simple Meditation).
Ch'un Ou Chai (Springtime Lotus-root Studio).
T'ing Hung Lou (Tower for Listening to the Wild Geese).
Chih Hsiu Hsüan (House for Display of Beautiful Flowers).
Hsü Pai Shih (Chamber of Silent Meditation).
Fo Yü I So (Buddha's Home), popularly known as *Ta Yuan Ching* (Great Round Mirror).
Especially famous are the long winding galleries called *Wan Tzŭ Lang* (Swastika Gallery).

2. THE " MIDDLE SEA " LAKE (CHUNG HAI)

Wending our way north from the Fêng Tsê Yüan we come to the Chung Hai. The first of the more important buildings in it is the *Chü Jên T'ang* (Hall of Exalted Aim), erected as a residence by Yüan Shih-k'ai in 1912-13 in the vast park called *Chieh Fan Chi* (Happy though Burdened with Affairs of State). Yüan Shih-k'ai knew his history ! He selected the name Chü Jên T'ang from a passage in Mencius. When the king's son asked Mencius : " What is the business of an unemployed scholar ? ", the Sage replied : " To exalt his aim ! " Asked what that meant, Mencius continued : " Setting it simply on benevolence and righteousness, he thinks that to put a single innocent person to death is contrary to benevolence, that to take what one has no right to is contrary to righteousness.   One's dwelling should be benevolence and one's path righteousness.   When benevolence is the dwelling-place of the heart, and righteousness the path of life, the business of a great man is completed."

Whatever may be one's opinion as to whether Yüan Shih-k'ai " exalted his aim " in his political career, he certainly cannot be said to have done so as builder and architect, for all

the buildings that have been erected or " restored " by him
are in the worst possible taste.

To the north of the Chü Jên T'ang is the *Huai Jên T'ang*
(Palace Steeped in Compassion). This vast complex of buildings consists of a succession of courtyards leading into one
another, with beautiful gardens, artificial rockeries covered
with creepers, open and covered-in galleries, pools and so
forth. It was the residence of the Empress-Dowager, when
she lived in the Lake Park. The *Yen Ch'ing Lou* (Tower of
Prolonged Prosperity), a large two-storeyed building in the
central courtyard beautifully decorated in brilliant colouring
and with sculptured balustrades, carved doors, and latticed
windows, was specially built for her.

One of the most important palaces of the whole group is
the *I Luan Tien* (Hall of Ceremonial Phœnixes). The " I "
stands for the suite of an Empress or Empress-Dowager, and
the " Luan " for the phœnix which is the insignia of an Empress,
corresponding to the dragon of an Emperor. The name
is taken from an ancient palace at Loyang in Honan, the eastern
capital of China under the Eastern Han Dynasty (A.D. 25).

It was in the I Luan Tien that the dramatic Council of
War was held on June 20, 1900, when the decision was taken
to declare war against all the Foreign Powers. And it was
from here that the Empress-Dowager Tz'ŭ Hsi issued her
valedictory decree just prior to her death at three o'clock in
the afternoon on November 15, 1908. Her remains dressed
in robes of state embroidered with the imperial phœnix were
placed in the coffin which she kept permanently in readiness
on this spot and were borne at midnight to the T'zŭ Ning
Kung in the Forbidden City, to await an auspicious day for
burial.

Another important building is the *Ta Li T'ang* (Grand
Ceremonial Hall). The ceremonial hall was formerly in the
Nan Hai in an annex to the *Chêng Shih T'ang* (Government
Affairs Office), next to the Pi Shu Lou. President Hsü
Shih-ch'ang used to receive foreign visitors there. When
Ts'ao K'un became president, he removed the Ta Li T'ang to
this enclosure.

Continuing our walk north past the public swimming-
pool, opened in 1933 on the site of an ancient park called

Liu Shui Yin (Sound of Flowing Waters), we come to one of the most interesting edifices in the Chung Hai. This is the *Tzŭ Kuang Ko*, usually translated " Throne Hall of Purple Effulgence." This incorrect designation arises from the fact that *Tzŭ* has been taken for the colour, although there is not a sign of purple in the whole structure, the tiles being all green or yellow. As in the case of the *Tzŭ Chin Ch'êng* (Forbidden City) the character Tzŭ is taken from *Tzŭ Wei* (The Pole-star) around which the other stars revolve. For was not the Emperor called " Son of Heaven," and did not all tribute-bearers, envoys and similar lesser stars flock to this palace to be received by him in audience ? And did not Ch'ien Lung in his famous letter to King George the Third say : " My capital is the hub and centre about which all quarters of the globe revolve ? " But Ch'ien Lung had a precedent, none less than the Great Sage Confucius who said that " A virtuous ruler is like the Pole-star, which keeps its place, while all the other stars do homage to it."

It has also been stated by foreign writers that the palace was built during the Ming period. But at that time there was only a terrace here called *P'ing T'ai* (Level Terrace) from which the Emperors used to enjoy the view. It was the Manchu Emperor Shun Chih who erected the present structure, shortly after his arrival in Peking in 1644. He used it to hold military reviews, whilst from here K'ang Hsi watched archery competitions and wrestling matches by Mongol tribesmen. It was not till 1761 that Ch'ien Lung started the practice of receiving Mongol and other envoys and tributary princes in audience in the Tzŭ Kuang Ko.

Here too, in more recent times, the envoys of the Foreign Powers were received in audience, because the ceremony, from which the three kneelings and the nine prostrations had perforce to be omitted, could be conducted in this hall with less loss of face than in the sacred precincts of the Forbidden City. The first of such audiences took place on Sunday the 29th of June, 1873, shortly after the beginning of the reign of T'ung Chih. The Emperor arrived and mounted the throne at 9 a.m. sharp. The Japanese Ambassador was first received by himself, and then the other ministers together were led in by Prince Kung. The Russian Minister as dean of the Diplomatic Body delivered

T'UNG CHIH'S AUDIENCE IN THE TZŬ KUANG KO

a speech of congratulation, and each envoy laid his letter of credence on the table in front of the Emperor. The latter speaking through Prince Kung expressed his amicable feeling for the rulers represented, and the audience terminated, having lasted barely half an hour.*

A short distance north, in the angle of the wall is the *Shih Ying Kung* (Seasonable Palace) in which refractory members of the Imperial seraglio were kept in durance vile. To the right is the *Fu Hua Mên* (Happy Flowery Gate), the northern entrance to the Middle Sea.

Across the lake, on the east side, is a cluster of temple buildings known after the main hall, the *Wan Shan Tien* (Hall of Ten Thousand Virtues). It can be reached either by boat from the west side, or by the east entrance, the *Hsi Yüan Mên* (West Park Gate).

The main hall, originally dedicated to the worship of the constellation of the Great Bear, was a meeting-place of Buddhist scholars. It was here that the Emperor Shun Chih welcomed the pilgrim monks Ying P'u, Yü Lin, and Ch'iung Ch'i. In later years the Hanlin scholars used to wait in this hall for the Emperors when they came to pray for rain.

The shrines which are arranged in a series of three—a main shrine with a minor one on either side—contain the statues of Buddha and his attendants. They are flanked by two lines of Lohans of nine each, with a background of blue and white cloud looking as fresh as if painted only yesterday. The ceilings, too, are fine specimens of craftsmanship and merit attention.

Altogether, the hall is in a remarkably good state of repair, due probably less to the fact that it was the resort of many Emperors and their consorts, than that it has been patronized in quite modern times by presidents of the Republic, such as Yüan Shih-k'ai and Ts'ao K'un. The votive curtains hanging in front of the various shrines are gifts of these latter.

Leaving this hall we come to the *Ta Pei Tien* (Hall of Great Sorrow) which contains the idols of the *San Ta Shih* (Three Great Teachers).†

---

*See " Notes " at end.
†Confucius, Lao Tze, Buddha.

At the back is the *Ch'ien Shêng Tien* (Hall of a Thousand Saints), a beautiful circular pavilion with a seven-storeyed wooden pagoda, that used to hold one thousand Buddhas, now completely disappeared.

This whole group of buildings was constructed in the reign of the Ming Emperor Chia Ching, though they have been repaired at a much later date.

The side buildings in this enclosure contain the most extraordinary collection of gods to be seen anywhere—even in China. There are no less than twenty-four Dragon Kings who preside over the sun, moon, land, water, air, seas, rivers, lakes, and so forth. In another room are the Twelve Dragon Gods who control the Twelve Zodiacal Signs. At either end of this room are the statues of the God of Thunder (*Lei Kung*) with hammer and thunderbolt, and of the Goddess of Lightning (*Shan Tien Niang Niang*) with a mirror in each hand. The peculiar style of the hats worn by some of these deities should be noted. They are called *Mien Liu* (Crown Gems) and are the same as those worn by kings in the days of the Chou dynasty.

In a couple of small rooms on the west side is a collection of votive tablets inscribed by the Emperor Ch'ien Lung and the Empress-Dowager Tz'ŭ Hsi. The tablet over the door at the back is by the former and reads " We bestow favours on all good and honest men." One of the principal tablets is by Tz'ŭ Hsi and reads " Hall of Ceremonial Phœnixes." It has probably come from the palace of that name. Standing out in the lake all by itself—the bridge which formerly connected it with the mainland has disappeared—is a pretty little pavilion with the picturesque name *Shui Yün Hsieh* (Kiosk of Clouds reflected in the Water). It was considered one of the " Eight Famous Sights of Peking."* On a stone tablet inside the kiosk are engraved the four characters *T'ai I Ch'iu Fêng* (Autumn Wind of the Pool of Fertilizing Spume).

We now leave the park by the eastern entrance, the *Hsi Yüan Mên* (West Park Gate), a name, by the way, that reminds us of the old Ming name for the Lake grounds.

*See " Notes," page 326.

CHAPTER VIII.

THE ALTARS OF HEAVEN AND AGRICULTURE

IN the Chinese or South City, at the end of the broad Ch'ien Mên Street lies the *T'ien T'an* (Altar of Heaven) which, in historical importance as well as artistic beauty, excels all the temples not only of Peking, but of the whole of China.

It was built in the 18th year of Yung Lo (1420), the same year in which he rebuilt the wall of the South City. Only once since then has it been repaired, in 1754, when Ch'ien Lung issued an edict ordering the Board of Rites to have the Altar of Heaven repaired without delay, as it was falling to pieces. Since that time, the numerous buildings in the enclosure have been left to the wear and tear of the elements.

The entire grounds are about three and a half miles in circumference and are divided off by walls into an inner and outer enclosure. The latter has two gates, on the west side only; the former has six: one each on the south and north, and two each on west and east. The inner enclosure, again, is divided into a northern and a southern section by a wall running east and west.

The outer enclosure contains nothing of interest except the ancient cypress trees, most of which, however, have been cut down in recent times. Two sets of buildings on the west side, the hall for musicians and the stables for sacrificial animals, have been turned into a wireless station and a medical experimental station, since the establishment of the Republic. We might add that the famous "Peking asparagus" is grown here.

We enter the inner enclosure by the northernmost of the two western gates. Immediately to the south is the HALL OF ABSTINENCE (*Chai Kung*) which is surrounded by a moat; the bridge, balustrades and staircases leading to the various halls are all of white marble. Here the Emperor performed his ablutions and spent the night fasting, in preparation for the ceremonies on the following day.

Turning south from here, we go out through the gate in the wall running east and west, and taking a path going diagonally south-east come to the actual Altar of Heaven, called *Huan Ch'iu* (Round Mound) or *Nan T'an* (South Altar), both names of great antiquity. The altar is enclosed by a double wall : a circular inner, and a square outer one. Both walls have a triple marble gateway at the four cardinal points of the compass, called *Ling Hsing Mên* (Starry Wicket Gate). Between the south gate of the Inner Enclosure and the south outer Ling Hsing Mên is a flagstone pavement on which the Imperial tent was erected.

The altar is arranged in three terraces of white marble representing—from the top—Heaven, Earth, and Man. The upper terrace is 90 feet in diameter, the middle 150, and the lower 210 ; that is to say 3 by 3, 3 by 5, 3 by 7. Odd numbers only have been used, because the categorical numbers for Heaven are odd—and for Earth even—according to Chinese metaphysical doctrine.

In the centre of the upper terrace is a circular slab of marble, surrounded by 9 smaller ones, then 18, 27, and so on in successive multiples of 9, until in the outermost circle the square of 9, 81, the Chinese lucky number, is reached. In the pavement of the middle terrace the circles increase from 90 in the innermost, to 162 or 81 by 2 in the outermost ; and in the lower terrace from 171 to 243, or 81 by 3.

The circular balustrades of white marble in cloud design, surrounding each of the three terraces, have 72 (9 by 8) pillars

---

KEY

A Outer Gates
B Hall for Musicians
C Stables for Sacrificial Animals
D Hall of Abstinence (*Chai Kung*)
E Altar of Heaven (*Tien T'an*)
F and L Depository for Utensils
G and M Depository for Sacrificial Vessels
H Slaughter-house
I Temple of God of the Universe (*Huang Ch'iung Yü*)
J Hall of Annual Prayers (*Ch'i Nien Tien*)
K Hall of Imperial Heaven (*Huang Ch'ien Tien*)
N Covered Passage-way
O Stone Causeway

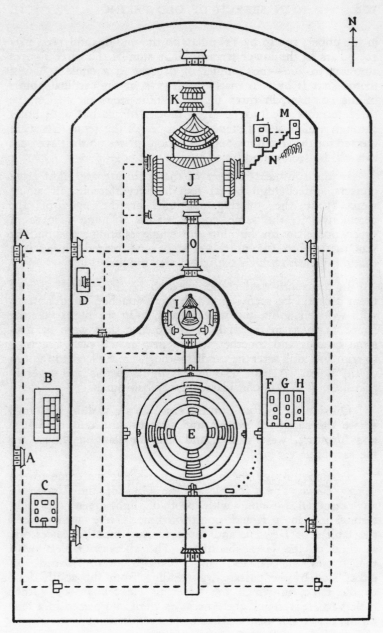

13. ALTAR OF HEAVEN

in the upper, 108 (9 by 12) pillars in the middle, and 180 (9 by 20) pillars in the lower terrace. The sum of the three figures amounts to 360—the number of degrees in a circle. Ascent to the altar is by four marble stairways, at the cardinal points of the compass, in three flights of nine steps each. On the three terraces used to lie large blocks of marble with holes through which were fastened the ropes of the tents that were erected for the ceremony ; and at various places on the pavement can still be seen round holes for the tent poles.

In the south-east corner of the enclosure are eight large cressets, 9 feet high by 21 feet in circumference, in which were burnt the offerings of silk at the end of the ceremony. In the same corner stands a huge furnace of green porcelain for burning the whole offering ; the bullock was carried up the porcelain steps and placed on an iron grating, beneath which the wood was kindled.

In the south-west corner used to be three poles—one of them can still be seen—to which were attached huge lanterns with wooden floors and wire screens. On the night that the Emperor spent in the Hall of Abstinence they were lit with large candles and together with a man inside each lantern— to trim and look after the candles—they were hoisted to the top of the poles. A man who let his light go out was severely punished, as it was considered a very bad omen.

Outside the low wall on the east side are various buildings where the sacrificial vessels and utensils, the tent coverings and furniture, were stored, and also the slaughter-house for the sacrificial victims.

Passing through the northern stone gate we come to the *Huang Ch'iung Yü* (Temple of the God of the Universe), an octagonal building with roof of light-green tiles and terminating in a round point of blue. Here were placed the tablets of Heaven, and those to the Imperial Ancestors, at time of the Great Sacrifice. The ancestor tablets with the names in Chinese and Manchu were placed on either side of the passage-way leading from the south door to the table on which the tablet of Heaven stood. Other tablets to Heaven and the Ancestors were also placed in a tent on the north side of the Altar of Heaven itself.

Leaving this temple by the same gate and turning north we pass through the gate of the wall that divides the Inner Enclosure from east to west, the *Ch'êng Chên Mên* (Gate of Complete Virtue). From there by the raised marble causeway which is still in excellent condition we come to the *Ch'i Nien Tien* (Hall of Annual Prayers), a triple-roofed circular building, 90 feet high, standing on a marble terrace; the pinnacle-shaped dome is covered with blue enamelled tiles, while the ball at the top is thickly gilded with fine gold leaf. This majestic edifice, by reason of its great height, perfect proportions, and wonderful colouring, is the most striking object in the whole park, and is, therefore, often wrongly called by foreigners the Temple of Heaven. As a matter of fact, it was never regarded by the Chinese as an important building, because it had nothing whatever to do with the worship of Heaven. In this hall prayers were said and sacrifices offered for a propitious year, and especially for a bountiful harvest. The ceremony took place during the first *hsin* (Eighth of the Ten Celestial Stems) at the Festival of the Commencement of Spring (*Li Ch'un*). This *hsin* character was an important factor in the ceremony; it means toil, hardship, and industry; and the Emperor's wishes during the sacrifice were that his husbandmen would toil diligently, so as to produce good crops by the *hsin* period in autumn, when the harvest was gathered.

The Ch'i Nien Tien is quite modern. It was struck by lightning in 1889 and completely burnt down. This, by the way, was considered a very inauspicious omen, so much so, that the calamities of the Emperor Kuang Hsü's reign were later always ascribed to the fact that, in spite of this warning, he took over the reins of government in that year. According to the popular version, the disaster was caused by a centipede daring to climb up to the golden sphere at the top, for which sacrilege it was struck by a thunderbolt. The temple took ten years to rebuild and cost, it is said, over twenty million taels.

To the north of the main temple is the *Huang Ch'ien T'ien* (Hall of Imperial Heaven) in which the tablets of Heaven and the Imperial Ancestors were permanently enshrined. In the circular openings of the windows were placed bluish glass rods, thus tinging the interior with an ethereal blue, the colour of Heaven.

From the east gate of this enclosure runs a winding covered-in passage-way of seventy-two compartments, each ten feet in length, leading to another store-house for sacrificial vessels and slaughter-house. The passage-way served as a shelter in bad weather.

In an open space in the grounds south of this passage-way lie seven curiously-shaped small blocks of stone, called *Ch'i Hsing Shih* (Seven Star Stones), because according to legend they are supposed to have fallen from the sky. But they are certainly not meteorites; more probably simply blocks of stone left over, when the temple was built.

The sacrifice at the Altar of Heaven, the most important of all the state observances of China, was a highly complicated ceremony with a deeply spiritual meaning. It is not possible, within the scope of this work, to give more than a general outline, but those who are further interested should consult G. Bouillard's *Le Temple du Ciel* which gives the fullest details.

On the day previous to the Winter Solstice the Emperor proceeded in his elephant chariot to the temple grounds, accompanied by a retinue of over two thousand persons, members of the Imperial family together with high military and civil officials, and entering the outer enclosure by the northernmost of the two west gates, went straight to the south gate of the Inner Enclosure. Here he alighted from his chariot and proceeded on foot to the Temple of the God of the Universe where he burnt incense and prostrated himself before the sacred tablets. Then, after a tour of inspection to see that all was in order for the next day's ceremony, he returned in his chariot to the Hall of Abstinence. Here he spent the night in fasting and meditation, his eyes fixed on a life-size brass image (*T'ung Jên*)—said to be that of a certain eunuch of the Ming dynasty who had changed his earthly for an ethereal form—and implored the spirit to intercede with Heaven on his behalf.

The next morning, about two hours before daylight, officials of the Sacrificial Court came to announce that all was ready. The Emperor having donned his ceremonial robes of plum-coloured silk, with a black satin cap and blue satin boots, went in his chariot to the south gate of the inner enclosure, there to wait in the specially erected yellow silk tent until the sacred tablets had been invited to emerge from their shrine. He then ascended the altar by the south staircase to the middle terrace where he stood facing north. The service opened with peals of music. When everybody had taken up their proper positions, the Emperor ascended to his place on the top terrace, facing the tablet of Heaven and between that of the Imperial Ancestors, where he remained standing whilst the whole burnt offering was placed on the sacrificial furnace. Then kneeling down before the tablets he performed the nine prostrations and offered up bundles of silk, jade cups, and other gifts to the accompaniment of more sacred music. In all, there were three distinct and separate sacrificial services, between each of which the Emperor retired to his position at the foot of the staircase on the middle terrace. When the services had been concluded according to ritual, the round blue gem, the symbol of Heaven, was carried back in a special sedan to its resting-place in the Temple of the God of the Universe. The Emperor having watched the burning of the various offerings, then returned to the Imperial tent to wait until the tablets had been replaced in their shrine, when he ascended his chariot and went back to the palace by the way he had come.

With the overthrow of the Manchu dynasty this impressive ceremony which had been performed for hundreds of years without interruption came to a sudden end. Yüan Shih-k'ai attempted to restore the worship—with slight alterations— during his presidency, but without success. Modern China desired to break with the past. It is, however, interesting to note that when the Kuomintang or Nationalist Party came into power, they found it necessary to create some form of State religion, and so started the worship of Sun Yat-sen. The official ceremonies on the birth and death day of this patron saint of Modern China can thus be said to have taken the place of the ancient sacrifices at the Altar of Heaven.

In modern days the Altar of Heaven has undergone some strange vicissitudes. In 1900 the British forces were camped there, and the terminus of the Peking-Tientsin railway was

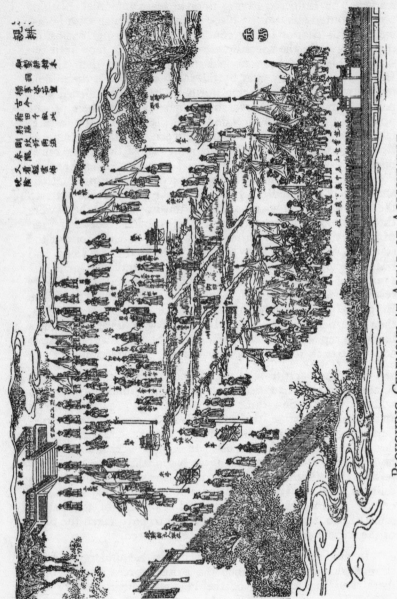

PLOUGHING CEREMONY AT ALTAR OF AGRICULTURE

brought right up to its west gates, until 1902 when it was removed to its present site. In 1917, during General Chang Hsün's ill-fated attempt to restore the Manchu dynasty, his troops occupied the grounds and put up their last fight there. Since then, the outer enclosure has been used for various government bureaus, and Chinese troops have camped here repeatedly in recent times. It is doubtless only a matter of time, before the whole place will be razed to the ground and converted into a municipal swimming-bath or a stadium, or some other equally utilitarian structure.

To the west of the Altar of Heaven is the so-called ALTAR OF AGRICULTURE, built in the reign of the Ming Emperor Chia Ching and repaired under Ch'ien Lung. The Chinese name is *Hsien Nung T'an* (Altar of Agriculture), but this is rather a misnomer, because the temple was devoted to several forms of worship, there being altogether four different altars, each dedicated to a particular deity.

The enclosure was surrounded by a high wall about two miles in circumference and planted with wonderful old cypress trees which, unlike those of the Altar of Heaven, were planted irregularly throughout.

To these grounds the Emperor used to come each spring to plough, as did also some of the city magistrates, in order to give the People an example of industry. Special plots of ground were set aside for this purpose, that used by the Emperor being kept quite apart ; and if for some reason he was unable to attend, it was left untouched. Rice and four varieties of millet were the cereals employed in the ceremony ; the former was the crop sown by the Emperor himself. All the instruments used in the ploughing ceremony were of yellow colour, as also were the oxen. The Emperor, guiding the plough, had to trace eight furrows starting from east to west ; the President of the Board of Finance followed on his right with a whip, and the Viceroy of the Metropolitan Province on his left with the box of seed which a third high official sowed. Princes and other high officials ploughed eighteen furrows of their own, and finally some aged peasants completed the work. The grain gathered in the autumn from this ceremonial sowing was kept in a special granary and could only be used for sacrificial purposes.

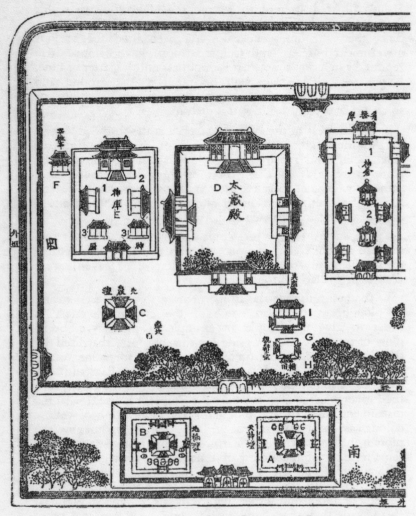

北

太歲殿

14. OLD CHINESE MAP OF THE

NORTH

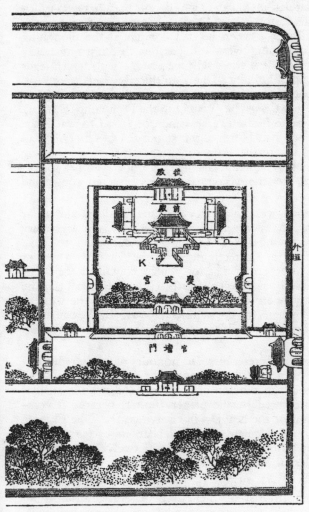

ALTAR OF AGRICULTURE

A Altar to the Spirits of Heaven.

B Altar to the Spirits of Earth.

C Altar to the God of Agriculture.

D Hall of the Year God.

E 1. Hall where Spirit Tablets were kept.

2. Kitchens for sacrificial foods.

3. Wells.

F Slaughter-house for sacrificial animals.

G Terrace for watching the ploughing.

H Ploughing ground.

I Emperor's dis-robing Hall.

J 1. Store-room for musical instruments

2. Store-room for sacrificial utensils

K Palace where Empress await-ed Emperor.

Entry to the enclosure was by the southernmost of the two east gates. On the right is the *Ch'ing Ch'êng Kung* (Palace for the Congratulations on the Completion of Work), so-called because here the Empress used to come to tender her congratulations to the Emperor when he had completed the ploughing ceremony. Continuing west and passing through a gateway in a wall running north and south we reach a path which leads north to a group of buildings where sacrificial vessels were kept. Directly in front of us, looking west, lies a raised terrace fifty feet square called *Kuan Ching T'ai* (Watching the Ploughing Terrace), where, as the name indicates, the Emperor stood to watch the ploughing operations. North of this stands the *Chü Fu Tien* (Hall for Disrobing) where the Emperor, preparatory to performing the labours of a husbandman, changed his Imperial robes for ordinary clothes, to the accompaniment of sacred songs and music.

To the north-west, close to the inner wall, is the Altar of Agriculture itself, erected in honour of the legendary Emperor Shên Nung (2838 B.C.) who is supposed to have invented agriculture. Directly north of the Altar is a group of buildings, the northern rooms of which contained the spirit tablets of the Gods of Heaven, Earth, Hills and Rivers ; in the eastern rooms were stored the sacrificial vessels ; in the western ones were the kitchens for the sacrificial foods. In the courtyard are two pavilions over wells from which the water was drawn for libations.

The religious ceremonies in honour of the traditional Father of Agriculture would, however, not have been considered complete without the worship of the Year God, who in ancient times was represented by the planet Jupiter, because it completes the circuit of the heavens in twelve years. The Chinese used formerly to calculate their calendar in cycles of sixty years, made up from the combinations of twelve " Branches " and " Ten Celestial Stems."

The Altar to the Planet Jupiter or the Year God (*T'ai Sui T'an*) lies north-east of the Altar of Agriculture in an enclosure of its own, which contains a large number of buildings. In the south-east corner was a huge stove in which the animals used for the sacrifice were boiled or roasted. The sacrifice to the Year God was performed on the penultimate day of the year and also on a lucky day specially selected from the first ten days of the year.

Passing out through the inner wall by the south gate we come to two more altars standing together in an enclosure by themselves. That on the east is the Altar to the Spirits of Heaven, and that on the west to the Spirits of Earth. On the north side of the eastern altar stand four beautifully carved marble shrines in which were placed—from east to west—the tablets of the Gods of Winds, Clouds, Rain, and Thunder. On the south side of the western altar are five marble shrines ; three carved with waving lines to represent mountains contained a tablet each, to the Five Sacred Mountains, to the Five Market Towns, and to the Five Hills ; the two others carved with a wave design to represent water, had a tablet each, to the Four Seas and to the Four Rivers.* On the east and west of this western altar there are two other shrines, to celebrated mountains and rivers of the Empire.

The sacrifices at both these altars took place on the same day in midsummer. On account of this worship the whole temple was sometimes also known as the Altar of Hills and Streams (*Shan Ch'üan T'an*). This Nature Cult is very ancient in China, going right back to the Chou dynasty, when sacrifices of this kind which had started as the local worship of individual hills and streams were already included in the regular State ceremonies.

Alas for the beauties and interest of this once famous Altar of Agriculture ! The buildings, when not in use as military barracks, are now used for a police station and other public offices, and are closed to the public. The northern half of the enclosing wall has been pulled down, the majority of the wonderful ancient cypress trees have been cut down, to be used as firewood by the soldiery.

The part of the grounds, north of the inner wall, has been turned into a public park, *Ch'êng Nan Kung Yüan* (South City Public Gardens) which is the name that it is best known by to rickshaw coolies and so forth.

---

* See " Notes " at end.

CHAPTER IX.

THE EASTERN HALF OF THE IMPERIAL CITY
AND THE COAL HILL

ABOUT a hundred yards to the west of the Peking Hotel, inside the south-east corner of the old wall of the Imperial City, lies a small building with yellow-tiled roofs. This is the *T'ang Tzŭ* (Ancestral Hall), a modern building erected in 1901, after the enforced removal of the original hall from its former site in the present Italian Legation (See Chapter 1).

In Chin times (about A.D. 1115) the present site was known as *Hsiao Nan Ch'êng* (Small South City). At the junction of two small streams on this spot the first Emperor of the Chin dynasty built a pavilion called *Ch'êng Shui Ko* (Pavilion of the Sparkling Waters) which name was changed by the Ming Emperor Wan Li in 1602 to *Yung Fu Ko* (Pavilion of Bubbling Happiness). When in 1900 a new site had to be chosen for the T'ang Tzŭ, this was the spot selected by the imperial astrologers as likely to be of good omen for the welfare of the dynasty, in which selection they cannot be said to have been highly successful, seeing that only a dozen years later the Manchu rule came to an end.

The T'ang Tzŭ was a kind of private family chapel of the dynasty, in contrast to the official Imperial Ancestral temple, the T'ai Miao. In times of war or distress the Emperor used to come here to report to his ancestors, and on New Year day he offered up sacrifices to their spirits. As the conquests of the Manchus were chiefly due to their cavalry, an image of the God of Horses (*Ma Shên*) was given a special place in the Hall, and sacrifices were offered up to him, whenever a campaign was about to start and the horses required special care. A Tartar ceremony called *T'iao Shên* (Exorcising the Evil Spirits) was performed here by Mongol witch-doctors (*Shamans*) of both sexes, on the 19th, 20th and 21st of the 1st

Moon. It was quite a festive affair. After the ceremony a quantity of flour dumplings and jars of wine were fought for by those present, each competitor trying to outdo the other in the amount he could eat and drink.

There is a mast about nine feet high standing in the courtyard called *Tsu Tsung Kan Tzŭ* (Ancestors' Pole). At the top is a bronze plate or bowl in which food for birds was placed. The origin of this practice is as follows :—

Once in his youth, T'ien Ming, the grandfather of the first Manchu Emperor Shun Chih, was being pursued by a band of robbers. Following the advice of an old woman whom he met, he hid himself behind a large tree on the branches of which a number of birds were perched. When the robbers came up and saw that the birds were sitting there quietly, and not circling overhead, as they usually do when disturbed, they thought that T'ien Ming must have taken another route and so gave up the pursuit. It was the custom for an Imperial Prince (or sometimes even the Emperor himself) to repair to the T'ang Tzŭ on the night of the 30th of the 12th Moon and offer up sacrifices to his ancestors at the foot of this pole which represented the tree that had saved T'ien Ming's life. At the same time, a new scarf was placed around the neck of T'ien Ming's portrait which stood in the hall. This latter ceremony, called by the Manchus *Huan Hata* (Changing the Scarf), was to commemorate a battle in which T'ien Ming had received a cut on the neck that left a scar for the rest of his life.

In 1926 the local council of the Kuomintang started to pull down the buildings and walls, but the ex-Emperor Hsüan T'ung is said to have hastened in person to Peking and prevailed on Marshal Chang Tso-lin to put a stop to this. Nowadays the premises are in private occupation.

The "river," really a creek, over which the Pavilion of Bubbling Happiness was built has recently been filled in and a road called *Nan Ho Yen* (South River Bank) constructed. In Manchu times the southern wall of the Imperial City was continuous, and this part could only be reached by entering through the Tung An Mên, on the east side. The Allied forces in 1900 broke a hole in the wall at this corner, which, however, was closed up again till 1912, when it was once more opened up. Just about this spot, immediately behind the high

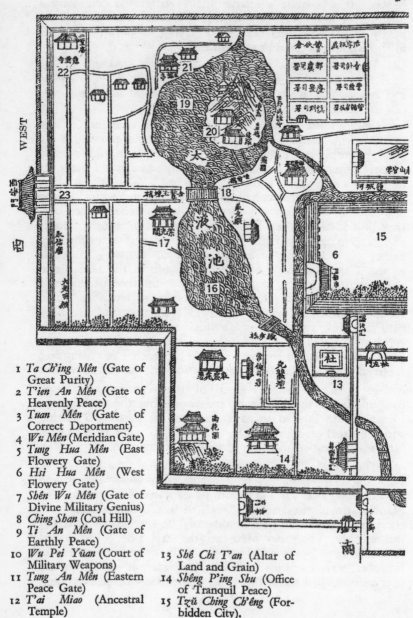

1 *Ta Ch'ing Mên* (Gate of
  Great Purity)
2 *T'ien An Mên* (Gate of
  Heavenly Peace)
3 *Tuan Mên* (Gate of
  Correct Deportment)
4 *Wu Mên* (Meridian Gate)
5 *Tung Hua Mên* (East
  Flowery Gate)
6 *Hsi Hua Mên* (West
  Flowery Gate)
7 *Shên Wu Mên* (Gate of
  Divine Military Genius)
8 *Ching Shan* (Coal Hill)
9 *Ti An Mên* (Gate of
  Earthly Peace)
10 *Wu Pei Yüan* (Court of
  Military Weapons)
11 *Tung An Mên* (Eastern
  Peace Gate)
12 *T'ai Miao* (Ancestral
  Temple)

13 *Shê Chi T'an* (Altar of
  Land and Grain)
14 *Shêng P'ing Shu* (Office
  of Tranquil Peace)
15 *Tzŭ Ching Ch'êng* (Forbidden City).

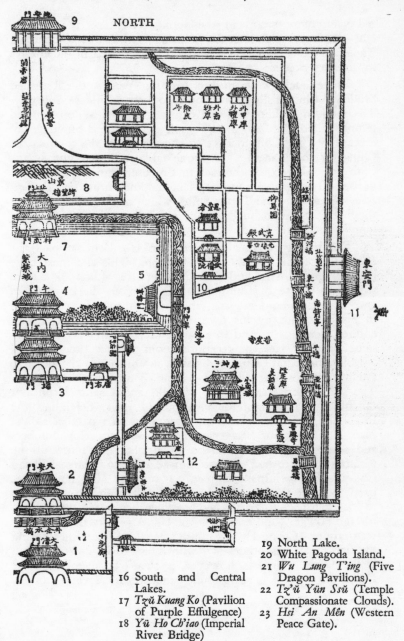

NORTH

16 South and Central Lakes.
17 *Tzŭ Kuang Ko* (Pavilion of Purple Effulgence)
18 *Yü Ho Ch'iao* (Imperial River Bridge)
19 North Lake.
20 White Pagoda Island.
21 *Wu Lung T'ing* (Five Dragon Pavilions).
22 *Tzŭ Yün Ssŭ* (Temple Compassionate Clouds).
23 *Hsi An Mên* (Western Peace Gate).

red wall, there stood in the summer days of 1900 a gun emplacement from which the British Legation was bombarded. The open space west of the T'ang Tzŭ was used in olden days for archery practice.

Immediately west, in the Nan Ho Yen, is the Returned Students' Club, distinguished by an old-style Chinese doorway. The modern buildings of this club stand on the site of an old temple called *P'u Shĕng Ssŭ* (Temple of Universal Subjugation) erected by Shun Chih in 1651 to commemorate the conquest of China by the Manchus. A stone tablet still standing in the Club grounds records the fact in Chinese, Manchu, and Mongolian. The temple and site is better known as *Shih Ta Tzŭ Miao* (Temple of the Tartar Shih), which name is derived from the fact that a Manchu Prince called Shih repaired the original temple and resided in it.

Continuing north along ,the Nan Ho Yen we pass the enclosure of the Peking Union Church. This site must have bad *fêng shui* (" Wind and Water," otherwise " Luck ").* Here stood the house of Ching Shan, the famous diarist in *China under the Empress-Dowager*, who was thrown into the well in his courtyard by his own son, when the Allied armies entered Peking. And in a house erected later on the very same spot—in fact the reception-room covered the courtyard —resided General Chang Hsün who in 1917 made the abortive attempt to restore Emperor Hsüan T'ung to the throne. The restoration lasted about a week, and Chang Hsün put up quite a stiff fight for a couple of days, defending the Imperial City wall which in those days ran parallel to the Nan Ho Yen, but was overwhelmed by superior numbers and equipment. There can be no doubt that most of the generals who turned against him—excepting Marshal Tuan Ch'i-jui—had originally agreed to support him but ratted, partly because they thought he was distributing too many jobs to his own friends, partly because they discovered that certain foreign powers—and especially the U.S.A.—were hostile to the restoration. Chang Hsün's house was set on fire, either during the fighting, or as others say, with intent to immolate himself in the flames. He was, however, rescued by a member of the Dutch Legation, where he found sanctuary for several months.

---

* See " Notes " at end

We next cross the broad street running between the Tung Hua Mên and the Tung An Mên, the eastern gates of the Forbidden and Imperial cities respectively ; the latter was pulled down in 1933. Continuing north up the *Pei Ho Yen* (North River Bank) we see across an open space on our left a large, ugly, foreign building of red brick. This is the PEKING NATIONAL UNIVERSITY, commonly known as " Peita "— the two syllables *Pei Ta* merely meaning " North Large." It started in 1894 as the " Imperial University " on the site of the old " Horse God Temple " which lies further west along the street. The modern building of red brick was erected in 1910, when the old university was turned into dormitories.

Under the Mings the *Ma Shên Miao* (Temple of the God of Horses) stood within the precincts of the Imperial stables on the north side of the street. In the 20th year of Ch'ien Lung (1755) the stables were removed to the south side of the street. In 1894, as stated above, the temple was reconstructed and the university installed therein. Both the university and the whole surrounding district are still referred to by the Pekingese as *Ma Shên Miao*.

Turning north up a street to the west of the modern university building we come to a group of temples known as " The Three in One." In the centre is the *Sung Chu Ssŭ* (Temple of Sacrifices to the Mountains) after which the whole group is named ; to the east is the *Fa Yüan Ssŭ* (Temple of Buddha's Expanse), and to the west the *Chih Chu Ssŭ* (Temple of the Knowledge of the Rosary). In the Fa Yüan Ssŭ is a fine bronze tripod, 6½ feet high ; and in the Chih Chu Ssŭ a bell inscribed with Sanskrit. These temples were built under K'ang Hsi on the site of two printing establishments for sacred books which stood here in Ming times. In former days over one hundred Mongol lamas resided in these temples who used to translate and print Tibetan and Mongol liturgical books. There are about fifty Mongol lamas left who still occupy themselves with book printing. These Tibetan books, printed from wood blocks on thick paper, in long strips piled over each other, with yellow covers, were sold to the Mongols who used to come down to Peking each winter.

Proceeding west we see before us the COAL HILL lying immediately to the north of the Forbidden City. This hill is

東｜東ㄱ
安ㄐ安ㄱ
橋門｜門ㄱ

TUNG AN MÊN

of artificial construction, formed from the earth taken out of the moat when the Forbidden City was built by Yung Lo. It is recorded that during the Liao dynasty a huge amount of coal and charcoal was stored here to be used in case of emergency. The coal laid the foundation of the present hill which was later covered with the earth dug out of the surrounding area which forms the "Three Seas." And as the charcoal was placed in a deep pit alongside of the coal, the hill in those days was called *Mei Shan T'an Hai* (Coal Hill and Charcoal Sea). The hill was constructed for geomantic reasons—like the mounds on the north side of graves—to guard the Imperial Palaces against evil influences coming from the north. During the Mings it was called *Wan Sui Shan* (Hill of Ten Thousand Years), also *Pai Kuo Shu Yüan* (Garden of One Hundred Fruit Trees), which names were afterwards changed by the Manchus to *Ching Shan* (Prospect Hill), though it is still popularly known as *Mei Shan* (Coal Hill) for the reason given above. The five pavilions—an odd number as usual—one at the top, and two on each of the western and eastern shoulders, were built in the 16th year of Ch'ien Lung (1758). The park was used by the ladies and officials of the Court to take the air in.

The entrance is in the middle of the south wall, immediately opposite the north gate of the Forbidden City. Having taken a ticket at the office we enter through the *Ching Shan Mên* (Prospect Hill Gate), and have in front of us a two-storeyed pavilion, the *Ch'i Wang Lou* (Beautiful View Tower). Inside is a tablet to Confucius, said to have been placed there, because close-by, on the left side of the gate, there used to be a school for the sons of members of the Eight Banners.

Following the path round to the east we come to a stone tablet on the hill-side, near a low mud wall round the remains of an ancient sophora. This was the tree on which the last Emperor of the Mings, Ch'ung Chêng, is said to have hung himself, when Peking was captured by the rebels in April 1643. Certain writers have challenged the truth of this story, but the stone tablet which was erected by the authorities of the Palace Museum in 1930 reads :—

"In respectful memory of the Emperor of the Mings who, remembering his ancestors, committed suicide on this spot rather than fall into the hands of his enemies."

Until recent years a heavy iron chain was fastened round this tree. It was not, as some writers have asserted, the chain with which the Emperor committed suicide, but was placed there by orders of the Manchu Emperors, as a reminder of the tree having been, so to say, an accessory to the death of an Emperor. The chain is said to have been removed by foreign soldiers in 1900. The tree is still known as " The Guilty Sophora " (*Tsui Huai*).

Ascending the hill by a stone path and passing the two eastern pavilions we come to the largest one, at the top and centre, called *Wan Ch'un T'ing* (Pavilion of Ten Thousand Springs). The large wooden Buddha is not old, as there was formerly a bronze idol which disappeared after the occupation by French troops in 1900.

From this point one gets a remarkable all-round panorama of Peking and its surroundings, one of the most picturesque in the world, especially towards the west, with the hills standing out boldly in the background and looking as if they were only just outside the city, instead of nearly twenty miles away. Directly south, at our feet, lies the Forbidden City with its splendid yellow roofs, whilst north and west one gets the impression of one vast park ; to the east, however, where Peking has been most modernized, this appearance is less noticeable.

Descending by the two western pavilions we turn north and come at the end of the enclosure to a group of buildings called *Shou Huang Tien* (Hall of Imperial Longevity). In the main building were kept the portraits of deceased Emperors, which were unrolled by the reigning Emperor and sacrifices offered up to them on New Year's day. These pictures were removed to the Palace Museum some years ago, and have now disappeared altogether, along with the other Palace treasures. The archway in front of the buildings is inscribed with characters reading : " Patterns for all ages, ancient and modern," in reference to the rulers whose portraits included all the Emperors from the legendary ruler Fu Hsi down. The Shou Huang Tien was erected in the time of Ch'ien Lung with materials taken from the Ming tombs. The halls are built in the style of the T'ai Miao.

The buildings in a separate enclosure on the north-east are of earlier construction and were used for storing the pictures, before the Shou Huang Tien had been built; and afterwards the coffins of deceased Empresses and Empress-dowagers were kept there while awaiting burial. The two towers at the corners of the north wall are of the Ming period. The large complex of buildings on the east side of the enclosure was used as a prison for princely offenders. The Emperor Yung Chêng at different times imprisoned no less than five of his brothers here, on the charge of conspiring against him.

All these fine buildings are now closed to the public and are rapidly falling into complete ruin.

Leaving the Coal Hill and returning east we come to the *Pei Ch'ih Tzŭ* (North Moat). Immediately at the corner on the east side is the *Fêng Shên Miao* (Temple of the God of Winds). It was built by Yung Chêng in 1728 and called by the more elegant name "Temple of the Diffusion of Tranquillizing Breezes" (*Hsüan Jên Miao*). It is now the headquarters of the Peking Medical Association.

Half-way down the street, on the same side, is the *Yün Shên Miao* (Temple of the God of Clouds). It was also built by Yung Chêng, in the year 1730, and was also provided with a more distinguished name, "Temple of Clouds joined in Harmony" (*Ning Ho Miao*). It is now a police station.

Just before we reach the main road leading to the Tung Hua Mên, on the west side, near house No. 88, there used to stand the *Wu Pei Yüan* (Court of Military Weapons), an armoury built in Ming times.

Crossing the main street into its south continuation, the *Nan Ch'ih Tzŭ* (South Moat)—in which by the way many foreigners reside—we take the first small turning on the left (east) and turning south by several small winding lanes come to a remarkable-looking building standing on a raised terrace high above the surrounding houses. This is the well-known *Mahakala Miao*, commonly known to foreigners as the Mongol Temple. It is a monastery inhabited by Mongol lamas who by the rules of the place are bound to read the Buddhist liturgical books in the Mongol language. The name "Mahakala" is the Sanskrit for Siva as Destroyer and refers to the idol called by the Chinese *Hei Hu Fa Fo* (Black Protector of Buddha's Law) which stands in the temple.

This powerful " Demon Protector " of the Lamaist world comes from the Hindu Pantheon where he is represented with a garland of skulls, seated on a corpse. Under this terrific shape Siva is adored as the destructive God of Time, as well as the Vanquisher of Death. The Chinese also refer to him as *Ta Shên Wang* (Great Spirit King) or *P'u Tu* (Saviour of the Universe). *P'u Tu Ssŭ* was the name given to it by Ch'ien Lung when he repaired it in 1776, and is still its present official name.

It was originally a palace in which, according to tradition, the Ming Emperor Chêng T'ung lived, after his return from captivity in Mongolia in 1457, until by a palace revolution he succeeded in recovering the throne after deposing his younger brother Ching T'ai who had become Emperor during his absence. The first Manchu Emperor, Shun Chih, when he took over the government, presented the palace to his uncle, Dorgun, otherwise known as Prince Jui, who had helped to conquer China and acted as regent during his nephew's minority. Dorgun who died in 1650, was posthumously accused of having tried to usurp the Imperial power and was struck off the roll of the Imperial clan, but his name was restored by Ch'ien Lung. In 1691 the Emperor K'ang Hsi converted the palace into the present Lama temple.

The temple has also a peculiarity in its construction, as the roof has two sets of eaves. The story of how this came about is as follows :—The contractor who was building the temple had made a mistake in his calculations, so that the slope of the roof was out of proportion, and seeing no way of putting it right had determined to commit suicide. On the evening when he took the fatal decision, the cook who prepared the workmen's food suddenly fell sick and a stranger took his place. When the workmen came to partake of the meal that the temporary cook had prepared for them, they found that too much salt had been put in all the dishes. The strange cook was called to explain, but all he would say was : " *Chia Chung Yen* " (By mistake I have put in too much salt). They then complained to the contractor who also called on the man to explain his behaviour, when he again only repeated the same three words. Not another syllable could they get out of him. As the contractor was pondering over this strange reply, a light suddenly dawned on him, and he saw that it was a pun on the three words which might also mean—in different tones—"Add an extra set of eaves." He sent for the man, but he was not to be found, although the gate-keeper said that no one had left the premises. The contractor realized that this must be *Lu Pan* (The God of Masons) of whom we have already heard. So he burnt incense to him, followed his advice, and the proper proportions of the building were restored.

Going south and west by more narrow lanes we arrive back in the Nan Ch'ih Tzŭ. On the east side, close to the south end of the street is a high red wall. Inside was the *Huang Shih Ch'êng* (Imperial Historical Archives), which was established during the Ming dynasty, for the purpose of preserving the secret Imperial records. According to the Chinese custom these archives were supposed never to be destroyed, so that it would be interesting to know, what has become of them.

CHAPTER X.

THE WESTERN HALF OF THE IMPERIAL CITY

TO reach the western part of the Imperial City we go past the Central Park (Chapter V) and through the gateway west until we reach a high archway on the north side, the entrance to the *Nan Ch'ang Chieh* (South Long Street). This street has been laid out since the Revolution. Here again, as in the eastern half, there being no opening in the wall, it was impossible in Manchu times to approach the Imperial City from the south. One could only reach this spot by entering through the *Tung An Mên* (Eastern Peace Gate) and then going right round behind the Coal Hill, a very considerable détour, as can be seen from the map, so that in former times it was one of the most inaccessible parts of Peking.

A short, broad street on the left, just north of the archway, leads to a large enclosure, formerly called *Nan Fu* (South Palace), now a Middle School. In this enclosure stood the *Shêng P'ing Shu* (Office of Tranquil Peace) which played quite an important part in Court life. In it the actors used to reside, when ordered to perform at Court, and here were kept all the paraphernalia required for Imperial performances, such as costumes, swords, coats of mail and so forth. The high wall round this enclosure is still the original one.

At the north end of the Nan Ch'ang Chieh we cross a broad street leading from the *Hsi Hua Mên* (West Flowery Gate), of the Forbidden City, to the *Hsi Yüan Mên* (Western Park Gate). This short piece of road played an important rôle in the latter days of the Manchu dynasty, for it was the route used by the Empress-Dowager Tz'ŭ Hsi, when going to and fro between the Forbidden City and the Central Sea. Moreover, the latter was the gate used by high officials going to audience with the Empress, when she was in residence in the Lake Palace. When at the beginning of the attacks on the Legations in June 1900 the Empress-Dowager removed from

the Lake Palace to the Forbidden City, a guard of honour
of Boxers was drawn up along this road. The Empress after
inspecting them, presented them with two thousand taels of
silver and congratulated their commander, Prince Chuang,
on their smart appearance.

It is well worth taking a stroll through some of the side
lanes round here, for they have a strange air of old-world
peace and calm, in strong contrast to the busy noisy streets
in other parts of the city.

Continuing north along what now becomes *Pei Ch'ang
Chieh* (North Long Street) we pass a group of temples, two
on the left, and one on the right. The first on the left is the
Lei Shên Miao (Temple of the God of Thunder), more elegantly
called, *Chao Hsien Miao* (Temple of Luminous Thunder),
built in 1732 under Yung Chêng. Sacrifices were offered
here by the highest officials in the capital on the first day of the
Second and Eighth Moons. A legend says that a certain Chang
Sêng-yao drew a pair of dragons on the wall of the temple for
a joke, but when he put in the eyes they flew off into the sky
amidst thunder and lightning. A damsel called Ah Hsiang
is said to push (*sic!*) the chariot of the God of Thunder whose
whip is supposed to be the flash of lightning.

The next temple on the same side is the *Hsing Lung Ssŭ*
(Temple of Prosperity). Originally, in Yung Lo's reign, it
was an imperial armoury in which was an effigy of Lu Pan,
the God of Carpenters, who was worshipped by the workmen. According to a stone tablet in the courtyard the armoury
was abolished by K'ang Hsi in 1700 and turned into a temple
called *Wan Shou Hsing Lung Ssŭ* (Temple of Prosperity of Ten
Thousand Ages), afterwards changed to the present name.

Immediately across the road is the *Fu Yu Ssŭ* (Temple of
Blessed Protection), built during the 1st year of Yung Chêng
(1723). There is a tablet in the temple in honour of K'ang
Hsi inscribed by Yung Chêng with the following eulogy
" Great Imperial Ancestor, achiever of great deeds, whose
great and meritorious actions merit his becoming a Buddha."
There are two small rooms one on each side of the main hall
where the tablet is, one contains the books that Yung Chêng
used to study, and one his throne on which he rested
after performing sacrifices to his father. This temple is still

in a good state of repair and worth a short visit ; unfortunately
it is not open to the public, as it has been converted into offices
connected with the Panchan Lama of Tibet.

We have now reached the north-west corner of the moat
round the Forbidden City and turning to the right have before
us, at the south-west corner of the Coal Hill, the *Ta Kao Tien*
or *Ta Kao Hsüan Tien* (Hall of High Heaven). It was built
by the Ming Emperor Chia Ching and repaired in the reigns
of Yung Chêng and Ch'ien Lung. The supreme deity of the
Taoists, Yü Huang (The Jade Emperor), is worshipped here
who, as a Nature God, was supposed to send or withhold rain.
For this reason, when occasion called for it, the Emperor used
to proceed in state to this temple to pray for rain. It was
here too, that the eunuchs and maid-servants of the
palace were instructed in their duties and in correct deportment. At the back of the compound is a circular pavilion
with a beautiful roof of blue tiles, in imitation of the colour
of Heaven, which forms a striking object, when seen from the
Coal Hill or the pagoda in the North Lake. The south gateway
is flanked by two beautiful ornamental arches, carefully restored
in recent times, and outside each of them is a stone tablet
inscribed in six languages (Chinese, Manchu, Mongol on one
side ; Calmuck, Turkish and Tibetan on the other) ordering
all passers-by to dismount from their horses or carts. On
the south side of the road, within a red wall, stand a pair of
beautiful pavilions with no less than 72 roof ridges in yellow
tiles.

This curious construction is accounted for by the following popular tale. The contractor who had been ordered
to build the pavilions in this style was in great difficulties, as
it was so complicated that he could find no one who could
draw him a design or make a model. One of his workmen,
a youth noted for his filial conduct towards his old mother,
happened to be sitting in a tea-house, when an old man with
a long beard entered carrying in his hand a wicker-work cage
for crickets, of a very curious and ingenious design. The
workman was much taken with it and wanted to buy it, but
when the old man said it was worth a thousand taels he cried
out : " You're mad ! how do you think a common workman
like me can find that sum." " I didn't ask you to buy it,"

said the old man, " I'll give it you as a present." The young man refused saying he only wanted it for his contractor. "Well, he can afford to pay a thousand taels," said the old man. Whilst they were arguing, one of the foremen came in and, seeing that the cage was just the design they were looking for, rushed off to find the contractor. When the latter arrived he asked to see the cage, saying he would pay a thousand taels. The old man said he had not got the cage, but pointing to the workman added : " If you pay over to him straight away one thousand taels, you will find it in his house on his mother's table," and took his departure. The contractor would not believe this at first, but finally paid the workman the sum, and they went together to the latter's house, where, sure enough, they found the cage on his mother's table. The old lady said that a short while before an old gentleman with a long beard had called and left it with her saying it was payment for some money they had lent him. This, of course, was our old friend, Lu Pan, to whom they went and burnt incense. And the pavilions, as you can see, were successfully erected.

The Ta Kao Tien is now occupied by a government bureau and is closed to the public.

From here we proceed due west and crossing the Imperial Canal Bridge come on our right to a large red gateway. This is the entrance to the NATIONAL LIBRARY (*Kuo Li Pei P'ing T'u Shu Kuan*). It was built in 1932 on the old site of a temple which was erected in 1513 in the reign of the Ming Emperor Chêng Tê, called *Yen Shou Ssŭ* (Temple of Bountiful Crops). There was a building called *An Lo T'ang* (Hall of Peace and Happiness) attached to the temple in which aged women were cared for. Before that time a palace stood here in which in 1481 the Emperor Hung Chih was born.

The Library, though quite modern, is well worth a visit— apart from its functions—as it is one of the few modern buildings in Peking where the attempt has proved successful of combining Chinese architecture with western structural and mechanical improvements.

Diagonally across the road from the Library is a gate which leads to the offices of the Municipal Government. In Ming times there was a building on this site known as the *Pai Niao T'ang* (Hall of a Hundred Birds), because thousands of singing-birds were kept there. Prince Ch'un, the Prince-Regent, father of the Emperor Hsüan T'ung, started to convert this hall into a palace for himself, because by custom he was supposed to move out of his own palace, where "a dragon had been born," so that it could be converted into an Imperial shrine. But before the new palace was completed, the revolution broke out; it was afterwards used for Cabinet offices under the Republic, and has now been further demoted to Municipal offices.

To the north of the Library is a short wide street running to the wall of the Park, which is called *Chan T'an Ssŭ* (Temple of the Red Sandalwood Buddha). The name is all that now remains to remind us of one of the largest and most famous temples in Peking, which once stood on this street, on the site now occupied by military barracks. This temple was completely destroyed by the Allies in 1900, because it was the head-quarters and drill-ground of the Boxers, whilst the Lama priests attached to it took a leading part in inciting the populace and troops to attack the neighbouring Catholic cathedral.

It was built under the early Mings and originally called *Ch'ing Fo Tien* (Hall of the Pure Buddha), later changed to *Hung Jên Ssŭ* (Temple of Exalted Benevolence). The name Chan T'an Ssŭ dates from the 15th year of K'ang Hsi (1676), when the temple was reconstructed and dedicated to the Chan T'an Buddha. It consisted of three large buildings, one of which, the *Ta Pao Tien* (Hall of the Great Jewel), contained a very famous and miraculous idol.

This was a statue of Buddha five feet high in red sandalwood, covered with black varnish, which used to change colour according to the temperature and hour of the day. In the reign of the Ming Emperor Wan Li it was gilded over. According to a stone tablet of the 6oth year of K'ang Hsi (1722) that used to stand in the temple, this idol was carved in the days of the Chou dynasty and came of itself to China from the West, at the time when Buddha appeared on earth. Thirty-two similar idols were made at the same time, but Buddha is said to have declared that this Chan T'an one was the only true likeness. From the time it was made to the above year of K'ang Hsi was a period of 2,710 years according to the Chinese records. The idol was carried from place to place in different parts of China—the details of its pilgrimage, if true, form a really remarkable record—until it finally found a resting-place in this temple. What became of the idol eventually is not known.

Amongst the numerous other idols in this temple was one called in Chinese *Lu Chi Fo Erh* which has a curious resemblance to Lucifer, probably the only instance where Satan himself is to be found in the Chinese pantheon. The temple was well endowed by the Manchu Emperors, and several hundred Lamas resided there. A Living Buddha also had his residence there and used to hold a grand prayer-meeting with " Devil Dances " on the 8th of the First Moon.

We continue west along the main street and, just before reaching a triple gateway, the *Hsi An Mên* (Western Peace Gate), of the Imperial City, turn north up a short broad street to the *Pei T'ang* (North Cathedral). The cathedral was originally situated close to the west wall of the Central Lake, near where the Municipal offices now are, in a place called *Ts'an Ch'ih K'ou* (Entrance to the Silkworm Moat), where in Ming times mulberry leaves were dried and silkworms reared. This site was presented in 1693 by the Emperor K'ang Hsi to the Jesuit fathers, Gerbillon and Bouvet, out of gratitude to them, for having cured him of an attack of malaria by means of quinine, then a new medicine. The chapel built by them on that site, with Imperial permission, was dedicated in 1703 and remained in being until the persecution of foreign missions under Tao Kuang in 1827, when it was closed up and after a nominal payment of Taels 5,000, demolished, and the property given to one of the Imperial princes. By the treaty of 1860, all the property formerly belonging to the Catholic missions had to be restored to them, and so the old site was handed back to the missionaires who erected a new church there in 1867, all that remained of the former mission buildings being the stone steps of the old cathedral.

When in 1885 the Empress-Dowager Tz'ŭ Hsi moved into the palaces on the Central Lake which had been specially restored and enlarged for her, she objected to the proximity of the cathedral on the score of *Fêng Shui* (i.e. lucky omens). It is however probable that this played a smaller part in her objections than her fear lest her movements should be spied on by the "foreign devils" from the top of the building, the towers of which rose high above the walls, even after the latter had been specially raised. According to a local tradition it was quite a minor official, a Mongol named En Yu, Deputy Lieutenant-General of the Bordered Blue Banner Corps, who succeeded in carrying out the autocratic old lady's wish to have the edifice removed, after all the other ministers had failed to find a remedy, owing to their fear of getting into trouble with the French. He arranged the matter with a native friend of his, who was a Catholic priest, through whose good offices he got the Church and then the French Legation to agree to the cathedral being removed to its present site, *Hsi Shih K'u* (Western Ten Store-rooms), by which name it is still known to the Pekingese.

The original Hsi Shih K'u was a building composed of ten rooms used during the Ming and Manchu dynasties to keep various government stores, chiefly valuables confiscated by the state from cashiered officials. In the store-rooms which had been officially sealed up for many years, a large quantity of valuable goods was found. This was in addition to the Taels 350,000 (about the same in gold dollars, in those days) which they received as compensation. The old site was handed over in 1887, and the present cathedral opened on December 9th, 1888. Inscribed over the main door of the cathedral in Chinese are the words: "Catholic Church built by Imperial Order, 13th Year of Kuang Hsü."

En Yu, by the way, must have done quite well over his stroke of diplomacy, for he died a rich man some years ago, having survived the siege of the cathedral where he had hidden himself from the Boxers who were looking for his head, because of his friendship with the Catholics.

The Pei T'ang continued to enjoy an undisturbed existence on its new site until 1900, when it was caught in the maelstrom of the Boxer rising. Its heroic defence under Bishop Favier is an epic far surpassing that of the Siege of the Legations, on account of the fierceness of the attacks and the limited means of the defenders. The Boxers made a dead set at the place, probably because they thought it would be an easy job and that they had only to deal with their own countrymen. There were assaults almost every day; at one time as many as fourteen cannon were turned on it ; and no less than seven different mines were sprung causing heavy loss to the defence. It was defended by about 3,000 native converts, a small number of whom were armed with swords and spears, thirteen foreign missionaries, and a hundred seminarists some of whom where armed with rifles, and by 11 Italian and 40 French marines under Sub-lieutenant Paul Henry who fell on July 29. The attacks started on June 5, and the place was not relieved till August 16, nor was there any period of truce, as at the Legations. Moreover they were very hard up for supplies. Repeated sorties were made by the defenders, in desperate efforts to find food, and to dislodge sniping parties of the besiegers. It is amusing to read in Chinese accounts the high moral indignation at the wicked converts venturing to come out " to plunder shops and burn down houses." Luckily for the defenders, the Boxers proved themselves completely useless at any serious fighting. On more than one occasion they obtained respite while the attacking forces were fighting amongst themselves. As with the Legations, there was an element of comedy intermixed, when on two occasions the Empress-Dowager sent express orders to stop the bombardment for the afternoon, as the noise of the guns made her head ache during her picnic on the adjoining lake.

The cathedral and other buildings in the Mission, though badly knocked about, remained standing, whereas the whole surrounding district from the walls of the Lake Park to the Shun Chih Mên Main Street and for hundreds of yards north and south, was completely wiped out, which accounts for the markedly modern appearance of this particular part of the city, with its numerous semi-foreign buildings.

At the back of the Pei T'ang, divided from it by a wall, lies a compound called *Jên Tz'ŭ T'ang* (Hall of Compassionate Humanity). It was formerly a temple called *Tz'ŭ Yün Ssŭ* (Temple of Compassion reaching to the Clouds) which was taken over by the Catholic Church in 1885, when they occupied the Hsi Shih K'u site, and renamed as above, probably to avoid any question of Buddhistic influence. It is now a nunnery and orphanage, and work and food are provided for the poor.

Further north lies the old French Cemetery in which are buried the soldiers and officers of the two campaigns of 1860 and 1900.

Across the main street, on the south side, there used to be another famous temple, the *Kuang Ming Tien* (Hall of Glorious Brightness). It was originally a Taoist temple called *Wan Shou Kung* (Palace of Ten Thousand Ages) built by the Ming Emperor Chia Ching in 1557. The Emperor being a religious devotee used to live here for weeks on end practicing with a favourite monk the Taoist religious exercises called " *Wu Wei Erh Wu Pu Wei* " (Through non-action everything can be attained), so that it is not surprising that the Empire went to pieces in his reign. Ch'ien Lung repaired the temple twice and changed the name to its present form. It was a large complex of buildings the most striking of which was a high circular hall in the front courtyard, of the same construction and colouring as the famous temple at the Altar of Heaven, except that it had only two, instead of three roofs. It stood on a two-storeyed marble terrace with six separate flights of stairs of 24 steps, and was the most conspicuous building in this part of the city. The Kuang Ming Tien suffered severely in the fighting round the Pei T'ang and never recovered ; the buildings were allowed to fall into ruins and the temple has now practically disappeared.

The street to the east of this temple site, the *Fu Yu Chieh*, brings us back to the Hsi Ch'ang An Chieh, at the corner of the South Lake grounds.

CHAPTER XI.

THE SOUTH-EAST QUARTER OF THE TARTAR CITY

OUR wanderings thus far have taken us among the more spectacular and architecturally more striking parts of Peking, where the former rulers had their palaces and temples. We shall now extend our walks, in search of Old Peking, to humbler, but no less interesting, portions of the city.

We commence this survey with the south-east quarter of the former Tartar City, the section which is best known to foreign residents, because the Legation Quarter is included in it and the majority of foreigners live in this part of the city.

Leaving the Legation Quarter at the north end of Marco Polo Street and crossing the broad *Ch'ang An Chieh* (Eternal Peace Street) we proceed north along a busy thoroughfare called *Wang Fu Ching Ta Chieh* (Main Street of the Well of the Prince's Palace) which derives its name from the well, a small hole on the west side of the roadway, opposite the police-station. It is covered over nowadays with a piece of iron sheeting, but is still in use. This street is better known to foreigners as MORRISON STREET, after Dr. George Morrison, the famous "Times" correspondent who used to live at No. 98, on the west side, now occupied by a foreign firm.

Dr. Morrison, now almost a legendary figure of Peking, came out to China in the early 'nineties, and soon made a name for himself by his brilliant dispatches to the "Times." He took an energetic part in the defence of the Legations in 1900, until severely wounded, and afterwards, during the occupation by the foreign armies became still more famous, by his frank criticism of their doings, especially of the Germans who wanted to have him court-martialled, because he had exposed some of the excesses during their punitive expeditions. As correspondent in the Russo-Japanese war he made another famous scoop by reporting the naval sortie of the Russian fleet from Port Arthur, before it actually took place. In 1912, after the revolution, he was made advisor to the Chinese government by President Yüan Shih-k'ai, which post he held till his death in 1920, taking part in the Versailles Conference with the Chinese delegation.

Before reaching No. 98 we pass a lane on the same side called *T'i Tzŭ Hutung* (Ladder Lane), on which used to be the main entrance of the offices of the *Ching Pao* or PEKING GAZETTE. The name " Ladder " referred partly to the fact that in former days the lane used to ascend by short rises, every ten feet or so, like the rungs of a ladder, and partly to the grades, or steps, through which the memorials and edicts (that appeared in the " Gazette ") were sent to and from the provinces. A dispatch from a district magistrate, the lowest grade, would pass to the next in rank and so on to the viceroy and from him to the Throne. The " Peking Gazette," according to some authorities goes back to the T'ang Dynasty (A.D. 618-907). It was not actually a government paper, but an organ published with permission of the government. It contained no opinions or comments of any kind, but was merely a record of official happenings, chiefly in the form of Imperial edicts and memorials to the throne, announcements of official promotions or degradations, and so forth. It was published in three editions: one in a red cover, the largest, every other day, with all documents in full ; one in a white cover, daily, with only brief notices ; and one a cheap, popular edition. A Red Book issued quarterly from these offices was, however, a strictly official publication, corresponding to our Civil Service or Army Lists. The premises in which the " Peking Gazette " was situated, are now occupied by the offices of a Chinese newspaper and some shops.

The next street, north, on the opposite side of the main road, leads to the Peking Union Medical College, or P.U.M.C., as it is known to all foreign residents, an institution built, equipped and maintained by the Rockefeller Foundation. The site originally belonged to Prince Yü, one of the eight " iron-capped princes," that is to say descended from one of the princely Manchu families that helped to conquer China. After the death of the original Prince Yü, his descendants one after another, gradually squandered all his wealth, until the property was finally sold to the Rockefeller Foundation. But the

Pekingese, when speaking of this hospital, invariably refer to it as the *Yü Wang Fu* (Palace of Prince Yü), though the actual Chinese name is *Hsieh Ho I Yüan* (Union Hospital).

Continuing along Morrison Street we come on the east side to a large arched gateway with crowds going in and out at all times of the day and innumerable bicycles stacked outside. This is the famous *Tung An Shih Ch'ang* (Eastern Peace Market), a kind of covered-in miniature town of its own, crammed with small shops and stalls, where you can buy anything from a cent's worth of melon seeds to the latest in radio sets, and everything at very reasonable prices. Whilst, to cater for amusement, there are restaurants of every kind and class, billiard saloons, and theatres. It is well worth spending a few minutes strolling along the narrow passages and watching the busy crowd of shoppers. The market is comparatively modern, having only been in existence since the last years of the Manchus.

Leaving the market by the northern entrance into *Chin Yü Hutung* (Gold Fish Lane) which, as the name indicates, was formerly a market for rearing and selling gold-fish, a few steps west bring us back on to the main street opposite the broad *Tung An Mên Ta Chieh* (Main Street of the East Peace Gate) which leads to the *Tung Hua Mên* (East Flowery Gate) of the Forbidden City. It was from a tea-house at the corner of these two main roads that the bomb was thrown on January 16, 1912, in the attempt to assassinate Yüan Shih-k'ai when he was premier. As his carriage was just turning into Morrison Street, the assassins hurled the bomb from a window in the upper storey, but just too late, for it fell behind the carriage killing several innocent bystanders and two of the escort but leaving Yüan not only unharmed, but so completely unmoved that he did not even drop the cigarette that he was holding. The horses of his carriage reared up and then bolted straight down Gold Fish Lane without stopping until they reached the Foreign Office where Yüan was then living.

Proceeding north up Morrison Street, the first turning on the left is *Hsi La Hutung* (Pewter Lane), which has sometimes been called the " Park Lane " of Peking, because many of the Manchu nobility and high Chinese officials had their residences here, amongst them Yüan Shih-k'ai himself, who lived there for some time on his return to public life during

the revolution of 1911. But its chief claim to fame is that
in one of the houses Miss Yehonala, as she then was, was
born and brought up, later to become the famous Empress-
Dowager Tz'ü Hsi. On June 16, 1852, she left her
home in this lane for the last time, in order to proceed to the
palace where she was selected from amongst sixty other Manchu
beauties as the concubine of the Emperor Hsien Fêng. Ladies
who enjoyed the high honour of having been selected for the
Imperial harem were very rarely allowed to leave the precincts
of the Palace, and certainly not to mix with ordinary mortals.
Only once again was the Concubine Yi, as Yehonala had then
become, to see her home in Pewter Lane, in January 1857,
when as a special favour for having given birth to an heir
to the Throne, she was granted permission to visit her family.
When she arrived in the Imperial yellow sedan at her old home,
all her relatives were waiting for her on their knees, with the
exception of her mother ; for filial respect rises superior even
to Imperial favour. At the ensuing banquet, however, the
mother took a seat lower than that of her daughter, in order
to show her respect for the mother of the Heir Apparent,
although at that time nobody in Pewter Lane could have
imagined the heights of power and fame to which the young
lady was one day to ascend.

North of Pewter Lane, on the east side of the main street
we have the *Tung T'ang* (Eastern Church). First erected in
1666 by Father Verbiest, after the death of Father Adam Schaal
on the site of another of the properties given him by K'ang
Hsi, it was closed and pulled down in 1812. Rebuilt in
1884, it was again destroyed in 1900, being burnt to the
ground by the Boxers on the night of June 13, when hundreds
of unfortunate native Christians who had taken refuge in its
precincts were massacred amidst scenes of fiendish barbarity.

The lane running along the north wall of the mission
grounds is called *Ch'un Shu Hutung* (Ailanthus Tree Lane),
a name that reminds us of tree worship in China. It is recorded
that during the Ming dynasty a noise like the clicking of dice
was heard in the branches of a very ancient ailanthus tree
growing in the lane which only ceased, when a sufficient
number of incense sticks had been burnt before the tree, to
placate the spirit that dwelt in it. This particular tree was

later destroyed by fire, but history does not relate what became of the tree-spirit, though as there are several ailanthus trees still standing in the lane, it may have moved into one of these.

Whilst on the subject of trees, we might note that there are two kinds of ailanthus: the fragrant (*hsiang*) and the unpleasant-smelling (*ch'ou*). The Chinese believe that, if the latter kind grows to a great height, the family living in that courtyard will have bad luck. This does not apply to the fragrant kind, because its leaves are used for food. There is also a well-known saying, that one must not plant a mulberry tree in front of a private house, nor a willow at the back. This is because *sang* (mulberry) has the same sound as *sang* (sorrow), while *liu* (willow) may exercise an unhealthy influence on the ladies of the household who usually occupy the apartments at the back, as the willow is symbolical of lust, frailty, and so forth. There is, however, no objection to the mulberry and willow being planted in public parks or in the courtyards of public offices, thus showing a delicate distinction between private and public morals. You will often see a strip of red cloth or paper attached to some tree or plant. This is done to protect a valuable plant against evil spirits that might cause it to wither and die.

The next turning north, on the same side, is a broad street called *Têng Shih K'ou* (Lantern Market Mouth). Under the Ming and Manchu dynasties this street was lined with shops and stalls that specialized in lanterns of every kind and during the Lantern Festival—from the 13th to 18th of the First Moon—was crowded with people who came to see the show of lanterns. The Republican authorities have repeatedly attempted to suppress this festival, and the lantern shops have long ago all disappeared.

A short distance up *Pao Fang Hutung* (Newspaper House Lane), the third turning north of Têng Shih K'ou, is the ancient temple, *Fa Hua Ssŭ* (Temple of Buddha's Glory). There are two temples of this name in Peking: this one, the " Upper House " which controls the other, the "Lower House" in the Chinese City (Chapter XVI). The temple was built in 1451 by Liu T'ung, chief eunuch of the Ming Emperor Ching T'ai. The six stone tablets in the main courtyard, five of which were erected by various Ming Emperors and the sixth by Ch'ien Lung in 1778, give particulars of the lives and teachings of the Three Great Teachers, after whom the main hall is named *San Ta Shih Tien*. In front of this hall is a very fine bronze incense burner, dated 58th year of Ch'ien Lung (1793); and in front of the second hall, *P'i Lu Tien*, (Hall of Vairocana Buddha), is a replica in white marble of the same year. In the back courtyard are drum and bell towers. Several private families now occupy the temple compound which is still in quite good repair; on religious festivals incense is burnt and services are still held here. The temple is of historical interest from the fact that the preliminary peace negotiations in 1860 between the British and French envoys and the Chinese Commissioners were conducted in the above two halls, though the actual signing of the Treaty took place at the Board of Rites (Chapter I).

Continuing east along Pao Fang Hutung and turning south down Hatamên Street we pass on our left the *Nei Wu Pu Chieh*, a street on which, as the name indicates, the Board of Interior used to be situated. The continuation of this street is the *Ta Fang Chia Hutung* (Lane of the Great Fang Family), half-way up which at a corner on the north side is a small dilapidated temple to a God of the Soil (*T'u Ti Miao*). This particular idol, strange to relate, has two wives. According to legend, two of these Gods of the Soil were shaking dice one day, just for a joke, with their wives as stakes. The loser had no intention of handing over his wife, nor did he even mention the wager to her. He was therefore greatly surprised, when he woke up in the middle of the night to find that his spouse had disappeared, and still more when on hastily calling on his colleague at this temple, he found her enshrined here. Anybody who thinks it worth while to visit this temple, will find the lucky god sitting here with his two wives, whilst those whose sympathy for the bereaved husband has been aroused, may seek him far away in the north-west quarter of the city where they will see him sitting dejected and alone in a small shrine in the *Chui Tsei Hutung* (Catch Thief Lane).

These gods of the Soil—there is one for each ward of the city—have many functions. One of the most important is transmitting messages from dying persons or those in distress. It is believed that, if a person in distress, far away from his home and friends, cries out aloud, the God of the Soil will pick up the message—just like our modern wireless—and transmit it to the person that the distressed one is thinking of, and that furthermore the receiving party can send a return message via wireless—we mean God of the Soil—thus preserving the person's life.

On the east side of Hatamên Street facing the Têng Shih K'ou stands a tiny temple that one might easily pass without notice in the noise and bustle of the modern traffic. Nevertheless, it is a very interesting temple well worth peeping into, for its origin goes back to the remote past. This is the *Erh Lang Yeh Miao* (Temple of Mr. Erh Lang) or better known to foreigners as the DOG TEMPLE. In front of the temple stands an urn, probably of the T'ang period, and a stone memorial tablet erected by Shih Wên-chu, the controller of the Imperial granaries in the reign of K'ang Hsi, which gives an account of the origin and history of the temple. In the third year of the T'ang Emperor Chên Kuan (A.D. 629) a shrine was erected on this spot in honour of Li P'ing, called the God of Irrigation, whose effigy was first placed here, but was afterwards replaced by that of his son, Erh Lang. (The mythology would appear to have become a bit mixed, as Erh Lang is supposed to have lived in the Yin period, a matter of a few thousand years before his father!) The tablet says that an "Earth Dragon" (*chiao*) suddenly appeared at this spot causing a flood in which hundreds of people were drowned. A Taoist priest named Hsiao Tao-ch'êng happened to come along and, seating himself on the ground quite undisturbed, began invoking the gods to destroy the dragon. But to the amazement of the bystanders he suddenly assumed the shape of Erh Lang and struck the dragon with his sword, whereupon the waters subsided, Erh Lang disappeared, and the monk Hsiao was sitting there, as before, in an attitude of prayer. The shrine was reconstructed in the second year of the Sung Emperor Yüan Yu (A.D. 1087), and again by K'ang Hsi in 1696.

There are numerous legends connected with Erh Lang, who was a kind of Hercules, but most of them are about his Celestial Dog, almost more famous than its master. The one best known to the Pekingese is the following which has a direct reference to this temple. Next to the temple there was once a butcher's shop which did a very good business. Every night a dog used to crawl into the shop and carry off

TÊNG

SHIH K'OU

a piece of pork. The butcher thinking he would put an end to these thefts lay in wait for the dog one night and stabbed it with his carving knife, but it managed to get away. Following the trail of blood he found to his alarm that it led into the temple. From that time on the dog never turned up again, and the butcher's business was ruined.

Inside there is very little room, as the building is less than twelve feet square and crowded with altars, shrines, and a miscellaneous collection of temple appliances. Underneath the table close to the shrine is a small kennel with a mud image of the celebrated dog. Erh Lang himself one can scarcely see, as he is sitting right at the back in the dark. Still, he is a very powerful personage in the faith-healing line, as is proved by the numerous votive tablets and pieces of orange-coloured cloth hanging from walls and ceiling, placed there by grateful patients, whose various ills he has cured in answer to their prayers and the burning of a sufficient quantity of incense sticks. What is still more interesting, is that his famous dog performs the same services for the canine race, which is the reason for the piles of small plaster dogs lying around the altar that have been placed there by owners whose dogs are sick. In fact, the Celestial Dog would seem to be a faith-healing vet, an art to which even we moderns have not yet attained. The small shrines on the side-tables have nothing to do with Erh Lang or his dog, but are, so to say, mere paying guests, minor deities favoured by certain families who pay rent for their favourites being allowed to bask in the rays of the more powerful deity. The temple is served by a family called Hsiao who claim to have been connected with it from the start, over thirteen hundred years ago, and to be descended from the Taoist priest mentioned in the story above; the temple attendant generally appears to be some elderly female belonging to this family.

Proceeding south down Hatamên Street we come to the *Wai Chiao Pu Chieh* (Foreign Relations Board Street), the fifth turning on the left, on which is situated the old Foreign Office, an uninteresting, ugly, modern building erected in 1911. Prior to 1860 the Chinese, believing China to be the centre of the universe and only having direct dealings with tributary states, had never felt the need for an institution of this kind. When, however, in that year they were very reluctantly forced to grant foreign envoys the right of residence at the capital, a Board of some kind had to be created where the latter could meet the Chinese officials. Instead of selecting one of the Six Great Boards for this purpose, the Chinese specially created a new subordinate office called *Tsung Li Ko Kuo Shih Wu Ya Mên* (Board for the General Management of the Affairs of all Countries), usually known as the TSUNGLI YAMEN. After the Boxer madness in 1900 this office was abolished and reconstructed as a proper Foreign Office, of the same standing as the other Boards, called *Wai Wu Pu* (Board of Foreign Affairs) which name was changed in 1911 to *Wai Chiao Pu* (Board of Foreign Relations). The Tsungli Yamên was situated in the street north of the Wai Chiao Pu Chieh, directly behind the former Foreign Office.

At the back of the Tsungli Yamên was the *T'ung Wên Kuan* (College of Universal Learning) established in 1860 for the purpose of training interpreters for the Foreign Office and the Maritime Customs. It was the first government college to be instituted in China with courses in foreign languages and other modern subjects.

The site has an interesting association with the tragic Empress, Aleuté, the wife of T'ung Chih, who was born here. The property which formerly belonged to her grandfather, Saishanga, a Prime Minister of Mongol extraction, was confiscated by the government, when he was thrown into prison for his ill-success against the Taiping rebels. His son, Ch'ung Ch'i, however, restored the family fortunes, firstly by taking a high degree in the Triennial Examinations—a rare performance for one of Manchu or Mongol descent—and secondly because his daughter, Aleuté, a maiden of great accomplishments and virtue, became the wife of the Emperor T'ung Chih. Her reign was a very short one, for on the early demise of T'ung Chih in 1875, she is supposed to have committed suicide, as a virtuous widow, either by starvation or by swallowing gold leaf. Other, and more likely, accounts have it that she was "assisted on high" by her mother-in-law, the Empress-Dowager Tz'ŭ Hsi, because she was known to be with child, and if it had been a male, Aleuté would then have become Empress-Dowager, whilst the other would have been relegated to the background. Ch'ung Ch'i himself who after the death of his daughter was put on the retired list for over twenty years ended in the same way. In 1900, after the Allies had entered Peking, he fled to Paotingfu and committed suicide there, in despair at the hopeless state of the country, although actually he had been steadily against the Boxer movement.

Close to the corner, on the north side of the Wai Chiao Pu Chieh, there used to be a large temple called *Shuang Chung Tz̆'ŭ* (Ancestral Hall of Two Loyal Men). It was erected during the reign of Yung Chêng in memory of two Manchu generals who fell in action suppressing a rising in Tibet.

The next turning on the south is the *Tsung Pu Hutung* (Principal Cloth Lane), a little way up which, on the north side, is a temple with the usual red walls, but with roofs of glazed black tiles. This is the Ancestral Temple of the famous Chinese statesman LI HUNG-CHANG, which was erected in his memory as a special honour by the orders of the Empress-Dowager. In one respect it is unique, as it is the only Ancestral Temple in Peking erected to a "commoner." It is now occupied as a private residence.

Spanning the Hatamên Street, just at the entrance of this same lane, there stood formerly the so-called KETTELER MEMORIAL, a large marble archway which the Chinese government erected to the memory of the German Minister, Baron von Ketteler, who was murdered on this spot by Manchu soldiery on the 20th of June, 1900, when he was on his way in a sedan-chair, unarmed and unescorted, to the Tsungli Yamên to discuss the protection of the Legations. The subsequent fate of this archway is an interesting commentary on the evanescence of things political. Erected in 1901, to be an "everlasting" reminder of this crime—as the inscription said—it was pulled down in 1918 at the end of the Great War; the original inscription was erased and replaced by a new one to Right and Justice; and the arch was re-erected as a War Memorial in the Central Park where it can be seen to-day.

Further south on the east side of Hatamên Street we come to a wide gateway, at No. 166, inside which is the former PALACE OF PRINCE I (Harmonious), a title conferred by the Emperor Yung Chêng in 1723 on Yün Hsiang, the only one of his numerous brothers who had not attempted to conspire against him. A descendant of this prince, in the reign of

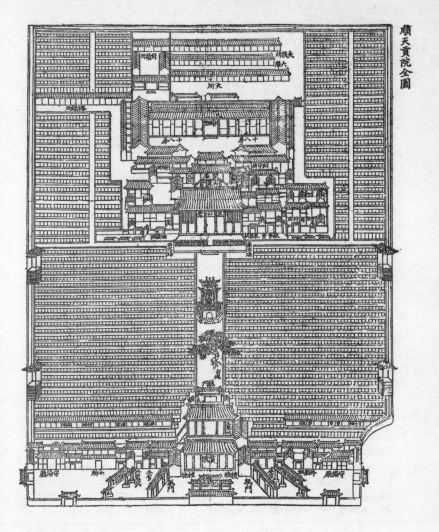

Tao Kuang, converted the palace into a temple called *Hsien Liang Ssŭ* (Temple of Worthies) and moved to another palace near the Ch'ao Yang Mên (Chapter XIII).

Just before reaching the glacis we leave Hatamên Street turning east down *Kuan Yin Ssŭ Hutung* (Lane of the Temple of Kuan Yin), at the end of which we see in front of us a large waste piece of ground, now the dumping place for the city's rubbish. On this site used to stand the HALL OF EXAMINA-TIONS, officially known as *Kung Yüan* (Public Halls). As these examinations played such an important part in the historical development of Old China, we shall perhaps be forgiven, if we describe these Halls at some length, even though they have now completely disappeared. The Examination Halls were built in the reign of Yung Lo on the site of the old Board of Rites of the Yüan dynasty. They covered, as can be seen, a vast area, which was surrounded by high walls pierced by two large gates on the south side and a smaller one on east and west. Inside was a second enclosure with triple gateways and ornamental arches facing each of the outer gates. At the southern end of the inner enclosure between the two gates stood a three-storey tower with a pavilion at each corner, called the *Ming Yüan Lou* (Round Bright Tower) from which the roll of the candidates was called. North of this in the centre was the *Shih Pa Fang* (Eighteen Rooms), a building occupied by the Grand Examiner, Examination Superintend-ents, and Examination Assistants. To the east and west were ranged long rows of buildings containing nearly 8,500 tiny cubicles, ten feet in height and five feet square, in each of which a candidate was confined for the whole duration of the examination. The door of each cell bore a different character which was the one that the candidate affixed to his papers, instead of his name. In the reign of Kuang Hsü, the number of candidates having very greatly increased, several more rows of cabins were built and also two additional pavilions.

According to tradition, the Emperor Ch'ien Lung wishing to assure himself that the examinations were being properly conducted once took part as a candidate in disguise. He was put into a cell in the south-east corner of the compound marked with the Character for " heaven," which being the first character in the famous " Thousand Character Classic " corresponds to our No. 1.   Though how the Emperor who was supposed to be there incognito just happened to get that particular cell, tradition does not record.   In front of this cell stood an ancient sophora tree, and as the sun shone directly on his face, the Emperor wished that it would extend one of its branches so as to give him some shade.   No sooner had he expressed this wish than a violent wind got up breaking off a branch of the tree which fell in front of the window thus providing the desired shade.   In return the Emperor ennobled the sophora by giving it the title *Lung Chiao* (Dragon's Claw)—Dragon being the special emblem of the Manchu dynasty—the name by which this tree is known to the Pekingese at the present day.

Under both the Ming and Manchu dynasties the Metropolitan Examinations were held here every third year.   From five to six thousand candidates who had taken their degree in the provincial examinations, *Chü Jên* (Promoted Scholar), flocked to Peking to take part in them.   The examination was similar to that in the provinces : the themes were taken from the same works, and the essays were but little else than repetitions of the same train of thought and argument ; but the examiners were of much higher rank.

Before the examination commenced, the candidates were required to change their own clothing for garments specially provided on the spot, so as to prevent the possibility of their smuggling in with them any books, papers, notes or other means of aid.   When the candidates entered their cells in which they were to be confined for three days and two nights and which were only furnished with a stool, table, and writing materials, the examination papers were handed to them, and the door of each cell was carefully sealed up, and could not be opened again, under any pretext whatever, until the examination was over and the papers had been collected.   During the whole time deputies patrolled day and night the narrow lanes between the rows of cells to see that nothing was handed in to them. The strain on the candidates was terrific ; some went raving mad, others died of exhaustion or committed suicide.   In the latter cases, as the door could not be unsealed, a hole had to be cut in the wall to pull the bodies out.

Many were the superstitions connected with these examination halls.   As soon as the candidates had started work a couple of men would walk up and down the lanes between the cells waving a flag and crying out in a loud voice: " Whoever has an enemy here, may now take his revenge ! " or " Anybody who has a grievance, can now redress it ! "   These words were addressed, *not* to the competitors, but to the shades of the departed who were supposed to be hovering overhead in the void, to inform them that now was their opportunity to revenge themselves on any of the candidates who had wronged them. Candidates, therefore, who fell ill or failed in the examination, would put the blame on their dead enemies.   For instance, if a fly or other insect happened to alight on the writer's pen, thus spoiling a character or otherwise interrupting his work, it was an enemy who had done it.   There were, however, also friendly spirits who helped them.   A candidate who had omitted a dot from a certain character, an omission that would have certainly ploughed him, had the dot put in by a fly which alighted on the exact spot.   This was his reward for never having killed a fly !

The flag mentioned above was that of K'uei Hsing, the God of the Pole Star, the distributor of literary degrees.   It contained the seven white stars of the Great Bear on a black field with a white border.   This deity was a special favourite of aspirants to literary honours who frequented his temple before the coming examination to find out by means of a planchette, whether they would be successful or not.   Lü Tung-pin, one of the Eight Immortals, was another of the deities specially worshipped by the candidates.   For all you had to do to obtain success at the examination, was to burn a few bundles of incense sticks before his image, when he would send you in a dream the theme that would be set you at the examination, thus enabling you to prepare the answers beforehand.

Under the Mings, and right up to the latter days of the Manchus, these examinations were, with very rare exceptions, the only way of entering official life and serving the State. Whatever we may think, in these later times, as to the suitability of literary essays as a test of a man's capacity to govern his fellow-men, this system had, at any rate, the one great recommendation, that it kept open the door of public service to talent only, irrespective either of wealth or position.   In this the Chinese were centuries ahead of us Westerners, who only in the last century introduced competitive examinations for

Examination Halls

the public services.   Since the establishment of the Republic
they have retrograded from this system.

The examinations were continued in Peking right up to
the Boxer outbreak in 1900.   During the occupation of the
Allied armies most of the cells were pulled down for firewood,
and one of the punitive demands of the foreign Powers was
that the Triennial Examinations should be discontinued for a
period of five years.   Before that term had expired, the whole
system was changed, and the old examinations were never
re-instituted.   The halls fell into disuse and were razed in
1913, the first intention being to erect parliament buildings on
the site.   This was never carried out and, as we have said, it is
now used as a rubbish dump.

At the south-east corner of this open space is a small lane
called *Li Yü Hutung* (Carp Lane), which has an interesting
association with the examinations.   The majority of scholars
from the provinces entering for the Triennial Examinations
arrived in Peking by boat via the Grand Canal, Tientsin,
and Tungchow.   A number of merchants formed a shipping
company and opened an office in this lane, close to the
examination halls, so that the students could book their
return passages.   This shipping company's house-flag was a
carp, thus giving the name to the lane.   It was a clever piece
of modern advertising on their part, because the carp was
symbolical of success at the examinations, and every candidate
would naturally be anxious to return under that flag.

The entrance to the ASTRONOMICAL OBSERVATORY (*Kuan
Hsiang T'ai*—Watching the Luminaries Terrace) is on the north
side of a small lane directly under the wall.   The observatory
was built in 1296 in the reign of the famous Mongol Emperor,
Kublai Khan, on the south-east corner of the city wall.
But when Yung Lo rebuilt Peking, the walls were removed
further south which accounts for its present seemingly non-
descript position.   Under the Mongols there was an octagonal
tower on the terrace at the top of which a quadrant was placed.
The Ming Emperor Chia Ching reconstructed the observatory
in the second year of his reign (1522); a tall flag-staff for
studying the winds, and an observation tower forty feet high
were added five years later.   These various erections have
long since disappeared.

The two copper cisterns in the small east garden are all that remain of a famous water-clock from Ming times of which Edkins who still saw it in the 'nineties of last century gives the following description: "Five copper cisterns are arranged one over the other beside a staircase. At eclipses the time is taken by an arrow held in the hand of a copper man looking to the south; the arrow is three feet one inch in length; it is marked with hours from 12 noon to 11 a.m. The arrow rests on a boat which floats in the fourth cistern and ascends as the water in the cistern rises. The quantity of water and the size of the cistern are so adjusted that the time marked on the arrow agrees with the time of day as known by astronomical observation. A new supply of water is needed for each day."

We pass through a room to an inner courtyard at the foot of the steps leading to the terrace. Here used to stand two huge bronze armillas constructed by a famous Chinese astronomer, Kuo Shou-ching, in 1427. (An armilla or armillary sphere is an arrangement of rings to show the relative positions of the principle circles of the heavens). These two armillas were taken away to Nanking in 1933.

We ascend the steps to the terrace which overtops the city wall against which it is built; there is no means of exit from the terrace to the wall. The position of the various instruments is shown by the following rough sketch:

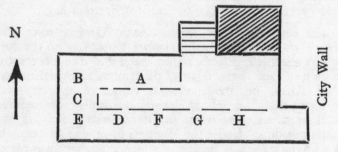

A. New Armilla   .. 1744   E. Ecliptic Armilla .. 1674
B. Quadrant (Dragons) 1674   F. Theodolite   .. 1715
C. Celestial Globe   .. 1674   G. Sextant   .. 1674
D. Altazimuth   .. 1674   H. Zodiacal Armilla .. 1674

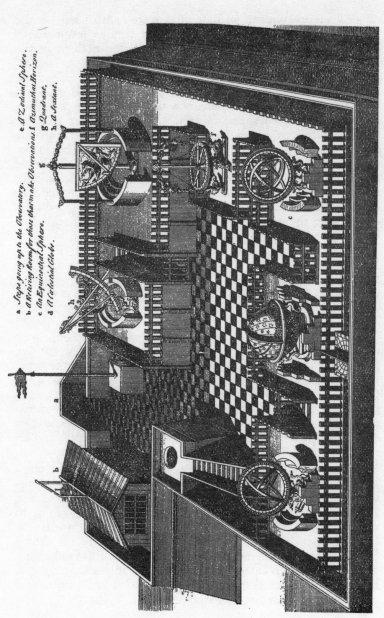

a Steps going up to the Observatory.
b A Writing Room for those that make Observations.
c An Equinoctial Sphere.
d A Celestial Globe.
e A Zodiacal Sphere.
f An Azimuthal Horizon.
g Quadrant.
h A Sextant.

THE OBSERVATORY AT PEKING IN THE 17TH CENTURY

All the instruments of date 1674 were constructed on the orders of the Emperor K'ang Hsi by the famous Jesuit priest, Father Ferdinand Verbiest; with the exception perhaps of the altazimuth (E) which according to some sources is said to have been a present from Louis XIV of France. Of these instruments the most noteworthy is the huge celestial globe on which each star is represented by a tiny bronze button. (For further details see Appendix H.). After the Boxer troubles the Germans carried off most of these beautiful instruments and re-erected them in one of the parks at Potsdam; but at the end of the Great War they were returned to China—one of the minor benefits of the Versailles Treaty. The brick building at the corner of the terrace is, needless to say, of quite modern date. Before descending, we will do well to take a good look round from the terrace, as the view of the city and the eastern outskirts is particularly fine.

The buildings in the yard below are all comparatively new. In the central courtyard is a small celestial globe which was copied from the large one, when the instruments were taken to Germany. Close to a well on the left of the gate is a stone tablet erected by Yung Chêng in 1728 recording an extraordinary celestial phenomenon that was observed in the eastern sky at daybreak on March 15, 1725 : the sun and the moon rose together (*sic !*), as if bumping into one another, whilst the five planets each of a different colour were all visible at the same time, hanging together like a string of pearls. (The name of the Chinese astronomer who observed this is not given, and it would be interesting to know whether any foreign astronomer noted a similar phenomenon on this date). As this was considered a most auspicious omen for both the Celestial Empire and its ruler, this stone tablet was set up to commemorate the event.

One of the chief duties of the astronomers was the compiling of the official calendar. Towards the end of the Mings this was in such complete confusion that even the Board of Astronomy seemed unable to put it right. When he came to the throne, K'ang Hsi who was well-inclined towards the Catholic missionaries owing to the influence of Father Adam Schaal, his tutor, called in Father Verbiest to assist in reforming the calendar. It is interesting to note that in the long debates at the Grand Council on this question the Manchu princes and officials were in favour of Father Verbiest, whilst the Chinese backed their own countrymen, adopting the view that the prestige of the Empire would suffer, if foreign methods were adopted, and that a faulty calendar was better than one tainted by foreign interference. However, the Emperor was too enlightened a ruler to be moved by chauvinist arguments of this kind in a scientific question, and he dismissed the Chinese President of the Board of Astronomy, putting Father Verbiest in his place with orders to set to at once and correct the calendar. In order to do so, it was necessary to cut out a whole month, which provoked quite a strong anti-foreign feeling. Plaintive protests poured in from all quarters of the Empire, the common people asking: " What has become of that month, and where has it been hidden away ? "

As you leave the Observatory, you will notice a narrow, dry ditch running down towards the south-east corner of the city wall. Looking at this very dilapidated, ugly and neglected part of the town where all open spaces are used as rubbish dumps, it is difficult to picture to oneself that this district was once famous for its scenic beauty. But so it is. The ditch is what remains of the once famous *P'ao Tzŭ Ho* (Bubbling River) which was dug out in the Mongol dynasty. Officially it was known as the *Hui T'ung Ho* (Favourable Communications River) and had its source at the Jade Fountain, to the north of the city. On its banks which were planted with willows several famous temples were situated, and it was a favourite spot for boating parties and picnics.

We return along a lane called *Piao Pei Hutung* (Pasteboard Lane). This name comes down from Ming times, when there were here establishments of paper-hangers. In former days it was the fashion to paper the walls and ceilings of palaces and the mansions of the wealthy with pictures of dragons, phœnixes, lions, tigers, or other designs, such as flowers, leaves and insects. Each animal or flower was appropriately matched: a dragon with a phœnix, a crane with a deer, a butterfly with a flower, and so forth. These decorative artists—for that is what they really are—also design out of paper horses, boats, carriages, and all the other paraphernalia that a person uses during lifetime. They are carried in a funeral procession and burnt, so that the deceased can enjoy the use of them in the next world. These workers in paper are experts whose art is in constant demand, not only by the living, but also by the dead.

CHAPTER XII.

THE SOUTH-WEST QUARTER OF THE TARTAR CITY

FOR this tour we leave the western entrance of the Legation Quarter and cross the space in front of the Chung Hua Mên to the *Hsi Chiao Min Hsiang* (West Intercourse with the People Lane). At one time it was intended to make this the " Wall Street " of Peking. This is the reason why numerous bank buildings are to be found here, of a size now out of all proportion to the financial activities of present-day Peking. Following the tram line we turn north into the *Ssŭ Fa Pu Chieh* (Ministry of Justice Street). The former Ministry of Justice was the building in the grounds on our left, now occupied by the Headquarters of the Kuomintang or Nationalist Party. In Ming and Manchu times this whole block was the site of the notorious BOARD OF PUNISHMENTS (*Hsing Pu*). Here were sent all the more important cases from the provinces, as also all the criminals awaiting execution. The prison attached to the Board consisted of about twenty-four separate one-storey buildings surrounded by a very high and thick wall. (There is a portion still standing on the west side). It was several feet below the level of the road, so that one descended to it, as into a basement, and at the time of the summer rains not only the courtyard, but also all the cells, were flooded. Altogether, it was a most unpleasant place in every respect, as Sir Harry Parkes himself had occasion to find out who was confined there for eleven days in 1860, with chains round hands, feet and neck. It was doubtless the fact that an official of the British Foreign Office had himself experienced the horrors of a Chinese prison which made the British government of those days so adamant in maintaining the extraterritorial rights of its nationals.

The modern building with a large three-face clock, further north along the street is the former Supreme Court (*Ta Li Yüan*) erected in 1915 on the site of the CENSORATE (*Tu Ch'a Yüan*—Court for Examining Everything). This office dates

Hsi Yang Lou

back to the later Han dynasty (A.D. 25-220), but the building was first erected in the Mongol dynasty under this name. The members were drawn from the Six Boards, and each Board had also a censor attached to it. The Emperor sometimes selected his own candidate known for integrity and fearlessness. In actual fact, the censors were nothing but paid government spies, camouflaged under high-sounding titles, who pried officially into the public and private lives of the official classes. They were often dispatched to the provinces on tours of inspection. They were even privileged to censure the Emperor himself for any act they considered illegal or harmful to the country, and in theory were supposed to be exempt from punishment if they did so. But numerous are the cases recorded in Chinese history where a censor was put to death, or still oftener sent into exile, for giving unpalatable advice. A common name for them was *Erh Mu Kuan* (Ear and Eye Officials). The office was abolished after the Revolution in 1911.

Continuing north till we reach an open-work wall and following this west we come to the broad street running past the entrance to the South Lake. Opposite this gateway, on the south side of the road was the site of a Mohammedan quarter, called *Hui Tzŭ Ying* (Mohammedan Camp). This so-called camp was constructed by Ch'ien Lung in 1760 for the accommodation of his Mohammedan soldiers who had been enrolled in the Eight Banner Corps. There were 147 small rooms for the soldiers built round a square in the centre of which stood a pavilion for the officers, called *Hsi Yang Lou* (Western Ocean Tower),—alluding to the fact that the Mohammedans came from the west,—with four bronze turtles at the top pointing in the four directions of the compass. It was at this tower—sometimes called a mosque—that Ch'ien Lung's famous "Fragrant Concubine" (*Hsiang Fei*) used to gaze longingly with thoughts of her far-distant home in the west. (Chapter VII). When Yüan Shih-k'ai became First President of China in 1912, he pulled down this pavilion, ostensibly because the turtle on the north pointed directly at the main entrance to the South Lake where his palace was situated, which was supposed to be an inauspicious omen, but more probably because the palace grounds were overlooked from the top of the tower. There is no record of what has become of the four turtles. Yüan Shih-k'ai also tore down the quarters of the Mohammedan Bannermen and erected buildings in which were to be lodged the Six Boards that he intended establishing, when he became Emperor. As is well known, he failed in his attempt to ascend the throne, and the buildings are now occupied by private tenants and not by ministers of state.

On the opposite corner on the north side of the street are the ugly modern buildings of the former Ministry of Communications. The western end—occupied at one time by the Directorate-General of Posts—was the site of the old *Wang Yeh Miao* (Prince's Temple), of which a stone tablet recording the building of the temple is all that remains. In Manchu times it was said that terrible howlings and wailings and the cracking of whips were heard here, because it was supposed to be the punishment place of the King of Hades; but no such goings-on were ever reported after the Posts were established there.

Further west, on the north side of the road, we espy two small pagodas rising above the shops in front. These are all that remain of the once famous *Shuang T'a Ssŭ* (Temple of Double Pagodas), erected in 1190 by the Chin Emperor Ming Ch'ang who was a devoted follower of Buddhism and built a large number of temples and monasteries in Peking and other parts of China. The two pagodas stood at the western end of the monastery; one is nine, the other seven storeys high. The pagodas are well-known to the Pekingese from the popular play " The Four Scholars," who in this temple took the famous oath that, if they were successful in their examinations, they would never accept bribes or oppress the people. Three of them, however, broke their oath and did take bribes for which they were tried by the fourth who had risen to be Governor.

Turning south along the Shun Chih Mên Main Street we pass on our right, about half-way towards the gate, a lane with the curious name of HUMAN HAIR LANE (*T'ou Fa Hutung*), which originates from an explosion; not one that made the hair stand on end, but that " froze it together." According to Chinese records, on the 1st day of the Fifth Moon of the 6th Year of the Ming Emperor T'ien Chi (1625) the huge arsenal north of the Elephant Stables blew up, destroying this section of the town and killing over five hundred people.

The force of the explosion was said to have been such, that some women who were riding in a cart had all their clothes torn off their backs, which clothes were deposited at Ch'ang P'ing Chou, near the Ming tombs, a distance of over 25 miles ! The only survivor on the actual scene of the explosion was a young lad found buried unharmed amongst the ruins who said that he was working with thirty men unloading kegs of powder when the explosion took place. The usual crowd having rushed to the spot and seeing a pile of what appeared to be human hair lying there, at once jumped to the conclusion that it had been blown off the heads of these men. Hence the name of this lane. That, at least, is how the matter is recorded in the local annals.

Immediately within the gate on the east side facing the wall is the *Nan T'ang* (South Cathedral). It was erected in 1650 on the site of the residence of the Catholic missionary, Father Ricci, by his successor, Father Adam Schaal who obtained special permission from the Emperor Shun Chih. In 1775 it was burnt down, but was rebuilt with the help of a large subscription from the Emperor Ch'ien Lung, and survived the numerous persecutions of the Catholic religion, until it was closed up in 1827 under Tao Kuang. In order to save it from being confiscated, the Catholics made over the property by deed to the Russian Ecclesiastical Mission who preserved it for them till 1860, when after the Franco-English expedition it was handed back and reopened. In the early days of the Boxer troubles it was stormed by a fanatical mob and burnt to the ground, hundreds of Chinese converts who had taken refuge there being massacred or burnt alive. The present building, therefore, is quite modern.

The *Shun Chih Mên* (Gate of Direct Rule), also called *Hsüan Wu Mên* (Gate of Proclaimed Military Strength), the west gate of the south wall of the Tartar City, has been reconstructed in recent times, the whole outer wall having been completely removed. It has always been considered an unlucky gate for two reasons. Firstly, because from a geomantic point of view it is in the " unlucky " or " cutting-off of life " quarter. For this same reason, in all Chinese houses, only subordinate buildings, such as kitchen, storehouses and so forth, are erected in the south-west corner. Secondly, because through this gate those condemned to death were taken to the Execution Ground (Chapter XVI).   Hence it is still popularly known as the Gate of Death (*Ssŭ Mên*), as, of course, none of the criminals who passed through it ever returned alive.   And for these reasons this gate was never used by any of the Emperors.   In the outer courtyard of this gate there used to be three short round pillars of brick, about 2½ feet high, the remains of five water-levels installed at the time of the rebuilding of the walls by Yung Lo. The top of these pillars was level with the surface of the lake at the Summer Palace and also, it was said, with the top of the pagoda at T'ungchow, to the east of Peking.

Following the street that runs west under the wall we come to the PARLIAMENT BUILDINGS, uninteresting, modern types, erected by Yüan Shih-k'ai in 1912, and now occupied by colleges.   Here the first Chinese parliament held its interminable, turbulent, and futile sessions, often interrupted by lengthy " holidays," until its natural death in 1924, or thereabouts— there seems to be no exact record of this unimportant event. This first effort at parliamentary government in China, apart from being an extremely costly method of conducting the country's affairs, as the vote of each of the five hundred odd deputies had to be bought before any measure could be passed, was distinctly not a success and has left no mark whatever on the history of the country.

Much more interesting is the fact that the site on which these buildings stand was that of the famous ELEPHANT STABLES (*Hsiang Fang*).   The " Elephant Quarter " covered a vast area and was, to all intents and purposes, a small city of its own, even to the extent of having its own particular temple to the tutelary deity of elephants.   The buildings consisted of six rows of eight stables, each 36 by 18 feet, with massive brick walls six feet thick, lit by a skylight in the gable-shaped roof. The exit from the enclosure was by a heavy iron-bound wooden door built over the centre of a wide and deep trench that ran all round the inside of the outer wall, into which the keepers could jump, when the animals became unruly.   When they were taken out for duty this door was laid down flat so as to cover the trench and form a bridge for them to cross. These elephant houses were built in the 6th year of the Ming Emperor Hung Chih (1495).

Elephants were known in China during the reign of the Great Yü (2205 B.C.) and were said to have been fully trained during the T'ang and Sung dynasties and used in Imperial ceremonies. In Ming and Manchu times the elephants formed part of the tribute from the kingdoms of Burma and Annam and were used in public ceremonial processions.

They were employed on duty in two ways : in the first duty six of them took up their position at daylight outside the Wu Mên facing each other in three pairs. When the bell sounded for the officials to enter the palace, the elephants knelt down and remained in this position, until everyone had passed in, when they rose and each pair facing crossed trunks, thus forming a barrier through which no one was allowed to pass. As soon as the Court was over, they withdrew their trunks to let the officials pass out, when they returned to their quarters. Their other duty was to draw a specially constructed Imperial chariot which the Emperor used when he went to worship at the Altar of Heaven and at the T'ai Miao (Ancestral Temple). Both K'ang Hsi and Ch'ien Lung used elephants to carry the Imperial Genealogical Register (Chia P'u), which was corrected to date every few years, to Mukden in Manchuria, to be deposited in the Ancestral Temple there.

The elephants, though attended by specially trained keepers, were under the direct orders of the Emperor himself. If an elephant fell sick whilst on duty, the keeper at once sent in a memorial to the Emperor who wrote out a slip ordering the sick elephant to be sent back to his quarters and another one to take his place. The Emperor's order, it is said, had to be read out aloud for all the elephants to hear, as otherwise not one of them would move. But if the order was read aloud, the elephant next for duty would step forward and follow the keeper to his post. If an elephant injured any one of the public while on duty, or otherwise misbehaved himself, the Emperor would order an appropriate punishment. If it was to be a whipping, two elephants would wind their trunks round the offender and force him on to his knees, so that the keeper could flog him ; when it was over, he would rise and bow several times, as if thanking the Emperor for the punishment. If it was only to be a light punishment, such as demotion, the offender was shifted from the first, or whatever rank he held, to a lower place; for these elephants ranked with princes and other dignitaries and received the same emoluments.

Their rations were allotted according to their duties; that of standing still on guard being considered more onerous, the elephants performing this duty received a larger ration than the ones that drew the Imperial chariot. Unfortunately for the elephants, the money allotted to them as salary had to pass through so many hands that by the time it came to their share for fodder even, there was barely sufficient to keep them alive. The keepers, too, had to get their rake-off which they tried to make by cutting down on the cooked rice that was placed in the centre of the bundles of rice-straw supplied to the elephants. The latter knowing the wiles of their keepers would carefully weigh the bundles with their trunks and, if they found the weight too short, would start a rough house; it was then that the keepers had to make for the above-mentioned trench.

Another perquisite of the keepers was the disposing of the elephants' dung to the ladies of Peking who after washing it thoroughly used the strained-off water to wash their hair with, as it was supposed to give it a brilliant gloss. It was also used by men to cure the scars which, in the days of the queue, were often exposed on the shaved crown of the head. For this reason, a slang term for persons who put on airs was *Hsiang La Ssŭ* (Elephants' Dung).

The keepers of these Imperial elephants were Annamites, and the post descended in the same family from father to son. Only once a year were the elephants allowed outside for a stroll, on the 6th of the Sixth Moon, when they were taken down to bathe in the moat outside the wall of the Tartar City. They were, however, not allowed to go right into the water on account of the difficulty of getting them to come out again. This day was a Peking holiday, and it used to be a popular amusement to go and see the elephants taking their bath.

In the spring of 1884, whilst practicing with the chariot, one of the elephants escaped and caused a tremendous panic in that part of the city through which he promenaded. For several hours the whole life of the city was interrupted, until he was found by the keepers in a narrow alley in which he had lost himself and was taken back to the stables. After this incident elephants were no longer employed in Court ceremonies. In any case, when soon afterwards Annam and Burma ceased to be tributary to China, no further elephants were sent up, and the existing ones gradually died of starvation.

Continuing along the street under the wall, and turning north before we reach the south-west corner, we come to a large enclosure with high walls, inside which can be seen numerous buildings with yellow-tiled roofs. These buildings are now a school, but were formerly the PALACE OF PRINCE CH'UN (*Ch'un Wang Fu*). He was the seventh son of the Emperor Tao Kuang and better known as the father of the Emperor Kuang Hsü, and the brother-in-law of the Empress-Dowager Tz'ŭ Hsi, and was the only one of the elder princes who managed to keep on good terms all his life with this formidable lady. From all accounts he would seem to have been a comparatively honest, well-meaning, and somewhat stupid, person, but an ardent upholder of the rights of the Manchus. A famous saying of his in 1885, when a war with France was in progress and a rebellion threatening in South China, that he would rather see the Empire handed over to the foreign devils than to the Chinese rebels, did not increase his popularity amongst the Chinese. Luckily for his peace of mind, he did not live to see the disasters of the Japanese War or the Boxer madness. After his death in 1891, the Empress-Dowager issued a special edict praising him for his modesty in not availing himself of the high honour that had been granted him of using yellow curtains in his sedan-chair and generally for not attempting to push himself forward as the father of the Emperor. By her orders too, his palace was divided into two parts, one for an ancestral hall to himself, and one, according to precedent, as a shrine for his son who had become Emperor. This palace was occupied by the staff of the British forces in 1900-01.

It was from here that on a bitterly cold night in January, 1875, in the midst of a violent dust-storm, the future Emperor Kuang Hsü, weeping bitterly, as if foreseeing the evil destiny that awaited him, was fetched in the Imperial yellow sedan-chair with eight bearers to the palace where he at once had to perform the ceremony of kotow before the corpse of his predecessor.

BATHING

Elephants

In view of its disastrous results not only for the whole of China, but also for the Manchu dynasty and for Peking itself, we ought perhaps to dwell shortly on the circumstances of the selection of the son of this Prince Ch'un as Emperor. The Emperor T'ung Chih, whose personal name was Ts'ai Ch'un, died without an heir. The lineal descendants of an Emperor in the same generation all bore the same first character in their names : for instance, those of the same generation as T'ung Chih were all called Ts'ai something, and their sons again were called P'u something. It is as if the names of the sons of an English king, for instance, all commenced with Eg-, that is to say, Egbert, Egmont and so on, and those of their sons with Ed-, Edwin, Edward, etc. Now, according to the laws of ancestor worship, an equal (i.e. one of the same generation) could not perform the ancestral sacrifices to an equal ; nor could a man for this reason adopt an equal as his son. Kuang Hsü whose personal name was Ts'ai Tien was a cousin of the same generation as T'ung Chih, so that his selection as the latter's successor was a complete breach of these laws and offended the dynastic feelings not only of the Manchus, but also of all loyal Chinese. A certain censor, Wu K'o-t'o, even committed suicide at the Emperor's grave as a protest, after composing a famous memorial on the subject.

As a matter of fact several candidates more suitable than Kuang Hsü were available at the time in the lower (and there-fore correct) generation : P'u Lun, the grandson of Tao Kuang's eldest son ; P'u Chün grandson of Prince Tun ; and P'u Wei grandson of Prince Kung. But the Empress-Dowager who was primarily responsible for the selection rejected all three and chose the son of Prince Ch'un, partly because he had married her sister and partly because she wished to continue in power herself. For if P'u Lun, the most suitable, had been chosen, she would immediately have been relegated to the background, as he was already seventeen years of age. (For a more detailed view of the succession of the Emperor Kuang Hsü see Appendix F.).

At the back of this palace, in an angle of the high walls, is a small shrine to the local deity of the district (*Ch'êng Huang*) who, to judge by the hundreds of votive tablets and strips of yellow cloth that cover the walls in both directions, must be a particularly efficacious deity.

Continuing north through a maze of small lanes we come to the small, but well-preserved, *Wo Fo Ssŭ* (Temple of the Sleeping Buddha) situated in a lane of that name, and with a large idol of the Buddha in a prone position. The temple was built by a monk called Chiu Fêng in the T'ang dynasty, in A.D. 648, repaired by K'ang Hsi in 1665 and again by Ch'ien Lung in 1761. The latter ordered the stone tablet to be placed in the temple courtyard, where it still stands, recording the history of this monastery. About twenty rather dirty and miserable-looking young acolytes reside in this temple where they are being trained as monks.

We now turn east along the lane and its continuation, called Old Board of Punishments Street (*Chiu Hsing Pu Chieh*) because in Mongol times the Board was situated in this street, and come out again on to the Shun Chih Mên Main Street. The second turning north on the same side bears the curious name *Shê Fan Ssŭ Hutung* (Free Distribution of Rice Temple Lane) from a temple of this name situated on the north side. According to tradition, during the reign of the Ming Emperor Chia Ching a scholar from the province of Kiangsu resided in a small temple in this lane. He was so poor that during the day he had to beg in the streets to earn his living, whilst at night he worked hard at his studies for the public examinations. He registered a vow that, if he succeeded in obtaining a degree—all that a scholar required so that he need do no more work for the rest of his life—he would repair the temple which had fallen into decay and would provide food gratis to all the poor living in the neighbourhood. Having been successful in the examination, he made good his vow and distributed grain free for three years.

On the opposite side of the main street, almost facing this lane is the *Hsi Tan Shih Ch'ang* (Market at the West Single Archway) which corresponds, here in the west, to the market in the east city (Chapter XI).

A few yards further north we come to *Shih Hu Hutung* (Stone Tiger Lane), formerly called Lion Tiger Lane (of same sound). We would mention that in Chinese the words "lion," "stone," and "lost" have the same sound, but different characters. At the far end of this lane can be seen, to this day, a stone lion, and close to it on the north side, up against the wall of a coal-yard (No. 1.) a small stone tiger. The story is as follows :—In the North City, off the An Ting Mên Main Street, is a lane also called Stone Tiger Lane (formerly known as Lost Tiger Lane—of same sound). In that lane there were once two stone tigers one of whom went off for a walk one day and meeting in the lane we are describing the stone lion became rooted to the spot (from fright ?), so that he could not return to his own lane. Therefore in the former " Lost Tiger Lane," as the name once indicated, there is only one tiger to be seen to-day, while in the former " Lion Tiger Lane," as the name also showed, we find both the lion and the tiger. This story, we are afraid, is slightly confusing, because the Peking police, lacking a sense of humour, have renamed both lanes " Stone Tiger Lane."

Going back along the main street to the Hsi Ch'ang An Chieh we return by the way we came.

THE NORTH-EAST QUARTER OF THE TARTAR CITY

IN order to reach this part of the city we continue up Morrison Street (Chapter XI) to the north end, and then west into the An Ting Mên Main Street. A street on the right called Iron Lion Lane (*T'ieh Shih Tzŭ Hutung*) derives its name from an iron lion that used to stand in this lane, in front of the former palace of Prince Ho, the fifth son of the Emperor Yung Chêng. In a turning on the north side, the *Ch'i Lin Pei Hutung* (Unicorn Tablet Lane), there was a beautifully-carved unicorn in stone, about five feet long by four feet high. It was said to date from the T'ang period and had been placed there by Prince Kung, the fifth son of the Emperor Shun Chih, at the entrance to his palace, which has long since disappeared. Both the lion and the unicorn have been taken away in recent times and now adorn the Propaganda Offices of the Kuomintang at the Drum Tower.

Turning west up the street opposite Iron Lion Lane, called Broad Street (*K'uan Chieh*), we pass a small stone, camel-backed bridge with the curious name of *Tung Pu Ya Ch'iao* (East Not-dented-in Bridge). The origin of this name is as follows : on the opposite, west, side of the *Hou Mên* (Back Gate) is a similar bridge, called *Hsi Ya Ch'iao* (West Dented-in Bridge), because formerly the wall of the Imperial City bulged here and ran along the centre of the bridge, thus " denting it in." But on the eastern bridge the wall did not encroach and so it was called " Not dented-in."

On reaching the Hou Mên, officially known as *Ti An Mên* (Gate of Earthly Peace) we turn north along the *Ku Lou Ta Chieh* (Drum Tower Main Street) and see in front of us the famous DRUM TOWER (*Ku Lou*). It was built by Yung Lo when he moved his capital to Peking. It is 99 feet high, constructed of brick up to the top storey, and then of wood. The materials for its construction were taken from the old

Drum Tower of Mongol times which stood in the then centre of the city at the southern end of what is to-day called " Old Drum Tower Main Street," about one hundred yards west of the present tower. The original name was *Ch'i Chêng Lou* (Mustering for Duty Tower), as a signal drum was beaten before daylight for all government employees to assemble.

In this tower was a kind of water-clock, called " The Brass Thirsty Bird " (*T'ung K'o Niao*), said to have been invented by one Li Lan who lived in the Sung dynasty. The upper jar was in the form of a bird through whose beak the water seeped into a lower jar with a bamboo rod, showing divisions of a quarter of an hour, at each of which a watchman struck a large cymbal (*ch'a*) eight times. The Manchus did away with the " Thirsty Bird," using an ordinary jar instead, and replaced the cymbal by a drum, which was only struck at nightfall. This custom of sounding the watches was continued right down to the early years of the Republic, but was abandoned when the new régime established the Propaganda Quarters of the Kuomintang in this ancient and historical building.

A short distance to the north lies the BELL TOWER (*Chung Lou*). Built during the reign of the Mongol Emperor Chih Yüan (A.D. 1285), it was removed to its present site by Yung Lo. It was later destroyed by fire and not rebuilt till 1745 under Ch'ien Lung. It is ninety feet high and constructed of bricks and stone.

Whenever the drum in the Drum Tower was beaten, the bell was tolled immediately afterwards. It was cast under Yung Lo and is estimated to weigh twenty thousand pounds ; the Chinese say that its chimes could be heard forty *li* (13 miles) away.

There is a romantic story in connection with the casting of this bell. For some reason or other the foundry could never obtain a perfect casting ; no matter how they tried, there was always something wrong with it. At last the Emperor Yung Lo becoming impatient at the constant delays, threatened to have the owner of the foundry beheaded, unless he completed the bell within a definite time. The bell-founder's daughter noticing her father's distress and learning the cause, persuaded him to take her to the foundry when the next casting took place, although women were strictly forbidden to be present, as the feminine principle (*Yin*) was supposed to have an evil influence. Just as the molten metal was being let out into the mould, the girl suddenly jumped into it. Her father made a desperate clutch at her to try and save her, but only succeeded in catching hold of one of her shoes which came off in his hand. This time the bell was perfectly cast, without a blemish, but according to popular belief, it has ever since given forth the sound "*Hsieh*!" (Shoe) when struck.

Like the Drum Tower, the Bell Tower was also in use during the first years of the Republic, but later, in accordance with the claims of Modern Progress, was converted into a cinema hall.

Going back to the Drum Tower and then east along the main street of that name (*Ku Lou Ta Chieh*) for about a mile, we pass on the north side of the street the *Shun T'ien Fu* (Shun-t'ien Prefecture). This department was first established by Kublai Khan in 1264 and called *Ta Tu Lu* (Big Capital Road), because it was the headquarters of the Generalissimo, under whose orders the troops were dispatched along the various trunk roads leading from Peking. It was changed to the present name under the Mings. *Shun T'ien* (Obedient to Heaven) is the name of the prefecture in which the city lies, which was then, as it still is, under the jurisdiction of the Mayor of Peking and includes the entire province of *Chihli* (Direct Rule), —now Hopei—with the exception of Tientsin which has its own mayor.

Turning north up the main street we come to the *An Ting Mên* (Gate of Fixed Peace). This gate, the easterly of the two north gates, the starting-point of the road to Ku Pei K'ou and Jehol, was occupied in 1860 by the British who dragged their guns up the ramp and posted them on the wall commanding the city. The only other point of interest about the gate is that, before it was reconstructed for the round-the-city railway, the outer gate, in the barbican, faced east, outwards, instead of west, inwards. The two northern gates were, therefore, not facing each other, as was the case with the pairs of gates on the other three sides. The reason for this is that, as we have mentioned elsewhere (Chapter I), Peking was built to resemble *No Cha*, a mythical personage, with three heads and six arms. The two northern gates, representing his feet, were therefore built with their outer gateways turned the same way like human feet. The following sketch will make this clear :—

Ch'ien Mên

An Ting Mên   *Tê Shêng Mên*

Crossing An Ting Mên Street and continuing straight on east we reach Hatamên Street. The junction of the two main roads, paved with large flag-stones, part of an ancient causeway, is called *Pei Hsin Ch'iao* (North New Bridge), although no bridge has stood here within the memory of man. The name is accounted for as follows :—At the north-east corner is a small temple with a well at the back, down which there hangs an iron chain. When this is pulled, a curious sound, as of a strong wind, comes up from the bottom of the well, said to be caused by a " pig-dragon " that is chained up there. According to the popular story, a bridge stood on this spot in the Sung dynasty, spanning a pool in which the " pig-dragon " lived. There had been no rain for over three years, and as the " pig-dragon " was suspected of being the cause of the drought, a priest belonging to the temple put him in chains. On the " pig-dragon," asking how long his imprisonment would last, he was informed that he would not be released, as long as a bridge spanned the creek. When later on the bridge was pulled down and a causeway built instead, the name " North New Bridge " was given to the causeway, so as to deceive the " pig-dragon " ; and this name has remained ever since.

Turning north up the main street we come on the right (east) side to the Lama Temple or *Yung Ho Kung*, whilst across the road, in the *Ch'êng Hsien Chieh* (Complete Worthies' Street) lies the Temple of Confucius. These two temples are dealt with separately in Part Two of this chapter.

Adjoining the Lama Temple on the east is another group of temple buildings situated in a beautiful, sequestered spot, called the *Pai* or *Po Lin Ssŭ* (Cypress Grove Temple). The bark of this tree is used for making a yellow dye. The temple was built during the reign of the Mongol Emperor Chih Ch'êng, in 1347. In the main courtyard is a tablet bearing the characters *Wan Ku Pai Lin* (Cypress Grove of Ten Thousand Ages) presented to the lamas by the Emperor Ch'ien Lung, by whom the temple was repaired and a special " Rest-house " built there for himself. The side buildings were used by the higher lamas of the Yung Ho Kung as a kind of summer retreat. In recent times it has been turned into a school, at times even into a barracks, and all the images and old relics have disappeared.

About a quarter of a mile to the east lies the large compound of the Russian Mission, called *Pei Kuan* (North Hostel). This part of the city was originally occupied by the Albazin prisoners whom the Emperor K'ang Hsi brought to Peking in 1685. Albazin was a small Cossack settlement on the Amur River whose inhabitants were constantly raiding Chinese territory, until the Emperor sent a special expedition to suppress them. The prisoners, amongst whom were thirty or forty Russians including a priest, were given land and a small temple in this north-eastern corner of the city close to the present Mission grounds. Later on, permission was granted for priests to be sent to them to attend to their spiritual needs, and these formed the nucleus of the North Hostel. The Albazins themselves intermarried with the Manchus and in the course of time became indistinguishable from the rest of the population. They remained attached to the Orthodox Church, and there are, it is claimed, families bearing Russian names still living in this district. In 1858 the Russian Ecclesiastical Mission from the *Nan Kuan* (South Hostel) was transferred to the Pei Kuan (Chapter I).

The grounds, though extensive, contain little of historical interest, because all the old buildings were completely destroyed during the Boxer outbreak in 1900, when several hundreds of the native Christians were murdered, many of them being thrown down the well that is still to be seen in the garden.

In the north-east part of the grounds is a Memorial Chapel to the victims. After 1900 the property was considerably enlarged, and new buildings erected which are totally different from those destroyed by the Boxers. The monks have a flour mill, dairy, bee-hives and a printing-press.

Leaving the Mission in a southerly direction we come to the main street leading to the *Tung Chih Mên* (East Straight Gate). This is one of the four gates that has no second official name. It is also the only other one of the nine original gates that was provided with a bell instead of a gong. There are three different stories accounting for this. One is the same as at the Hatamên (Chapter XVI) and refers to the "pig-dragon" at the North New Bridge who was told that, in addition to the bridge taboo, he could not be released until the gong was sounded at this gate. So here, too, they went and replaced the gong by a bell.

The other story is that a Bachelor of Arts, who was on his way to Peking to take the Metropolitan Examination, fell in with a tortoise disguised as a scholar. When they reached the capital they put up at an inn outside this gate, and the tortoise said to the B.A. "You will take a first degree in the coming examination, so when you see the Emperor, please ask him when I may come into the city and go up for my examination." The B.A. having passed successfully, as prophesied, on returning to the inn was asked by the tortoise, whether the Emperor had fixed a date for his examination. "Yes," replied the B.A., "He told me to tell you that, when the gong at the East Straight Gate is struck, it will be the summons for you to appear at the examination." He then rushed back to see the official in charge of the gate and asked him at once to change the gong for a bell. (The point of this tale is that tortoises are believed to cause floods, so that it was desirable neither to offend him nor to let him into the city). The change was made, and it is said that the simple-minded tortoise is to this day hiding in a deep hole outside the gate waiting for the gong to summon him to the Metropolitan Examination.

The third reason given for the change from gong to bell is more prosaic and more modern. It is said that the bell was placed there on the orders of the Emperor Tao Kuang in honour of a conscientious guardian of the gate who refused to open it after closing time, even for the Emperor himself.

To the south of the Tung Chih Mên, under the city wall, is a lane that is closely associated with a famous episode in Chinese history. This is *Shan Tzŭ Shih Erh Hutung* (Rocky Mountain Lane), so called from a pile of rocks, discoloured· by fire, that once stood in a garden on this spot, the property of Wu San-kuei's father. This garden was specially created for the famous " Round-Faced Beauty " (*Ch'ên Yüan Yüan*) who was the unwitting cause of the Manchu conquest of China.

There are several versions of how Wu San-kuei, the Chinese Commander-in-Chief, obtained possession of the maiden. One story is that he bought her for a fabulous sum during a visit to Soochow. But the correct version is probably, that he first met her at a banquet in the house of one of the ministers of state, T'ien Wan, where she was employed as a maid-servant, and that he fell in love with her at first sight, attracted as much by her beautiful voice as by her good looks.

Wu San-kuei who was defending the important pass of Shan Hai Kuan against the Manchu invasion in 1643, had left the " Round-Faced Beauty " behind him in Peking under the care of his father. But when Li Tzŭ-ch'êng, the robber chief, captured Peking, she fell into his hands. On learning of the fate of his favourite, Wu was so overcome with passion that in his desire for revenge he tendered his allegiance to the Manchus, surrendering up to them the pass. Afterwards Li sent the " Round-Faced Beauty " to Wu's camp, in the hope of appeasing him, but it was too late ; for in the meantime the Manchus had entered Shan Hai Kuan, from where they advanced against Li and, after defeating him decisively with the aid of Wu San-kuei, themselves captured Peking. Yet though this fair lady was thus one of the determining factors in the establishment of the Manchu dynasty, the only memorial of her is this blackened mass of rocks in an obscure side-alley.

Retracing our steps west up the Tung Chih Mên Main Street, we turn south down a street called very suitably—in view of its narrowness—*Pei Hsiao Chieh* (North Small Street). The large buildings on the east side are the GRANARIES where formerly the Tribute Rice was stored. They are now either completely in ruins or have been adapted for other uses, but in Manchu times were of considerable importance in the life of Peking. For it was from them that the Manchu Bannermen drew their allowance of free rice or, as we moderns would call it, the dole.

This brings us to the main street leading to the *Ch'i Hua Mên* (Gate of Unmixed Blessings), officially known as *Ch'ao Yang Mên* (Gate Facing the Sun), the southern gate in the east wall. At the corner of the main street and the Pei Hsiao Chieh, on the west side, is another PALACE OF PRINCE I whom we have previously mentioned (Chapter XI). It is now a school. A descendant of this prince, Tsai Yüan by name, attempted to usurp the regency after the death of the Emperor Hsien Fêng at Jehol in 1860, where he had fled before the advance of the Anglo-French armies. But the conspirators met their match in the Empress-Dowager Tz'ŭ Hsi, who was then the mother of the new Emperor and here, for the first time, showed that energy and courage which marked her rule during the rest of her life. As the usurping regents were bound by custom to accompany the Imperial coffin all the way back to Peking, the Empress who had to go on in front in order to receive the coffin on its entry into the capital, was able to take counter-measures with the help of Prince Kung, one of the late Emperor's brothers. The regents had laid plans to have her assassinated at the pass of Ku Pei K'ou, but were frustrated by Jung Lu, the commander of the Manchu bodyguard, who left the cortège at night and hastening ahead escorted her safely to Peking, for which service he was ever afterwards in high favour with her. On their arrival at the city gates the three conspirators were surrounded by an overwhelming force and arrested. Prince I and Prince Chêng were made to commit suicide, whilst the third, a Manchu commoner, Su Shun, was publicly beheaded. The descendants of Prince I were deprived of the title; the property was confiscated; and, as if to add insult to injury, this palace of his was assigned as the residence of the "Barbarian Chief," Lord Elgin, during his short stay in Peking. This was but poetic justice, because Prince I had always been a great hater of the "Outer Barbarians." Moreover, apart from his having been the leader of the War Party, it was on his direct orders that Parkes and the others were taken prisoners which led to the burning of the old Summer Palace. In 1864, in thanksgiving for the suppression of the

T'ai P'ing rebellion, the hereditary princedom of I was restored. But anti-foreign tendencies must, one supposes, have been deep-rooted in the family for another Prince I, the grandson, was made to commit suicide in 1900 for his alleged complicity in the Boxer movement.

A little way to the east lies the palace of another even more famous princely personage, namely Prince Tuan of Boxer fame. His palace, known as *Wu Yeh Fu* (Palace of the Fifth Prince) because his father was the fifth son of the Emperor Tao Kuang, lies on a street called very suitably "Burnt Wine Lane" (*Shao Chiu Hutung*), seeing that he was rather fond of the bottle. Except for his prominent part in the Boxer movement—which in this era of historical whitewashing some might even palliate as merely an excessive form of the nowadays popular nationalism—he does not seem to have been at all a bad fellow, and still preserved some of the virility of his Manchu forbears. He was a tall, sturdy man, with a red face and rough manner, very honest and outspoken, a heavy drinker and with a peculiar taste for dogs' meat which he used to buy himself at a special shop outside the Tung Hua Mên. In pre-Boxer days he was a well-known figure in Peking society, of whom many amusing tales are told, especially of the way in which he stood up to the formidable Empress-Dowager whom he was inclined to look down on as an outsider, being himself the grandson of Tao Kuang.

On one occasion when he wanted to present a special dish of salmon to the Empress-Dowager, the eunuchs in attendance demanded a large tip, before taking it in. Thereupon, the prince picked up the dish and carried it into her presence with his own hands. He disapproved of the Empress-Dowager's penchant for naughty stories with which her eunuch attendants used to entertain her. Once, when a story of this kind was being told in his presence, he suddenly jumped up from his chair, twisted his queue round his head—in the style of a low comedian—and started strutting up and down singing a popular vulgar song at the top of his voice. The Empress merely said : " Take him away. He's drunk," but she took the hint and forbade these stories in public for the future. On another occasion, when an obscene play was being performed at the palace, Prince Tuan began applauding loudly. To one of the princes who was sent by the Empress-Dowager to reprimand him for this serious breach of etiquette, he replied in a voice audible all over the place : " Oh, I quite forgot. I was so taken with the play, I thought I was at one of the public theatres."

Considering the leading part that he played in the Boxer rising, Prince Tuan would appear to have got off very lightly. Instead of losing his head—as the Powers originally demanded— he was permitted to go into exile in the far distant province of Kansu. After the revolution of 1911-12 he returned to Peking for a short time ; but this was too much for the Foreign Powers, and at their request the new Republican authorities who had not the slightest sympathy for him ordered him to go back to Kansu where he died in the early 'twenties of this century.

His son, P'u Chün, commonly known as Ta Ah Ko, had, at one time, a very good chance of becoming Emperor, having been appointed Heir-Apparent to the Emperor Kuang Hsü in January 1900. When, as a result of his father's participation in the Boxer disasters, he was deposed, he retired to this palace, the Wu Yeh Fu, where he spent the remainder of his life trying to drown in dissipation the memories of the glorious future that had once been within his grasp.

Turning west along the main street, we pass, on the north side, a large temple with roofs of glazed green tiles, now a police station. This is the *San Kuan Miao* (Three Officials Temple), also known as the *Yen Fu Kung* (Palace of Prolonged Happiness). The name San Kuan Miao refers to the three deities, Heaven, Earth and Sea, whose worship dates back to the Yin dynasty (1766-1122 B.C.). This temple has a tragic association with the end of the Mings. When the Emperor Ch'ung Chêng had finally decided to defend the City against the rebel chief, Li Tzŭ-ch'êng, he proceeded with a large retinue to this temple in order to find out by drawing lots whether his decision was approved of by the gods. Having performed the required sacrifices, the Emperor took the bamboo tube containing the lots—narrow slips of bamboo—and was about to draw forth the fatal slip, when the whole contents of the tube fell to the ground. Taking this as an omen of disaster, the Emperor in despair hurled the tube to the ground and cursed the temple for evermore, desiring that the hopes of all future applicants should be disappointed in the same way as his had been. Ever since that day the temple has been avoided by worshippers and is known to the people as the " Cursed Temple."

Crossing Hatamên street, and taking the fourth turning on the right, we come to the *Lung Fu Ssŭ* (Temple of Prosperity and Happiness). It was built in 1451 under the Ming Emperor Ching T'ai. More than ten thousand workmen were employed in its construction ; most of the wood and marble was brought from the Hsiang Fêng Tien, one of the palaces in Nanking, occupied by the first Ming Emperor Hung Wu. In 1731 it was repaired by Yung Chêng who took a special interest in this temple. Formerly a large community of monks resided here, but it is nowadays of no religious importance, its chief claim to notice being the fair that is held four times a month, for three days at a time.

CHAPTER XIII.—PART TWO.

THE TEMPLE OF CONFUCIUS AND THE LAMA TEMPLE

THE TEMPLE OF CONFUCIUS (*K'ung Miao*) or " Temple of Great Perfection " (*Ta Ch'êng Miao*), is also known as *Wên Miao* (Civil Temple) or *Hsien Shih T'an* (Altar of the Master Teacher), which is the official name.

During the Ming and Manchu dynasties the temples of Confucius were called *Wên* (Civil) in contradistinction to those of the God of War which were called *Wu* (Military). Under the Republic all Confucian temples were changed back to the ancient name, *K'ung Miao*. Confucian temples are to be found all over China, the most important being at Ch'ü Fu in Shantung where the Sage was born in 550 B.C. This, the first temple in his honour was built by Duke Ai of the State of Lu, some time in 478 B.C., a year after his death. It was perhaps only right that Duke Ai should have built the first Confucian temple, because it was he who captured the unicorn (*ch'i lin*) whilst on a hunting expedition in the west in 481 B.C. When this news came to his ears, Confucius gave up his labours saying that his own death was close at hand—the *ch'i lin* was considered a supernatural creature, therefore of evil omen—and died two years later, as he had predicted.

The Peking temple was built towards the end of the 13th century, in the reign of the Mongol Emperor, Chih Chêng, and repaired by many later rulers, especially by K'ang Hsi in 1689, and again by Ch'ien Lung in 1737, when the ordinary grey tiles of the roofs were replaced by Imperial, yellow ones.

As is the case with all Confucian temples, a stone tablet at the entrance orders civil and military officials to descend from their horses or sedan-chairs, as a sign of reverence.

We enter by a western side door; the central one was only used by the Emperor on his official visits. Passing

through the *Hsien Shih Miao* (Temple of the Master Teacher)
enter courtyard where there are a large number of stone
tablets inscribed with the names and addresses of all the
scholars who were successful in the Triennial Examinations.
The oldest are three that date back to the Mongol dynasty, so
that these tablets represent an almost complete record for seven
centuries. The two huge stone tablets standing on the backs
of tortoises inside pavilions on either side contain historical
notices about the temple.

In the verandah on the north side of the *Ta Ch'êng Mên*
(Gate of Great Perfection) which leads to the main enclosure,
there used to stand ten drum-shaped blocks of black granite,
the famous " STONE DRUMS." They are said to belong to the
Chou period (1122-255 B.C.), though there is still a certain
amount of argument in learned circles on this point, as the
characters with which they are inscribed are not only difficult
to decipher, but have become in parts quite illegible.

About seven miles south of Fênghsiang, in the province of
Shensi, is a place still called Shih Ku Yüan (Stone Drums'
Origin) which is probably the spot where they were first hewn
out. This locality lay once in the ancestral territory of Tan Fu,
the founder of the Chou dynasty, who lived for a time at the
foot of Mount Ch'i, in the present district of Ch'i Shan, the
southern end of which was his favourite resort for hunting
expeditions. And it is quite possible that the stone drums
were made in commemoration of at least one of same. They
were rediscovered in the early part of the T'ang dynasty, about
the 8th century, lying half-buried in the ground.

When the Liao Tartars invaded China, the Sungs fled to
the south taking the drums with them to Pien Liang (the
modern K'aifêng) where they had established their new
capital. After its capture by the Min-chih Tartars in A.D. 1126,
the drums were carried off to Peking. In 1307, in the reign
of the Mongol Emperor Ta Tê, they were placed here, in the
gateway of the Confucian temple, where they remained until
May 1933, when the Nationalist government ordered their
removal south, replacing them by modern replicas. Inside
the same gateway are ten facsimile stones, which were cut
by the order of Ch'ien Lung, in order to preserve a record of
what remained of the inscriptions.

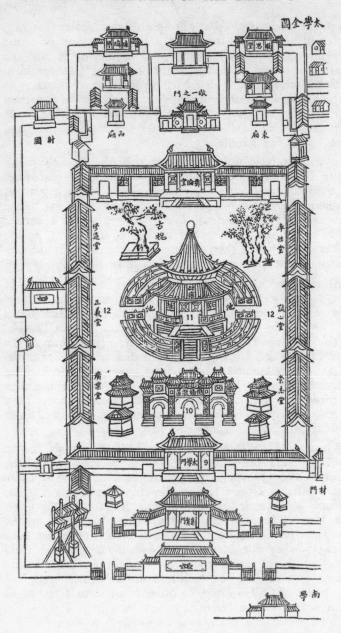

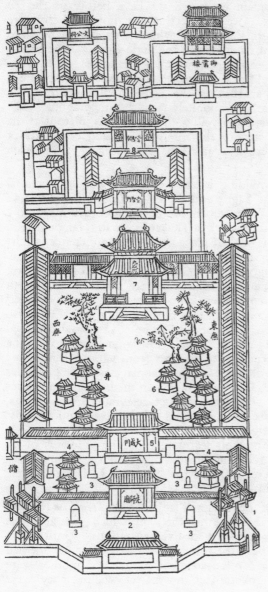

1 Entrance

2 *Hsien Shih Miao* (Temple of the Master Teacher)

3 Tablets to Scholars

4 Pavilions

5 *Ta Ch'êng Mên* (Gate of Great Perfection)

6 Victory Memorials

7 *Ta Ch'êng Tien* (Hall of Great Perfection)

8 *Ch'ung Shêng Tien* (Hall of Reverence to the Sage's Ancestors)

9 *T'ai Hsüeh Mên* (Gate of Great Learning)

10 Triple Archway

11 *Pi Yung Kung* (Imperial School-room)

12 Cloisters with classics.

Entering the main courtyard we have before us the *Ta Ch'êng Tien* (Hall of Great Perfection), an imposing structure about fifty feet high, the roof of which is supported by large teak pillars brought from Burma and Indo-China. The broad, handsome marble terrace on which it stands is called *Yüeh T'ai* (Moon Terrace) and is approached by three sets of seventeen steps, the central set having the usual " spirit staircase," a single block of marble elaborately carved with dragons. The eleven stone tablets under yellow-tiled pavilions in front of the " Moon Terrace " record the foreign wars and conquests of the Manchu Emperors, K'ang Hsi, Yung Chêng, and Ch'ien Lung.

In the main building itself, the central wooden ancestral tablet is that of the Sage ; and the inscription, in Chinese and Manchu, reads : " The tablet of the soul of the most holy ancestral teacher, Confucius." The tablets of four famous sages, of whom Mencius is one, are placed in pairs on either side, whilst eight minor sages occupy a lower position in the background. In T'ang and Mongol times, under the influence of Buddhism, images of the Sage and his followers were placed in Confucian Temples but were removed again under the Mings, on the ground that they were contrary to the idea of spiritual power. The rush matting with which the floor used to be covered was a special importation from South China. The numerous handsome tablets round the ceiling are presents from various Emperors : each inscription is different and pays homage to some particular virtue of the Sage. The stone tablets in the buildings on either side are inscribed with the names of celebrated Confucianists, of whom eighty-six were disciples of the Sage ; on the east side are seventy-eight virtuous men, and on the west side fifty-four famous for their learning. But the followers of no other teacher or religion, however learned or virtuous, are allowed a place here, which is the " Temple of Fame " of the Confucianists exclusively.

At the back of the main hall is the *Ch'ung Shên Tien* (Hall of Reverence to the Sage's Ancestors) in which are kept the spirit-tablets of his ancestors for five generations. Until recent times, it had ever been the rule in China that when anyone had done good service for the state, his father and mother were honoured by the government, no matter whether they were dead or alive ; and when the person had done something quite unusual the honour might be conferred as far back as three generations. Confucius, however, was honoured in the same way, as if he had been the founder of a new dynasty.

Services with elaborate ceremonial and sacrifices were held in this Temple of Confucius in the spring and autumn and especially on the 27th of the Eighth Moon, the birthday of Confucius, in which all the noted scholars of the day and the representatives of the Emperor took part. Similar services, on a smaller scale, were also held at the other Confucian temples all over China. For a time, the official worship of Confucius was continued under the Republic, then dropped for a time, to be restored once more in 1934.

Adjoining the Confucian Temple on the west is the HALL OF CLASSICS (*Kuo Tzŭ Chien*). Originally a private school during Mongol times, it was enlarged and converted into a national university by the Emperor Yung Lo. The present structure, however, is not the same as the original building, but was erected by Ch'ien Lung in 1783 under the name of *Pi Yung Kung* (Imperial School Room), as is recorded in the antithetical tablets hanging from the pillars. In the beautiful central pavilion surrounded by a pool across which lead four marble bridges the Emperors used to expound the classics in the Second Moon of each year. The Emperor was seated on a large throne inside the hall, in front of the famous " Five Mountains " screen, while the assembled scholars stood outside on the steps and bridges leading to the hall. Many of the old cypresses in the enclosure date back to Mongol times, having been planted by one of the Principals of the college in those days. The beautiful triple archway of yellow porcelain leading to the Pi Yung Kung bears the characters *Fu T'ien Chiao Tsê* (All under Heaven receive Benefit by Instruction), a sentence from the Confucian Analects. The pool called *Yüan Ho* (Round River) used to contain numerous golden carp and beautiful lotus flowers, but since the establishment of the Republic has become totally neglected. In the cloisters at each side of the courtyard are about 300 stone monuments engraved, back and front, with the complete text of the Nine Classics. The idea was copied from the times of the Han and T'ang dynasties when, to guard against a recurrence of a similar disaster such as the Burning of the Books under the Emperor Ch'in Shih Huang in 213 B.C., this method of preserving an accurate record of the Classics was adopted. The text on each stone is divided into pages of a convenient size, thus facilitating the reading of the inscriptions.

The LAMA TEMPLE (*La Ma Miao*) or *Yung Ho Kung* (Palace of Concord and Harmony) was originally the palace of the fourth son of the Emperor K'ang Hsi who afterwards became Emperor under the reign title Yung Chêng. In 1745 his son, the Emperor Ch'ien Lung, who was born here converted the palace into a temple, in accordance with the ancient custom to which we have already referred, whereby the palace of a prince who ascended the throne could not be inhabited by his descendants or other relatives and had therefore to be transformed into a temple. The inscriptions on the stone tablets in the front court, composed by Ch'ien Lung himself, refer to this custom.

We reach the temple grounds by the gate on the east side of the main street, and turning north under an ornamental archway pass down a long narrow enclosure between red walls—behind which are the dwellings of the lamas—until we reach the main gate, the *Chao T'ai Mên* (Gate of Shining Glory), through which we enter into the front court. Immediately to our left and right are a Drum and a Bell Tower; the bell dates from 1484. Beyond, on each side, are two open octagonal pavilions containing stone tablets. That on the left is in Chinese and Manchu, the one on the right in Mongolian and Tibetan. The inscription is an account by Ch'ien Lung of the building of the temple. The two fine bronze lions are of Ch'ien Lung period; the curious marks on them are patches to cover up faults in the casting.

We take our ticket at the office on the east side and enter through the *Yung Ho Mên* (Gate of Concord and Harmony) the building on the north. This is the *T'ien Wang Tien** (Hall of the Four Heavenly Kings) who guard against evil spirits, as can be seen from their huge images—two on either side—each of which holds down a couple of demons under its feet. The idol in the centre is that of the Coming Buddha (*Mi Lei Fo*). It should be noted that in this hall there is nothing specifically Lamaistic or in any way different from ordinary Chinese temples.

*See "Notes" at end.

From here we pass into the second court. The fine bronze incense burner is of date 1746. The large square-shaped marble tablet under a double-roofed pavilion bears an inscription giving the history of Reformed Lamaism in four languages (Mongolian on the east face, Manchu on the south, Tibetan on the west, and Chinese on the north). The central building in this court is the *Yung Ho Tien* (Hall of Eternal Harmony), which contains the images of numerous Buddhas, the central one of which is Sakyamuni Buddha. In the side buildings are figures of different Buddhas and of the innumerable saints and demons of Lamaism. Under the verandah on the east side are two large prayer-wheels inscribed in Sanskrit with "*Om Mani Padme Hum*," an invocation to the Divinity within symbolized as the "Jewel in the Lotus." These wheels are filled inside with strips of paper wound round the axle and inscribed with prayers, so that you can thus deliver yourself of an incredible number of them by a single turn of the drum.

We next pass into the third court through the *Yung Yu Tien* (Hall of Eternal Divine Protection) in which there are three Buddhas ; that in the centre is the Buddha of Longevity (*Ch'ang Shou Fo*). The incense-burner in this court dates from Tao Kuang (1839). The main building, in the form of a cross, is the *Fa Lun Tien* (Hall of the Wheel of Law), the roof of which is especially notable for its peculiar and beautiful architecture. As the name is intended to show, this hall is used for teaching the doctrines of Buddhism. Here the lamas assemble five times in twenty-four hours for services, sitting cross-legged at their low tables covered with yellow silk, under the presidency of the Head Lama who is seated on a chair. At the back of this hall, facing north, is a large screen carved in coloured terra-cotta portraying scenes from the life of the Buddha. The building on the west side of the court, the *Hsi Pei Tien* (Western Hall of Propriety), contains various images. That on the east, the *Tung Pei Tien* (Eastern Hall of Propriety) is more interesting, as in it are the images and altars of the five principal Tibetan deities, known as "The Defenders of the Law." Of these the two most important are : at the north end, the terrible goddess Lha Mo (Tibetan for Kali, ante p. 127) worshipped by Hindu Tantrists and the Red Sect of Lamaism; immediately next to her, with a

KEY

1 *Chao T'ai Mên* (Gate of Shining Glory)
2 Drum Tower
3 Bell Tower
4 Pavilions with Stone Tablet
5 *T'ien Wang Tien* (Hall of the Heavenly Kings)
6 *Yung Ho Tien* (Hall of Eternal Harmony)
7 *Chiang Ching Tien* (Hall of Expounding the Sutras)
8 *Wên Tu Sun Tien* (Tibetan name)
9 *Yung Yu Tien* (Hall of Eternal Divine Protection)
10 *Fa Lun Tien* (Hall of the Wheel of the Law)
11 *Chieh T'an* (Altar of Vows of Abstinence)
12 *Yao Shih T'an* (Altar of Master of Medicine)
13 *Hsi Pei Tien* (Western Hall of Propriety)
14 *Tung Pei Tien* (Eastern Hall of Propriety)
15 *Wan Fu Ko* (Pavilion of Ten Thousand Happinesses)
16 *Yen Sui Ko* (Pavilion of Perpetual Peace)
17 *Yung K'ang Ko* (Pavilion of Everlasting Happiness)
18 *Sui Ch'êng Tien* (Hall of Established Peace)
19 *Ya Mu Tê K'o Lou* (Tower of Yarmantaka)
20 *Chao Fo Lou* (Tower of Buddha's Splendour)
21 *P'u Sa Tien* (Hall of Pu-sa)
22 *Kuan Ti Miao* (Temple of God of War)
23 *Ch'an T'ang* (Hall of Contemplation)
24 *K'o T'ung* (Guest Hall)
25 Passageway to Imperial Library
m, m—Masts   L L—Bronze lions   i, i—Incense-burners

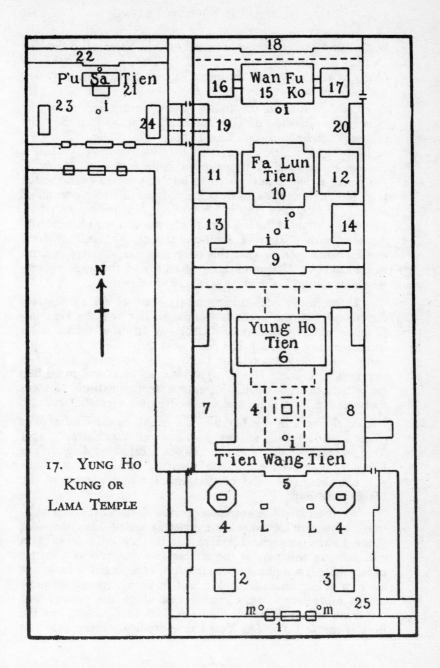

22

P'u Sa Tien
21

23

24

18

16 Wan Fu
    15 Ko   17

19   20

11 Fa Lun
    Tien
    10   12

13   14

9

N

Yung Ho
Tien
6

7   4   8

T'ien Wang Tien

17. YUNG HO
KUNG OR
LAMA TEMPLE

5

4   L   L   4

2   3

25

m   m

1

bull's head and carefully covered up, is Yama, the God of Death. To the west of the Fa Lun Tien, is the *Chieh T'an* (Altar of the Vows of Abstinence) in which the ordination of the novices takes place.

Passing on into the fourth court we see before us the *Wan Fu Ko* (Pavilion of Ten Thousand Happinesses), the most striking building of the whole Yung Ho Kung. The two aerial bridges which connect up the side pavilions give it a unique appearance. It contains a huge statue of Maitreya, the Buddha that is next to come into this world. The statue is 75 feet high and is said to be carved out of a single trunk of cedar. The coronet on the head of the idol indicates that he has not yet attained the full dignity of a Buddha who is generally depicted with a kind of skull-cap inlaid with shells. When the Emperor used to visit this temple in the old days, a lamp hanging above Maitreya's head was lit, and the huge prayer-wheel standing on the right was set in motion.

Through the side building on the west we enter a separate compound : on the north is the *P'u Sa Tien* or *Kuan Yin Miao* (Temple of the Goddess of Mercy) in front of which is an incense-burner of K'ang Hsi date. On the walls of this temple hang some very interesting pictures, eight on each side, of the Buddhist saints (*Lo Han*) whose red faces are more like caricatures than the usual stereotype representations of them that we find elsewhere, and are well worth a careful study.

At the back of this building is a temple to the God of War (*Kuan Ti Miao*) with an incense-burner of Tao Kuang (1835) The presence of this god, who is not a Buddhist deity, in the Lama Temple need not excite surprise, because, as we have said elsewhere, the God of War was the patron saint of the Manchu dynasty.

We return to the entrance court. Here on the east side, north of the ticket office, is a gateway called *Shu Yüan Mên* (Gate to the Imperial Library). It is very difficult to gain admission to this part of the temple grounds, and as a matter of fact there is not much of any interest, as most of the buildings are now falling into ruins. We will, however, enumerate some of the more important. Passing east along the passage-way we come to the *P'ing An Chü* (Hall of Tranquillity) ; at the back is the *Ju I Shih* (As You Please Studio). From here you

enter the *Shu Yüan Chêng Shih* (Principal Imperial Schoolroom) ;
south-east is the *Wu Fu T'ang* (Hall of the Five Happinesses) ;
west the *Hai T'ang Yüan* (Begonia Park).   North of this is
a passage-way leading to the *Yen Lou* (Tower of Perpetual
Years) ; west of the tower is the *Tou T'an* (Altar to the God
of the Pole-star).   East of this is the *Fo Lou* (Buddha's Tower).
In front of the tower is the *P'ing T'ai* (Level Terrace) with the
Ta Fo T'ang (Great Buddha's Hall).   Here used to be kept a
large number of idols, especially of the kind called *Huan Hsi Fo*
(Joyful Buddhas), in all stages of crude animalism, said to be
symbolical of fecundity.   These have now been moved to
other places.   The lama guides make a great to-do about
showing these figures to tourists and demand an extra tip
before doing so.   Visitors are recommended to save their
dollars.   The figures are very crude indeed and, as a porno-
graphic exhibition, disappointing.

We might add here a word of warning on another point.
Visitors are advised not to venture alone into the maze of
buildings with any of the lamas.   In former days the
Yung Ho Kung had a very bad reputation indeed for assaults
on foreigners and sometimes the complete disappearance
of solitary sightseers.   Even in quite recent times there
have been numerous authentic cases where single foreign
visitors have undergone very unpleasant experiences there.
As recently as 1927 one of the authors was enticed into one
of the buildings on the pretence of being shown some rare
ornaments and nearly had the door closed on him.   When
he pulled out his revolver which from experience he had taken
along, the lama at once let go of the door explaining
that he had only closed it, because he did not want the Head
Lama to see him showing visitors around.   He was, however,
not satisfied with this explanation and reported the man's
action to the Head Lama and had the pleasure of seeing him
give the rascal a good thrashing until he shouted for mercy.

The famous ceremony of the " Devil Dance," as it is
called by foreigners, is still held at the Lama Temple towards
the end of the First Moon.   The Chinese call it *Yen Kuei* or
Ta Kuei (Exorcising or Beating the Devils).   The performance
given here is, however, only a very poor reflection of the real
dances that take place in Tibet and is scarcely worth going to

see owing to the crush, disorder, and noise of the Chinese
crowds, which not only hinder the performance, but prevent
one seeing anything. Moreover, considerable portions have
been cut out by order of the police, especially the more exciting
and horrible parts. From the performance seen at the Lama
Temple it is therefore impossible to obtain any correct idea
of the artistic and religious value of these Tibetan plays.

The chief attraction in the Dance is the gorgeous robes
and the huge grotesque masks worn by the performing lamas.
These masks, by the way, are stored in the building called
Chao Fo Lou (Tower of Buddha's Splendour) in the back court ;
for a consideration the priests will bring them out and pose
for you.

Chapter XIV.

THE NORTH-WEST QUARTER OF THE TARTAR CITY

WE commence this tour from the *Ti An Mên* (Earthly Peace Gate) popularly known as the *Hou Mên*, the "Back Gate" of the Imperial City. The broad street which runs west past it leads in about one hundred yards to an insignificant-looking "camel-back" stone bridge, called *Hsi Ya Ch'iao* (West Dented-in Bridge), mentioned in the first part of the last chapter. This bridge is, however, unique in another respect: it was the only public edifice in the whole city that was inscribed with the characters *Pei Ching* (Northern Capital).

The following legend accounts for this :—At the time, when the Emperor Ch'ien Lung came under the influence of the Yellow Sect of Lamaism, a Living Buddha chanced to visit Peking. He was received with semi-divine honours, and obtained such an influence over the Emperor that he succeeded in persuading him to substitute Lamaism for pure Buddhism. The head-priest of *T'an Chüeh Ssŭ*, an important centre of Buddhism in the Western Hills (Chapter XXIV), became alarmed at the Emperor's change of faith and determined to interview the Living Buddha.

On entering the latter's presence, the priest, instead of performing the usual prostrations, threw his alms-bowl into the air. It remained suspended above the head of the Living Buddha, who fell flat on his face, and gradually increasing in size slowly descended covering him completely. When the Emperor, who was present at the interview, asked the meaning of all this, the priest replied that the Living Buddha was neither a god nor a man, but an evil spirit, and lifting up the bowl revealed a large toad squatting underneath. Addressing the toad he said : "I will not hurt you, but you must at once return whence you have come." "You just wait ! I'll get even with you," replied the toad and with one bound disappeared. The priest then turned to the Emperor saying : "That's bad.

We must take care." " Well, why did you let him go ? "
asked the Emperor reasonably enough. The priest explained
that, as this evil spirit had not done them any harm, it could
not, according to the Sacred Law, be punished, adding : " It's
not for myself I fear, but for the city of Peking which he may
destroy by flood." " What's to be done ? " asked the Emperor.
" Dig a bed for the waters to run off, build a bridge over it
with the characters *Pei Ching*, and they will then flow through it
without flooding the town." And that is why this bridge
bears these two characters.

On the north face of the bridge is the carved head of a
ch'ih wên, a member of the Dragon family, supposed to be able
to prevent the waters from rising and causing floods, and
therefore, in view of the above story, a very suitable ornament
for this particular bridge.

Retracing our steps to the Hou Mên and along the main
street running north to the Drum Tower, we turn left along
the *Ku Lou Ta Chieh* (Drum Tower Main Street). Any one
of the lanes on the south side will bring us out on to the banks
of a long narrow stretch of water, popularly known as *Shih
Chi Hai* (Stone Relics of the Sea). The correct name, however,
is *Shih Ch'a Hai* (Ten Temples of the Sea), and is so marked
on all maps. The lake dates from the Mings by whom it is
said to have been dug out, in order to have a miniature souvenir
of the scenery in the South, with its rice-fields and lotus
ponds. The water which comes from the Jade Fountain
(Chapter XXII) enters the city by an opening under the north
wall, flows through this Shih Ch'a Hai and out again under
the bridge we saw above, into the North Lake. At the west
end there stood in olden times a beautiful pagoda the *Lung
Hua Miao* (Temple of Civilizing Influences) which, together
with numerous other temples, was built by an official of Shensi
province, San Tsang-shih. The whole work was completed
under the Ming Emperor Wan Li. Whatever may have been
the original number of temples there are only three left
now. During the summer months this " Sea " is a favourite
resort of the lower classes who come here in thousands to
take the air and to spend the day in the numerous tea-houses
along its banks listening to story-tellers, ballad-singers or
other musical entertainments. At night-time, however, it

is a place to be avoided, less on account of foot-pads, than because quite a number of suicides take place in the lake, so that their spirits are abroad looking for victims. According to the inhabitants of the district, the voices of ghosts can often be heard wailing at night.

If we walk along the bank a short distance west, we come to a large temple in a very good state of repair. This is the *Kuang Hua Ssŭ* (Temple of Great Religious Transformation) which derives its name from the following legend :—During the Mongol Dynasty a mendicant monk took up his abode on a vacant plot of ground where the temple now stands. Here he sat in meditation for twenty years reciting the Buddhist sutras, his neighbours supplying him with rice. As he finished each chapter of his bible, he would take up a single grain of rice and place it in his alms bowl. Part of it he ate, the remainder he saved up to sell, in order to obtain funds with which to build this temple. The people seeing him full of zeal in such a worthy cause subscribed sufficient money to enable him to complete the building. As he had transformed (*hua*) the rice that he did not eat into a religious temple, it was named as above. The details of this story are inscribed on the memorial tablet that stands in the main courtyard, placed there by a eunuch, Ts'ao Hua-ch'un, who repaired the temple in 1634.

Returning to the main street and proceeding along it for about half a mile, we see on the north side of the road some wonderful yellow roofs. These belong to the *Tz'ŭ T'ang* (Ancestral Hall) of Prince Ch'un who acted as Prince Regent from 1908 to 1912 for his son, the ex-Emperor Hsüan T'ung. Although only about thirty years old, it is well worth a closer inspection, as the roofs and walls are in excellent repair and offer a fine example of green and yellow glazed tiling. The buildings have now been turned into a school—in the modern fashion of utility before art—and at the back of the main hall, behind the table on which the ancestral tablet used to stand, hangs the picture of Dr. Sun Yat-sen, the inveterate enemy of the Manchus.

In a street north-east of the Hall is a large temple, the *Nien Hua Ssŭ* (Toying with Flowers Temple), so-called from a legend that Buddha when jumping off a rock was saved by landing on a lotus floating in the pool below. In the rear hall of the temple is a fine bronze image of the Buddha surrounded by numerous smaller ones.

A few yards west of the Ancestral Hall is an archway leading to a small lane called *T'ieh Ying Pi Hutung* (Iron Shadow Wall Lane), at the north end of which stands the " Shadow Wall," a solid block of dark brown stone, about twelve by six feet, carved with dragons on both sides. This is an interesting relic of Ming times. During the reign of Yung Lo a foundry stood on this spot, for the special purpose of casting the numerous bells required by the Emperor when he was rebuilding and embellishing the city. The " Shadow Wall " stood at the entrance of this foundry to prevent evil spirits from getting in and spoiling the castings. It is called " Iron Shadow Wall," because the smoke from the furnaces, in the course of time, impregnated the stone to a great depth giving it the colour of iron. When the foundry fell into disuse, a lane was built through it, but the " Iron Shadow Wall " was left standing.

The high walls on the south side of the street surround the palace of the above-mentioned Prince Ch'un, known as *Shê Chêng Wang Fu* (Prince-Regent's Palace) or *Ch'i Yeh Fu* (Palace of the Seventh Prince) because his father who built it was the seventh son of the Emperor Tao Kuang. The entrance is on the lake side. The last Manchu Emperor, Hsüan T'ung, was born here, whose subsequent bad luck has been attributed to the fact that his father, the Prince Regent, instead of at once removing from this palace, in accordance with custom, because a "dragon had been born" there, continued to reside in it while his new residence in the Imperial City was being built (Chapter X).

It was close by here that Wang Ching-wei, one of the leaders of the Kuomintang and afterwards Prime Minister of the Nationalist Government, made his famous attempt to blow up the Prince Regent in 1910. At the north end of the lake is a street called *Shih Ch'a Hai* (same name as the lake), with a bridge at the one end, under which Wang and a fellow-conspirator had succeeded in fixing a bomb. On the night of March 28 they were hopefully waiting for the Prince Regent to pass this way, as usual, to the early morning audience at the Palace, when the barking of some neighbouring dogs attracted the police to the spot thus forcing the conspirators to decamp. After searching about, the police discovered the bomb and connecting wires. Wang remained some days in Peking before the police got on to his tracks. Eventually, according to his biographer, he betrayed himself to the detectives who were looking for him, owing to his innate politeness. For when he was saying goodbye at the station to two lady friends who were also involved in the plot, he raised his hat, thus revealing his false queue (attached to the hat)—in those days the mark of a true revolutionary. He was followed to his lodgings where much incriminating literature was found, arrested, and put on trial. According to the Kuomintang version the Manchus were so afraid of him, that he was only condemned to imprisonment for life, instead of being chopped into little pieces, the punishment that he might ordinarily have expected. His confinement only lasted for a short time, as he was liberated after the Revolution of 1911.

Continuing west along the main street we come to the *Tê Shêng Mên* (Gate of Righteous Victory), the west gate in the north wall of the Tartar City and one of the four that have no second, or official, name. The vault of the inner tunnel is unusually high, the appearance of height being increased by the absence of the tower over the gateway which was pulled down in 1921 on the grounds that it was unsafe. In the former gate enclosure, close to the railway track stands a small pavilion containing a stone tablet with a poem written by the Emperor Ch'ien Lung in 1797. The poem is a kind of literary pun on the name " Righteous Victory " and says that the gate is powerful enough in itself to protect all interests without offending anybody.* It was through this gate that the Empress-Dowager Tz'ŭ Hsi made her entry into the city on her return from Jehol in 1860, when she carried out the *coup d'état* that first placed her in power. And again, it was through this gate that she fled in the early hours of the morning of August 15, 1900, after the foreign troops had entered the city. Dressed in ordinary peasant's clothes and sitting in a common Peking cart she was held up for quite a long time by the mob of refugees pouring out through the gate, amongst whom she passed unnoticed.

---

*Since writing above, this famous tablet has been pulled down, the inscription erased, and the marble block shipped away !

The opening to the west, about fifty yards south of the gate, brings us to another, smaller, lake which has three names : *Lien Hua P'ao Tʒŭ* (Lotus Pond), *Ching Yeh Hu* (Lake of Tranquil Learning), and *Chi Shui T'an* (Heaped-up Waters Pool). The first is the popular name, the second derives from a small dilapidated temple on the north bank, *Ching Yeh Ssŭ*, and the third from a picturesque little temple situated on a hillock at the north-west corner. This last is a very ancient temple which was repaired by Ch'ien Lung in 1761 under the name of *Hui T'ung Tʒ'ŭ* (Ancestral Hall of the Passage of Whirling Waters). In front of it stands a stone tablet of that date with an inscription by the Emperor extolling the beneficial influences exerted by the waters of the Jade Fountain which flow into this lake. The tablet formerly stood inside the courtyard and is almost black from the number of rubbings taken from it. The head-piece is strangely carved, indicating that the tablet was erected to suppress any supernatural influences that might encourage the monks of the temple to become immortal. (Ch'ien Lung who was very superstitious probably wanted to reserve that distinction for himself !) Outside the temple, at the back, is a curiously-shaped stone on a marble pedestal, said to be a meteorite. Looking west from this spot one gets a very good idea of how the city wall curves southwards.

Proceeding to the south side of the pond, we pass a stone tablet erected to the memory of a well-known scholar who despairing of his country drowned himself at this spot. South we have the *Kao Miao* (August Temple), the entrance to which is through a gate a little to the east of the actual temple. The official name of this temple which was built by a Palace eunuch in the 16th century is *P'u Ch'i Ch'an Lin Ssŭ* (Buddhist Asylum for the Poor). Its chief claim to fame is that it was here that Parkes and Loch were imprisoned in September 1860. They had been treacherously seized by the Chinese when they had gone to their camp under a flag of truce during the advance of the Anglo-French forces on Peking.

The prisoners were loaded with chains and first lodged in the common prison attached to the Board of Punishments, the Chinese seeking in vain by every means, both threats and actual maltreatment, to force Parkes to write to Lord Elgin and induce him to stop the Allied advance. However, on

September 29, Parkes and Loch were removed from the prison and brought to this temple. Although more comfortable and better treated here, they were by no means out of danger, as the Chinese threatened to execute them at the first shot fired against the city. It may be imagined therefore, with what feelings Parkes and his companion cooped up in this little temple heard the sounds of heavy guns to the north of the city on October 7, which luckily for them was only a salute being fired in the Allied camp. They thought their last hour had come, but it was not till much later that they learnt, how near to death they had really been. For Hêng Chi, one of the more reasonable high Manchu officials, having learnt on the 8th, through private advices in advance, that the Emperor Hsien Fêng, then in residence at Jehol, had issued orders for the immediate decapitation of all the prisoners, managed to persuade Prince Kung to release them that same morning. They were liberated barely a quarter of an hour before the courier arrived from Jehol with the Imperial Decree. This, it must be added, was a very lucky escape for the city of Peking too, in view of the already inflamed feeling amongst the Allied forces.

The room in which Parkes and Loch were confined was a small one on the left-hand side of the entrance leading to the second courtyard. In the adjoining hall were quartered the Manchu guards, and on one of the pillars was a mark, six feet five and a half inches from the ground, showing the height of one of these men whom they had measured during their detention. On the wall of the courtyard in which they were allowed to take exercise was a rough map of the world drawn by Loch to while away the time, and on that of the room they occupied an inscription in Chinese ink reading :—

" H. S. Parkes

H. B. Loch

Brought here 29th September, being 7th October—this the 8th. From 18th to 29th September with 1 Sikh and 2 French in prison of Hing-poo."

This inscription was still to be seen in the late 'nineties.

The original buildings associated with Parkes' imprisonment stood where the present wide front-courtyard is to-day. They were pulled down in 1920.

Leaving the Kao Miao and taking any one of the turnings west until we come to the Shun Chih Mên Main Street, we turn south till we reach the street running to the *Hsi Chih Mên* (West Straight Gate), the northerly of the two west gates. Although it is one of the gates without an official name it has a second popular name, " The Open Gate " (*K'ai Mên*), because it leads to the Summer Palace, and was therefore liable to be opened at any time of night, when the Empress-Dowager was in residence there. It was completely reconstructed in 1894 at the time when the new Summer Palace was built. Except for the P'ing Tsê Mên, on the same side, it is the only gate that has remained unchanged from olden times.

About half-way to the gate, on the south side of the main street, lies the *Hsi T'ang* (West Church). Built originally by Father Pedrini in 1725 it was partially destroyed by an earthquake in 1730, and was finally closed up and pulled down under Chia Ch'ing in 1811. A new church erected on the same site in 1867 was destroyed in 1900, and rebuilt for the third time, as it stands to-day.

On the north side of the main street, about a quarter of a mile from the gate, is a lane called *Ma Hsiang Hutung* (Horse Physiognomist Lane). During the Ming dynasty a veterinary surgeon named Fan lived in this lane : it was then called *Shou I Hutung* (Veterinary Surgeon Lane). But as Mr. Fan was an expert on the points of a horse and could tell at a glance its age, without even looking at its teeth, and was also able to calculate the number of years it had to live, and whether it was docile or not, and many other things besides, the neighbours regarded him as a kind of " Horse Physiognomist " and named the lane accordingly.

The Chinese say that there are thirty-two points of a horse, of which the eye comes first. It should be like " a hanging bell " (i.e., protruding, like the eyes of a gold-fish). The colour too is very important: red, bay, white, yellow, black, and grey is the order of preference. A red horse with a long streak of white on its nose or with one white foot is unlucky, as this indicates mourning. But if a red horse has a curl or a circle on its forehead, this is lucky, as it indicates old age—for the owner. A horse—of any colour—with a curl or circle in the middle of the spine is said to be " carrying a corpse "

(*t'o shih*), and its rider will meet with an accident, if not death.
A horse with a circle beneath one or both eyes is "weeping"
(*t'i lei*) and will cause its owner all sorts of trouble and worries.
All four feet should be straight and the ankles small; the
upper part of the legs longer than the lower; the head large
and lean; the neck curved like a bow; the ears small, round,
and slightly pointing forwards; the belly small; the flesh on
the hip joint or whirlbone firm; and the tail should hang down
from the root spreading out like a bamboo broom. Such would
be a first-class animal "able to do a thousand *li* in one day";
in fact a celestial horse would not be able to compare with it
for speed, vitality, and fire. If some of the Peking racing
"fans" choose their pony according to these points, they will
doubtless be able to spot a winner every time!

Retracing our steps, we turn south along the Shun Chih
Mên Main Street, and then east up the *Hu Kuo Ssŭ Chieh*, which
street takes its name from the *Hu Kuo Ssŭ* (Protect the Country
Temple) lying on the north side. We have here a famous
relic of Mongol days. Originally it was the residence
of a Mongol Prince T'o T'o of the Yüan Dynasty who after
rising to become minister of state was suspected of disloyalty
and banished to Yünnan in 1355, where he died of poison.
About ten years after his death, his reputation was vindicated,
and his residence turned into a temple in his honour, the *Ch'ung
Kuo Ssŭ* (Temple of Veneration for the State), which in late
Manchu times was changed to its present name. The huge
property embraced two temples, of which the eastern one
has completely disappeared, whilst that on the west is the
present temple, still popularly known as *Hsi Ssŭ* (Western
Temple). It has been repeatedly repaired: three times under
the Mongol dynasty, and again later in both Ming and Manchu
times. There are two small pagodas, called *Fo Shê Li* (Buddha's
Relics) and a large number of stone memorial tablets of Mongol,
Ming, and Manchu periods. One of these, dated first year
of Huang Ching (1312), was inscribed by the famous painter
Chao Mêng-fu. By the side of one of the halls stands a dilapidated
figure of T'o T'o himself together with his wife, dressed
in red robes. Several years ago, there was a stone image of
a famous monk, Yao Shao-shih, sitting in an attitude of abstraction,
with a stone tablet behind him. The figure has disappeared—probably sold to some curio-dealer—but the tablet

is still there. A fair is held in this temple three times a month, one of its specialities being trees, shrubs and flowers of all kinds.

Not far from the north-east corner of the temple grounds is a lane called *Tou Chi K'êng Hutung* (Fighting Cocks Pit Lane). From Ming times right down to the latter part of the reign of Tao Kuang there was a large pit in this lane in which cock-fights were held. The pit was oval in shape covering an area of 3,000 feet by 30 feet deep, with sloping sides down which the public gained access to the flat arena at the bottom. In the spring of each year the " fans " brought their birds here to be weighed and measured by the pit-keepers, after which the bets were made. Cocks of equal size and weight were matched for a fight and put into a pen ; some grain was thrown in for which the cocks started scrapping, and the fight was on. Very heavy betting is said to have taken place at these cock fights, not only between the owners, but also among the general public ; thousands of dollars changed hands at each fight. The pit-keepers charged ten per cent on each cock, according to the amount wagered by its owner.

To the east of the Hu Kuo Ssǔ, at the corner of the Tê Shêng Mên Main Street, is the PALACE OF PRINCE CH'ING, the Manchu statesman who together with Li Hung-chang had the unpleasant task of cleaning up the Boxer mess and signing the Peace Protocol of 1901 for China. He was Prime Minister at the outbreak of the Revolution in 1911. Still further east, on the site of another prince's palace, is the CATHOLIC UNIVERSITY erected in 1930.

In the lane south of the Hu Kuo Ssǔ Chieh is the PALACE OF PRINCE CHUANG, one of the leading spirits of the Boxer movement in 1900, whose military activities never took a more exciting form than superintending the massacre of native converts. It was at the gates of this palace that the Boxers, under his guidance, held so-called trials, in one of which no less than nine hundred perfectly innocent persons of both sexes and of all ages were done to death in cold blood. This butchery was too much even for the Empress-Dowager who remonstrated with him and ordered him " to keep his men in better order." When the Boxer movement had failed and the incensed Western Powers were insisting on the punishment

Kublai Khan

of the chief criminals, Prince Chuang's head was one of the first they demanded. As he had fled into the interior an Imperial Commissioner was sent after him to convey to him the Imperial Decree ordering him to commit suicide. He was then taken to a room at the back of his residence where a special red silk cord had been tied to a beam in readiness for him, which he himself fastened round his neck with the greatest sangfroid, thus expiating his very considerable crimes.

We proceed south along the main street, until we reach the road leading to the *P'ing Tsê Mên* (Gate of Just Rule). The official name, seldom used, is *Fu Ch'êng Mên* (Mound Formed Gate). As mentioned above it is the only other gate that still retains its original form and thus gives you a good idea of an old Peking gate, with circular barbican and a small temple therein, and an outer side-gate leading to a road lined with food-shops and eating-houses, between the gate and the suburb.

On the south side of the tunnel of the inner gateway about six feet from the ground you will see a brick carved with a flower. This has an interesting historical origin. In olden times a thief was branded, for the first offence with a mark on the left arm, for the second on the right arm, and for the third offence on the left temple. (In order to hide this latter mark, the criminal was sometimes able to bribe the executioner to pull the skin down tight, so that the brand-mark was covered by the hair. On the other hand, if no bribe at all was offered, the executioner might pull the skin upwards, so that the brand appeared on the cheek). When the rebel chief, Li Tzŭ-ch'êng took Peking in 1643, he entered the city through this gate. Therefore, the Manchus who shortly afterwards ascended the "Dragon Throne," in order to emphasize their disapproval of the crime of rebellion, had one of the bricks carved in this way, thus branding the gate for the crime of having let a rebel pass through.

Leaving the gate and returning east along the main street we come, on the north side, to the *Pai T'a Ssŭ* (White Pagoda Temple). Erected in the reign of the Liao Emperor Shou Lung in A.D. 1092 to commemorate his accession to the throne, it was repaired in 1272 by Kublai Khan, who was a devout Buddhist and spent large sums in improving and restoring the temple buildings which in those days were used as public offices. The Ming Emperor T'ien Shun in 1458 changed the name to *Miao Ying* (Marvellous Powers of Manifestation), which is still the official name, as shown by the characters over the entrance, though it is only known to the populace as the " White Pagoda Temple." Both K'ang Hsi and Ch'ien Lung repaired the temple, and there is a stone tablet erected by the latter inscribed with Chinese, Manchu, Mongol, and Tibetan characters.

The White Pagoda is said to have " the form of a bell and the colour of silver." It is surmounted by a huge brass plate on which stands a small pagoda of the same metal. Kublai Khan, who used frequently to visit this temple, fearing that the brass pagoda might fall down and kill someone, had a marble balustrade built round it and the whole covered in with brass netting. Beneath its foundations are said to be buried twenty beads, two thousand clay pagodas, and five books of Buddhist prayers.

There is a popular Peking rhyme about this pagoda which runs as follows :—

Pai-t'a-ssŭ	At the White Pagoda Temple
Yu pai t'a.	Is a White Pagoda
T'a shang yu chuan . .	On the pagoda are bricks
Mei yu wa.	But no tiles
T'a t'ai-erh lieh-la . .	On the pagoda's pedestal there showed
I tao fêng.	A great crack
Lu-pan-yeh hsia lai . .	Master Lu Pan came down
Chü shang t'a.	And repaired the pagoda.

According to the legend to which these verses refer, some time in the early days of the Manchu dynasty the pedestal showed a wide crack, and the whole pagoda threatened to tumble down. Popular tradition says that a man dressed in mason's clothes suddenly appeared from nowhere and walked several times round the pagoda shouting " I'll mend it ! I'll mend it ! " The next day, to the astonishment of the credulous Pekingese, it was found that the crack had actually been filled up, and there were marks of a mason's trowel on the fresh mortar. This job was at once ascribed to the intervention of Lu Pan, the protecting Genius of masons and carpenters, whom we are constantly meeting with during the course of our wanderings.

A fair is held in this temple four times a month.

Further east, also on the north side of the street, its main gateway flanked by two ornamental archways which span the street, is the *Li Tai Ti Wang Miao* (Temple to Successive Generations of Emperors). It was built in the reign of Chia Ching (1523) on the old site of a temple called *Pao An Ssŭ* (Temple of Precious Peace).

In it were placed tablets to all past Emperors, except tyrants, usurpers, enemies of literature, or those who had been assassinated or had lost their throne, even though through no fault of their own. In this way were the judgments of History to be confirmed and her lessons impressed on the minds of future generations. The spirit-tablet of the famous Mongol Emperor, Kublai Khan, the patron of Marco Polo, was at first admitted to this pantheon and retained in spite of the protests of the literati. It was, however, removed later by the Ming Emperor Chia Ching in response to a particularly persuasive memorial by an ultra-patriotic censor. The Manchu Emperor K'ang Hsi restored the tablet to its former place and added that of Hung Wu, the first Emperor of the Mings, as well as those of the Emperors of the Liao and Chin dynasties. In 1776 Ch'ien Lung added the spirit-tablets of all the Ming Emperors with the exception of Wan Li and T'ien Ch'i whom he did not consider worthy of a place here, owing to their "love for debased eunuchs." He also had the ordinary grey tiles on the roofs replaced by Imperial yellow ones.

The temple has been modernized and is now the headquarters of the Red Swastika Society (Chinese Red Cross). The spirit-tablets, however, are still there.

On the north side of the street, close to the corner of the Shun Chih Mên Main Street, is a temple that dates from very ancient times, known as the *Kuang Chi Ssŭ*, its official name being *Kuang Chi Ch'an Ssŭ* (Temple of Universal Rescue and Profound Meditation). During the Chins a temple called *Hsi Liu Ts'un Ssŭ* (Temple of Mr. Liu's West Village) stood on this spot. In 1457, when he resumed the reins of government, the Ming Emperor T'ien Shun enlarged the temple; and it was repaired by K'ang Hsi who changed the name to

Hung Tz'ǔ Kuang Chi Ssǔ (Temple of Great Compassion and Profound Rescue).   It is recorded that a large library of ancient books was preserved here ; that in the courtyard stood many " Iron Trees " ; and that an expert sculptor Liu Kung-pei, a Southerner, carved a ten-foot Buddha out of a single piece of sandal-wood which he presented to the temple, when the name was changed to its present form.   There are still a large number of monks residing here, though the temple has been shorn of most of its former glory, quite especially since the great fire in 1932 in which a large portion of the buildings was destroyed.

CHAPTER XV.

THE WESTERN HALF OF THE CHINESE CITY

WE enter the Southern or Chinese City by the *Ch'ien Mên* (Front Gate), the central and most important of all the gates of the Tartar City, lying as it does in a direct line with the main entrances and ceremonial halls of the Forbidden City. It was built in the reign of Yung Lo, taking nine years to build, being completed in 1419 and renamed *Chêng Yang Mên* (Straight towards the Sun Gate) which is its official name. Its present appearance differs very considerably from that of former times when it had an outer enceinte and four gates, as is shown on the accompanying sketch:

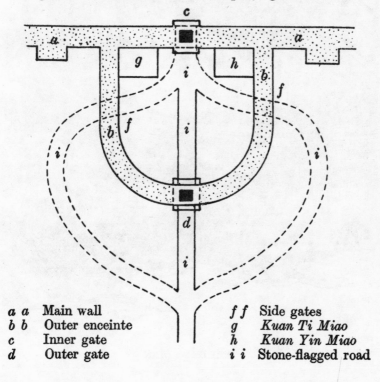

a a	Main wall	*f f*	Side gates
b b	Outer enceinte	*g*	*Kuan Ti Miao*
c	Inner gate	*h*	*Kuan Yin Miao*
d	Outer gate	*i i*	Stone-flagged road

内城

城闉

正陽外門

CH'IEN MÊN

The outer gate was kept permanently closed and only opened for the Emperor when he went to worship at the Temples of Heaven and Agriculture. The towers over the inner and outer gates were both burnt down in 1900. The outer one was set alight by the flames from some shops outside which had been fired by the Boxers, because they were selling foreign goods; the inner one fell a victim to the carelessness of the Indian troops of the Army of Occupation. Luckily for the appearance of the city, the Chinese in those days were still " superstitious " enough to believe that their capital could not prosper without the towers over the Main Gate, and so they at once rebuilt them. In 1916 when the requirements of modern traffic made an extension of the gate imperative, the outer enceinte was completely removed and the whole rearranged in its present ugly form, though a few minor alterations would have been quite sufficient. The grotesque-looking outer tower built by a German architect is, needless to say, quite modern, and houses an exhibition of native products.

In the old days, prior to 1900, the Ch'ien Mên was closed every evening at dusk with a certain amount of ceremony. About a quarter of an hour before closing-time an iron gong hanging in a wooden frame outside the guard-room was beaten, the strokes being slow and deliberate for the first five minutes, and gradually quickening until they formed one continuous sound. The gong then suddenly ceased, when some of the guards went to the end of the tunnel and gave long, loud warning cries for another five minutes. After that the gates were closed and bolted with a huge wooden beam which was fastened with a large iron Chinese lock. As they returned to their quarters the guards emitted a chorus of long-drawn howls, corresponding to our " All's well ! " This gate alone, of all the others, was opened again for a few minutes shortly after midnight, to allow officials who had been spending the evening at the haunts of amusement in the Chinese City to get back in time for the Imperial Audience which took place in the small hours of the morning. After 1900 the Ch'ien Mên was never closed at all.

The two small temples up against the wall outside the inner gate date back to Ming times, as is recorded on the stone tablets still standing in both of them. That on the east is the *Kuan Yin Miao* (Temple of Kuan Yin). A certain amount of confusion exists regarding this deity whom most foreigners call the Goddess of Mercy. But every true Chinese believer will tell you that Kuan Yin is a deity who appeared in a number of different places and under various forms, but always as a male. The Chinese female deity with whom he has been confused was worshipped in South China long before the advent of Buddhism, also under the name of Kuan Yin. She is said to have been miraculously transported on a lotus leaf to the sacred island of P'u T'o near Ningpo. Her father— supposed to be Chuang Wang (723-696 B.C.)—of the Chou dynasty having fallen sick, she cut off a piece of flesh from her arm and made it into a brew that saved his life. To show his gratitude, he ordered a statue to be erected in her honour " with perfect eyes and perfect arms." But the sculptor misunderstanding the word *ch'uan* (perfect) for *ch'ien* (thousand) carved a statue with a thousand eyes and arms, the form under which her memory has been revered ever since.

The temple on the west side, *Kuan Ti Miao* (Temple of the God of War) is historically more interesting. As he was the patron saint of the Manchu dynasty, the Emperors used to stop and offer up sacrifices at this temple, whenever they passed through the gate. On her return from Sianfu in 1901 the Empress-Dowager stopped here to burn incense at the shrine before entering the city, although one would scarcely have thought that she had much cause to be thankful to the God of War, seeing that he was also the patron saint of the Boxers.

The God of War is one Kuan Yü who lived during the time of disunion and strife, usually known as the period of the Three Kingdoms, and is regarded as the most striking figure in a very romantic epoch of Chinese history. He was born in A.D. 162 and was killed in 219. The influence of the drama, coupled with that of the famous historical novel *San Kuo Chih Yen I* (History of the Three Kingdoms) have raised Kuan Yü to a pitch of popularity almost unknown amongst other nations. Napoleon, in Chinese eyes, was a mere bungler compared to him, who enjoys greater honours and titles than the Corsican ever dreamt of. From the time of the Sungs right down to the Republic, each Emperor has bestowed on him a title higher than the last.

On entering the temple you see directly in front of you the God of War seated in his niche, gilded all over and wearing a red robe. The life-size figures standing on either side are as follows :—

EAST SIDE (Right) :

1.—Kuan P'ing, his adopted son who fell with his father. He is carrying in his hands the God of War's seals of office.

2.—The central figure is Liao Hua, one of his generals, who holds his helmet.

3.—The next is Wang Fu, another of his generals holding Kuan Yü's precious sword, who on learning of his death threw himself down from a wall and perished.

WEST SIDE (Left) :

1.—Chou Ts'ang, Kuan Yü's armour-bearer, with the famous " Black Dragon Sword." He, too, committed suicide on hearing of his master's death.

2.—In the middle is Chao Lieh who was in charge of Kuan Yü's commissariat, with his coat of mail.

3.—Finally there is Ma T'ung, leading his famous war-steed, the " Red Hare," the stuffed figure of which stands close-by. The faithful animal refused to eat, after its master's death, and soon died.

There are no less than ten temples dedicated to this god inside the walls of Peking alone, to say nothing of several outside. This temple is, however, the most popular ; large numbers of all classes still coming to worship here, even in these modern times, on the 1st and 15th of each Moon.

Crossing the bridge and proceeding along Ch'ien Mên Main Street we take the fourth turning on the right, a very narrow, busy street, the *Ta Cha La* (Large Gate-Posts), so-called from the wooden gates at each end. These gates were a common feature of Chinese cities in former times ; they divided off the wards and were closed at night, as a protection against thieves and looting mobs. This street, known to foreigners as " Silk Street " from some large silk shops therein, used to be the chief shopping-centre of the old capital, and was especially noted for its " Foreign Goods " stores, when the strange devices of the West were still a novelty. Though it has lost much of its glory in recent times, it is still worth a visit, especially at night, when the mixture of gorgeous flags and signboards with modern electric light signs gives a very picturesque effect. We might add that it leads to the restaurant and amusement quarter to which we refer in a later chapter.

The continuation of this street is *Kuan Yin Ssŭ Hutung* with a temple to Kuan Yin at its western end. This lane brings us into touch with a society that has a vast membership in North China, the *Tsai Li Hui* (Total Abstinence Society), an off-shoot of the White Lily Sect. Members of this Society who are forbidden to mention the name of Kuan Yin simply refer to streets of this name as *Ta Hutung* (Main Lane). By the rules of the Society they are bound to abstain from all alcoholic beverages and tobacco, do not burn incense or offer up sacrifices and, strangest of all, are not allowed to keep cats, dogs, or chickens, as these animals are considered unlucky. They only use Kuan Yin's name in cases of extreme distress, when, if they pronounce it three times, it is said to bring immediate relief.

The temple to which an interesting local legend is attached lies between the fork of two lanes, at the east end of what used to be one long, unbroken block of buildings, said to represent a dragon : the temple was the head ; the temple gate the mouth ; two flag-poles that formerly stood in front of the temple were the horns ; two holes for the well outside the temple were the eyes ; the long block of buildings was the body ; and a small temple with a single flag-pole at the west end was the tail. In Manchu times there was a prophecy that from this dragon a second Emperor would arise, presumably some-body living in this block. So, to prevent this, the two very short lanes which exist to-day were driven through it from north to south, thus killing the dragon.

Taking the north fork we come by a number of winding lanes to the *Liu Li Ch'ang* (Glazed Tile Factory), a street of con-siderable interest in the cultural history of Peking, because it was—and to a lesser extent still is—the centre of old book-shops, also of old pictures and curios. Here Manchu princes and high Chinese officials used to stroll up and down looking into the shops and inspecting the old books and pictures. The name of the street comes from the kilns that once stood here in which was produced an opaque, glass-like substance used in the manufacture of coloured glazed tiles for the Imperial Palaces. After the kilns were closed down, the area in which they stood, on the north side of the street, was for many years a market for curio dealers, known as *Ch'ang Tien* (Leased Enclosure), because they were charged ground-rent. In an enclosed square at the end of the street as well as in the Fire God Temple (*Huo Shên Miao*) in the middle, a large annual fair is held from the 1st to the 15th of the First Moon. It was formerly chiefly a fair for curios, and many good pieces could be picked up at very reasonable prices. But it has now become a general fair, and is visited by enormous crowds every year. The iron gate leading to the square bears the characters *Hai Wang Ts'un Kung Yüan* (Public Garden of the Village of the Sea King), a name that takes us back to very ancient times. According to local tradition, during the reign of the Liao Emperor Pao Ning, about A.D. 977, someone set himself up as contractor for boats to convey grain across the numerous creeks that in those days intersected this district. Owing to his extortions he was given the name *Hai Wang* (Sea King), and the village that stood on this spot was called after this nickname, which has thus been preserved to the present time.

Leaving the Liu Li Ch'ang we turn south down the main street that leads from the *Ho P'ing Mên* (Gate of Peace and Harmony), the tenth and newest gate of the Tartar City, opened in 1925. From here we reach the main street running from the west gate of the Chinese City, the *Chang I Mên* (Gate of Prolonged Righteousness), officially known as the *Kuang An Mên* (Broad Peace Gate).

At the junction of these two streets there used to be a large open space, called *Ts'ai Shih K'ou* (Vegetable Market). Up till 1901 this was the EXECUTION-GROUND and has therefore a notoriously evil sound for the ears of the Pekingese. To tell a person to go to the Vegetable Market is akin to our telling a person to go and hang himself. Except in very important cases the executions took place at daybreak, after which the market was opened for business, all traces of the early morning tragedy being covered with lime. The criminals were brought from the Board of Punishments in open carts, similar to the famous tumbrils of the French Revolution. On the night before their execution they were given whatever they wished to eat and drink, were allowed a theatrical show, and women were even admitted to console their last hours.

At one end of the closed-off space was a mat-shed where the condemned had to wait for the arrival of the Imperial Decree for their execution, whilst in another shed at the opposite end sat the officials of the Board with a red-buttoned mandarin at their head. On one side was a small altar on which were laid the executioner's instruments, such as swords, ropes, tourniquets. In front of the altar was a stove with a large cauldron of boiling water to warm the swords. These were short, broad blades, almost like choppers, with a long wooden handle carved with a grotesque head. They had been in use for hundreds of years and were regarded as spirits. There were five of them, each with its own name : Great Lord, Second Lord, and so on. When not in use they were kept at the Chief Executioner's house, a tower on the wall, where according to popular belief they could be heard at nights singing songs about their gruesome deeds. Each was supposed to have its particular characteristic : some were skittish and playful, dallying and toying with the heads of the victims, others were more sedate and took them off at a blow.

When the fatal decree arrived, the prisoners were led out in turn before the officials and made to go through the pretence of acknowledging the justice of their punishment. They were then handed over to the Chief Executioner, *Kuei Tzŭ Shou* (Devil's Hand) who was stripped to the waist, except for a blood-stained apron of yellow leather. The condemned was made to kneel down, a string was passed round his neck and under his chin, and his head held up by the assistant executioner. With a shout of " *Sha la jên la !* " (I've killed my man) the Chief Executioner wielding the sword with both hands severed the head from the trunk at one blow. If the head fell at the first stroke, the crowd of spectators would all shout " *Hao Tao !* " (Good Sword), partly in praise of the executioner's skill, but partly from a supersititous hope of warding off the same fate from themselves. The executioner was only supposed to take one stroke to lop off a head, and if he failed he was reported to the Throne and severely punished. But so expert were they that it very seldom happened that they did not sever the head at one stroke, even when there was a whole row of persons to be decapitated. As no one could be executed except on the Emperor's express orders, it sometimes happened, in the case of the death or serious illness of the Emperor, that there were as many as fifty or sixty awaiting execution at one time.

For fear lest the shades of the decapitated might return to seek their revenge on the living, the execution-ground was surrounded with a " Spirit Barrier. " The entrance on the east was given the name *Hu Fang Ch'iao* (Tiger Guarded Bridge) so that the spirits of the departed would not dare to break out on this side for fear of being devoured ; an iron gate was specially set up on the north side to prevent them entering the city ; whilst on the south the entrance was called " Spirit General " who would certainly not let them pass that way. The only exit left open was that to the west, the idea being that the shades should be allowed to find their way to the Western Paradise, the Buddhist Heaven.

About half a mile from the Kuang An Mên is a broad opening on the north side of the street up which lies the *Pao Kuo Ssŭ* (Recompense the State Temple). It is believed to be the oldest temple in Peking, as it is recorded to have been built in the Chou dynasty. It was certainly repaired by the Liao Emperor Ch'ien Tung in 1103. In the courtyard there is a stone tablet dated 1466 stating that the Ming Emperor Ch'êng Hua again repaired this temple which, he found, had been built originally by an Empress-Dowager Chi Hsiang of the Chou dynasty out of her private purse. As the Chou dynasty was about 2500 years earlier, this statement must be taken with a grain of salt, especially as no other record of the lady exists.

Crossing some open spaces in an easterly direction we come to the *Ch'ang Ch'un Ssŭ* (Temple of Everlasting Spring) on the *Hsia Hsieh Chieh* (Lower Slanting Street). This temple was built about 1560 by the mother of the sensual and extravagant Emperor Wan Li whose reign ushered in the downfall of his dynasty. When in his boyhood he was taken seriously

ill and on the point of death, his mother made a vow that, if
he recovered, he should become a monk and enter a monastery.
But when he did regain his health she changed her mind and
procured another monk as substitute who thus, to all intents
and purposes, was the Emperor himself. She therefore had
this temple specially built for him, placing in it a large image
of herself studded with valuable gems which she called *Chiu
Lien P'u Sa* (The Nine Lotus Buddha)—the lotus being the
Buddhist symbol of purity. On the walls of the main hall
used to hang one thousand pictures of Buddha which have
long ago disappeared, as have, needless to say, the valuable
gems on the idol.

Continuing south and crossing the main street we come
to *Niu Chieh* (Cow Street), a Mohammedan quarter, on the
east side of which is a mosque (*Ch'ing Chên Ssü*), the largest
in the city. There is no definite record of the date when
Mohammedans first settled in Peking, but it is certain that
they were already practicing their religion here in the reign
of K'ang Hsi (1662-1723), when they were so "suspect"
that special officials were appointed to keep an eye on their
doings. Later on, when the Chinese had become used to
them, and more probably, after they had shown themselves
such excellent soldiers in the various campaigns of the great
Manchu Emperors, they were accepted as part of the general
population and allowed to practice their rites without
interference. The main road is called "Cow Street" because it
runs through the quarter where the Mohammedans live who
are popularly supposed to eat more meat than the ordinary
Chinese, though actually it is rather mutton than beef. The
Chinese are very prejudiced against Mohammedans, accusing
them of being too sharp, clannish, and ill-natured. Occasionally,
out of pure spite, a Chinese opens a pork shop opposite
that of a Mohammedan butcher and, in order to frighten off
the sheep that are brought to the Mohammedan shop, has
the picture of a ferocious tiger painted across the front of his
own shop. The other then retaliates by hanging up a large
mirror in which appears the reflection of the tiger that will
then, of course, devour the pigs !

Apart, however, from minor pleasantries of this kind,
the two communities live together in peace, at any rate in Peking,

where one never hears of anti-Mohammedan riots. The reflections of the Chinese against Mohammedan honesty will not be borne out by foreign residents who have had dealings with them, though some people perhaps may have their doubts when they hear that nine-tenths of the curio dealers are of that persuasion.

Taking a lane opposite the mosque and going south-west across open ground we come to a district called *Pai Chih Fang* (White Paper Quarter), because the local inhabitants have been manufacturing paper here for many centuries. In the vicinity is the *Ts'ung Hsiao Ssŭ* (Temple of Supreme Service). First built during the reign of the T'ang Emperor Chên Kuan in A.D. 627 under the name of *Tsao Hua Ssŭ* (Date Flower Temple) on account of the large number of date trees planted there. Later during the same dynasty a certain Liu Chung, noted for his filial piety, took over the monastery and changed the name to Temple of Supreme Filial Piety. It was changed to its present name under the Mongol Emperor Yüan Chêng (1295-1307) by whom it was extensively repaired. The Mings also took a great interest in this temple : T'ien Shun rebuilt it completely ; Chia Ching was a great patron and erected a large library adjoining it, called *Ts'ang Ching Ko* (Chamber for Preserving the Diamond Sutra) ; and the Emperor Lung Ch'ing in 1568 set up here the celebrated *Wan Yen Pei* (Tablet of Ten Thousand Destinies). The Chinese consider this tablet to be a marvellous piece of sculpture, which it certainly is. At the top of the tablet is engraved the picture of a beautiful mansion ; in the centre is carved another tablet, about fourteen inches long, on which are inset 156 square pictures each of which is a representation of the house. Furthermore, and still more wonderful, the tablet is inscribed with the names of thousands of scholars and other persons who contributed towards its erection by order of the Emperor. Both the Library and the tablet still stand in the temple grounds, but the sutras have been removed to an unknown destination.

The best time to visit this temple is in May or June—at the festival of the " Commencement of Summer " (*Li Hsia*) when the peonies for which the temple is still famous are in full bloom, and thousands come to see the celebrated flowers. Anyone who considers himself a poet goes there to compose poems about the *Mu Tan* (peony), the " King of Flowers," which the Chinese so much admire. These particular plants were first brought to this temple by one of the head priests in the early days of the Manchu dynasty from Tsao-chou Fu in Shan-tung which is famous all over China for its peonies. Ever since then these flowers have been specially cared for and are still from the original roots—a matter of over three centuries ! There is a strange thing about them, that, if the flower is picked, the plant does not blossom again for two or three years.

The original temple endowments having disappeared, the temple is now in very low water, and the few remaining monks seek to keep it up by charging a small entrance fee and by letting out rooms for a few dollars a month.

Returning to " Cow Street " and continuing east we come to the *Fa Yüan Ssŭ* (Temple of Buddhist Origin), one of the oldest and most interesting temples of Peking. It was built in A.D. 645 by the Emperor Chên Kuan, under the name of *Min Chung Ssŭ* (Temple to Loyal Warriors), in memory of the soldiers who fell in his numerous campaigns against Korea and other border states. Their bones were buried under the stone altar in the temple compound. The Sung Emperor Hui Tsung (1101-1125) was kept prisoner for a time in this temple. When the first Ming Emperor Hung Wu drove out the Mongols, he altered the name to *Ts'ung Fu Ssŭ* (Temple of Supreme Blessings) in thanksgiving for his victory. The Manchu Emperor Yung Chêng again changed the name to *Fa Yüan Ssŭ*. The story goes that his grandmother, the Empress-Dowager, claimed to have heard the temple bell one night. As this was the only instance when the chimes from this temple had ever been heard in the Palace precincts, she said that they must be *Fa Yüan* (Source of Buddha's Law) sent to her expressly.

Among the numerous tablets standing in the temple grounds two are of particular interest. One is said to have been inscribed by Li Shih-min, the second and greatest of the T'ang Emperors, eulogizing An Lu-shan, the Turk, who was then governor of Peking. When the latter revolted, the Emperor had the words in his praise obliterated from the stone. It was during this revolt that the famous Chinese heroine Yang Kuei Fei met her death.

The other tablet records the story of Ts'ao O, a young lady who drowned herself in a river near Ningpo because she failed to find her father's body. When Hsieh Fang-ta, a faithful minister of the Sung dynasty, was compelled to accept a post in Peking by the Mongols who had overthrown the Sungs, he came to live in this temple. After seeing Ts'ao O's tablet he went on what is probably the first hunger strike on record, saying that if a young girl could not forget her father, how could a loyal minister desert his Emperor.

In the early days of the Manchu dynasty a famous fair was held here on the 8th of the Fourth Moon, when the temple was thrown open to the general public. According to local tradition, the fair was forbidden by the Emperor Ch'ien Lung, for the following reason :—The Emperor, who was fond of going about the city incognito took it into his head one day to visit the temple and go on a religious diet. Although he entered the temple by the front gate, like one of the ordinary public, he was recognized by the abbot who was determined that even this august visitor should not be allowed to infringe any of the rules of the monastery. The Emperor, however, made no mistakes and conducted himself with strict propriety, until towards the end of the meal, when instead of quietly laying down his chopsticks straight out in front of him according to the monastery etiquette he threw them down carelessly just anyhow. Thereupon the abbot struck him a blow with his wand and ordered the front gates to be closed and locked, so that His Imperial Majesty had to make his exit through a back-door. On his return to the palace the Emperor at once issued a special edict that the front gates of this monastery were never again to be opened. Nor were they, until the establishment of the Republic!

A more likely reason for the ban against the fair is, that it often lasted till late into the night, when numerous scandals took place which coming to the ears of the Censorate were reported to the Emperor, so that the fair was closed down for good.

The temple is now but a sorry reflection of its former glory. The only excitement—if such they can be called—are the services for the dead that are still held here. It is also famous for its old-style Chinese block printing.

A little way to the east, on the *Ch'i Ching Hutung* (Seven Wells Lane) is the *Lien Hua Ssŭ* (Lotus Flower Temple). It

was an obscure monastery in the time of the Mings and had
fallen into decay, until Ch'ien Lung discovering that there
was a large pond there covered with beautiful lotus, rebuilt
the temple at enormous cost.   At one time it was used as a
residence by candidates from the provinces when preparing
for the Metropolitan Examinations.   To-day the Lien
Hua Ssŭ is the centre of painting in Peking.   It is the Mecca
of all those who love art for art's sake.   One of the best
painters in Peking, a monk named Jui Tan lives in the temple
to whom all budding artists go for instruction.

Going east from the Fa Yüan Ssŭ we reach the *T'ien Ch'iao*
(Heaven's Bridge), which is no longer a bridge and is nowadays
only indicated as such by the marble balustrades.   In former
days this bridge enjoyed a very unpleasant notoriety from the
swarms of beggars who gathered here and pestered passers-by.
Although this has now been stopped, the whole district enjoys
even to-day a by no means savory reputation.

We return along the Ch'ien Mên Main Street.

Those who feel sufficiently energetic to take a walk right
down to the south wall of the Chinese City will find two
interesting ancient sites.

About a quarter of a mile west of the Altar of Agriculture
and in line with its southern wall is a group of buildings
standing on a terrace well above the level of the surrounding
reed ponds.   This is the *T'ao Jan T'ing* (Joyful Pavilion), said
to date from Sung times.   Originally the temple here was called
Tz'ŭ Pei An (Compassionate Monastery).   In the reign of
K'ang Hsi a certain Chung Tsao erected a pavilion here where
he entertained his friends, so that gradually the original name
became forgotten, everybody referring to the place as the
" Joyful Pavilion."

On a mound north of and close to the Pavilion stands
a small house surrounded by a mud wall.   At the south-
west corner of the wall are two small dark-grey tombstones.
These are said to mark the spot where Hsiang Fei, the
" Fragrant Concubine," whom Ch'ien Lung loved in vain lies
buried (Chapter VII).

CHAPTER XVI.

THE EASTERN HALF OF THE CHINESE CITY

IMMEDIATELY adjoining the east end of the Legation Quarter lies the easternmost gate of the south wall of the Tartar City, popularly known as the *Hata Mên*, a name that comes down from Mongol times, when a Mongolian Prince Hata, had a palace in the vicinity. The official name, inscribed over the south face of the inner tunnel, is *Ch'ung Wên Mên* (Noble and Refined Gate). The outer gate which lay formerly on the west side of the enceinte was moved to its present position directly in line with the inner gate, when the Bengal Sappers and Miners brought the railway past here in 1902. For the same reason as at the Tung Chih Mên (Chapter XIII) a bell, instead of the usual gong, was sounded here at nightfall. A "pig-dragon" who lived under the bridge outside the gate used to cause floods in the city whenever he came out of the water ; so he too was chained up and told that he would be released, as soon as the bell struck.

On the site of the first buildings across the bridge on the east side there stood the Head Office of the notorious PEKING OCTROI, in former times a very lucrative and much-sought-after post. It was abolished when the Kuomintang moved the capital to Nanking in 1928,

The seventh turning on the left is the *Hua Erh Shih* (Flower Market), a street famous for its artificial flowers and cheap jewellery, and therefore a favourite shopping centre for visitors of the fair sex. A short distance up this street, on the north side, is a Temple to the GOD OF FIRE (*Huo Shên Miao*). It was built under the Mings in 1568 and reconstructed in the last year of Ch'ien Lung (1776). Local tradition says that one very hot summer day, during the reign of the Ming Emperor Ch'ung Chêng, a Taoist priest was burning incense at the altar in the temple, when an earthquake occurred causing the God of Fire to sway about so that he nearly tumbled from his niche. The priest was so deeply engrossed in his devotions that he had not noticed the earthquake and thought that the god was trying to get down from his throne and go out for a walk. He therefore seized him by the knees beseeching him not to leave the temple, lest by so doing he should add to the already unbearable heat.

Whilst on the subject of earthquakes, we might add that, although the city of Peking does not lie in a volcanic or even mountainous region, it has suffered from several very bad shocks during the course of its existence. There are records of severe earthquakes in 1624, 1679, and 1680 when the palace caught fire ; another on November 13, 1731, the worst ever experienced in China, when over one hundred thousand of the population of Peking alone are said to have perished ; and again, as late as 1830.

There are altogether no less than eleven of these temples to the God of Fire in Peking, three of which were built by the Emperors, and the others by the people themselves. It will be noticed that in all these temples the Gods of Fire have blackened faces and terribly scorched bodies, less probably from their association with fire, than from the constant burning of incense with which they have been fumigated.

At the east end of " Flower Market Street " we turn north until we reach a small temple lying immediately south of the *Tung Pien Mên* (Eastern Wicket Gate), the north-east gate of the Chinese city. This is the *P'an T'ao Kung* (Spiral Peach Palace), a temple dedicated to *Hsi Wang Mu* (The Western Royal Mother).* In honour of her birthday on the " Feast of the Immortals "—3rd of the Third Moon—a fair is held here amidst great rejoicings from the 1st to 5th day of the Third Moon. The temple itself is an insignificant building with only two small rooms, in one of which is the image of the " Royal Mother " and behind her the mother of the God of the Pole Star. Legend accounts for the curious name of the temple as follows :—Close to the Eastern Sea (*Tung Hai*) is a hill called Tu So Shan on which grows a peach tree with a branch that extends spirally for thousands of miles. Hence the peaches (*t'ao*) were called spiral (*p'an*). As Hsi Wang Mu who dwelt on the K'un Lun Mountain many thousands of miles away could not visit the Eastern Sea,

*See at end " Notes " to page 83.

the peach tree stretched forth its branch laden with fruit so
that she could pluck it at her leisure.   On the 3rd of the Third
Moon Peking girls do up their hair in coils (*p'an*) as a sign
that they are of marriageable age.   A somewhat similar custom
takes place on the 2nd of the Second Moon, called *Lung T'ai
T'ou* (Dragon Raising his Head).   On that day women do no
needle-work, for fear of ruining their eyesight, while young
girls of fifteen or over coil up their hair as a sign that they
want a husband—if they can catch him!   More prosaically, the
name "*P'an T'ao*" for this temple probably originated from
the fact that a tree bearing the small flat peach (*p'an t'ao*)
grew there.

It is worth while taking a short walk outside the *Tung
Pien Mên* to see the pleasant river scenery on the stone-lined
banks of the canal that has its terminus here.   This is the
Tung Ho (East River) which connects via the town of T'ung
Chow with the Grand Canal at Tientsin and was formerly
the route by which the tribute rice was brought to Peking.
For this reason the ground between the moat and the east
wall as far as the Ch'i Hua Mên was lined with sheds where
the rice was unloaded and stored, prior to removal to the
granaries inside the city.   In former days the canal was a great
place for water picnics in summer, and for rides on the ice in
winter on toboggans (*p'ai tzŭ*) which are propelled by a man
standing at the back with a pole between his legs, in fact a
kind of "ice-punting."

Returning to Flower Market Street and taking the second
large turning on the left, called *Nan Yang Shih K'ou* (South
Sheep Market Mouth) we reach a broad street running east
and west.   Close to it is a tiny alleyway with the strange name
Chu Li Pa (Bamboo Wattle Lane). Nobody would imagine
that this name is connected with pigeons and, incidentally,
one of the most interesting historic lanes of the old capital.
In former days a number of pigeon fanciers—or thieves, to
be more exact—used to rear pigeons in this alley and teach them
the gentle art of stealing.   These birds which were trained to
steal the rice from the Imperial Granaries were called by the
expressive term "Food Distributors."   Their crops were
artificially expanded to more than twice the size of that of an
ordinary pigeon.   When let loose they flew straight to the

granaries and fed on the best rice until their crops were full.
On their return they were given a shallow bowl of water with
alum in it to drink, which caused them to retch and bring up
the contents of their crops. After it had been washed and
dried, this rice was either sold retail or used in the family. A
man with a flock of one hundred pigeons could, it was reckoned,
in this way collect about fifty pounds of rice per day. These
pigeons, though well housed and cared-for, were never fed
until after their day's work was over, and then always in the
early evening, so that they were all the hungrier for their task
next day. As they were kept in cages of closely woven bamboo
wattles—as a protection against cats—the lane was called by
this name. And though, since the fall of the Manchus, the
Imperial Granaries have all been closed up, and the thieves
have lost their livelihood, the name of this lane still preserves
the memory of their little tricks.

We might add here that in former days, quite apart from
the above malpractices, the Pekingese were greatly addicted—
and still are, though to a very much less extent—to the more
innocent amusement of flying pigeons. At the numerous
city fairs you will still see many pigeons on sale which fanciers
buy, after a very careful inspection, and carry home neatly
slung up in a piece of cloth. The attraction of this sport,
the Chinese say, is to watch the flock circling round, sometimes
standing out black against the sky and then suddenly almost
invisible, according as the sunlight catches them, and last
but not least, they enjoy the music of the pigeon-whistles which
are attached to the tail of several of the flock. These
whistles, made of bamboo, are said to have been used originally
to frighten off hawks and other birds of prey. They work
on the principle of an organ pipe, the pigeon's flight forcing
the air through the tube of the whistle produces a curious,
melancholy, wailing sound, which may not greatly appeal to
foreign ears.

These pigeons are trained to recognize certain colours,
so as to guide them back to their home. In most cases a row
of coloured tiles is laid on top of the ordinary grey roof tiles ;
in others when the owner wishes to call the flock home he
waves a long bamboo pole with a flag of the particular colour
that the birds have been trained to recognize as their own.

Crossing the main street we continue south through a network of lanes until we arrive at the *Fa Hua Ssŭ* (Temple of Buddha's Glory), built by the chief eunuch of the Ming Emperor Ching T'ai in 1451. This temple has the additional characters *Hsia Yüan* (Lower Court), as it is under the control of the temple of the same name in the Ta Pao Fang Hutung (Chapter XI).

South of it is the *Hua Yen Ssŭ*, named after a Diamond Sutra. It was built by K'ang Hsi in 1662, in honour of Tou Mu, the mother of the God of the Pole Star, whose image is enshrined in the temple. He subsequently changed the name to *Yü Ch'ing Kuan* (Pure Palace of the Jade Emperor) by which it is best known. In the courtyard is a stone tablet of the Chin dynasty with an inscription in Sanskrit. The pagoda of thirteen storeys, to the south-east, is called *Fa T'a Ssŭ* (Buddha's Pagoda Temple), but the common people think of it as the " Tired Pagoda " (same sound), because there was a legend that the pagoda had walked here all the way from the West.

About three quarters of a mile due east, close to the wall, is a temple with many historical associations, the *Nien Hua Ssŭ* (Temple of Picked Flowers). It was built in 1581 during the reign of Wan Li, under the name of *Ch'ien Fo Ssŭ* (Temple of a Thousand Buddhas). When the Manchus came into power, a minister named Fêng P'u seized the place for himself and altered the name to *Wan Liu T'ang* (Hall of Ten Thousand Willows), as it is popularly called to this day. His arbitrary action was much resented by all admirers of the temple, but as he was the favourite minister of the Emperor Shun Chih, nothing could be done. When K'ang Hsi came to the throne, he took back the property and gave it to a favourite minister, Shih Wên-tsu, who built the " Balcony of Great Sympathy " (*Ta Pei Ko*) adjoining the temple. Later on, K'ang Hsi changed his mind again, seized the property for himself and rebuilt the whole place under its present name. It became once more a favourite rendezvous of scholars and officials. One day when the Emperor was taking a stroll here he found a large number of famous scholars enjoying the beauties of the temple ; so he ordered them to write an eulogy of the " Hall of Ten Thousand Willows." The best poem was written by two Hanlin scholars, Mao Chi-lin and Ch'ên

Chi-nien, who in consequence were given a banquet by their Imperial patron. To-day this once famous temple has fallen into decay, and nothing remains of the former splendid lotus pools, pavilions, and arbours that graced its extensive grounds under the early Manchu Emperors. There is still a small pond, called " The Pool for Liberating Living Things " (*Fang Shêng Ch'ih*), that once stood in the grounds. Close by is a small temple to which people still resort to set free captive birds, in order to acquire merit according to the rules of Buddhism.

We return to the Fa Hua Ssŭ and go due west skirting the north wall of the Altar of Heaven. A short distance from the north-east corner of the enclosure is a street called *Tz'ŭ Ch'i K'ou* (Porcelain Mouth), popularly known as *Tz'ŭ Ch'i K'êng* (Porcelain Pit), from the popular tradition that when digging up earth to repair a temple in this neighbourhood, in the reign of the Ming Emperor Chia Ching, many pieces of ancient porcelain were discovered, so that for a time the place became a veritable paradise for curio dealers.

In one of the small lanes off this street is the famous THIEVES' MARKET which is held in the small hours of the morning, before it is light enough for either the seller or his goods to be seen too distinctly. It is generally believed that all the articles sold here are stolen goods and can therefore be picked up for a song. No doubt, a considerable portion have not been acquired on strictly commercial principles by those offering them for sale. On the other hand many of the articles have probably been quite honestly come by, but are brought here, in the hope that the " honest " purchaser will thus be deceived into thinking them stolen goods and that he is therefore getting a cheap bargain. By the Chinese the market is merely called *Hsiao Shih* (Small Market) ; " Thieves' Market " is the name by which it is known to foreign residents.

To the north of the Altar of Heaven there used to be numerous small ponds called *Chin Yü Ch'ih* (Gold Fish Ponds) in which, gold-fish are said to have been reared as early, as the 12th century. On this spot there once stood a temple called the " Jasper Pool Temple," after the famous lake of Chinese legend on which Hsi Wang Mu, the " Western Royal Mother," used to disport herself. At one time there were dozens of gold-fish ponds in and around Peking, all said to be off-shoots of this " Jasper Pool." For the past twenty years or more, gold-fish have been mostly reared in tubs in which they do not seem to thrive as well as they did in these ponds, probably owing to the lack of certain insects on which they feed.

Leaving the wall of the Altar of Heaven at the north-west corner we turn north up a lane called *Ching Chung Miao Hutung*, in which stands a temple of that name. The *Ching Chung Miao* (Loyal to the Last Temple) was dedicated by the Emperor Ch'ien Lung to the loyal hero, Yüeh Fei, as is stated on the stone memorial tablet standing in the compound. Yüeh Fei was executed by the orders of Ch'in K'uei, a Prime Minister of the Sung dynasty, because he was an obstacle to the peace negotiations with the Mongols. When he was thrown into prison, Yüeh Fei bared his back on which were imprinted the characters " Loyal to the Last." In front of the temple are stone figures of the traitor minister Ch'in K'uei and his wife in a kneeling posture. Passers-by whose patriotic feelings became too strong for them would often stop to spit on these effigies, as on account of this cruel and treacherous murder Ch'in K'uei has been held up to execration by the Chinese all through the centuries. On the Lantern Festival, the 15th day of the First Moon, people used to make an image of Ch'in K'uei out of charcoal, place it before the idol of Yüeh Fei and set it alight, until it was totally destroyed. Thus was Yüeh Fei's loyal spirit appeased by seeing his murderer sacrificed before him at least once a year. From this custom, by the way, is derived the name of a common form of Chinese food, the fritters fried in oil, which are called *Yu Cha Kuei* (Boiled in Oil Devil). The following further notes on Ch'in K'uei, in this connection, may perhaps be of interest :—In 1895, at the close of the disastrous war against Japan, the citizens of Hangchow destroyed Ch'in K'uei's image altogether, as a sign of their disapproval of the terms of the Peace Treaty. A few years later the Financial Commissioner of Hangchow, Yün Tsu-yi had four new images made, representing Li Hung-chang, Shao Yu-lien, Chang Yin-huan, the three plenipotentiaries who signed the treaty; the fourth was that of Gustav Detring, a former Commissioner of Customs then advisor to Li Hung-chang. These images were treated in the same way as that of Ch'in K'uei !

Yüeh Fei, on the other hand, had all his titles posthumously restored to him by the Sung Emperor Hsiao Tsung in 1162 ; his remains were buried with full honours and a special shrine was erected to his memory, under the title of " Loyal Hero." His image now stands next to that of the God of War in most of the latter's temples, and under the Republic he was given equal rank with him.

In the Ching Chung Miao is also an image of Lu Pan, the patron God of carpenters and masons.

From the temple a few steps to the west bring us out on to the Ch'ien Mên Main Street.

CHAPTER XVII

THE NORTHERN SUBURBS

ABOUT a quarter of a mile outside the An Ting Mên on the east side of the road lies the ALTAR OF EARTH (*Ti T'an*). When Yung Lo first built the Altar of Heaven (Chapter VIII), he called it *T'ien Ti T'an* (Altar of Heaven and Earth), following the system laid down by Hung Wu, the founder of the Ming dynasty, that Heaven and Earth should be worshipped together. At the request of his court astrologers the Ming Emperor Chia Ching, in the 9th year of his reign (1530), selected this site, belonging to an old temple of the Yüan dynasty, and built here a separate Altar of Earth which was at first a very modest affair. It remained so until the Manchu Emperor Chia Ch'ing began to take an interest in this worship. The reconstruction of the altar took several years and cost a large sum of money, as numerous additions were made at different times, until it was completely remodelled.

It is composed of three sections which, unlike those of the Altar of Heaven, are square—for in Chinese geomancy the square is associated with the Earth and the circle with Heaven. At the end of the approach from the main road there stands a tall *P'ai Lou*, one of the most imposing in Peking. There is nothing in the first section except a former " Poor-house," at one time occupied by soldiers who cleared out the paupers and took possession themselves. At the entrance to the second section is the ticket office of the Metropolitan Park which was opened to the public in 1925 but has now been closed again. Passing through a second gate we have another park on our left, the *Shih Chieh Yüan* (Park of the World), which used to have a relief map, showing the location of the various countries of the world, with their mountains and principal cities. A little further on is a pavilion with five angles, called the Republican Pavilion, symbolical of the Five Races of China.

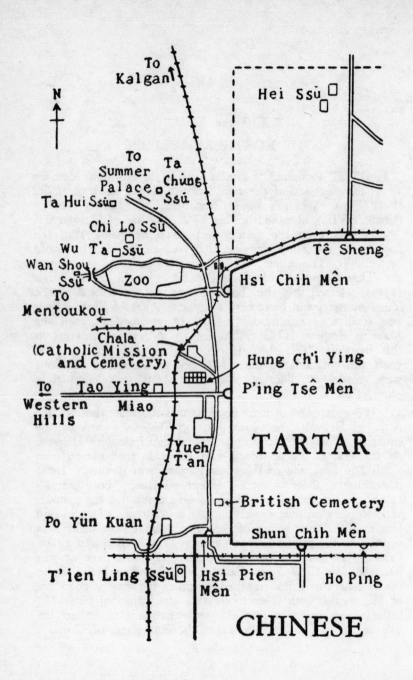

To Kalgan

N

Hei Ssŭ

To Summer Palace
Ta Chung Ssŭ
Ta Hui Ssŭ

Chi Lo Ssŭ

Wu T'a Ssŭ

Wan Shou Ssŭ

Zoo

Tê Sheng

Hsi Chih Mên

To Mentoukou

Chala
(Catholic Mission and Cemetery)

Hung Ch'i Ying

To Western Hills

Tao Ying Miao

P'ing Tsê Mên

Yueh T'an

TARTAR

British Cemetery

Po Yün Kuan

Shun Chih Mên

T'ien Ling Ssŭ

Hsi Pien Mên

Ho Ping

CHINESE

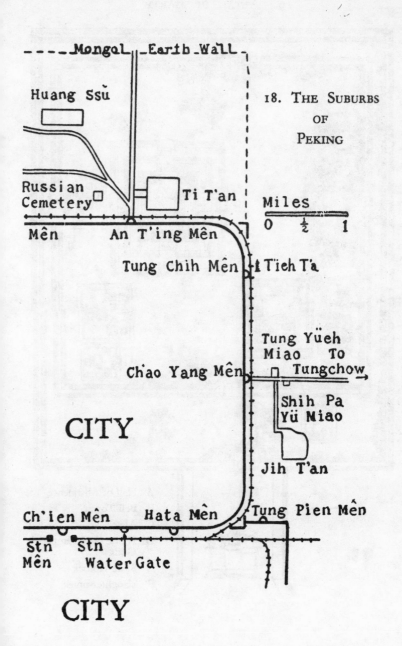

18. THE SUBURBS
OF
PEKING

Mongol Earth Wall

Huang Ssŭ

Russian Cemetery

Ti T'an

Mên

An T'ing Mên

Tung Chih Mên

Tieh T'a

Miles
0   ½   1

Tung Yüeh
Miao   To
Tungchow

Ch'ao Yang Mên

Shih Pa
Yü Miao

CITY

Jih T'an

Ch'ien Mên

Hata Mên

Tung Pien Mên

Stn
Mên

Stn
Water Gate

CITY

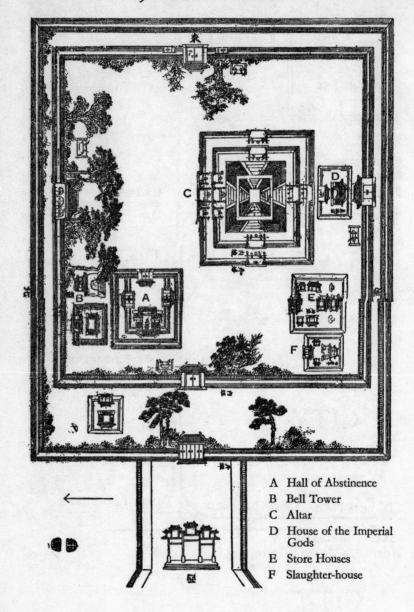

A Hall of Abstinence
B Bell Tower
C Altar
D House of the Imperial
   Gods
E Store Houses
F Slaughter-house

At the back of the " Park of the World " are the neglected remains of what was once a beautiful palace, the *Chai Kung*, where the Emperor fasted and changed his robes prior to performing the annual sacrifice. The chief object of interest is the altar itself which is surrounded by two low walls with yellow tiles. There are three handsome arches on the north, and one on each of the other three sides. The altar of white marble is approached from four sides by four steps to each of the two terraces ; the lower terrace is 106, and the upper 60 feet square, the height between the two being six feet. It is surrounded by a moat about eight feet wide. Close to the altar on the south is the *Huang Chih Shih* (House of the Imperial Gods), in which were kept the spirit-tablets, until they were used for firewood by soldiers in recent times. To the southwest lay another imposing palace, now also in ruins, where the princes and high officials who took part in the ceremony used to rest. Adjoining it is a pavilion where the sacrificial animals were slaughtered.

The roofs of the buildings and the walls are covered with yellow tiles ; the gem, the symbol of the object worshipped, which was placed before the tablet of Earth, was yellow and square, in conformity with the Chinese idea of the colour and shape of the earth ; whilst the robes worn by the Emperor at the ceremony were of the same colour. The annual sacrifice at the Summer Solstice was very similar to that performed at the Altar of Heaven.

We retrace our steps towards the gate, and take a road on the west side that leads to the Yellow Temple. About half a mile along this we see on our left the RUSSIAN CEMETERY belonging to the Mission at the Pei Kuan (Chapter XIII). Its only feature of interest is the memorial tablet standing up against the west wall.

SACRED

TO THE MEMORY OF

Captain L. R. BRABAZON, R.A.

Lt. B. R. ANDERSON, Fane's Horse

Private S. PHIPPS, 1st Dragoon Guards

W. DE NORMANN, Esq., Attaché H.B.M. Legation

T. W. BOWLBY, Esq., Correspondent of the " Times "
and
EIGHT SIKH SOLDIERS
who
treacherously seized in violation of a flag of truce
on the 18th September, 1860,
sank under the inhuman treatment during their captivity
This stone replaces the original memorial destroyed by the
Chinese in June 1900.

The bodies were first buried here, but in the 'seventies were removed to the British Cemetery outside the Hsi Pien Mên (Chapter XVIII). As a matter of strict historical accuracy, the body of Captain Brabazon, was never buried here, as it was never found, nor, indeed, was his actual fate ever definitely known. Rennie in his " Peking and the Pekingese " describes how the poor old father came out all the way from England— quite an undertaking in those days—in search of his son. He even offered a reward of £20,000 and wanted to visit the camp of the famous Mongol General Sêng K'o Lin Ch'in, who had opposed the Allied armies in their advance on Peking, being convinced that his son was still held prisoner by him. The British diplomatic representatives of those days threw cold water on the idea. The Emperor Hsien Fêng having just died, they were much more concerned, as to whether they should send their condolences to the Chinese Foreign Office on black-edged note-paper or not, than to clear up the fate of Captain Brabazon. While the Chinese, for their part, put an end to the proposed visit by pointing out that, if anything happened to the father, other relatives would then come out to hunt for him, and so the business might go on *ad infinitum*. How little does the world really change !

Continuing north for about a mile across the plain which in former times was, and still is, used as a review and drill ground, we come to a large complex of buildings. This is the famous Lama temple commonly known as the YELLOW TEMPLE (*Huang Ssŭ*), built during the Ming dynasty under the name of *P'u Ching Ch'an Lin* (Monastery of Universal Peace). As there are two establishments, the Chinese refer to them as the east (*tung*) and west (*hsi*) temples. They were both destroyed, when the rebel leader, Li Tzŭ-ch'êng, invaded Peking in 1643. The eastern temple was rebuilt by Shun Chih in the 8th year of his reign (1651), as a temporary residence for the Dalai Lama who visited Peking in the following year. And a year later the western temple was added to house the Dalai Lama's staff. The temple was then allowed to fall into disrepair until the 9th year of Yung Chêng (1731), when several important Mongol dignitaries visited Peking, who resided here and provided the funds for its repair and for the numerous large brass idols which it at one time contained. In the grounds are a number of stone tablets recording the history of the two temples, and the rules to be observed during worship.

The temple formerly housed a large community of Mongol Lamas and was an important centre of Lamaism, famous for the " Devil Dances," known as " Whipping the Devils," which were held here on the 13th and 15th of the First Moon. It has now fallen on evil days : the greater part of the buildings are in ruins or are occupied as barracks, and the Lamas have all departed, except for a few caretakers. The only portion worth visiting is the enclosure on the western side, where the buildings have recently been repaired, and in which stands the so-called " Marble Pagoda." This is a beautiful octagonal marble stupa over a handsomely carved mausoleum, erected by Ch'ien Lung in 1781 to the memory of a P'an-ch'ên Lama, who died of smallpox during a visit to Peking. On its eight sides are engraved scenes from the Buddha's life, such as the preternatural circumstances of his birth, his entrance to the priesthood, struggles with the unbelieving, teaching of disciples, and death. The Lama's body was taken back to Tibet, but his clothes are said to be buried beneath the mausoleum. The circumstances of the Lama's visit and the erection of this mausoleum are mentioned in Turner's " Embassy to Tibet."

In 1900 many of the marble carvings were badly defaced by the foreign soldiery. They were afterwards repaired, only to be again defaced, this time by Chinese soldiers quartered there in recent times.

Outside the temple grounds, away to the north-east, up some narrow alleyways, is a small temple called *Ts'an T'an*

(Altar of Meditation) where the bodies of the dead lamas are
kept in curious square-shaped wooden coffins. For those who
think it worth while the guide will, for an extra 20 cents, lift
the lids for you to see the decaying remains !

Proceeding in a north-westerly direction for about a mile,
we strike the road that leads to the Tê Shêng Mên. To the
north of us, on the west side of the road can be seen the
black-tiled roofs of a temple which in consequence is popularly
known as the *Hei Ssŭ* (Black Temple). There are really two:
the front (*ch'ien*) and the back (*hou*) temples which are
completely separated from each other. They were built
in the years 1645-46 and contain several relics of the Ming
dynasty, such as iron bells cast in the reign of Wan Li,
and a large bronze bell of the 10th year of Chêng Tê (1515).
Both temples have been turned into barracks.

From here we re-enter the city by the Tê Shêng Mên and
leave it again by the Hsi Chih Mên. Instead of turning north
along the main road to the Summer Palace, we continue straight
on west for about a mile to the entrance of the ZOOLOGICAL
GARDENS (*Wan Shêng Yüan*). This is one of the oldest and
largest of all the parks in Peking and has had many ups and
downs during its existence. It was originally the property
of one of the sons of the Emperor Shun Chih and was called
Lo Shan Yüan (Pleasure Gardens). In the course of time it
fell into ruins, but in the 12th year of Ch'ien Lung (1747)
was reconstructed in honour of his mother's sixtieth birthday.
Later on it became the property of a younger brother of the
Emperor Hsien Fêng, and hence is still known as the *San Pei
Tzŭ Hua Yüan* (Flower Garden of the Third Prince). This
prince, like so many Manchus of later days, totally
neglected his property, so that for many years it became a
kind of " No-Man's Land." After her return from Sianfu
in 1901, the Empress-Dowager began to take an interest
in it—probably because it was close to her route to the Summer
Palace—and spent large sums in developing it. When a certain
high Manchu official, Tuan Fang, visited " Seventeen Foreign
Countries " in 1902-3, he bought in Germany a large collection
of animals and birds, as well as hiring a few keepers, and had
them shipped to Peking as presents for the Empress-Dowager.
(Tuan Fang, by the way, was the Viceroy of Shensi who in

1900 saved the lives of the missionaries in that province by ignoring the edict ordering their destruction).

This menagerie, which is said to have cost a million taels, was placed in the park, when the name was changed to *Wan Shêng Yüan* (Park of Ten Thousand Animals). The Chinese director got into trouble with the old lady on her very first visit, because, when she asked him the name of one of the animals, he was unable to tell her, and was dismissed on the spot. Like so many other things in this country, the " Ten Thousand Animals " have now become less than one hundred, if as many. All that is left of the original collection are a few poor specimens of various animals, and last but not least, one solitary elephant, who is kept chained up for weeks on end in a cubicle hardly large enough to hold a baboon. The poor fellow has some cause to welcome visitors—but for whom he would starve to death—as he humbly holds out his trunk for a tiny bundle of " rice-straw," weighing less than an ounce, for which the keeper charges four coppers. The remainder of " The Ten Thousand Animals " have been stuffed—certainly the only time that this term could be applied to them after their arrival at the Gardens—and are to be seen in a museum in the grounds. Nevertheless the park is well worth visiting for a quiet ramble.

One of the pleasure trips used to be to the " Little Island of Japan " with several Japanese houses which the Empress-Dowager is said to have ordered at a time when she was contemplating visiting the Land of Cherry Blossoms. Since her death the house have been allowed to fall into ruins, and the island is seldom visited since Japan has become so unpopular in China these many years. By the side of a small lake is an unsightly foreign-style house, called *Huai Jên Lou* (Reception Room for Distant Guests). It was built by the Empress-Dowager for the special purpose of entertaining her foreign lady friends ; after her death it was converted into a restaurant which has recently closed up through lack of customers. There are a number of " experimental farms " for cotton and various kinds of fruit trees, as well as a museum for insects. But, strange to say, the very insects that are exhibited, in order to show people what they look like and how to destroy them, are the same as those that are

eating the plants and trees of the experimental farms just
outside ! Recently the name of the Park has again been altered
to *Chung Yang Nung Shih Yen Ch'ang* (Central Experimental
Agriculture Ground), but the local people still call it by the
old name of *San Pei Tzŭ Hua Yüan*.

People often ask where they can see a eunuch. If they
visit this park, they will see two giant eunuchs—there used to
be four of them—standing at the entrance gate ; one of them
measures seven feet six inches, and the other seven feet four
inches. They were favourites of the Empress-Dowager, her
special bodyguards.

Leaving the gardens we continue west along the road
that skirts the wall of the park until we come to a bridge over
the canal leading from the Summer Palace, called *Pai Shih
Ch'iao* (White Stone Bridge). A short walk from here across
the fields in an easterly direction brings us to the *Wu T'a Ssŭ*
(Five Pagoda Temple). This is the common name ; the correct
official name is *Chên Chüeh Ssŭ* (Awaken to the Truth Temple).
It was built during the 1st year of the Ming Emperor Ch'êng
Hua (1465). The records state that in that year a Hindu
named Pantita arrived in Peking with gifts for the Emperor
consisting of five golden Buddhas and a model of Buddha's
Diamond Throne in Central India where Sakyamuni attained
to Buddhahood. In return the Emperor bestowed on him
a golden seal together with the title *Ta Kuo Shih* (Great State
Bodhisattva), as also this plot of ground on which to build a
temple.

The massive square foundation, called by the Chinese
Pao Tso (Throne), has a distinctly Indian style of architecture.
It is fifty Chinese feet in height ; the sides are decorated with
rows of Buddhas ; whilst on the flat roof stand five pagodas.
The original staircase having completely disappeared you
ascend to the top by means of a ladder provided by a self-
appointed guardian against a small payment.

The central pagoda has imprints of Buddha's feet in hollow
relief, emblematical of his many wanderings during which his
feet became festered. There is a peculiarity about these imprints,
which are of stone let into the brick pagoda, that even on the
hottest day they are quite cool to the touch. This is ascribed to
their supernatural origin. The pagoda next on the east is

symbolical of Buddha's body, that on the same side represents
the place where Buddha's mother mourned for him after his
death. The pagoda on the west indicates the spot where
his body was kept for seven days prior to burial, the other
on that side is symbolical of his feet. With the exception of
the central pagoda, they are all inscribed with the sutras in
Sanskrit.

All the buildings were repaired under Ch'ien Lung, but
the original temple which stood in front of the Pao Tso have
completely disappeared, together with seven marble tablets
inscribed by seven famous scholars. The superstitious claim
that the fact of the " Throne " not having fallen into ruins is
proof of the sacredness of Buddha's immortal remains, of
which it is symbolical.

About a mile west of here, lying on the north bank of
the canal, is *Wan Shou Ssŭ* (Temple of a Myriad Ages). It
was built in 1577 by the Emperor Wan Li's favourite eunuch
Fêng Pao and is one of the finest and best preserved temples
in Peking. In former times the famous bell now in the Ta
Chung Ssŭ hung here. It was the favourite resting-place of
Tz'ŭ Hsi and the Emperor Kuang Hsü when they went to and
from the Summer Palace. In the eastern courtyard is a huge
pile of rocks from which the Empress-Dowager and the Emperor
used to view the surroundings. Within the temple is a *pei* or
stone tablet by Chang Chü-chêng, Grand Secretary under the
Ming Emperor Lung Ch'ing, whose tutor he had been. He
crushed the faction under Fêng Pao (who built this temple).
Although the Emperor Wan Li highly esteemed him and
loaded him with honours, yet in 1584 he took away all his titles
and confiscated his property on the grounds that he was arrogant
and too fond of engrossing power. There is also a *pei* by Ch'ien
Lung recording the history of the temple in Chinese, Manchu,
Mongolian and Tibetan script. Each year from the 1st to
the 15th of the Fourth Moon a fair is held in the temple, when
it is crowded with worshippers.

A short distance to the north-east of the Wu T'a Ssŭ is the
Chi Lo Ssŭ (Temple of Supreme Happiness). It was built in
the 1st year of the Mongol Emperor Chih Yüan (1260), and
repaired during the reign of the Ming Emperor Ch'êng Hua
(1466). In the courtyard is a small pagoda said to have been

erected by a monk, Yün Lang, and therefore called *Yün Lang Ho Shang T'a* (Pagoda of the Monk Yün Lang). There is also a stone tablet with an inscription extolling the beauties of the temple and its surroundings, written by Yen Sung, the chief of the " Six Wicked Ministers " of the Ming dynasty, but also the finest penman of those times. It seems to be a habit of wicked officials to try and condone for their sins and, at the same time, display their superior erudition and calligraphy, by endowing monasteries and temples with their masterpieces. Another tablet is by the famous minister of state, Yeh Hsiang-kao, lauding the flowers and other beautiful things, written in the 3rd year of the Ming Emperor T'ien Ch'i (1623). Yeh was of quite a different type from Yen Sung, and as he saved many good men from the vengeance of the execrated eunuch Wei Chung-hsien, he was driven from office by the eunuchs.

During the reign of Ch'ien Lung the temple was a favourite resort in the Fourth Moon for sightseers to view the blossoms of the *Hai T'ang* (Mules Floribunda), and other species which grew there in abundance. The place has now gone completely to ruin and is seldom visited.

About a quarter of a mile north of the Chi Lo Ssŭ, not far from the road to the Summer Palace, we come to the *Ta Hui Ssŭ* (Temple of Supreme Wisdom). It is usually referred to as the *Ta Fo Ssŭ* (Big Buddha Temple) from the huge copper idol of Buddha, fifty feet high, enshrined there. The temple was built in 1513 under the supervision of Chang Hsiung, the favourite eunuch of the Ming Emperor Chia Ching. In 1548 it was reconstructed and several halls were added. There are two tablets in the courtyard, one by the Minister, Li Tung-yang, and one by Li Sui, President of the Board of Works, recording the history of the temple from the time it was built down to 1592. In that year it was repaired and further enlarged by the Emperor Wan Li. In 1757 Ch'ien Lung had the copper idol patched, as it had lost some of its fingers and toes.

About one mile north of here across the road leading to the Summer Palace, lies the *Ta Chung Ssŭ* (Great Bell Temple), the official name of which is *Chüeh Shêng Ssŭ* (Awakened to a Sense of our former Existence). The huge bell in this temple was cast by the Taoist magician, Yao Kuang-hsiao, who persuaded the

Prince of Yen to ascend the throne as Emperor Yung Lo in 1402, and who three years later became Junior Tutor to the Heir Apparent. The famous bell is fifteen Chinese feet in height, fourteen feet across at the lower rim, thirty feet at its greatest circumference, and eight inches thick. It is inscribed on the inner and outer face with the Buddhist sutras written by Shên Tu, Sub-Chancellor of the Grand-secretariat under Yung Lo. Its actual weight is 87,000 catties, or 116,000 pounds. The bell used to hang in the Wan Shou Ssŭ, having been transported from there on massive hardwood rollers in the 8th year of Ch'ien Lung (1743). Inside the top of the bell hangs a brass cymbal at which visitors cast coppers through two small holes in the sides. It is believed that, if anyone makes a wish when throwing the copper and then succeeds in hitting the cymbal so as to make it give forth a sound, the wish will be fulfilled. A fair is held at the temple from the 1st to 15th of the First Moon, when thousands of men, women and children climb to the top of the bell-tower, in order to obtain a good view of the city. It is well worth visiting at that time.

CHAPTER XVIII

THE WESTERN SUBURBS

LEAVING the Tartar City by the south-west gate, the Shun Chih Mên, we turn west along the motor-road that runs parallel with the moat, and proceed out of the Chinese City by the *Hsi Pien Mên* (West Wicket Gate). From here we turn sharply down the paved slope on the left and in less than half a mile come to the *Po* (or *Pai*) *Yün Kuan* (White Cloud Temple), a Taoist sanctuary. The oldest part of this temple stands on the site of a T'ang dynasty structure that was repaired under the Chins in 1192, and lay inside the city of that day. It was rebuilt by Genghis Khan of the Mongol Dynasty, under the name of *T'ai Chi Kung*. (Chinese philosophers speak of the origin of all created things as T'ai Chi.) The famous Taoist priest, Ch'iu Ch'ang-ch'un, better known by his religious name of Ch'u Chi, lived in this temple. Upon his death here in 1227, at the age of eighty, a disciple, Yin Chih-p'ing changed the name to the present one. The fourth hall is dedicated to the memory of Ch'u Chi, whose portrait is still to be seen and whose remains are buried under the pavement in front of the altar.

The temple was repaired in the 27th year of Hung Wu (1394) by his son, the Prince of Yen, who was governor of the North, with his residence at Peking, thus showing incidentally that he was interested in Peking long before he ascended the throne as Emperor Yung Lo. In 1756 Ch'ien Lung had extensive repairs made to the temple and presented the monks with a large number of idols, amongst them that of the Taoist "Pope," Chang Tao-ling. In front of the altar to Ch'u Chi is a huge alms-bowl, said to hold no less than 140 pounds of rice, made out of the solid knob of a tree. It has an ivory tablet inscribed with verses by Ch'ien Lung himself, each character of which is filled with gold.

On the 19th of the First Moon vast throngs of people visit the temple, when Ch'u Chi's portrait is paraded for all to see. Beneath the marble bridge in the main courtyard a large bronze cash is suspended, with one of the temple priests sitting cross-legged behind it. Visitors throw coppers at the cash and are assured of good fortune, if they succeed in hitting it. As the bronze cash is so hung that it is very difficult indeed to hit, and as all the coppers go to fill the temple coffers, the priests make quite a good thing out of this harmless superstition.

On the night of the 19th the temple is crowded with visitors come to watch the arrival of the Eight Immortals who are supposed to descend from heaven about midnight. This festival is called *Yen Chiu Chieh* (the 9th day of the second decade of the " Moon Festival " of Peking), Yen being an ancient name for Peking. During the festivities, which actually last from the 1st to 19th, there used to be held in the road immediately west of the temple trotting races for men and cart races for women ; and a veritable orgy of gambling succeeded a few days of religious worship. In former days the fashionable society of the capital attended these races, in which even Manchu princes and nobles did not consider it beneath their dignity to take part. The races often led to violent brawls and clan fights. In recent times they have been given up, and nowadays the merry-making is restricted to the ordinary temple fair.

About a quarter of a mile to the south of the Po Yün Kuan can be seen a fine pagoda. It lies in the grounds of the *T'ien Ning Ssŭ* (Temple of Heavenly Peace), the entrance to which is on the south side. It is a very ancient site indeed, as it was first built during the reign of the Emperor Yen Hsing of the Northern Wei dynasty in A.D. 472 under the name of *Kuang Ling Ssŭ* (Temple of Buddha's Halo). The temple was repaired and the name changed under the Sui, T'ang and Chin dynasties. In Chin times it actually stood within the city of those days. It was completely destroyed by fire in 1367 during the fighting, in which the Mings overthrew the Mongols. The Ming Emperor Hsüan Tê rebuilt it in 1427 under the name of *Yüan Ning Ssŭ* (Heavenly Peace Temple). Extensive repairs were made to it in 1445 by his successor Chêng T'ung, and the name once more altered to *Kuang Shan Chieh T'an* (Warning Altar of Great Mercy), as a reminder to the monks of their vows or the Ten Buddhist Commandments. Ch'ien Lung repaired the temple at considerable cost in 1756

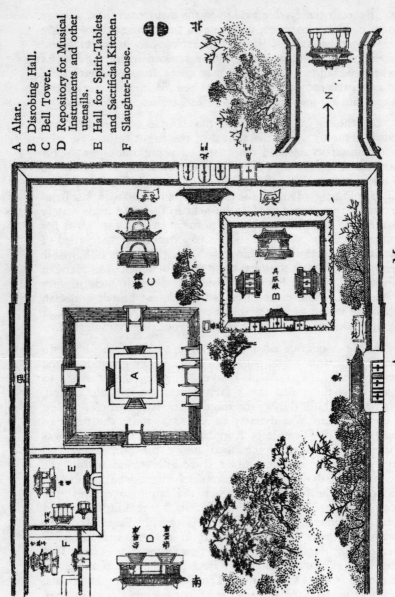

A Altar.
B Disrobing Hall.
C Bell Tower.
D Repository for Musical Instruments and other utensils.
E Hall for Spirit-Tablets and Sacrificial Kitchen.
F Slaughter-house.

20. ALTAR OF THE MOON

and finally changed the name to the present one. The *Po Yün T'a* (White Cloud Pagoda), which stands in the northern courtyard, a pagoda of thirteen storeys, covered with carvings of the Sung period representing different scenes from Buddhist mythology, holds a colossal Buddha. To its eaves there used to be suspended no less than 3,400 little bells with clappers which, when the wind was in the right direction, could be heard a mile away ; they have now mostly disappeared.

Returning to the road running north from the Hsi Pien Mên we come in about a quarter of a mile to the BRITISH CEMETERY. It dates from the early 'seventies of the last century. At the east end of the main avenue is a monument to four of the victims of 1860 who were captured at the same time as Parkes and Loch and who died of ill-treatment : Messrs. Bowlby, Phipps, Anderson and de Norman. Their remains were first interred in the Russian cemetery outside the An Ting Mên, where there is still a memorial stone giving full details (Chapter XVII), but were transferred here, when this cemetery was opened. There are also the graves of about a dozen persons who fell in the Siege in 1900. The cemetery was completely destroyed by the Boxers in that year, the coffins dug up, the bodies thrown out, and the tombstones broken up. Under the terms of the Protocol the Chinese government had to restore it to its former condition. The Latin inscription on the south side of the mortuary chapel says in terse but pointed language : " The mortuary chapel having been impiously destroyed by wicked persons in 1900 was rebuilt at the expense of the Imperial Chinese Government."

About a mile further on the left (west) side of the road, we come to the ALTAR OF THE MOON (*Hsi Yüeh T'an*). It lies about a third of a mile south of the road leading to the P'ing T'sê Mên. It was erected in the same year as the Altar of the Sun (Chapter XIX), in the 9th year of the Ming Emperor Chia Ching (1530), on an almost exactly similar plan, except that the wall round this altar was square, and the symbolical colour white.

Outside the north entrance stands a high *p'ai lou* bearing the characters *Li Shên Fang* (Portal to the Worship of the Moon Spirit). The entrance was by a triple gateway on the north side. To the west of it lay the Bell Tower and to the east the Hall where the Emperor changed his robes (*Chü Fu Tien*). Towards the centre was a low square wall, covered with white tiles, and pierced by a triple archway on the east, and a single archway on the other three sides. Inside this wall was the altar forty-four Chinese feet square and four and a half high, to which a flight of steps gave access on each of the four sides. In the south-west corner was the *Shên K'u*, where the spirit-tablet of the Moon was kept and the *Shên Ch'u* where the sacrificial animals were cooked. Adjoining this was the slaughter-house (*Tsai Shêng T'ing*), and to the east against the south wall were the *Chi Ch'i K'u* and *Yüeh Ch'i K'u* in which the sacrificial utensils and musical instruments were kept.

The ceremony took place on the Autumn Festival, *Li Ch'iu* (Beginning of Autumn), on the 18th of the Eighth Moon (about the beginning of August), at ten o'clock in the evening. As in the case of the sacrifices to the Sun, it was performed on alternate years by the Emperor himself. Dressed in white robes the Emperor ascended the altar from the east, in which direction the tablet of the Moon-Goddess was facing. Unlike the Sun she had participators in the sacrifice, namely the tablets of the Pole-star, of the twenty-eight main constellations, of the seven planets, and of the rest of the firmament. These tablets faced south and were covered over with an awning of white cloth. The symbolical gem used in the sacrifice was also white.

In recent times the whole enclosure has been converted into a kind of open-air school, and the buildings are now used as dormitories or class-rooms.

From the Altar of the Moon we proceed west along the main road that leads from the P'ing Tsê Mên. About a hundred yards beyond the railway crossing on the north side of the road is the *Tz'ŭ Hui Ssŭ* (Temple of Spiritual Wisdom). This is popularly known as the *Tao Ying Miao* (Temple of the Inverted Shadow), because low down in the door at the back of the main hall is a small hole, through which the shadow of a person standing or passing outside appears upside down (on the principle of the camera obscura). The temple was built in the 19th year of the Ming Emperor Wan Li (1591) by a eunuch at the command of the Empress-Dowager Tz'ŭ Shêng, as is recorded on one of the numerous stone tablets standing in the main courtyard.

The most interesting object, from a legendary point of view, is the small white stupa on the left-hand side in the front court-yard, called *Chih Chu T'a* (Spider Pagoda). A Buddhist priest named Yü An who was studying the Diamond Sutra on this spot, was constantly disturbed by a spider that climbed up the legs of the table and sat down beside him. Unlike Miss Muffet of the nursery rhyme, the priest was not frightened away, as the spider behaved with the greatest courtesy and kept constantly bowing to him, ignoring all his efforts to drive it off. This went on daily, until the priest had finished the whole of the Sutra, when the spider shed its envelope and disappeared. Yü An believing the insect to be the disembodied spirit of some famous Buddha, placed the envelope in a casket and buried it, erecting the stupa over it. There is a small tablet close by on which Yü An has recorded this story. At the back of the temple, to the north-west, was a cemetery called *Ching Lo T'ang* (Hall of Peaceful Joy) in which were buried the maid-servants and eunuchs of the Imperial concubines of the Ming Court.

Returning from the " Inverted Shadow Temple " towards the P'ing Tsê Mên and taking the last turning on the north, just before the bridge across the moat, we come in less than a quarter of a mile to a road on the west side, called *Liu Kung Fên Hsieh Chieh* (Six Public Cemeteries Slanting Street). On the south side of this street will be noticed a series of alleyways laid out in regular rows like a camp; this was the CAMP OF THE RED BANNER of the Manchu Banner Corps (*Hung Ch'i Ying*) and is still known by that name. On the north side of this " Slanting Street " lies the Catholic Mission. The entrance is at the last gate in the high wall close to the railway track. These grounds are popularly known as *Ch'a La'rh*, from the palisade which used to stand here in former days. The Mission, originally that of the Jesuits (Portuguese), is now a school of the Marist Brothers (French) and contains the CATHOLIC CEMETERY in which many famous missionaries were buried.

The site was originally presented to the Jesuits by the Emperor Wan Li in 1610 as a burial-place for Matteo Ricci. Here stood, at the time of the latter's decease, a Buddhist temple erected by a Palace eunuch called Yang, who had recently been condemned to death and whose property had therefore been confiscated. The Jesuit missionaries petitioned the Emperor for this site which was granted to them in spite of the opposition of the eunuchs. The temple was torn down and its materials used for building a mortuary on which were engraved the two characters *Ch'in Tz'ŭ* (Imperial Order). Up to about 1704 the other Jesuit missionaries who died in Peking were buried to the south of Ricci's tomb. Meanwhile, in 1666, the piece of ground immediately adjoining on the west, by special order of the Emperor K'ang Hsi, was converted into a separate cemetery for the Jesuit missionary, Adam Schaal, who was a special favourite of his. After 1708 the two portions were joined together, and the main avenue was moved to the centre between the two. This cemetery remained in the hands of the Catholics until they were finally driven out of Peking under Tao Kuang. It was then transferred to the care of the Russian Mission, who handed it over to the French missionaries after the treaty of 1860. In the troubles of 1900 the cemetery was completely wrecked by the Boxers who dug up the corpses, scattered the bones, destroyed the tumuli, and broke the gravestones in pieces, some of which, as can be seen, have been joined together again. Under the terms of the Protocol, the cemetery was repaired at the expense of the Chinese Government, but was never restored to its former beautiful and impressive appearance.

The small shrine standing on a raised terrace at the north end was erected to the memory of the martyrs of the Boxer year. The three large tombstones to the right (east) of it are those of: (1) The Dutch Jesuit, Adam Schaal, who had been tutor to the Emperor K'ang Hsi; (2) In the centre the tombstone with gilt lettering—a recent renovation—that of Matteo Ricci and (3) On the right the celebrated Belgian, Ferdinand Verbiest, the Astronomer-Royal of K'ang Hsi and the reformer of the Imperial Calendar. He died in 1688 and was buried with almost princely honours, the Emperor himself subscribing Taels 700 towards the burial expenses and deputing his own father-in-law and five high Court officials to represent him at the ceremony.

The church to the south was erected after 1900. Let into its walls are various tombstones which formerly stood in the old cemetery. Amongst those on the north side is that

of Joseph Castiglione (Lang Shih-ning), the famous Court
painter of the Emperor Ch'ien Lung.

The plan (overleaf) shows the cemetery as it was at the
end of the 17th century. The following is a description of
the old cemetery by Dr. Rennie (" Peking and the Pekingese ")
who visited it in 1861 :

" At the end of this avenue is the entrance to the cemetery,
which consists of a massive gate of solid marble in one large
slab" (This original gateway can still be seen from the road
outside). " On entering the cemetery a pathway is seen running up the centre, and at the end of it, in the distance, a marble
crucifix surmounting an altar of the same material, reached
by a flight of marble steps. On the right of the entrance is
a large and elaborate monument to Francis Xavier, who died
in 1736. In front of this the ground has been recently disturbed.
It was here that the French prisoners who died in the hands
of the Chinese in 1860 were originally interred. Their
remains have since been removed to the old French cemetery,
about seven miles to the westward of Peking. On the left
of the entrance there is a monument of similar design, erected
in 1745 in honour of the second centenary of the Jesuit mission
in Peking. The cemetery is oblong, and all the graves are
covered in by arched-roofed sarcophagi. They are arranged
in eight rows of ten in each, five graves of every row being
on each side of the central avenue. In front of every grave is
a tombstone placed at a little distance from the sarcophagus,
but the greater the distance, in like proportion is the honour.
The tomb of the celebrated Matthew Ricci stands on the right-
hand side, at the extreme end of the cemetery, near the altar.
It is a sarcophagus of the same shape as the others, and in front
of it there is an oblong monumental stone of marble, about
ten feet high, standing on a marble tortoise, the latter indicating
it to be an Imperial gift. It bears an inscription in Latin and
Chinese. On each side of the extremity of the avenue near
the altar there are two similar monumental stones, also standing
on marble tortoises. The one on the right is in honour of
the equally celebrated Verbist, erected in 1688, and that on
the left is to the memory of a Portuguese Jesuit of the name
of Pereira. On the same side, a little in front, is the tomb of
Adam Shall, a Dutch Jesuit, erected by the Emperor K'ang-hsi,

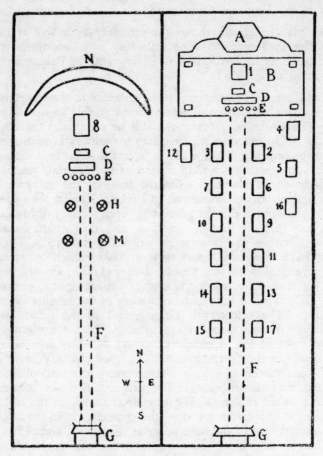

21. PLAN OF JESUIT CEMETERY AT END OF
THE 17TH CENTURY

(*According to Favier's " Péking "*)

A Hexagonal Chapel   F Avenue
B Terrace   G Gates
C Stone Tablet   H Stone Horses
D Stone Altar   M Stone Mandarins
E Stone Incense Burner, etc.   N Earth Mound

by whom he would seem to have been highly appreciated, from the distance in front of his grave that the monumental stone is placed. Near it is the tomb of another well-known man, Castilone, the painter who was employed for some years in decorating the palace. A dense vegetation surrounds the tombs, the whole of which are completely shaded from the sun by the rich foliage of the numerous trees that grow within the enclosure. Altogether I know no more interesting spot to visit in the neighbourhood of Peking than these curious relics of a bygone age."

In the old cemetery the tomb of Matteo Ricci was specially distinguished by the marble carving that stood in front of it, an altar with incense burner, candlesticks, and flower-jars, arranged in the order followed in all Buddhist temples. A few of the other graves, but only those near the north end—that is to say only the earlier ones—had this same ornamentation in front of them. This is historically interesting and significant.

Father Ricci had permitted his converts to retain the worship of ancestors and of Confucius among their rites; and after his death the Jesuits continued this liberal policy which powerfully aided the spread of the Catholic religion in China and brought in many converts who might otherwise not have joined the Church, especially amongst the educated classes and higher officials. Some time after Ricci's death the Dominicans strongly opposed this policy of the Jesuits. Violent dissensions broke out between the various missionary bodies which spread to the Court, so that already in the later days of K'ang Hsi the Catholics had fallen into disfavour. The dispute, known to history as "The Rites Controversy," was carried on for more than a century, greatly impairing the discipline

KEY

		died			died
1	Matteo Ricci, S.J.	1610	10	G. de Magalhaens, S.J.	1677
2	Jean Terenz, S.J.	1630	11	Louis Buglio, S.J.	1682
3	Jacques Rho, S.J.	1638	12	Ferdinand Verbiest, S.J.	1688
4	F. Christophor (Ch.), S.J.	1640	13	Francois Simois, S.J.	1694
5	F. Pascal Mendez (Ch.), S.J.	1640	14	Charles Dolzé, S.J.	1701
6	N. Longobardi, S.J.	1654	15	Louis Pernon, S.J.	1702
7	D. Coronatus (Franc.)	1666	16	F. Pierre Frapperie, S.J.	1703
8	Adam Schaal, S.J.	1666	17	C. de Broissia, S.J.	1704
9	E. de Sequeira (Ch.), S.J.	1673			

of the Church in China. In spite of repeated Papal decrees and special missions it was not finally settled until the issue of the Papal Bull *Ex Quo Singulari* in 1742, which definitely forbade every kind of Chinese rite and prescribed the form of oath of obedience to the Papal decrees on this question, that had to be taken by all the Catholic missionaries in China.

This decision had enormous effect in modifying the subsequent history of missions in China. From that moment commenced the persecution of the Catholics with the official sanction of the Emperor Yung Chêng, who made it a criminal charge against Christianity, that it interfered with the duty of paying honour to one's parents.

Although this decision undoubtedly stopped the flow of converts and greatly added to the difficulties of missionary work in China, it is now generally admitted that it was the only logical step to take. For if the more liberal policy of the Jesuits had been adhered to, it seems more than likely, that, with the Chinese facility for absorbing extraneous civilizations, Catholicism would in time have completely disappeared and been merged in some form of Chinese worship.

CHAPTER XIX

THE EASTERN SUBURBS

ABOUT a third of a mile outside the Ch'i Hua Mên, on the north side of the road, is a temple flanked by a pair of ornamental wooden *p'ai lou* and with a triple archway of green and yellow tiles facing the entrance. This is the famous Taoist temple, the *Tung Yüeh Miao* (Temple of the Eastern Peak), one of the most interesting places in Peking, in which are assembled many of the deities of the Chinese pantheon.

It is dedicated to Huang Fei Hu who, according to legend, rebelled against and killed the wicked tyrant Chou Hsin, the last of the kings of the Shang dynasty, who was infamous for his terrible cruelties. For this action which brought peace to the empire, Huang Fei Hu was deified as the supreme god of the sacred mountain T'ai Shan in Shantung. He is also called *T'ien Ch'i* (Equal to Heaven), because the T'ai Shan itself is considered equal to Heaven. Construction on the temple was started under the Mongol Emperor Yen Yu, at the request of his tutor Chang Liu-shun ; it took eight years to build and was completed in 1329.

Huang Fei Hu's birthday falls on the 28th day of the Third Moon, but the festivities usually take place from the 15th to the 28th, on which day the Emperors used to depute high officials to burn incense at his shrine. A fair is held here on the 1st and 15th of both the Chinese and foreign months which is attended by large crowds of worshippers who come to pay their devotions to the particular deity favoured by them. Thousands of bundles of incense-sticks are burnt, garlands of artificial flowers are placed before the shrines, and paper sheets stamped with coins in the shape of cash offered up—the popular mind attributing to its deities the same desire for wealth as exists amongst mortals. Many of the spirits are consulted by drawing lots, and worshippers armed with feather dusters may be seen performing the pious task of clearing away the dust and cobwebs that have accumulated during the year, not only from the furniture, but also from the gods and goddesses themselves.

The chief centre of interest is the second courtyard in which stands the main temple and around the sides of which run rows of small cubicles open to the front except for a wooden railing. Each of these cubicles contains an idol—sometimes two— representing some form of human activity or force of Nature. To enumerate a few of the more important : there are the tutelary deities of the seas, mountains, rivers, rain, thunder and light- ning ; the guardian spirits of birds and domestic animals, of commerce, official rank, riches, literature ; and those that control both good and bad deeds, often a separate spirit for each deed. In all there are seventy-two such deities called *Ssŭ* (Chiefs of Departments). In front of them, on either side, stand subordinate spirits or demons, sometimes shown in the act of punishing or leading off a sinner. Not all these spirits enjoy the same popularity. As can be seen, the cells of the more popular, that is the more powerful, are decorated with wooden votive tablets or streamers of yellow cloth bearing the words " Pray and you will be heard," and similar testimonials, the presents of grateful supplicants. The cells of these more important deities have sometimes been expanded into small temples, which is the case, for instance, with those of Wealth, Birth, Long Life, Official Promotion and others.

As we pass into this courtyard through the side gate on the right we shall notice hanging on the wall a large *suan- p'an* (abacus) with the characters *Hao Li Pu Shuang* (Without the Slightest Error). It is intended as a warning to the entering worshippers that their smallest faults will not escape a reckoning. Turning to the right along the south verandah, the first cubicle next to the door is that of the warrior Yüeh Fei ; the figure on the right being led away by a demon is the traitor minister Ch'in K'uei. (See Ching Chung Miao, Chapter XVI). In the south-east corner is the *Ch'ang Shou Ssŭ*, the spirit controlling age, and therefore the deity to be worshipped in order to ensure a long life. Turning north along the east verandah we come to the *Fang Shêng Ssŭ* (Spirit who lets loose living things), a kind of Inspector of the Cruelty to Animals Society, from whom one can obtain good marks by setting free caged birds, or even fish. In the middle of the east verandah is a large shrine, expanded into a temple, to the twin gods of Wealth, the *Wên Wu Ts'ai Shên* (Civil and Military Spirits of Riches) who are, needless to say, much patronized. On each side stand eighteen subordinate deities representative of the different forms of wealth. The fourth cubicle from the north end on the east side contains another very popular spirit—as can be seen from the numerous votive tablets adorning the walls— the God of Official Promotion.

Ignoring the main temple for a moment and continuing our tour of the cubicles, the second large cubicle on the north side to the west of the temple is that of Huang Fei Hu's son. Turning along the west verandah, the sixth cubicle contains the Spirit of Plagues and Boils. One of the attendant figures on the left has, it will be noticed, broken out into boils and looks a horrid sight covered with paper plasters. The big red hall in the centre is that of the Goddess of Birth and her husband. Small plaster dolls, the offerings of worshippers desirous of obtaining offspring, lie scattered about in front of the altar, whilst two huge demons, with anything but pleasing faces, are carrying bundles of babies (literally) which they are to deliver at the addresses indicated to them by the Goddess. Turning east along the south verandah, the last cell just before the gate is that of *Hsien Pao Ssŭ*, a kind of Lost and Stolen Property Office. This deity has two functions : one to punish thieves and those unable to distinguish between meum and tuum, and the other to restore lost or stolen articles to those who apply for his good services. This is performed by means of drawing lots of numbered thin slips of bamboo. Outside this cell there stands a rickety chest-of-drawers containing printed slips corresponding to the numbers on the lots with very rough directions of how to find the missing article.

On the north side of the courtyard is the main temple, the *T'ien Ch'i Tien* (Hall of Him Who is equal to Heaven), in which is enshrined Huang Fei Hu who acts as a kind of Rhadamanthus meting out rewards and punishments to mortals, in accordance with the reports received from the other spirits. He is therefore the chief object of worship and has the largest crowd of suppliants, most of whom perform their devotions on the terrace outside, though the more wealthy are allowed inside for an extra fee and may thus hope to obtain a more favourable hearing. In many cases worshippers consult the god on their private affairs by means of lots.

The God of Literature (*Wên Ch'ang*) shares the sanctum with the God of the T'ai Shan—which accounts for the rows of tables with blank writing-books, writing brushes, and plaster models of ink-slabs.

As even deities must conform to popular custom, Huang Fei Hu is naturally a married man, but as further according to custom he does not wish to appear in public with his wives, the two ladies are relegated to a special temple at the back where they sit with five hand-maidens on either side to wait on them, but otherwise totally neglected.

The two pavilions in the centre of the courtyard contain stone tablets dated the 17th year of K'ang Hsi (1678) which record the history of the temple in Chinese and Manchu. The other numerous stone tablets are inscribed with lists of names of admirers and religious societies which have subscribed towards the upkeep and repair of the temple.

Behind the main temple are two courtyards. In the smaller one, on the south and east side, is the *Chêng I Tien* (Straight and Only Hall) containing three idols. In the centre is *T'ien Shih* (The Heavenly Master); on the left is *Yao Wang* (King of Medicine) with a boy standing on either side, one holding a bundle of prescription books and the other a medicinal herb; on the right is Confucius, also with two pupils, one holding a set of books and the other with writing materials.

Passing into the larger and northern courtyard we come to the *Hsi Shên Tien* (Hall of the Spirit of Joy) who is worshipped by actors. In a room on either side are six wooden tablets— and one under the altar itself—making the Thirteen Tones (*Shih San Yin*) which are used in the drama.

Adjoining this room is the popular shrine of *Wên Ch'ang* (The God of Literature) with the famous jade-white horse (*Yü Ma*), that he rode on all his journeys, on the right, and a bronze mule (*T'ung Lotzü*) on the left. Of the two animals which are the chief attraction of this shrine, the bronze mule is the more popular, as can be seen from the way he has been polished bright by innumerable strokings of the faithful. It is believed that, if you stroke either of these animals, you will keep in good health or, alternatively, if you are sick, will be cured, and that the effect will be more certain, if you touch the animal on the same part of the body where you are suffering.

Further west, behind and directly in line with the main temple, is another building with a varied collection of deities. Immediately on the left of the door is a shrine with a small figure. This is Old Mother Wang (*Wang Ma Ma*). She is dressed in a blue gown, wears in her hair a pomegranate flower, and holds in her hand a large spoon. In front of her stands a tub supposed to contain water mixed with sugar (but the tub is always empty) called *Mi Hun T'ang* (Broth that confuses the Souls). It is believed that the moment a person dies, the soul flies direct to the old woman from whom it receives a spoonful of this broth which makes it forget its existence in this world. As Mother Wang is kept pretty busy handing out doses to the numerous souls that are coming to her all the time, it occasionally happens that one of them misses its spoonful of broth. And as such a soul would then remember its experiences during its former existence and would thus be an exceptionally bright spirit in the next world, a common form of sarcasm for a person who is too smart is *Mei yu ho kuo mi hun t'ang* (He has not drunk the broth that confuses the souls).

Next we have the Nine Goddesses (*Chiu Wei Niang Niang*), nine identical idols in three groups of three each. The one in the centre of the left group is the Goddess of Smallpox; the lady on the right of the centre group looks after the eyesight of children, for which reason she is holding a spare set of eyes in her hands; whilst all three in the group on the right, one of whom is holding a child at her breast, are responsible for childbirth and its varying accompaniments.

In the storey above (up a very steep and rickety staircase) is the idol of *Yü Huang* (The Jade Emperor), a kind of Chinese Jupiter, who has the rare distinction of being both a Taoist and Buddhist deity. Away in a far corner is a small shrine to the *Ta Hsien Yeh* (Great Venerable Fairies). These are: fox, weasel, snake, hedgehog and rat, which animals are supposed to have power to exorcize evil spirits and protect the faithful. This particular shrine is worshipped by travellers and is very popular, as can be seen from the numerous votive strips hung on the wall by those who have returned safely from a dangerous journey.

In a courtyard on the west of the front entrance are some more interesting deities. Immediately on the right is a small shrine in which sits a benevolent-looking old gentleman with a long beard, with festoons of red threads hanging down in front of him. This is the God of Marriage, *Yüeh Hsia Lao Jên* (Old Man of the Moon). If a person is without a wife and has difficulty in finding a suitable match, his friends or relations come to this shrine and take away with them one of the red threads hanging there. This they then fasten secretly across a door or the person's bed, or even to the legs of a table or chair that he uses. If he unknowingly runs up against the thread and breaks it, he is assured of finding a suitable wife in the near future. This is known as *Ch'uang Hun Hsien* (Accidentally breaking the marriage thread). If the result is successful, he must not forget to show his gratitude by coming back and hanging up a new thread for the " Old Man of the Moon," as otherwise there would be none left for subsequent wife-seekers.

Further inside, on the south, is the Temple of Medicine. Here *Yao Wang* (King of Medicine) is enshrined flanked by ten venerable-looking persons, his assessors, the Ten Celebrated Physicians (*Shih Ming I*). There are also the idols of various Spirits of Epidemics and Disease, most unpleasant-looking demons—as well they may be. At the side are two cupboards containing medical prescriptions which are drawn for by lot by sick suppliants, after the usual burning of incense and prostrations. Presumably these deities can make no mistake in their diagnosis, as otherwise it might be awkward, were one to draw a prescription for some skin disease, when suffering from an internal complaint.

Close by is the *Yên Wang Tien*, containing the idol of the so-called King of Hades. Originally he was President of the First Court of Hell, but was degraded to the Fifth Court, because he showed too great leniency in allowing souls to return to life. Probably for this reason it is believed that he can still procure—for a consideration—a prolongation of your span of life, and he is therefore invoked by younger persons who have fallen sick. As there is a popular superstition that anyone who wastes salt thereby cuts short his span of life, the individual who is ill promises to give Yên Wang a quantity of salt—so

SPIRIT OF LONGEVITY

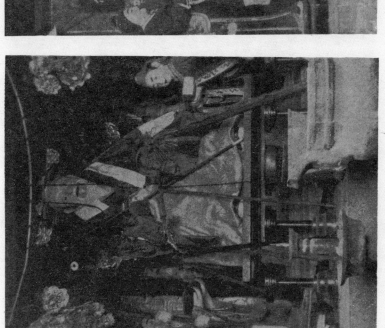

THE OLD MAN OF THE MOON

IDOLS IN THE TUNG YÜEH MIAO

many pounds for each year of life prolonged—if he recovers
from his sickness. If he does not recover, no salt is given;
the god has to go without it.

Finally we must not forget to mention the shrine of Lu
Pan whom we have come across so often in our search for
" Old Peking." He is the deity of the five crafts connected
with the building trade : carpenters, masons, bricklayers,
house-painters, and paper-hangers. His own temple is nowadays in rather a neglected and tumble-down condition, which
may perhaps be ascribed to the modern Trade Union representatives being jealous of his former activities.

A short distance from the Tung Yüeh Miao going west,
on the south side of the road, is a temple popularly known as
the *Shih Pa Yü Miao* (Temple of the Eighteen Hells). On
either side of the courtyard are crude sets of plaster figures
enacting the punishments meted out in the next world for
various crimes committed in this. Sawing in two between
boards, boiling in oil, tearing out tongues with red-hot pincers
are a few of the more striking pleasantries. Those who enjoy
horrors of this kind will find it worth a visit.*

To reach the ALTAR OF THE SUN (*Ch'ao Jih T'an*) we take
the road south immediately opposite the entrance of the Tung
Yüeh Miao. (*Ch'ao* here means " to worship " at the Sun
Altar, and not " facing," as it has sometimes been translated).
The entrance is from the west. At the north-west angle is
an imposing *p'ai lou* with the characters *Li Shên Fang* (Portal
to the Sun-Spirit Worship). The altar was built in the 9th
year of the Ming Emperor Chia Ching (1530), at the suggestion
of a Court astrologer who memoralized the Throne stating
that a man named Hsiao Ying had a piece of property 810
Chinese feet square which was just right for an altar to the
Sun and which he was willing to present to the Emperor.

The first pavilion on entering the enclosure, on the left
(north), is the *Chü Fu Tien* where the Emperor changed his
robes. Beyond it is the Bell Tower, and then the *Yüeh Ch'i
K'u, Chi Ch'i K'u*, and *Tsung Chin K'u*, in which were kept the
musical instruments, the sacrificial vessels, and the carpets and

*For a full description of these tortures See H. A. Giles " Strange
Stories from a Chinese Studio " (Appendix).

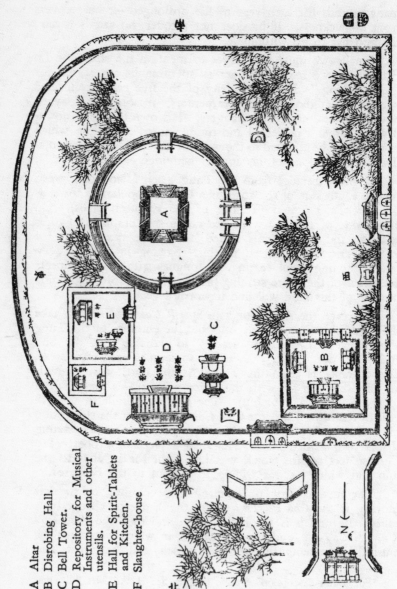

A Altar
B Disrobing Hall.
C Bell Tower.
D Repository for Musical
   Instruments and other
   utensils.
E Hall for Spirit-Tablets
   and Kitchen.
F Slaughter-house.

22. ALTAR OF THE SUN.

rugs. To the east is a compound with the *Tsai Shên T'ing*,
where the sacrificial animals were slaughtered, the *Shên K'u*
in which the spirit-tablet of the Sun was kept, the *Shên Ch'u*
where the sacrificial animals were cooked, and the *Têng K'u*,
Lamp room.

Towards the centre of the enclosure is a low red-tiled
ROUND wall, with a triple stone gateway on the west and a single
one at each of the other three sides. The altar itself is a low
square terrace surrounded by a marble balustrade and approached
by a flight of steps on each of the four sides. The tiles of the
enclosing wall are red, as was also the round gem that was
used as the symbol of the sun in the ceremony. The altar
is supposed to have a remarkable echo: if anyone stands on the
centre stone of the terrace and utters a word or sentence in
an explosive tone, a distinct echo is said to come up from the
ground below one's feet.

The sacrifices took place on the 15th of the Second Moon,
the Spring Festival, *Li Ch'un* (Beginning of Spring), about
two hours before sunrise. They were performed on alternate
years by the Emperor and by officials deputed by him in the
intervening year. The tablet of the Sun was placed on the
eastern side of the terrace facing west, from which side the
Emperor ascended the altar.

Most of the buildings in this enclosure having, as usual,
been occupied by soldiery are fast going to ruin.

About a mile outside the Tung Chih Mên is the IRON
PAGODA (*T'ieh T'a*), an octagonal brick structure about thirty
feet high and twelve feet across, surmounted by a small iron
pagoda. Enshrined at the foot of the latter is a miniature idol
of Kuan Yin. This turret-like edifice was originally called
Hsiao Yao Ch'êng (City of Transcendental Bliss), because Kao
Hsü, Prince of Han, the second son of Yung Lo, was roasted to
death here. For many years his charred skeleton could be seen
in a recess at the rear of the ground floor. But in recent times
it has been covered with plaster and draped in a yellow robe,
making quite a handsome-looking prince.

According to the story—which is historical,—Kao Hsü
who was an expert archer and cavalry leader and always in the
forefront of the battles during his father's successful rebellion,
aspired to succeed him. He was, however, disappointed in

these hopes by the appointment in 1404 of another prince as
Heir Apparent.   This was the result of the misrepresentations
of his enemies, especially the eunuchs, so that, for the rest of
Yung Lo's reign, he took every opportunity of attacking them
and the Heir Apparent.

His father, discovering that, while he was away on an
expedition against A-lu-t'ai in 1417, Kao Hsü had started a
rising in Nanking, wanted to degrade him.   But through the
intervention of his elder brother the punishment was commuted
to banishment to Lo-an in Shantung.   There, on the accession
of his nephew Hsüan Tê in 1426, Kao Hsü raised the standard
of rebellion.   The new Emperor hastened to the scene in person
and by means of his artillery suppressed the rising.   Kao Hsü
was forced to surrender, brought back to Peking in chains, and
taken to this spot, where he was placed in a huge cauldron and
roasted to death.

Each year during the 8th, 9th, and 10th day of the Fourth
Moon a fair is held within the pagoda grounds, when incense
is burnt before the remains of this prince whose tragic death
is thus still kept in memory even at the present day.

CHAPTER XX.

" WINE, WOMEN AND SONG"

THE Chinese are hedonists par excellence. This accounts for their good temper and their habit of always looking on the bright side of things, no matter how afflicted they may be, rich and poor alike. Their hedonism is a practical combination of egoism, in that the supreme aim of the individual is to enjoy the good things of this life, and of altruism, in so far as the right of everyone to enjoy himself in his own way is admitted absolutely and without question. As a result, the Chinese have developed one of the most tolerant social systems that anybody can desire.

The rickshaw-man can ring his bell, the chauffeur toot his horn, the hawker cry his wares on the street at all hours of the day and night. Private theatricals raise a perfect pandemonium until the early hours of the morning, whilst the racket kept up at Chinese dinner-parties by the " morra " players, the high shrill voices of the sing-song girls, and the discordant notes of the various musical instruments is something that must be heard to be believed. No one minds it in the least. Sidewalks are crowded with rickshaws, hawkers and their stands ; carts and camels block the pedestrian's road ; cyclists (without lights, despite police regulations) rush to and fro to the danger of life and limb ; motor-cars dash at breakneck speed through the crowded streets, often without lights, others with only one light; rickshaws, cars, and carriages obstruct the street crossings, the guardian of the law standing idly by and making no attempt to clear the traffic.

Yet no one ever dreams of making the slightest complaint. It is all taken as part of the day's work, on the principle of letting the other fellow enjoy himself as he likes. Indeed, nothing less than a revolution, riot, or an attack of bandits is considered here the equivalent of our " disturbance of the peace."

Everybody, except the fussy foreigner, takes all this for granted ; and no one is seemingly a penny the worse for it. Time and noise simply do not count.

Nevertheless, though the Chinese may appear to us strangely indifferent to the, perhaps passive, pleasures of quiet, order and comfort, they certainly show a keen enough appreciation of the more active ones, such as the palate, love, and the drama.

And of the three the first is to them by far the most important, so much so that the western quotation which we have taken as title to this chapter would scarcely be appreciated by the Chinese who would rather put it : " Eating, Women, and Song." In fact, the Chinese equivalent of our greeting " How do you do ? " is " Have you had your food ? " If ever, by chance, you are desirous of avoiding an interview, or wish to break one off, it is no good claiming a prior engagement. A Minister Plenipotentiary, a Prince, or even a lady friend, would appear to be no valid excuse in the eyes of a Chinese. All you need say is *Wo hai mei yu ch'ih fan* (I have not yet had my meal), and all is forgiven, everything is understood.

It is therefore not strange that the Chinese who so wisely attach this importance to the simple pleasure of eating should have brought the preparation of their food to a fine art unequalled by any other people in the world. It is no exaggeration to say that Chinese dishes can be reckoned, not in hundreds, but in thousands. Each province, nay even each city, has its own peculiar way of preparing certain dishes. Peking too has its own specialities, as we shall note below, but Peking is famous for more than that. It is, or rather we should say it was, the Mecca of all the gourmets of the Chinese Empire. As it had been the capital for so many centuries to which flocked vast numbers of officials from every part of China— not to mention the thousands of students from the provinces for the Triennial Examinations—it naturally contained restaurants to suit every possible taste. In Peking there are even to-day over a thousand restaurants. Nowadays, it is true, Peking is but a shadow of its former self, but the tradition of good living still exists ; and in some of the older restaurants it is still possible to get a really first-class Chinese dinner in the old style.

1.—RESTAURANTS

We herewith submit a list of some of the better-known restaurants with the dishes for which they particularly cater.

IN THE EAST CITY:

Tung Hsing Lou (Eastern Prosperity House). On the north side of the Tung An Mên Ta Chieh. Shantung style. First established during the reign of Tao Kuang (1830) under the name of *Chiu Ho Hsing*. Their present chef used to cook for the late Empress-Dowager. Specialities are: fish; mandarin duck; eggs in various ways; and white fungus.

Fu Shou T'ang (Hall of Happy Old Age). In the Chin Yü Hutung, opposite the north entrance of the Tung An Market. Shantung style. Established eighty years. The late Empress-Dowager used to favour the food prepared by this restaurant, but her chief eunuch, the infamous An Tê-hai, recommended the Tung Hsing Lou instead (probably because he received a "squeeze"). Specialities: birds' nests; shark fins; Peking duck; sea-slugs; pork, Soochow style.

I Ya I (The First in Asia). In the Pa Mien Ts'ao Hutung, continuation of Morrison Street. Cantonese style. Specialities: awabi, a shell-fish, boiled or fried in lard (a sumptuous dish); fish cooked in bean-curd "grains"; duck soup with native wine.

Yü Hua T'ai (Restaurant of Rich and Fine Viands). In the Hsi La Hutung, off Morrison Street. Yangchow style. Specialities: *kan pei* (scallops); shrimps; and perch.

OUTSIDE CH'IEN MEN:

Chih Mei Chai (House of Exquisite Beauty). On the west side of the Mei Shih Chieh. Shantung style. Established one hundred years. Specialities: large shrimps; finely ground turnip cakes; several varieties of mushrooms; chicken.

Fu Hsing Chü (Happy Prosperity House). On the north side of the Kuan Yin Ssŭ Ta Chieh. Shantung style. Specialities: various kinds of fish cooked in wine; winter bamboo shoots; *kan pei* (dried scallop).

Hou Tê Fu (Unbounded Virtue and Happiness). In the Ta Cha La. Peking style. Specialities: fish sliced and served with soy; bears' claws, boiled and served with various condiments.

Fêng Tsê Yüan (Fruitful Garden). On the west side of the Mei Shih Chieh. Peking style. Specialities : fat Peking duck steamed, with cabbage; fish lips fried in lard and served with soy.

Chêng Yang Lou (Facing the Sun House). In the Hsien Yü K'ou. Peking style. Specialities : crabs ; roasted meats ; scalded mutton.

Ch'üan Chu Tê (Accumulated Virtue). In the Hsien Yü K'ou. Peking style. First established in the reign of Ch'ien Lung. Speciality : roast Peking duck (very good indeed).

T'ai Fêng Lou (House of Abundant Peace). On the west side of the Mei Shih Chieh. Shantung style. Specialities : sheep tripe ; chicken blood.

Kung Tê Lin (Restaurant of Abundant Merit). On the north side of the Li T'ieh Kuai Hsieh Chieh. Peking style. This establishment specializes in lenten-fare (no meats of any kind), and is much patronized by various religious sects, and especially by monks and nuns.

IN THE WEST CITY :

Chung Hsin T'ang (Hall of the Loyal Heart). On the Hsi Ch'ang An Chieh. Foochow style. Established over a hundred years. The chef of this restaurant used to cook for the ex-emperor Hsüan T'ung who is now in Manchoukuo.

Ch'ien Yang Kuan (A literary name for Kueichow). On the Hsi Ch'ang An Chieh. Kueichow style. Old establishment. Specialities : *mo-p'o-tou-fu* (old pock-marked woman) consisting of a mixture of mushrooms, bean-curd, soft and dried, with red peppers ; mutton boiled in soy and native wine and a Japanese condiment.

Ta Lu Ch'un (Great Land of Happiness, i.e. China). On the south side of the Hsi Ch'ang An Chieh. Szechuan style. Speciality : *pan-san-ni*, a mixture of several kinds of beans and dates, made into a congee and sweetened with sugar (recommended for invalids).

Ch'ing Lin Ch'un (Prosperous Spring Forest). On the south side of the Hsi Ch'ang An Chieh. Szechuan style. Specialities : steamed chicken ; cooked turtle.

Tung Ya Ch'un (Mirthful East Asia). On the north side
of the Hsi Ch'ang An Chieh. Szechuan style. Specialities:
shredded ham, with sea-slugs and bamboo shoots; pork and
cabbage, mixed with mushrooms and bamboo shoots, and
rolled up in the rind of bean-curd; pork done up in balls, with
sea-slugs and bamboo shoots.

Hsin Lu Ch'un (New Great Land). On the south side of
the Hsi Ch'ang An Chieh. Szechuan style. Specialities:
chicken stewed in milk; pig's marrow boiled in pig's blood
(very good eating, especially for invalids).

Ch'ieh I (The Best of Everything). In the Jung Hsien
Hutung. Szechuan style. Specialities: cows' sinews, well-
boiled and served in soup; glutinous part of flour separated
in water, first fried in oil and then boiled in chicken and duck
soup (an excellent dish); young chicken cut very fine and
served with chilli peppers.

Jung Yüan (Hibiscus Flower Garden). In the Jung Hsien
Hutung. Szechuan style. Specialities: black fish-spawn boiled
in vinegar and red pepper; ham and eggs sliced and fried in
lard and stuffed with chicken (very tasty); *lu-wei-p'in-p'an*, a
mixture of ham, fresh pork, bamboo shoots, pigs' tripe, and
pigs' tongue, served with a thick gravy; fish gills and lips
made in to a clear soup.

Hsin Kuang Tung (New Canton House). In the Hsi Tan
Shih Ch'ang (Western Market). Cantonese style. Specialities:
boiled cows' sinews with bamboo shoots; dried salt meats
boiled with pork, bamboo shoots, pigs' tripe and tongue;
stuffed chicken (After the entrails have been removed it is stuffed
with various condiments and hung in the air for several months,
with feathers intact. When thoroughly dried the feathers and
the condiments are removed, and the chicken is stewed. Makes
very good eating) pigs' trotters roasted and boiled, served with
soy (highly recommended).

There are several Mohammedan restaurants called by the
Chinese *Yang Jou Kuan* (Mutton Houses) which serve chiefly
mutton and vegetables.

WINE.—Of Chinese wines there is not much good to be
said. In this respect it must be confessed that the Sons of
Han fall far behind us Westerners. The best quality wine is

called *Shaohsing* (also known as *Hua Tiao* or *Ch'in Shao*), a mellow, yellow-coloured wine, something like a very mild sherry, of which one can partake considerable quantities without suffering any serious effects, especially if taken hot. Another light wine is the kind called *Liang Hsiang* which comes from a place of that name in the province of Hopei. A very fiery, strong wine is that called *Kao Liang*, made from millet and mixed with pigeon-droppings to give it a good body. It is commonly known as *Shao Chiu* (Fired Spirits), but vulgarly as *Pai ka erh* (Pure Alcohol). Another, if possible stronger, kind is *Fên Chiu*, made in Fênchow in the province of Shansi. Foreigners not used to strong drink will do best to stick to *Shaohsing*. There are a few modern grape wines, from Shantung and Shansi, but they are very uninteresting, resembling our grape juice, rather than a proper wine.

2.—Singing Girls

The Chinese call a certain kind of woman *Chi Nü* (Joy Girl). The original meaning of *chi* was "women's trinkets," denoting something of small value—a mere trifle. The names of the demi-monde are interesting. For instance we have :

Yin Kuei (Silver Cassia Flower) ; *Chih T'ing* (Iris Pavilion) ; *Hsiang Yü* (Fragrant Jade) ; *Yen Wu Chai* (Beauty of the Five Continents) ; *Shui Hsien Hua* (Water-Spirit Flower, i.e., Narcissus) ; *Hsüeh O* (Snow Bug) ; *Yü Han* (Jade Lotus-bud) ; *Hsüeh T'ao* (Snow Peach) ; *Yü Fêng* (Jade Phœnix) ; *Hsiao Yün* (Little Cloud) ; *Yüeh Hsiang* (Moonlight Fragrance) ; *Hua Ssŭ Pao* (Flower of the Four Precious Arts, i.e., singing, playing "morra," music, and literature) ; and a hundred others.

It is to be noted that these so-called sing-song girls often change their abode and, when they do so, generally adopt a fresh "flower name," unless they are already well known.

In the newspapers and in public they are referred to, under even more poetical titles, such as "Miss Chang the Stately Beauty"; "Miss Liu, a Fairy of the Moon"; "Miss Wang, the Bright Little Night Pearl from Shanghai"; "Miss Li, the Affectionate Love Bird"; and so forth.

These girls make their living in various ways : entertaining guests, singing, playing games, and attending dinner-parties.

Many of them are not to be tempted in any way. A common saying amongst them is " we sell our songs, but not our body." And in many cases this is literally true. We have seen quite a number of foreigners, taking for granted a sing-song girl's bewitching smile as something not included in the menu, very much surprised at the cool way in which his advances are received. There are three classes of sing-song girls : the free girls who make money for themselves; those mortgaged, where the family receives part of the earnings ; and those sold outright who receive nothing except their food, clothes and some cheap jewellery. Many are bought by rich patrons, to become their wives or concubines.

The common name for their houses is *Pan* (Company, Class). Outside the door hang tablets with names such as, " The Three Happinesses "; " The Four Seas "; " Pine and Phœnixes " (i.e., like the pine which remains fresh the winter through); " Garden of Beautiful Fairies "; " Garden of Transplanted Flowers " (referring to those transferred from some other domicile); " Fairies inhabiting the vast, cold, Moon "; " Cassia and Lotus Flower Garden "; " The Fragrant Clouds " (a euphemism for sexual intercourse).

The Chinese mostly do not visit these *Pan* for any carnal desire, but simply to while away a few hours of social pleasure, to drink tea with the girls—in fact these visits are called *Ta Ch'a Hui* (Tea Meetings)—to listen to their songs, hear them play on their favourite instruments, to have a little flutter in gambling, and so forth. And unless the visitor becomes involved in an intrigue, it only costs him a few dollars per " tea-meeting."

Once every three years an examination of all the demi-monde is held. Those who excel in the various arts and blandishments required by their calling, such as looks, figure (thin ones preferred), singing, music, " morra," painting and literature, are rated Prima, Secunda, Tertia, corresponding to the honours given to college graduates. Their names are written on a " list " which is posted in their rooms for the edification of their admirers.

The " Gay Quarter " lies outside the Ch'ien Mên, and a fancy name for it in recent years is *Ch'ing Yin Hsiao Pan* (Clear-gonging-and-drumming small bands), in contrast to their

competitors on the real stage where the noise of drums and
gongs, big and little, is anything but clear. However, the
sing-song houses, as we call them, are as well patronized as
the theatres, or more so, since after the shows are over, a long
queue of pleasure-seekers wend their way to them, to enjoy
themselves till daybreak, and often after.

3.—THEATRES

Foreigners when visiting Peking should on no account
miss going to see a Chinese play of some kind, if they wish to
understand Old China. For it is only at the theatres that
the costumes worn by the various classes of men and women
in any particular dynasty, or in ancient times generally, can
still be seen, as well as the curious weapons, queer head-
dresses and armour, and the other paraphernalia of court
and camp, to say nothing of many strange ceremonials and
customs.

The principal play-houses are as follows :—

OUTSIDE THE CH'IEN MEN :

Kuang Ho Lou (Tower of Extensive Harmony). In the
Jou Shih. This is the oldest theatre in Peking.

Kuang Tê Lou (Tower of Extensive Virtue). In the Ta
Cha La.

Ch'ing Lo Yüan (Garden of Joyful Merriment). In the Ta
Cha La.

San Ch'ing Yüan (Garden of the Three Congratulations, i.e.
Happiness, Matrimony, and Longevity). In the Ta Cha La.

Ti I Wu T'ai (Premier Dancing Stage). In the Hsi Chu
Shih K'ou.

K'ai Ming Hsi Yüan (Theatrical Garden of Diffused Refinement). In the Hsi Chu Shih K'ou.

Chung Ho Hsi Yüan (Theatrical Garden of Equilibrium and
Harmony). In the Liang Shih Tien Chieh.

IN THE EAST CITY :

Chi Hsiang Hsi Yüan (Theatrical Garden of Happiness and
Merriment). In the Tung An Shih Ch'ang.

IN THE WEST CITY :

Ha Erh Fei (A name given to it by the famous actor Mei Lan-fang after his first tour to the U.S.A., said to represent the Chinese sound for "Harvard.") In the Chiu Hsing Pu Chieh.

The performances take place in the afternoon and evening, and do not consist of a single play, as with us, but of about half a dozen different, short plays ; so much so, that one of these is often merely a portion of some longer play the continuation of which is given on another day. The names of the chief actors and of the more famous plays are advertised daily in the Chinese newspapers. The more popular plays are generally put on towards the latter part of the show, so that foreigners desirous of seeing a particular piece or actor need not worry about arriving early. Nor need they have any compunction about disturbing the audience. For in a Chinese theatre the playgoers arrive at all hours ; not only are people continually entering and leaving the hall, but a general buzz of conversation is going on most of the time. The Chinese theatre (of the old style at any rate) has only two kinds of seats : those in the main body of the hall, the cheaper seats, corresponding to our pit ; and an upper gallery with open boxes, somewhat more expensive, which is used chiefly by the womenfolk. Foreigners are advised to take the latter.

On looking at the stage which generally is not closed off by a curtain—though this modern device has been adopted in a few of the theatres—it will at once be noticed that it is completely devoid of scenery in our sense of the word. The external part of a Chinese play is indicated by signs and make-believe, by a few simple devices, and by the movements and dresses of the actors themselves. These are all fixed absolutely rigidly by convention and therefore well-known to every Chinese playgoer. But as they may not be so apparent to the uninitiated, we will give a few of them herewith :—

SYMBOLIC :

Two tables, one on top of the other covered with red cloth, and with a chair on top, indicate a throne or a judgment seat.

Two bamboo poles with some calico attached represent a city wall or gate.

A boat is generally represented by an old man and a girl with an oar who move at a fixed distance from each other.

A snowstorm is represented by a man carrying a red umbrella from the folds of which he shakes out a shower of white slips of paper.

A chariot is indicated by two yellow flags, with a wheel drawn on each, one held in each hand.

A whip held in the left hand shows that the actor is dismounting from, in his right hand is mounting, his steed.

ACTOR'S MOVEMENTS :

Lifting his foot high up indicates he is stepping over the threshold of a door.

Bringing the hands slowly together then closes the door.

A fan held close up to the face shows that he is walking bare-headed in the sun.

Walking slowly round the stage with both hands extended and feeling to both sides indicates walking in the dark.

Slowly moving the hands across the eyes denotes weeping.

Standing stiffly behind a pillar, he is in hiding.

Lifting the skirts, bending down at the waist, and walking with slow measured steps indicates the ascent of a ladder or stairs, or crossing a narrow plank on to a boat.

COLOUR AND DRESS :

A red painted face indicates a sacred, loyal personage, or a great emperor.

A black face—an honest, but uncouth fellow.

A white face—a treacherous, cunning, but dignified person.

A white patch on the nose—a villain.

Devils have green, gods and goddesses gold or yellow faces.

An emperor's robe is always yellow, embroidered with coiled dragons winding up and down.

High officials also wear yellow, but have dragons flying downwards.

A warrior's hat is bedecked with two long peacock feathers.

A beggar is indicated by a silk robe with gaudy patches.

A gay woman is covered with jewellery and gaudy silks and satins.

A virtuous one is always clad in a plain black gown with light-blue trimmings on the sleeves.

A ghost is represented by an actor with a black cloth over head and face, or with a slip of white paper stuck on the cheek, or with a long curl of white paper suspended from the head.

Death is indicated by a red cloth thrown over the face.

Two men carrying black flags show that evil spirits are roaming about looking for victims.

SOUNDS:

Blowing of trumpets off stage heralds the approach of cavalry.

Fireworks indicate the appearance of a demon.

Two or three blasts of the trumpet indicate an execution taking place off stage.

The Chinese audience is very critical of all these movements and posturings, and quick to spot the slightest mistake, of which they at once show their disapproval by loud shouts of contempt. They do not applaud by clapping, as we do, but by shouting out *Hao* (Good !) at the top of their voices, which may be observed, when they applaud the dancing or singing of some particular stage favourite.

Finally, as a further assistance to the intending playgoer, we include the synopsis of five well-known Chinese plays which can be recommended. It may be observed that, though to our taste they may appear somewhat lacking in point, they provide occasion for certain popular airs, ballet dances, and witty dialogue.

4.—PLAYS

Chai Hsing Fu. Manchu Period. Time 45 minutes.

A young student, called Lo Hung-hsün, whilst on a journey falls into the hands of a gang of bandits who are in league with the military officer in charge of the post at Chai Hsing Fu (name of the play), and who hand him over to this officer

as being a " wanted " robber. The news of his arrest comes to
the ears of his intended father-in-law, Hua Chên-fang, whose
daughter, Miss Pi Lien, entreats her father to save her fiancé.
Hua Chên-fang enlists the assistance of his friend Pao Tz'ŭ-an
and his daughter, Miss Chin Hua, and together they lead a
party to the rescue of the student. A furious battle takes place,
the officer and the brigands are defeated, and Lo Hung-hsün
released. The hero of the play is Lo's servant Yü Ch'un-lo
through whose courage the fight is won.

Wu Lung Yüan (Black Dragon Park). Also called *Tso
Lou Sha Hsi* (Sitting in a tower and killing Hsi). Sung Period.
Time 45 minutes.

Sung Chiang, the hero (or villain) of the piece falls in love
with a beautiful courtesan by name of Yen P'o-hsi. He builds
for her a beautiful and expensive villa and garden called the
Black Dragon Park (name of the play). Later he discovers
that she has a paramour in the person of one of his clerks, and
to make matters worse, refuses to have anything more to do
with him. He therefore calls on her, and as they are talking
quietly, suddenly draws a dagger and plunges it in her heart.
He then makes his escape to Liang Shan P'o in Shantung,
joining a band of robbers there whose leader he eventually
becomes. (He is the Chinese Robin Hood and Liang Shan
P'o is his Sherwood Forest).

Nieh Yin Niang. A Ballet piece. Time 70 minutes.

This is the name of an amazon who lived during the T'ang
dynasty. When ten years of age she was abducted by a nun
and taken to a cave in the mountains. Here the girl is instructed
in sword exercises, and when she has become an adept, is detailed
to kill a wicked official and his whole family. The official
himself she has no compunction in slaying, but cannot
bring herself to kill the wife and children. For this soft-
heartedness she is upbraided by the nun and sent back home,
with the admonition to keep up her sword practice and to
harden her heart. At the end of twenty years a white monkey
will be sent to bring her back again. On the way home she
slays a tiger that attacks her. Nieh Yin Niang's parents wish
her to marry someone they have selected, but she will only
marry the man of her choice which falls on a youth named Mo
Ching whom she instructs in her art. Their skill becomes

famous throughout the whole Empire, and they are urged
by a high official to proceed to Honan to kill a wicked governor
there, but on arriving at their destination and finding that he
is, on the contrary, a very worthy official much beloved by the
people, they give up their intention and join his staff instead.
Mo Ching gives him a jade necklace advising him to wear it
always—which he does and thus escapes an attempt at assassina-
tion. The twenty years having expired, the white monkey
turns up and takes Nieh Yin Niang back to the cave in the
mountains—Mo Ching is left behind—where she meets a woman
who was kidnapped at the same time as herself. Together
they show off their prowess in sword practice and posturing.
(This is the climax of the piece, a great ballet dance, which
never fails to bring down the house.) After that Nieh Yin
Niang becomes the Immortal of the Sword (*Chien Hsien*)
and disappears from mortal ken. (Ch'êng Jên-ch'iu, the famous
female impersonator, is the most popular actor taking the part
of Nieh Yin Niang at the present day. In this piece the orchestra
is augmented by bells, small drums, and so forth, playing a
strongly rhythmic tune which accelerates the dance and sword
play).

Shuang P'a P'o (The Two Henpecked Husbands). Also
known as *Pei Têng* (Carrying a Stool). Time 30 minutes.

Two henpecked husbands have a bet. Mr. Shih bets
Mr. Pu that if he goes home with him (Pu), Mrs. Pu will refuse
to serve them with wine at her husband's order. When they
arrive home, Mrs. Pu obeys her husband without a word and
pours out the wine. Mr. Shih seeing his money lost, grabs
hold of it and rushes off saying he has stomach-ache. Mrs. Pu
incensed at thus losing the money for the bet (which of course
they had arranged beforehand) makes her husband go down
on his knees and kotow to her, and in addition ties a stool to
his back and orders him to go out on the street and shout
in a loud voice : " Because I have fooled my wife, I am forced
to carry this stool." At the cross-roads he meets Mr. Shih
with a stool upside down on his head, his wife following behind.
He had been punished for coming home in a drunken condition. (The explanations given by the two husbands and their
antics are screamingly funny and invariably bring the house
down.)

T'ien Ho P'ei (The Mating at Heaven's Bridge).

The play opens with Hsi Wang Mu (Western Royal Mother) and Yü Huang (The Pearl Emperor)—the latter is sometimes left out in modern plays—disporting themselves in the Jasper Pool, with eight fairy maidens in attendance. They are waiting for Chih-nü (The Spinning-Damsel) who arrives late. For her unpunctuality, Hsi Wang Mu banishes her to earth for a period of seven days, which represents seven years, as one day in Heaven is equal to a year on earth. Hsi Wang Mu also sends for Chin Niu Hsing (The Golden Ox Star), and informs him that he is to descend to earth in order to protect Niu-lang (The Oxherd), who later becomes the Spinning-Damsel's husband. Here we have the representation of the engagement between Lyra (Chih-nü) and Aquila (Niu-lang), separated by the Milky Way (T'ien Ho).

The scene now changes. Niu-lang appears with his elder brother and the latter's wife. Niu-lang's brother who is about to leave for a distant place to collect debts, instructs his wife to keep a watch on the boy to see that he pursues his studies. After his departure, the wife who is not too fond of Niu-lang, tells him that he must either do the household work or go out and look after the animals and cut firewood. On his refusing she gives him a thrashing, whereupon Niu-lang clears out and takes his ox to the hills to graze. While he is lamenting his fate, the ox suddenly addresses him saying : " If your sister-in-law offers you anything to eat, refuse it, as she intends to poison you." Thoroughly amazed, Niu-lang asks the ox how it came to know what was in his sister-in-law's mind. " Never mind how I know," replies the ox, which is really the spirit of the Golden Ox Star. " Do what I tell you, and if she insists, say you are going to leave the family. Further, ask her to give you myself, an old cart, and a couple of boxes to carry your clothes in." Niu-lang returns home and, true enough, his sister-in-law meets him with a smiling face and offers him some cakes which she says she has made specially for him ! Niu-lang is now certain that what the ox had told him was true, and refuses the cakes. As he is on the point of leaving, his brother comes in, and on being told that Niu-lang wishes to depart implores him not to. The woman is finally compelled to sign a document granting Niu-lang's wishes, who

departs with his ox. When they have gone some distance,
the boy asks the ox where they are to procure food and money.
The ox replies that all he has to do is, to wave his knife or
sword, and he shall have whatever he wishes for. Niu-lang
waves his weapon, and money comes ; he waves it again, and
food is provided.

Niu-lang then tells the ox that he wishes to have a beautiful
wife. " I'll take you to a river " says the ox, " where you'll
find a beautiful and charming maiden."   On arrival at the bank
of the river (The Milky Way) Niu-lang sees nine maidens bathing
in the stream, their clothing lying on the bank.   The ox points
to the ninth maiden who, of course, is the Spinning-Damsel
saying " Seize her clothing."   Now, when the fairies see a
mortal in their midst, each seizes her clothing and decamps.
But the Spinning-Damsel, having no chance to escape because
her celestial robes are in the possession of a mortal, and being
in a nude state, is compelled to compromise by becoming his
handmaid. They live happily together for several years,
during which twins are born to them, a boy and a girl.   The
ox, who feels that his days are numbered, one day says to
Niu-lang " Master, I am getting old and must soon leave you.
When I am dead, cut off my head and preserve my stomach,
in which conceal the robes that your wife wore on the day you
captured her, and hang it to the beams of the house.   Should
your wife attempt to escape back to Heaven, take a stick and
rap on my head, strap your children to a carrying-pole and
follow her wherever she goes." After the ox's death Niu-lang's
wife suddenly remembers one night that the seven years of her
banishment to earth have elapsed.   So she takes her robes out
of the ox's belly, embraces her children and escapes from the
house, on her way back to Heaven.

When Niu-lang awakes to find her gone, he remembers
the ox's instructions and after rapping on the ox's head pursues
her to the River of Heaven taking his children with him.   Here
he sees her standing on the opposite bank together with Hsi Wang
Mu who waves to him to go back. (Note : Hsi Wang Mu is
seen throwing a strip of white cloth across the stage to represent
the Milky Way. Sometimes, too, there is a boat revolving
like the disk of a gramophone with the Spinning-Damsel
sitting in it. This scene represents the swirling of the waters

in the River). Niu-lang, his two children, and the Spinning-Damsel, all set up a terrible howling. Hsi Wang Mu touched by their grief also starts weeping and promises to allow them to meet each other EVERY SEVENTH DAY but which they mistake for the 7th day of the Seventh Moon.

On the 7th day of the Seventh Moon, magpies are believed to form a bridge, over which the Maid and Cowherd pass to embrace each other. At day-break on that day no birds, the Chinese say, are to be seen in the sky, as they are assisting to build the bridge. Children often take a pan of water which they place beneath a grape-vine arbour to watch by the reflection in the water whether any birds are to be seen in the sky for good luck ! They also believe that the weeping and wailing of the two lovers can be plainly heard in the Heavens above ; and the children start weeping in sympathy.

PART II

CHAPTER XXI.

THE SUMMER PALACE

THIS beautiful park, known to foreigners as the SUMMER PALACE, lies outside the Hsi Chih Mên, seven miles to the north-west of the city. By the Chinese it is called *I Ho Yüan* (Park of Peace and Harmony in Old Age) or *Wan Shou Shan* (Hill of a Myriad Ages). Strictly speaking, *I Ho Yüan*, the name given to it by the late Empress-Dowager, refers to the whole enclosure, whilst only the hill is the *Wan Shou Shan*.

Under the Mings it was known as *Hao Shan Yüan* (Park of Beautiful Hills). In 1751 Ch'ien Lung altered the name first to *Ch'ing I Yüan* (Park of Pure and Rippling Waters) and later again to *Wan Shou Shan*, the name by which it is still best known to the common people.

At the same time he ordered a canal to be dug to lead the waters of the Jade Spring to feed the lake in the park, the *K'un Ming Hu* (Vast Bright Lake) which up to his time, under the name of *Hsi Hu* (West Lake) or *Chin Hai* (Golden Sea), was nothing more than a large lagoon. Ch'ien Lung took the name *K'un Ming* from a lake of that name south-west of Sianfu in Shênsi, which was dug out originally under the Emperor Yao (2357-2258 B.C.).

The park is enclosed by a wall about four miles round, pierced with thirteen gates of which, however, only one, the *Tung Kung Mên* (East Palace Gate), is in actual use. Up to 1891 the park had walls on the north and west sides only, when a Manchu Bannerman, Ying Nien, memorialized the Throne for permission to add walls on the other two sides. This being granted, the walls were built, and guards stationed at all important points.

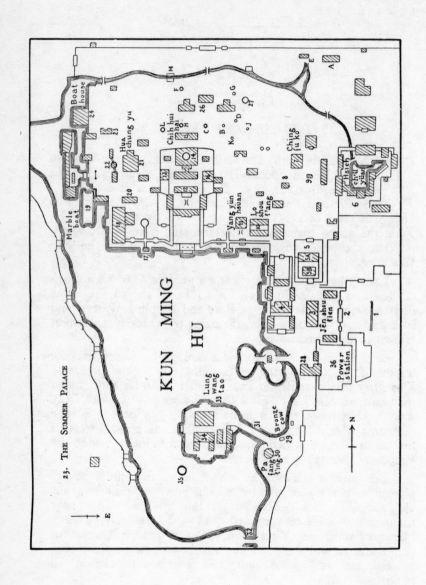

23. THE SUMMER PALACE

KEY

1 Screen
2 *Tung Kung Mên* (East Palace Gate)
3 *Jên Shou Tien* (Hall of Old Age and Benevolence)
4 *Yü Lan T'ang* (Hall of Jade-white Billows)
5 *Tê Ho Yüan* (Park of Pleasant Harmony)
5A *I Lo Tien* (Hall of Pleasant Smiles)
5B Theatre
6 *Hsieh Ch'ü Yüan* (Pleasure Garden)
7 *Ching Fu Ko* (Bright Happy Pavilion)
8 *Ju I Chuang* (As you like it Village)
9 *Tzŭ Tsai Chuang* (Happy Family Village)
10 *Lo Shou T'ang* (Hall of Happy Old Age)
11 *Yang Yün Hsüan* (Porch of Nourished Clouds)
12 *P'ai Yün Tien* (Hall of Serrated Clouds)
13 *Pao Yün Ko* (Pavilion of Precious Clouds)
14 *Fo Hsiang Ko* (Buddha's Fragrant Incense Pavilion)
15 *Chih Hui Hai* (Sea of Perfect Wisdom)
16 *Chuan Lun Tsang* (Tibetan Prayer Wheel)
17 *Yü Tsao Hsüan* (Fish amongst the Pond-weed Pavilion)
18 *Shih Chang T'ing* (Stone Man's Pavilion)
19 *Shih Fang* (Marble Boat)
20 *T'ing Li Kuan* (House in which to listen to the Call of Oriols)
21 *Hua Chung Yu* (Strolling in the midst of painted Scenery)
22 *Hsiao Yu Tien* (Little World)
23 *Yen Ch'ing Shang Lou* (Tower of Perpetual Pure View)
24 Boat House
25 The *Shih Erh Ch'u* (Twelve Small Places):—
　　A *T'iao Yüan Chai* (Long-distance View Tower)
　　B *Hsiang Yu Tsung* (Fragrant Royal Grotto)
　　C *Ying Chih Ko* (Impressed in Memory Pavilion)
　　D *Kai Ch'un Yüan* (Spring Terrace Garden)
　　E *Kou Hsü Hsüan* (Porch of Gutters and Ditches)
　　F *I Wang Hsüan* (Leaning against the Balustrade and viewing the Scenery)
　　G *Hua Ch'êng Ko* (Flower City Pavilion)
　　H *P'an Tso Lien T'ai* (Sitting cross-legged on the Lotus Terrace)
　　J *Ch'ing K'o Hsüan* (Green Vegetable House)
　　K *Chu Yü* (Bamboo Enclosure)
　　L *Hui Fang T'ang* (Artist's Studio)
　　M *Mai Mai Chieh* (Business Street)
26 *Hsü Mi* (Beautiful Heights)
27 *To Pao Liu Li T'a* (Most Precious Glazed Tile Pagoda)
28 *Wen Ch'ang Ko* (Tower of the God of Literature)
29 *T'ung Niu* (Bronze Cow)
30 *Pa Fang T'ing* (Octagonal Pagoda)
31 *Shih Ch'i K'ung Ch'iao* (Seventeen Arch Bridge)
32 *Hsiu I Ch'iao* (Bridge of Embossed Ripples)
33 *Lung Wang Tao* (Dragon King's Island)
34 *Lung Wang T'ang* (Dragon King's Hall)
35 *Fêng Huang Tun* (Phoenix Mound)
36 Power Station

Another but less well-known name for Wan Shou Shan is *Wêng Shan* (Pot Hill), from the legend that an old man had fashioned a large stone pot and cast it away on the west side of this hill. But according to another version this name really referred to an Empress of the Ming dynasty who was buried close-by. When repairs were being carried out at the Park a number of workmen came across a stone tablet on this spot with the inscription: "Tomb of the Empress Wêng. If you do not trouble me, I will not trouble you." Digging deeper they came to a layer of stones which on being opened up revealed a deep cavern full of water on which floated a boat. They placed a heavy stone on the boat which at once slid away through a cleft in the cavern and then as miraculously reappeared without the stone. The workmen reported this strange phenomenon to Prince Ch'ing who, knowing the superstitious nature of the Empress-Dowager, gave orders to have the place closed up again and nothing said about the find, and told her the story of the Pot as an explanation of the name Wêng Shan. The site of the supposed tomb is close to the Peking Electric Power main station, outside the park.

Close by is the tomb of the famous warrior and astrologer, Yeh-lü Ch'u-ts'ai, a descendant in the eighth generation of a prince of the House of Liao who in 1214 was Governor of Peking. When Genghis Khan captured the city he took a great fancy to Yeh and attached him to his staff. Besides being a great warrior, Yeh was also an astronomer and expert astrologer, whose warnings, it is said, when followed by the Great Khan, led to success, and when ignored, to disaster. Japanese astrologers to-day still study carefully Yeh-lü Ch'u-ts'ai's works on astrology, and it is said that Japanese generals only make war, when their astrologers report favourably. The Chinese have apparently lost the art, which perhaps accounts for the poor showing their armies make against the Japanese war-lords. The Japanese show great veneration for this tomb of his and, whenever they visit the place, burn incense before his spirit-tablet. Little seems to have been done to Yeh's grave until Tz'ǔ Hsi took an interest in it and built a temple there.

Most of the temples and other buildings in the Park were burnt down in 1860 by the British and French armies, at the same time as the old Summer Palace. At the coming-of-age

of the Emperor T'ung Chih in 1873 repairs were begun, to
prepare it as a place of retirement for the Empress-Dowager.
But the work was stopped on his death a year later, when she
once more assumed the Regency.   In 1889, when the Emperor
Kuang Hsü took over the reins of government, building was
once more started on it, the funds for this purpose being
appropriated from the revenues of the Board of Navy, on the
advice of Li Hung-chang.   This diversion of funds was one
of the main causes why the Chinese navy was in a state of
complete unpreparedness, when the war with Japan broke
out in 1894, so that the Summer Palace may be said to have
exercised a very important influence on the fate of China.
In 1900 the Park was occupied by various units of the Allied
armies and on the Empress-Dowager's return from Sianfu
was repaired thoroughly for a third time.

The Empress-Dowager was passionately fond of the
Summer Palace and spent as much of her time here as possible,
especially in the last years of her life, only returning to the
Forbidden City for the winter or unavoidable state occasions.
Even then, she used to leave the place with a heavy heart and
hastened back to it as soon as possible.   Every day, whether
wet or fine, she would wander round the grounds attending
to her flowers and fruit trees and tiring out her attendants by
her energy and vigour ; or she would go for picnics and water
pageants on the lake.   Those desirous of obtaining a more
intimate account of her life in these delectable surroundings
should read the books by Miss Catherine Carl and Princess
Der Ling.

The Summer Palace grounds were first thrown open to
the public in 1914.   The Chinese divide it into Eight Large
Sections (*Pa Ta Ch'u*) and Six Small Sections (*Liu Hsiao Ch'u*),
all on the southern face of Wan Shou Shan.

Entering by the *Tung Kung Mên* (East Palace Gate), the
first building we come to is the *Jên Shou Tien* (Hall of Old Age
as Reward for Benevolence), a name given to it by the
Empress-Dowager, who used it as an audience-hall.   In the
courtyard are several wonderful specimens of bronze dragons,
lions, unicorns, deer and phœnix, emblems of royalty and
longevity. At the back of her throne hung a large scroll with the
characters " Great Precious Mirror "—a gentle reminder that any

attempts at deception would be seen through, as though reflected
in a mirror ! It was formerly known as *Ch'in Chêng Tien* (Hall
of Diligent Government) where Ch'ien Lung used to receive
memorials when he stayed here. This enclosure contains a
huge natural boulder inscribed with complimentary verses, said
to have been brought from Manchuria. It was presented to
Tz'ǔ Hsi by Moêrhkên, a lineal descendant of Jui Wang or
Dorgun. (This Moêrhkên, by the way, owned the large
property, not far from here, now occupied by the Yenching
University).

To the west, adjoining the lake, is the *Yü Lan T'ang* (Hall
of Jade-white Billows) where, after the *coup d'état* of 1898,
the Empress-Dowager confined the unfortunate Emperor
Kuang Hsü, whenever she took him to the Summer Palace
with her. From within his prison walls he could have a good
view of the K'un Ming Lake. In 1904 she bricked in the Hall
which, up to that time, had no dividing wall,—presumably
to make certain that he could not escape, nor even view
the Lake !

To the north of the Jên Shou Tien is the *Tê Ho Yüan*
(Park of Pleasant Harmony). This court contains a large
three-storeyed building or tower, the lower floor of which was
used as a stage for theatrical plays. Opposite it is the *I Lo
Tien* (Hall of Pleasant Smiles) which was the Empress-Dowager's
private box, where, no doubt " she often smiled pleasantly "
when watching the plays staged for her special benefit—many
of them composed by herself—surrounded by the highest ladies
and gentry in the Empire.

Some distance to the north-east is the *Hsieh Ch'ü Yüan*
(Pleasure Garden). This name is taken from a line of verse
written by Ch'ien Lung : " A path, a kiosk, awaken pleasant
memories of rural scenes." It was originally called *Hui
Shan Yüan* (Park of Graceful Hills) and contains many
kiosks, pavilions, arbours, flowers, shrubs, and beautiful
summer-houses standing at the edge of a deep pool. It
was a favourite summer resort of the Emperor Ch'ien Lung,
and is well worth a visit, which can be made on our
way back.

To the north, on the hill, is the *Ching Fu Ko* (Bright Happy
Pavilion) where on bright moonlight nights the Emperor and

Empress used to take their evening meal. Nowadays the officials entertain their friends in it. There are two miniature villages just below the pavilion, the *Ju I Chuang* (As you like it Village) and the *Tzŭ Tsai Chuang* (Happy Family Village). These tiny hamlets were constructed on the orders of the " Old Buddha " after her return from exile in 1900-1, to remind her of the happy (?) existence of her peasant subjects in the interior of her empire. All the implements, whether farming or household, were made of pure mud, as also the tiny shacks containing them. The Ju I Chuang represents farm life, and the Tzŭ Tsai Chuang a peasant's life.

We return to the lake and proceeding west a few steps along the north bank come to a high, rounded arch. To the north of this is another group of buildings, called *Lo Shou T'ang* (Hall of Happy Old Age). This was Tz'ŭ Hsi's home when in residence at the Summer Palace. There is a massive boulder in the courtyard called *Ch'ing Chih Hsiu* (Cliff on which the Green Plant of Immortality grows). It is said to have been the property of Mi Wan-chung, a President of the Board of Works, who had it in the garden of his home at Ling-hsiang Hsien, in south Chihli. It was brought to Peking by order of Ch'ien Lung in 1751, and set up here.

At the back, on the west side, is the *Yang Yün Hsüan* (Porch of Nourished Clouds), used as a residence by the Court ladies.

From here one enters a long, painted gallery in two sections, its centre being in an exact line with the Fo Hsiang Ko, the four-storeyed pagoda on the peak of the hill. The total length is 1,170 feet; in addition there are several short side galleries leading off the main one to other small buildings at the foot of the hill.

The central and principal group of buildings is called *P'ai Yün Tien* (Hall of Serrated Clouds) which name actually only applies to the main hall facing the entrance. This entire enclosure was erected in 1889 on the old site of the *Ta Pao En Yen Shou Ssŭ* (Temple of Extended Life for Mercy and Favour Shown) which was built by Ch'ien Lung in 1751 in honour of his mother's sixtieth birthday, and destroyed by the Allied armies in 1860. At the entrance to the P'ai Yün Tien

CHINESE VIEW

SUMMER PALACE

is a small side-room containing four rickshaws, two of which have glass doors and windows, all handsomely decorated in Imperial Yellow. These were used by Tz'ŭ Hsi and her favourite ladies, when going about the park. The archway facing the entrance was erected during Ch'ien Lung's reign in 1755.

Visitors are not allowed to proceed directly to the top tower by the central path, but must ascend by the rough-hewn stone steps on the left (west) side, of which there are 112, and approach the principal buildings from that direction. Towards the top one comes to the BRONZE PAVILION, the *Pao Yün Ko* (Pavilion of Precious Clouds), built in 1755, according to Chinese reports, from castings made by the Jesuit missionaries. Tradition has it that this pavilion is haunted, for which reason the " Old Buddha " only once visited it.

Continuing our ascent we reach the beautiful four-storeyed tower, the *Fo Hsiang Ko* (Buddha's Fragrant Incense Pavilion) situated on the peak of the hill, on a high massive brick foundation, at a distance of 370 feet from the edge of the lake. Inside is a colossal gilt idol of Kuan Yin and her two attendant pages. An excellent bird's-eye view of the lake, islands, and bridges may be had from here, which will well repay the somewhat arduous climb.

At the back, outside the wall, is the *Chih Hui Hai* (Sea of Perfect Wisdom), also called *Wan Fo Tien* (Hall of a Myriad Buddhas), in which the " Buddha of a Measureless Age " is enshrined. This beautiful structure is built solely of glazed tiles (*liu li*) and does not contain a single brick or stick of wood.

Winding our way down through the passages in the rocks on the east side, we come to the *Chuan Lun Tsang* (Tibetan Prayer Wheel) of glazed tiles, with three figures representing Happiness, Emolument, and Longevity. Still continuing down-hill we reach the lower terrace on which stands a massive stone tablet bearing an inscription by Ch'ien Lung—" *Wan Shou Shan K'un Lun Hu* " (Hill of a Myriad Ages and Vast Bright Lake).

From here it is only a short distance to where we entered the enclosure. Proceeding westwards along the verandah we arrive at a small pavilion jutting out into the lake, called *Yü Tsao Hsüan* (Fish among the Pond-weed). It was from this place that Wang Kuo-wei, the Hanlin scholar and Dean of the Peking University, leaped into the water and drowned himself in 1928 in despair at the state of the country, then on the verge of going " Red."

The last pavilion at the west end of the verandah is the *Shih Chang T'ing* (Stone Man's Pavilion). The name is taken from the story of the Sung poet and artist, Mi Fei, who called a curious-shaped boulder " his brother." Leaving the small court in which the " Stone Man's Pavilion " stands we pass through a clean modern restaurant and come to the famous MARBLE BOAT (*Shih Fang*), built for Tz'ŭ Hsi out of the Navy funds. It is recorded that during Ch'ien Lung's reign a huge boulder, found embedded in the mud at the edge of the lake, was hewn into the form of a boat. The superstructure was added by the Empress-Dowager. Officially it is called *Ch'ing Yen Fang* (Clear Rivers and Quiet Seas Boat)—of the piping times of peace ! But the unfortunate Admiral Ting Ju-ch'ang who committed suicide at Wei Hai Wei after surrendering to the Japanese could have told the Empress-Dowager another story.

A delightful walk is to follow the paved path that leads past the Marble Boat to the Camel-back Bridge further west; then, turning to the right, before coming to the bridge, follow at a little distance the canal that circles the hills on the north. A boat can be hired to take you round this way; disembarking at the end of the canal we cross the foot of the hill at the east side close to, and behind the Jên Shou Tien.

We now return along the west section of the verandah and turning north from the Yü Tsao Hsüan come to the *T'ing Li Kuan* (House in which to listen to the call of the oriols). A little way to the south is a small two-storeyed theatre in which the Empress-Dowager used to enjoy the plays. To the north of this house, is a large enclosure called *Hua Chung Yu* (Strolling in the midst of Painted Scenery) ; and beyond this again, to the north-west, the *Yen Ch'ing Shang Lou* (Tower of Perpetual Pure View). In Ming times there was a small business street here, called *Mai Mai Chieh*, where the palace attendants could purchase their daily necessities from hawkers who were specially permitted to enter the park for this purpose. Later on it fell into disuse, until K'ang Hsi reconstructed it under the name of *Hsiao Yu T'ien* (Little World).

On the north side of the hill are twelve more small buildings (*Shih Erh Ch'u*), as follows :*

(*a*) *T'iao Yüan Chai* (Long-distance View Tower), commonly known as *K'an Hui Lou* (Seeing the Sights Tower) from where Tz'ŭ Hsi used to watch the yearly parades that took place from the 1st to the 15th of the Fourth Moon. They had an additional interest for her because of the large sums which she contributed to the various societies that took part in them.

(*b*) *Hsiang Yen Tsung* (Fragrant Royal Grotto). As many strange and valuable plants and flowers were grown here, it was compared to mountain heights, as for example *T'ai Shan* (The Royal Mountain) on which are grown plants supposed to confer immortality when eaten.

(*c*) *Yin Chih Ko* (Impressed on Memory Pavilion), where the Empress-Dowager usually had her photographs taken, i.e., they were scenes to be imprinted on one's memory !

(*d*) *K'ai Ch'un Yüan* (Spring Terrace Garden). Taken from an ode " Would that I were nine flights nearer heaven ! " Tz'ŭ Hsi, when visiting this terrace, no doubt imagined herself nearer to heaven !

(*e*) *Kou Hsü Hsüan* (Porch of Gutters and Ditches). There are numerous small water-courses running round and under this building. The floors are made of glass through which fish may be seen darting about, something after the style of the glass-boats on the Californian coast.

(*f*) *I Wang Hsüan* (Leaning against the Balustrade and Viewing the Scenery).

(*g*) *Hua Ch'êng Ko* (Flower City Pavilion), from the fact that the Empress-Dowager used to raise various species of foreign and Chinese flowers here.

(*h*) *P'an Tso Lien T'ai* (Sitting cross-legged on the Lotus Terrace). Here the " Old Buddha " used to sit in the costume of the Goddess of Mercy, with her favourite eunuch, Li Lien-ying, dressed as one of the goddess's pages, at her side.

---

*Their positions are only roughly indicated on the map.

(*i*) *Ch'ing Ko Hsüan* (Green Vegetable House). Vegetables for the Empress-Dowager's kitchen were grown here.

(*j*) *Chu Yü* (Bamboo Enclosure). All the buildings, balustrades, and so forth are made of various kinds of bamboo.

(*k*) *Hui Fang T'ang* (Artists' Studio). Tz'ŭ Hsi used to do much of her painting and writing here.

(*l*) *Mai Mai Chieh* (Business Street). The Empress-Dowager, allowed hawkers to open stalls and sell their wares to the eunuchs in this narrow alleyway. On one occasion a row broke out between the hawkers and the eunuchs, in which several of the latter got their faces scratched, so that the Empress-Dowager put a stop to the whole " business."

If we ascend the north side of Wan Shou Shan we shall see, close to the top, a mass of ruined temples of the Ming period, where are still to be found quite a number of gilt idols that were formerly in the Ta Pao En Yen Shou Ssŭ. This cluster of temples was known as *Hsü Mi*, a Mongol term, equivalent to " Beautiful Heights." The Empress-Dowager had intended rebuilding them, but the outbreak of the war with Japan in 1894 prevented her from doing so. The glazed-tile " dagoba " which stands a little to the east of these ruins, called *To Pao Liu Li T'a* (Most Precious Glazed-tile Pagoda), was built by Ch'ien Lung in 1751 and repaired by him in 1792. South of the " dagoba " is a large hexagonal stone pillar with inscriptions by Ch'ien Lung on each face. Having seen what is left of these Ming ruins we continue our walk east and south, and passing through the Hsieh Ch'ü Yüan arrive back near the entrance at the I Lo Tien.

There still remains to be visited the south-east section of the park, with the Dragon King's Island, which can be done either by hiring a boat for one dollar or by following the east shore of the lake. Taking the latter route we pass under the tower called *Wên Ch'ang Ko* (Tower of the God of Literature) and see before us on the foreshore the famous BRONZE COW (*T'ung Niu*). The official and correct name is *Chên Hai Niu* (Guard the Sea Cow). It was cast and set up on its present site in 1755 by order of Ch'ien Lung who wrote twenty-four lines of verse which are inscribed on its back. The bronze cow is a symbol of stability and according to popular belief was placed here to prevent the lake from overflowing. The Great Yü, 2205 B.C., when he had finished his labours of dividing the waters at Pa Ch'iu in Anhui province, set up an "Iron Cow," not only to prevent an overflow, but also to tranquillize the waves and stop the sea monsters from invading the land. Thus the "Bronze Cow," like the "Iron Cow," immortalizes the labours of the Great Yü. The natives of Peking have a saying that the "Bronze Cow" represents the Cowherd (Aquila), the lake the Milky Way, and the small shrine just west of the Marble Boat, called *Chih Nü Miao*, represents the Spinning-Maiden (Lyra), referring to the famous Chinese legend. (See Synopsis of Plays, Chapter XX).

Close-by is the *K'uo Ju T'ing* (Big Pavilion), also called *Pa Fang T'ing* (Octagonal Pavilion), standing at the approach to the *Shih Ch'i K'ung Ch'iao* (Seventeen-Arch Bridge) which spans the lake to the Dragon King's Island. Further south rises up the beautiful *Hsiu I Ch'iao* (Bridge of Embossed Ripples) more commonly, but less poetically, known as *Lo Kuo Ch'iao* (Hunchback Bridge).

On the island itself lies the *Lung Wang T'ang* (Dragon King's Hall). Its correct name, but seldom used, is *Kuang Jun Ling Yü Tz'ü* (Ancestral Hall of the Dragon King who blesses us with Seasonable, Plenteous and Moistening Rains). The Hall contains the idol of the Dragon King, with a blue face and crown on his head, dressed in an Imperial Yellow robe. In former days the Emperors used to proceed here to burn incense before him on his birthday (13th of the Fifth Moon), as also during prolonged droughts. He was supposed to control the waters of the K'un Ming Lake to see that they neither overflow nor dry up. These buildings are now used by the Chinese Nature Culture Society. A little way off, to the west of the island, is an islet called *Fêng Huang Tun* (Phœnix Mound) on which stands a lone and solitary tree. According to legend, during the early years of the Manchus, the palace ladies when nearing confinement were segregated in a building that once stood on this islet. But as too many girls (Phœnixes) were born, the Emperor Tao Kuang ordered the building to be pulled down, leaving nothing but the mound and the tree.

This brings us to the end of our trip round this beautiful park, which is usually done in three hours. Much too short a time to see everything properly; three days would be nearer the mark!

CHAPTER XXII.

THE JADE FOUNTAIN

THE extensive and beautiful park, *Yü Ch'üan Shan* (Jade Springs Hill), known to foreigners as "The Jade Fountain" lies about three miles north-west of the Summer Palace ("Jade" here simply means that the waters of the Springs are as pure and cool as jade). According to Chinese tradition the park is the foremost of the "Eight Famous Sights" of Peking.

It is first mentioned as the hunting-park of the Chin Emperor, Chang Tsung (A.D. 1190-1208), who had a hunting-lodge called *Fu Jung Tien* (Hibiscus Palace) on the crest of the hill where the *Yü Fêng T'a* (Jade Peak Pagoda) stands to-day. The latter, a hexagonal pagoda of seven storeys in a good state of preservation, is of much later date, as it was erected during the Ming dynasty.

Afterwards the grounds fell into disuse until 1680 when K'ang Hsi started to adorn it with pavilions, pagodas and rockeries, and planted many trees and shrubs, giving it a name for the first time, that of *Ch'êng Hsin Yüan* (Park of Transparent Waters—an allusion to the springs). In 1692 he changed the name to *Ching Ming Yüan* (Park of Cheerful Repose) and divided it into "Sixteen Views" (*Shih Liu Ching*), of which the "Jade Spring" was the first. There are two springs: the larger on the south-west slope of the hill, and a smaller one (with little water) at the foot of the hill south of the pagoda.

On entering the Park we follow the path called after the *Ku Hua Yen Ssŭ* (Ancient Maculated Grotto Temple) of which not a single trace remains. Halfway up the hill there are two grottos called *Hsia Hua Yen Tung* (Lower Maculated Grotto) and *Kuan Yin Tung* (Grotto of Kuan Yin). Continuing our ascent we come to the *Shang Hua Yen Tung* (Upper Maculated Grotto) on the site of the original temple of that name. The rock walls of the grotto are carved with over a thousand figures of

Buddhist saints together with their names. (The caretaker will let you enter for a small fee).

A fairly stiff climb brings us to the *Yü Fêng T'a* (Jade Peak Pagoda) from where we obtain a beautiful view over the surrounding country, including Peking, the Hills, and the Summer Palace. Close by are two stone tablets. One has an inscription by Ch'ien Lung reading "First Spring under Heaven"; the other some verses of his written by Wang Yu-tun, a Grand Councillor, whose penmanship was much admired by the Emperor.

That the park was a pleasure-resort in high esteem with the two great Manchu Emperors is evident from the poetical names that they bestowed on the "Sixteen Views":—A pavilion with roof of glazed tiles glittering in the rays of the sun is called "Reflection of the Sun on the Hibiscus Flowers." "Plucking Fragrant Herbs on Mountain Heights" was the name for a well-laid-out garden. "Melting Snow dripping from Mountain Crags sounds like the sweet music of a Lute" is a fanciful name for a gully. Another of the "Views" was called "Shadow cast by the Jade Peak Pagoda." More rural was: "The Wind soughing across the Reeds strikes pleasantly on the ear." "The Light on the Water is like Split Silk crackled in all directions" describes the reflection of the moon on waters ruffled by a gentle breeze. "The Chimes of a Bell on the Mountain Top sound from beyond the Clouds," of a temple bell ringing on mountain heights above the clouds. "The Old Hermit's Cottage" alludes to a mountain in the province of Kueichow on which a recluse studied alchemy.

All these are pure imagery by which the Emperors doubtless wished to show off their scholarship and refinement. The names are all that remain to remind us of the imposing and massive buildings with wide open gardens and spacious galleries, which spoke of the magnificence and artistic taste of those bygone days. They are now nothing but a heap of ruins scattered over the western slopes of the hill.

Among these stands a pagoda of glazed tiles, still in good repair. Close to it, on stone terraces, are two huge marble monuments, about thirty feet high, mounted on turtles some nine feet in length and six feet broad. The inscriptions by Ch'ien Lung are so weather-worn that they are scarcely discernible. The monuments and the pair of large iron urns date from 1788.

Quitting this scene of desolation we proceed in a south-westerly direction until we strike the path that leads to the *Lung Wang Miao* (Dragon King's Temple). It contains the idol of His Majesty who controls the waters of the Jade Fountain, together with several of his deputies. A wooden tablet over the door informs us that these waters " Eternally Fertilize the Imperial Domain." The Spring gushes out through sluices directly beneath the temple of the Dragon King. In front of the temple is a stone tablet dedicated to the Jade Spring by Ch'ien Lung on May 18, 1763, and inscribed with the characters *Yü Ch'üan Pao T'u* (The Jade Spring roars and leaps). This is taken from a poem about a spring of the same name, west of Tsinanfu in Shantung, by Chao Mêng-fu, the famous poet and artist, known for his wonderful paintings of horses. His verses run as follows :—

" There is not another such spring in the whole world.
Out of the earth it gushes forth, pure as ice in a jade vase."

From here we can either proceed to the pagoda situated on the south-west slope, or return to the entrance passing en route the beer and soda-water factory established in Republican times.

Close to it is a large pool and a boat-house where the notorious eunuch, Li Lien-ying, kept a boat in which he used to go fishing in his leisure moments.

We might mention that the water of the Jade Spring is believed to have great curative powers, due to the influence of a Fox Fairy who is reputed to live in a hole close to the spot where the water comes out through five sluices, a little east of the entrance. In consequence, many Chinese before entering the Park burn incense outside the wall here in order to propitiate the Fox Fairy and render the water still more efficacious.

It is also of interest to note that the Empress-Dowager had the idea of restoring this park to its former glory, from which it had declined during the reign of the parsimonious Emperor Tao Kuang. But as this would have run into hundreds of millions, Prince Ch'ing persuaded a geomancer to report that the *Fêng-Shui* of the place was bad, so that she gave up the idea and contented herself with the Summer Palace.

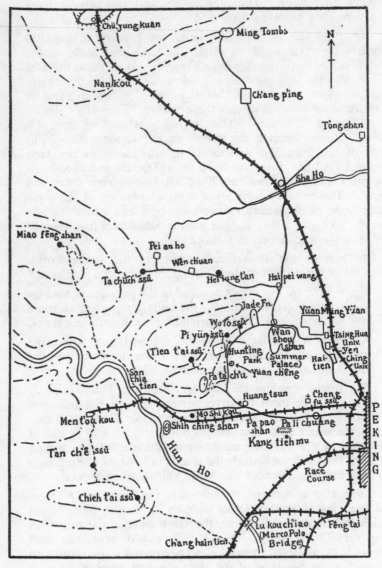

24. TEMPLES OF THE WESTERN HILLS

CHAPTER XXIII.

SOME TEMPLES OF THE WESTERN HILLS

Wo Fo Ssŭ (Temple of the Sleeping Buddha) lies up a side road, about two miles west of the Jade Fountain. This is the name by which it is generally known, but the official name is *Shih Fang P'u Chüeh Ssŭ* (The Whole Universe is Aroused to Our Sense of Charity,—i.e. Buddha, though asleep, is still conscious of what is going on in the world around him!) It is one of the oldest temples in the Western Hills, having been first built by the T'ang Emperor Chên Kuan (A.D. 627-649) under the name of *Tou Shuai Kung* (Bodhisattvas' Paradise). Kublai Khan changed the name to *Chao Hsiao Ssŭ* (Monastery of the Manifestation of Filial Piety). Later, also during the Mongol dynasty, the name was altered to *Hung Ch'ing* (Temple of Great Prosperity). The Ming Emperor Ch'êng Hua in 1465 had the temple repaired and changed the name to *Yung An Ssŭ* (Temple of Everlasting Peace). Yung Chêng in 1734 reconstructed the temple and gave it the official name it bears at present.

The rear hall contains the bronze idol of the " Sleeping Buddha " in a recumbent position fifty feet in length, fully clothed—except the feet, which are bare. The original idol was made of wood, but Ch'êng Hua replaced it by the present one which was cast in 1465. There is a smaller figure of Buddha, also in a reclining position, carved out of sandal-wood during the reign of Chên Kuan, which was apparently the first image of Buddha placed in the temple.

A fine avenue of old cypress trees leads to an archway of green and yellow tiles at the entrance through which one passes to the hall of the " Sleeping Buddha." In front of the temple are a pair of *P'o Lo* or *P'o Su* trees, supposed to grow in the Western Paradise and said to produce the fruit of eternal life. It is recorded that they were planted during the T'ang dynasty. On the west side of the temple, in the same courtyard,

is a large circular stone terrace on which stands a temple dedicated to *Kuan Yin* (The Goddess of Mercy). Through the
sluices beneath the temple there rushes out a clear stream of
water, which the Chinese believe to be a cure for all the ailments
that the flesh is heir to. There are no less than six stone
tablets (*pei*) standing in the temple grounds with inscriptions
by several Emperors. The most important is that by Ch'ien
Lung extolling the beauties of the temple and its surroundings.

About half a mile further west along the motor-road
we come to another side road leading to the famous temple of
Pi Yün Ssŭ (Temple of the Azure Clouds), a remarkable edifice
standing within a picturesque park. It was originally built
on the site of an old palace which belonged to Ahlichi, the
grandson of Yeh-Lü Ch'u-Ts'ai, the famous warrior and
astrologer who was Governor of Peking in 1214 (See Chapter
XX). The temple itself, was built at the close of the Yüan
dynasty (1366) and has been reconstructed and enlarged many
times since then. A favourite eunuch of the Ming Emperor
Chêng Tê, Yü Ching by name, repaired the temple in 1513 at
enormous expense with funds collected from the pious. During
the reign of the Emperor T'ien Ch'i the infamous eunuch
Wei Chung-hsien spent huge sums, which he had squeezed
out of the people, to further enlarge and beautify the temple.
Ch'ien Lung also contributed vast sums towards repairs in
1792, when he practically reconstructed or repaired most of
the temples in the Western Hills.

Passing through the archway we enter the outer courtyard
and find the once beautiful buildings mouldering in decay,
the gods capsized and lying about in all directions—in many
cases broken to bits by the collapse of the roof—wind and
rain peeling off their once beautiful coats of gilt. In a few
side buildings may still be seen the " Gods of Heaven and
Hell," poor relics of the past, resembling tattered scare-crows
in a cornfield.

The curious plaster frescoes representing the tortures of
hell look like snarling beasts baulked of their prey or the fierce
fiends of a distempered dream. One mounts to the top where
the so-called " Marble Stupa " stands, by four flights of stone
steps, with halls and annexes on each flight. These halls are
known as *Lo Han T'ang* and contain the eighteen personal

disciples of Buddha and the Five Hundred Saints.   The names
of these halls are :   *Ts'ang Chin Ko* (Hall in which the Sacred
Scriptures are Preserved), *Han Pi Chai* (Hall of the Great
Void), *Yün Jung Shui T'ai* (Clouds and Water Aspect Terrace),
Hsi Hsin T'ing (Pavilion of the Cleansed Heart), *Yüeh Hsiang
Shan Fang* (Mountain Cottage of Pleasant Memories).   A pool,
Cho Hsi Ch'üan (Buddhist Monk's Spring), is fed from a mountain
stream of that name.   Close to the pool is a large willow called
Ying Liu (Goitre Willow), because it has a large proturbance
resembling a tumour growing on one side of its trunk.   To
the east of this tree is a house containing a tablet bearing the
characters *Shui T'ien 1 Sê* (Sky and Water, One Colour), written
by the Ming Emperor Wan Li in 1575.

One of the kiosks bears the curious name *Hsiao Yün*
(Steaming Clouds), probably because it is situated on a mountain
height amidst the vapour of clouds.   Near-by, is a pool filled
with golden carp sacred to the monks, many beautiful lotus
and various species of bamboo.   There is also a building
called *Hsiang Chi Ch'u* (Cupboard of Accumulated Incense) in
which the monks keep their religious paraphernalia.   A long
covered-in gallery connects several of the temples and pavilions.
Last but not least, there is the famous *Chin Kang T'a* (Diamond
Sutra Pagoda), called by foreigners " Marble Stupa," though
not of marble at all, but of the famous *Talishih* or natural
coloured stone from Ta-li Fu in Yünnan.   A stone tablet
with an inscription by Ch'ien Lung recording the history of
the pagoda is still to be seen in the temple compound.   The
Pi Yün Ssŭ is visited by thousands of sightseers during the
1st to 15th of the Fourth Moon.   From 1926 to 1928 Sun
Yat-sen's brass coffin lay in a niche under the stupa until it
was removed, first to the Central Park in Peking and then to
the Purple Mountain at Nanking.

Adjoining Pi Yün Ssŭ, to the west lies the *Hsiang Shan*
(Fragrant Hills) or HUNTING PARK as it is generally called by
foreigners.   This beautiful wooded enclosure dates from the
Chin or Nüchên dynasty (A.D. 1115-1234), and was first used
by the Chin Emperor Ta Ting in 1170, when he built a
palace called *Hui Ching Lou* (Collected Scenery).   It was a large
game preserve, where hunting expeditions were the order of
the day down to the reign of Tao Kuang, in 1850 or

thereabouts. The ruins of the Hui Ching Lou are still to be seen, as also a tomb said to be that of one of the Liao Emperors. The game has now all disappeared, and instead of Imperial hunting parties, there are an Orphanage and a Sanatorium in a corner of the Park and a hotel called *Kan Lu* (Sweet Dew). This name was taken from that of a temple built on that spot by the Chin Emperor Ming Ch'ang in 1191, the *Yung An Ssŭ* (Temple of Eternal Peace), later altered to *Kan Lu Ssŭ* (Temple of Sweet Dew). It was repaired by Ch'ien Lung in 1745. The latter also changed the name of the park from Hsiang Shan to *Ching I Yüan* (Park of Peace and Harmony), enclosed it in walls, and divided it into twenty-eight sections or " Views "—twenty within the walls and eight outside of them. The first view (*ching*) was the *Hsiang Shan Ssŭ* (Temple of Fragrant Hills) which lay outside the south-west corner of the park and has now been turned into the above-mentioned hotel.

The other large building on the left, as one enters, was the *Chung Kung* (Central Palace) or *Hsü Lang Chai* (Studio of the Great Void). It has now been transformed into a school.

Outside the east wall is the *Ch'ao Miao* (Glorious Temple), built by the Emperor Ch'ien Lung in Tibetan style after a similar temple in Jehol. At the entrance stands a particularly fine *p'ai lou* of glazed tiles with inscriptions in four languages : Chinese, Manchu, Mongol, and Tibetan. It was erected by Ch'ien Lung in 1781.

The greater part of the remaining ancient edifices in this park have either disappeared or have been turned into bunga- lows which are let out as summer residences.

After leaving the Hunting Park the road crosses a spur from which we see below us, on our left, a circular construction with massive crenellated walls. This is the *Yüan Ch'êng* (Circular City) built by Ch'ien Lung in 1749 to commemorate the victorious campaign against the Tibetans conducted by his famous general, Fu Hêng. Nearby is a terrace with a high tower from which the Emperor used to watch the archery and other military exercises. Further along the road is a Lama temple, *Shih Shêng Ssŭ* (Temple of Real Victory), which was also built in memory of Fu Hêng's victory over the Tibetans. It is now deserted and fast falling into ruins. All this area has been converted into an agricultural experimental ground,

A number of queer-looking erections on the slopes of the hills and in the plains below are worth noting. These are the forts and block-houses erected by Ch'ien Lung for the purpose of training his troops to scale Tibetan strongholds. Originally there were no less than sixty-eight of them, containing 3,532 rooms in which his soldiers were quartered. None of the barracks are left, and very few of the block-houses.

Continuing along the motor-road for about seven miles we come to a group of temples known as *Pa Ta Ch'u* (Eight Big Places). These are eight temples situated one above the other in a defile of the hills, which are poetically known as *Ts'ui Wei Shan* (Blue-green Tinted Mountains), because they were mantled with grass of that tint. The hermit-monk, Lu Shih (See Pao Chu Tung below), is probably the founder of all the temples now known as Pa Ta Ch'u. The hills here, even to this day, are called *Lu Shan* (Lu's Mountain), a name that has been adopted by several shops in Peking. The tortuous outline of this chain of hills stands out sharply delineated against the pure and tender blue of the morning sky, but in the evening the wooded slopes darken and turn to purple, and lie like a black patch against a background of fiery sky, often incredibly red and dramatic.

From the hotel at the foot of the valley a stone path leads up past these temples. Starting from the bottom we have :—

1.—*Ch'ang An Ssŭ* (Temple of Eternal Peace), now practically completely in ruins and therefore called by the natives *P'o Ta Miao* (Great Ruined Temple). There is no record of this temple.

2.—*Ling Kuang Ssŭ* (Temple of Spiritual Light). It was first built during the Sung dynasty under the name of *Lung Ch'üan Ssŭ* (Dragon Spring Temple). The Chin Emperor Ta Ting in 1162 reconstructed it and changed its name to *Chüeh Shan Ssŭ* (Hill Temple of the Highest Intelligence, i.e. Buddha). It was repaired by the Ming Emperor Hsüan Tê in 1423, and again in 1478 by Ch'êng Hua who changed the name to the present one. This is one of the handsomest temples in this section of the hills. A beautiful eleven-storeyed white octagonal pagoda used to stand at the back of the temple. It was destroyed in 1900 by the Indian troops as a punishment, because Boxers had been harboured in the temple.

3.—*San Shan An* (Three Hills Monastery). No reason is
given for this name. It probably refers to three hills or peaks
in the vicinity of the temple. This, anyhow, was the name
given to it, when it was built in 1442 by the Ming Emperor
Chêng T'ung. In 1597 Wan Li reconstructed it, as also did
Ch'ien Lung in 1786. Locally the temple is known as *Ma Chia
An* (Ma Family Nunnery), probably because some female
member of a family called Ma retired to it.

4.—*Ta Pei Ssŭ* (Temple of Great Sorrow). It was first
built during the Sung dynasty under the title of *Yin Chi Ssŭ*
(Monastery of Peaceful Repose). The Ming Emperor Chia
Ching in 1550 made considerable repairs to it. K'ang Hsi in
1712 reconstructed it and changed the name to the one it bears
at present. A stone tablet, inscribed by the President of the
Board of Rites and dated the 2nd year of Yung Chêng (1724)
recording the history of the temple, is still to be seen in the
courtyard.

5.—*Lung Wang T'ang* (Dragon King's Hall), also called
Lung Ch'üan Ssŭ (Temple of the Dragon's Source). First
built during the Liaos (916) under the name of *Ch'i Yin Ssŭ*
(Temple of Retired Abode). The Emperor Ta Ting
reconstructed it in 1180, as also did the Ming Emperors Chêng
T'ung and T'ien Shun. Yung Lo spent a large sum in 1424
for repairs and changed the name to the one it bears at
present. In the southernmost of the two enclosures is a
beautiful little pool, from which the temple takes its name,
because it is supposed to be constructed in the shape of a
dragon out of the mouth of which the water pours into
the pool.

6.—*Hsiang Chieh Ssŭ* (Temple of the Fragrant World, i.e.
Buddhist Paradise). The original was built during the reign
of the T'ang Emperor Wu Tê in 619 under the title of *P'ing
P'o Ssŭ* (Temple of the Gentle Slope). The Emperor Hsüan
Tê, in 1426, reconstructed it and changed the name to
Yüan T'ung Ssŭ (Temple of the Omniscient Buddha). In 1678
K'ang Hsi repaired it and altered the name to *Shêng Kan Ssŭ*
(We are Grateful to Buddha). The name it now bears was
given to it by Ch'ien Lung in 1749 when the temple was repaired
and enlarged. A stone slab standing in the courtyard inscribed
by Ch'ien Lung gives the history of the temple.

7.—*Pao Chu Tung* (Precious Pearl Cavern). This is the highest of all the temples in this group. The ancient name was *Shih T'o Lin* (Sitting like a corpse, motionless, amidst the hills and woods). In 1326 the Mongol Emperor T'ai Ting changed the name to *Ta T'ien Yüan Yen Shêng Ssŭ* (Monastery to the Exalted Heavens, the Source of Prolonged Life for all Saints). Chêng T'ung in 1446 reconstructed the temple, calling it *Ch'ing Liang Ssŭ* (Pure and Cool Temple).

It is said that in the reign of the Sui Emperor Jên Shou (A.D. 601-4) a monk named Lu Shih (Lu the Teacher) arrived at the foot of the mountain by boat from Chiang Nan in the South, and retired to this cavern. Hence the hill was called *Lu Shih Shan* (Lu the Teacher's Mountain), and a temple built thereon later of the same name, *Lu Shih Ssŭ*.

According to a further legend, two little boys came to the monk and begged to be enrolled as his disciples. They went daily to the hills to gather firewood, prepared his meals, and waited on him generally. Then one day, in a season of drought, when the monk was offering up prayers for rain, the two boys suddenly jumped down a well and were turned into a pair of black dragons, one large and one small—whereupon rain fell copiously.

The name Pao Chu Tung is said to have originated from the black and white spots on the rocks near the temple which were supposed to resemble pearls. But as the entrance to the cavern is in the form of a huge oyster, and as oysters produce pearls, it is more likely that the name is derived from this, than from the spots on rocks. The entrance to the cave is also supposed to resemble the tail of a peacock. The idol of Buddha, represented as sitting or floating in mist or dew, is said to have been made in the 30th year of the T'ang Emperor T'ien Pao (A.D. 742). It is recorded that in ancient times there was a fine *p'ai lou* at the entrance to the cave, which has long since disappeared.

8.—*Pi Mo Yen* (The Cliff of the Mystic Demon). This is about half a mile south-west of Pao Chu Tung on the opposite side of the ravine. Legend says that this cliff was discovered during the reign of the T'ang Emperor Wu Tê (618-628); that there was a deep pool before the entrance of the cave; and that in the cave were idols of Lu Shih and his two page boys, known as the big and little black dragons. In the reign of the Ming Emperor Ching T'ai, in 1454, a tablet was set up on the face of the cavern stating that the *Ts'ui Wei Shan Ssŭ* (Blue Green Tinted Mountain Temple) formerly stood on this site. The present temple, *Chêng Kuo Ssŭ* (Monastery of Pure Salvation), was built during the reign of Wu Tê in 620 under the name of *Kan Ying Ssŭ* (Monastery of Equable Rewards and Punishments). This was altered to *Chên Hai Ssŭ* (Protector of the Seas Temple) by Ching T'ai who reconstructed it in 1454. Three years later his successor T'ien Shun repaired it again and changed the name to the present one. In the courtyard are to be seen three stone tablets recording the above facts. The latest is dedicated in the 5th year of Ch'êng Hua (1469) by Yao Kuei, the President of the Board of Rites.

About one and a half hour's walk from Pao Chu Tung, on the north side of these hills, lies *T'ien T'ai Ssŭ* (Monastery of Exalted Heaven). The official name is *T'ien T'ai Shan Fo Tzŭ Shan Ssŭ* (Temple of the Benevolent and Compassionate Buddha of the Exalted Mountain). The temple is commonly known to foreigners as the temple of the "Imperial Mummy," to which a lot of romantic legends are attached. It is impossible in a book of this description to go into all the various stories about the "Mummy." Suffice to say that we are very doubtful about this "Imperial Mummy" and think it is simply the mummy—more likely the wooden image—of some monk and not that of the Manchu Emperor Shun Chih who, as is fairly well established, died in the Yang Hsin Tien in the Forbidden City. A suspicious, although perhaps a negative, circumstance about this temple is that none of the Chinese books mention it in any way. It seems to have sprung to life, when the so-called "mummy" was placed therein.*

However, the "Mummy," whoever it may be, is well worth a visit. It is in the rear hall, seated on a canopied throne in front of an altar loaded with numerous offerings of the pious. The robe of Imperial yellow with which it is clothed is dusty with age, but the face is smooth and full-fleshed like that of a living man.

---

*For further details *cf.* R.F. Johnston "The Romance of an Emperor" in the *New China Review* Vol. II, Nos 1 and 2.

THE MUMMY AT T'IEN T'AI SSŬ

The main hall, too, should be visited. The ornaments on the altar are of beautiful blue porcelain. The bell, some five feet high, is a magnificent specimen of chiselled bronze, and the drum which faces it across the altar as fine an example of painted vellum as you will meet with in any of the temples in China. The chief glory of the temple, in our opinion, is the frescoed panel at the rear of the screen which stands behind the Buddha. It depicts Kuan-Yin in the form of a graceful figure floating on a pearly, rippling sea. The artist who painted it was a master of his craft.

Chinese flock to this temple in large numbers in order to offer up incense to one whom they believe to be a god-emperor. Consequently, the monks possessing such a valuable " relic " are never short of funds, and keep the temple in excellent condition. As long as they have this wonderful *jo jên* (flesh man) their rice basins will be full to overflowing !

Finally, there are three other places worth visiting, on the north side of the hills. They can all three be reached by motor-car along the road leading north from *Ch'ing Lung Ch'iao* (Green Dragon Bridge), at the back of the Summer Palace.

The first is *Hei Lung T'an* (Black Dragon Pool) or, as its full name is, *Hei Lung T'an Shên Miao* (Temple of the Black Dragon's Spirit). It lies on a small hill that rises abruptly out of the plain and is famous for a large and beautiful pool of clear water. At the top of the hill, from where you obtain an excellent view over the plain and the nearby mountains, is the shrine of the Dragon King. The temple was first built in the 22nd year of Ch'êng Hua (1486). In 1681 K'ang Hsi spent a large sum for its reconstruction. In 1725, owing to a prolonged drought, Yung Chêng deputed several high officials to visit the Black Dragon Pool to burn incense and pray for rain, which thereupon at once fell in copious showers. In memory of this event, he had an honorific tablet erected with the characters *Chao Ling P'ei Tsê* (The Glorious and Divine Spirit that Fertilizes the Earth with Seasonable Showers) which was hung up in the temple. The local people claim that, whenever the pool bubbles and is covered with mist or vapour, this is caused by the breath of the Black Dragon and is a sure sign that rain is coming.

Hei Lung T'an is well-known to foreigners residing in Peking. It is, however, probably not known that away in the hills—about 35 miles north of Miao Fêng Shan—there is a *Pai Lung T'an* (White Dragon Pool). It is said that, if after prayers have been three times offered up without success at the Black Dragon Pool, the White Dragon is appealed to, good results invariably follow and rain falls at once. The Manchu Emperors used to depute high officers to burn incense at both the Black and the White Dragon Pools during the spring and autumn of each year.

Continuing west we pass in about two miles *Wên Ch'üan* (Warm Springs), where there is a small hotel with medicinal hot baths. There is also a large school here and experimental plantations. It is well worth making a short halt here, as the place has a pleasant charm of picturesque tidiness, in great contrast to the ordinary Chinese village.

About two miles further on, a road branches off from the main motor-road and running west into the hills brings you to the temple of *Ta Chüeh Ssŭ* (Temple of Great Perception).

It was first built in A.D. 1069 in the reign of the Liao Emperor Hsien Jung under the name of *Ch'ing Shui Yüan* (Garden of Pure Waters). In 1191 it was reconstructed by the Chin Emperor Ming Ch'ang, and the name changed to *Ling Ch'üan Ssŭ* (Temple of Efficacious Springs). These names are doubtless derived from the springs which still flow down the hillside through the temple grounds, winter and summer alike. In 1428, under Hsuan Tê, the temple was again rebuilt and given its present name. Both K'ang Hsi, in 1720, and Ch'ien Lung, in 1747, repaired the temple, as they have recorded on the stone tablets standing in the courtyard. There are several other tablets giving the history of the temple: as for instance, one by a monk named Chih Yen, of the Liao dynasty, and one by Wang Yu, President of the Board of Works, dated 11th year of Chêng T'ung (1446). Near the temple is a seven-storeyed pagoda called *Hsing Ying T'a* (Pagoda of Nature's Silence). This temple lying in an easily accessible situation on the lower slopes of the hills, in a park of beautiful trees, and with a fine view over the plain, is a favourite summer resort of foreigners and Chinese alike.

CHAPTER XXIV.

SOME OTHER TEMPLES

ABOUT three miles outside Peking on the motor-road
that runs from the P'ing Tsê Mên to Pa Ta Ch'u lies
the village of *Pa Li Chuang* (Eight Li Village). Just
inside the east gateway, on the north side, is the temple of
Mo Ho An (Buddha's Mother Monastery), dedicated to Moho,
the immaculate mother of Sakyamuni. She is said to have
reappeared on her son's death and bewailed his departure.
It was built during the 25th year of Chia Ching (1546), who
provided the funds and delegated his favourite eunuch Chao
Chêng to superintend the building. The entire area originally
comprised some 250 mou or 41 acres of land. Much of it,
however, has been sold off in lots by the monks. The monastery
contains some ninety *chien* (divisions). The most interesting
sight—not generally known—in this temple are the fifty stone
slabs let into the walls of a building in the east enclosure. They
are inscribed with the Buddhist scriptures in different styles of
script. These were originally written in eighteen styles of seal
characters by a monk named Mêng Ying who lived during the
epoch of the Five Dynasties (A.D. 907-960). A high official of
the Ming dynasty, Wang K'o-shou, rewrote them in thirty-two
styles of script. During Wan Li's reign twelve of the best
Hanlin scholars translated and explained the texts, and inscribed
them on stone tablets. Later an abbot of the temple, Hsing
Hung, had them transferred to smaller slabs and placed them on
the walls where they may still be seen.

In the middle of the village, also on the north side,
stands a very fine pagoda of thirteen storeys, called *Yung An
Shou T'a* (Pagoda of Everlasting Peace and Old Age). The
piece of ground on which it stands was originally the property
of a eunuch named Ku Ta-ying, who intended to build his
tomb there. But as he died, whilst absent from the capital,
the land was confiscated by the Crown. The pagoda was

erected in 1578 with funds provided by the mother of the Emperor Wan Li, the work being supervised by a eunuch called Yang Hui. Adjoining it was a temple, the *Tz'ŭ Shou Ssŭ* (Temple of Compassionate Old Age), which has now completely disappeared. Close to the pagoda stands a tablet with an inscription by the Grand Councillor Chang Chü-chêng recording the history of the temple and pagoda. Across the road behind the large brick screen are two beautiful gingko trees which were probably planted when the temple was first built.

About two miles north of Pa Li Chuang, by winding country lanes, lies the village of Chêng Fu Ssŭ (Temple of True Happiness), close to which is the old FRENCH CEMETERY. The village takes its name from a temple that stood there in the reign of Wan Li, as also the tomb of a palace eunuch, Kao Ch'ing-hsiao who must have been an important person, as according to a stone tablet discovered on the spot in recent years, he was in charge of the Ch'ien Ch'ing Kung in the Forbidden City.

The site was purchased by the French Jesuits, probably as early as 1732, to serve as burial-ground and country residence. It lay at a convenient distance both from the city and from the old Summer Palace, where they had constantly to be in attendance as Court architects, artists and astronomers. The cemetery was repaired in 1777 and again in 1863, having in the meantime fallen into complete ruin during the persecutions under Yung Chêng. In the Boxer riots of 1900 the tomb-stones were broken to pieces and the vaults destroyed. The last restorations took place in 1907 and 1917, when the monument to the French soldiers who died in the Anglo-French expedition of 1860 was removed to the cemetery north of the Peitang in the city.

Some sixty-seven tombstones of the French missionaries are now set upright in the wall of the cemetery which is over-grown with vegetation. They record the names of many famous Jesuit missionaries, such as: Gerbillon* (1707), Bouvet (1730), Régis (1738), Parennin (1741), d'Entrecolles (1741), de Brossard (1758), de Maillac (1748), Gaubil (1759), Attiret

---

*Gerbillon was first buried in the Portuguese Cemetery of Chala and only re-buried here in 1735.

(1768), Amiot (1793). It was through the letters of these great missionaries that we have the fullest and most interesting descriptions of Manchu Court life, palaces, and parks, during the 18th century.

A few hundred yards west of Pa Li Chuang is the EUNUCHS' CEMETERY, originally known as *Ching En Chuang* (Border Village of Imperial Bounty), but now called *En Chi Chuang* (Village of Imperial Favour), because Yung Lo allotted this piece of ground for the purpose. There are about one thousand seven hundred graves, with a stone monolith in front of each mound, duly inscribed with the name, rank, date of death, and other particulars. They are all of the Ming and Ch'ing dynasties. The finest is that of Li Lien-ying, Tz'ŭ Hsi's favourite who died in 1911 at the age of sixty-nine.

This beautiful cemetery has unfortunately been desecrated in recent times by the soldiers of Marshal Fêng Yü-hsiang, who have overthrown many of the tombstones, broken the marble carvings, and cut down most of the old cypresses.

About one mile beyond Pa Li Chuang we pass the village of *T'ien Ts'un* (Heaven's Village), close to the Pa Pao Shan Golf Course. From here it is about one mile south across country to the village of Hsia Chuang, near which is a most interesting temple called *Kang T'ieh Mu* (Kang T'ieh's Grave), also known as *Kang T'ieh Miao* and *Hu Kuo Ssŭ*. The correct name, however, is *Hu Kuo Pao Chung Tz'ŭ* (Ancestral Hall of the Exalted Brave and Loyal). Kang T'ieh, whose distinguishing name is Ping,— hence frequently referred to as Kang Ping—was a general under Yung Lo. On one occasion when the Emperor went off on a hunting trip, he left Kang T'ieh in charge of the palace. Kang was much gratified by the confidence shown him by his royal master in giving him such an important trust. Fearful, however, that one of his enemies night endeavour to do him an injury by reporting some imaginary irregularity with the ladies of the palace, he determined to castrate himself. Having done so, he concealed the parts in the hollow of the Emperor's saddle. As he had anticipated, when Yung Lo returned, one of the ministers reported that Kang had had improper intercourse with certain of the Imperial ladies. In reply to this accusation, Kang T'ieh explained how he had made a eunuch of himself, imploring the Emperor to send for his saddle and examine it.

The Emperor did so and found the emasculated parts hidden in the saddle. Yung Lo was so struck with the loyal general's conduct that he made him his chief eunuch. After Kang's death, the Emperor deified him as the Patron Saint of Eunuchs, building this ancestral hall in his honour, and, as we said above, bestowed a large piece of ground to be used as a cemetery for eunuchs.

The Kang T'ieh Miao is a refuge for eunuchs. In 1934 there were still some thirty odd eunuchs living on the extensive premises which occupy no less than 17 acres of land and contain several courts, halls, and the ground at the back with Kang's tomb. The eunuchs are not " Buddhist monks " as has been stated, but eunuchs pure and simple. They all work on the premises, and several of them make their daily rounds to guard against thieves; for there are many precious relics kept in the various halls. The most valuable of these are two beautiful paintings which cover the two side walls in the main hall at the back, as well as a painting of Kang T'ieh himself. The wall paintings which look as fresh as if they were new are scenes from Kang's life as a warrior. The front courts contain several large stone tablets inscribed by the Ming Emperors Chia Ching and Wan Li, also by K'ang Hsi, and one of the 12th year of T'ung Chih (1873). There is a beautiful grove of pine trees, also six magnificent gingkos.

Several miles west of Pa Li Chuang, in the village of *Huang Ts'un* (Yellow Village), where the motor-road turns sharp north to Pa Ta Ch'u, stands a famous nunnery called *Pao Ming Ssŭ* (Temple for the Protection of the Ming Dynasty). This is a very ancient temple. It is recorded that when the Ming Emperor Chêng T'ung, on his way to a campaign against the Mongols, passed by this nunnery, the abbess approached him and on her bended knees begged him not to proceed as it would be fatal to him. His Majesty took no notice of her pleadings and went on his way. As the abbess had foretold, the campaign ended in disaster, costing thousands of lives, the Emperor barely escaping with his own. On his return to Peking Chêng T'ung visited the nunnery and thanked the abbess for her prediction. He also ennobled her with the title *Yü Mei* (Imperial Sister) and presented her with a large sum wherewith to repair the temple. It is for this reason that the people living in the neighbourhood always refer to the nunnery as *Huang Ku Ssŭ* (Temple of the Emperor's Sister).

The Emperor's generosity would, however, seem to have had a bad effect upon the morals of the nunnery. For in 1527, some eighty years later, the Emperor Chia Ching received a memorial from the Censor Kuei Ao to the effect that the nuns of the Pao Ming Ssŭ were nothing but a lot of harlots, that men of all descriptions were harboured in the premises day and night, and great carousals were being held there. Chia Ching not believing that such things were possible, deputed a high official named Huo T'ao to investigate the charges. Huo T'ao raided the place and found that the facts as stated by Kuei Ao were only too true. The Emperor on being informed became highly incensed and issued an edict that all nunneries were to be destroyed and the nuns driven out. The nuns of the Pao Ming Ssŭ, however, sent a delegate to the Palace and got the eunuchs to inform the two old Empress-Dowagers who, in turn, prevailed upon the Emperor to spare their temple, though all other nunneries were destroyed, as he had commanded. Chia Ching also issued a decree that all those nuns who had no homes to return to, were to live in the Pao Ming Ssŭ. Had it not been for the interference of the two Dowagers, it is possible that nuns in China would have ceased to exist from that date. A stone tablet called the *Hui Ni Pei* (Destroy Nuns Tablet) with an inscription by Huo T'ao still stands in the grounds of this nunnery, but the characters are nearly all obliterated.

If, instead of turning north at Huang Ts'un, we continue straight on, we shall come, on the south side of the road, to a hill rising abruptly out of the plain. This is *Shih Ching Shan* (Stone View Hill). There are three temples on this hill :—

1.—*Yü Huang Tien* (Palace of the Jade Emperor). Built during the reign of the T'ang Emperor Wu Tê, A.D. 620. The Ming Emperor Chêng Tê reconstructed it in 1614 and changed the name to *Chin Ko Ssŭ* (Golden Pavilion). This latter name is probably derived from the fact that all the idols therein are coated with gold leaf.

2.—*Yüan Chün Miao* (Temple to Almighty God). It was built in 1507, in the reign of Chêng Tê, by an official named Ch'ien Ning, who provided the funds. Owing to the very

shady proceedings in this temple, the Ming Emperor Chia
Ching ordered it to be destroyed. But later, some time during
Wan Li's reign (1573-1619), one of his eunuchs rebuilt the
temple on the old site, under the original name. For this
action he was severely criticized by a scholar named Tai To,
who wrote a book called Tai To Yeh T'an (Tai To's Night
Talks) in which he fearlessly attacked the eunuch, stating *inter
alia* that he did not even fear the Emperor himself. The latter,
however, ignored Tai To's ravings and favoured the eunuch
more than ever.

3.—*Pei Hui Chi Miao* (Northern Temple of Gracious
Salvation). Erected in 1729 in the reign of Yung Chêng. It is
recorded that, owing to the constant overflowing of the nearby
river, *Hun Ho* (Muddy River), and the resulting destruction
of crops, Yung Chêng granted huge sums for the building of
dikes, and AFTER the work was finished, erected the temple to
be the guardian of the waters. However, it is stated that no
floods have occurred in that district since the temple was built !

Several miles further down the river, close to where the
Peking-Hankow railway crosses it, at a distance of seven miles
from Peking, is the famous bridge of *Lu Kou Ch'iao* (Reed Ditch
Bridge). It is better known to foreigners as the MARCO POLO
BRIDGE, because he was the first foreigner to mention it in his
writings, having crossed it in the 13th century. His description
is as follows :—

" When you leave the City of Cambaluc [Peking] and have
ridden ten miles, you come to a very large river which is called
Pulisangkin and flows into the ocean, so that merchants with
their merchandise ascend to it from the sea. Over this river
there is a very fine stone bridge, so fine indeed, that it has very
few equals.

" The fashion of it is this : It is 300 paces in length and
it must have a good eight paces in width, for ten mounted
men can ride across it abreast. It has 24 arches and as many
water-mills, and is all of a very fine marble, well built and
firmly founded. Along the top of the bridge there is on either
side a parapet of marble slabs and columns made in this way :
At the beginning of the bridge there is a marble column, and
under it a marble lion, so that the column stands upon the
lion's loins, whilst on the top of the column there is a second

lion, both being of great size and beautifully executed sculpture. At the distance of a pace from this column there is another precisely the same, also with its two lions and the space between them is closed with slabs of grey marble to prevent people from falling over into the water. And thus the columns run from space to space along either side of the bridge, so that altogether it is a beautiful object."*

There are three points in this description worth noting, though we shall not enter into the controversy which they have aroused :

1.—The name Pul-i-sangin means in Persian " The Stone Bridge." It is probable that Marco Polo gave it this name, because it sounds something like the Chinese name of the river at that time, which was Sang Ch'ien Ho.

2.—The river, nowadays anyhow, is not navigable for boats with merchandise.

3.—The bridge has only 11 arches, not 24 as Marco Polo says. However, as it has been rebuilt since his day, this may account for the difference.

The bridge took five years to build (1189-1194) and it is recorded that thousands of workmen were employed in its construction. There is an interesting legend attached to the bridge as follows :—

When the bridge was completed, a monk named Wan Sung Lao Jên (Old Man of Ten Thousand Pines) appeared one day and said that as the ancient name of the river was *Sang Ch'ien Ho* (Mulberry Heaven River)—a name that always caused heavy floods because *sang* (mulberry) has the same sound as *sang* (sorrow) and *ch'ien* (heaven) the same sound as *chien* (sword), making 'Sorrow's Sword'—it was necessary, in order to avoid evil consequences, to set up a charm to control the waters. So he placed a large boulder beneath the central arch and carved thereon a Precious Sword, ôn which was inscribed in large characters, *Chu Lung Chien* (Exterminate the Dragon Sword). The charm, however, did not work, for in 1698 the bridge was destroyed by a flood. It was rebuilt by K'ang Hsi in the same year, when the name Sang Ch'ien Ho was

---

* Yule, The Book of Marco Polo, Vol. II, pp. 3-4.

changed to *Yung Ting Ho* (Everlasting Settled and Peaceful River). In July 1890 another serious flood occurred, in which several of the arches were washed away and have never been replaced.

The bridge has at present 11 arches. The number of carved lions on the balustrade and columns are said to total 280, but the exact number is in dispute. In the account of the bridge at the time it was repaired under the Ming Emperor Chia Ching it is specially stated that there are so many lions that it is impossible to count them, whilst local tradition has it, that several people have gone out of their minds in attempting to do so. Two pavilions were erected at each end by the Emperors K'ang Hsi and Ch'ien Lung respectively, and the marble tablets standing in them record the history of the bridge.

Across the far side of the Hun Ho, right away in the hills, lie two more well-known temples.

The first, *Chieh T'ai Ssŭ* (Ordination Terrace Temple), can be reached in four hours by donkey from the station of Ch'ang Hsin Tien on the Peking-Hankow railway.

It was originally a temple called *Hui Chü Ssŭ* (Wise Assembly Temple) built in the reign of the T'ang Emperor Wu Tê (A.D. 618-626). In the time of the Liao dynasty a famous monk, Fa Chün, retired to this spot and in 1070 erected an altar here for the purpose of ordaining monks, attracting a large number of followers. The dagoba containing his ashes stands below the north end of the terrace, and close by, on the terrace itself, is a stone tablet recording his meritorious deeds. After his death the temple fell into ruins and was not rebuilt till the 5th year Chêng T'ung (1441) under its present name. After the reign of the Emperor Wan Li the temple again fell into disrepair. The Emperor K'ang Hsi visited the place and, in the 24th year of his reign (1685), ordered it to be repaired. Ch'ien Lung stayed there repeatedly and did much towards its embellishment. The famous Manchu statesman, Prince Kung, who retired here when he withdrew from political life in 1888, subscribed a large sum towards the upkeep of the temple. The rooms he occupied are still shown.

On the north side of the first main hall is an enclosure in which is the *Ch'an T'ang* (Hall of Meditation) containing the famous wooden gong and ancient bell that were brought from

Honan by the Abbot Hsin Yang in the early 15th century.
The terrace above is famous for several very ancient trees,
amongst which, almost the first on your right as you enter, is
the *Wo Lung Sung* (Sleeping Dragon Pine) contorted in the
most fantastic way and supported by a fairly modern tablet.
At the north end of the terrace there is a famous White Pine.
The northern enclosure is called *Pei T'an* (North Altar).
In the temple in the centre of this enclosure, the *Hsüan Fo
Ch'ang* (Place of Choosing Buddha), the novices take their
vows. The initiation ceremony takes place once a year, and
the novices have to undergo considerable tests of endurance,
as for instance having lighted incense sticks applied to their
bare scalps until they leave a burnt scar. The buildings
running round this enclosure contain the idols of the Five
Hundred Lohans.

The temple is much frequented by both foreigners and
Chinese on account of its picturesque situation and the fine
view one obtains from the terrace.

In the neighbourhood are several caves with fancy names
such as " Cave of Great Antiquity," or " Kuan-yin's Grotto."
About a mile and a half west is a high peak, the *Hsiu Yüan T'o
Fêng* (Beautiful View of the Camel's Peak) also called *Chi Lo
Fêng* (Peak of Joy). Nearby, is a temple of the same name.
En route, there is a spring the waters of which are icy cold.
Each year during the 6th day of the 6th Moon, the monks
belonging to the Chieh T'ai Ssŭ and Chi Lo Ssŭ put out their
sacred books to dry in the sun, and each year during the 3rd
and 4th Moons thousands of sightseers swarm to the place
to worship, and view the scenery.

The other large monastery, *T'an Chê Ssŭ* (Monastery of
Clear Pools and Wild Mulberry), lies about six miles north-
west of Chieh T'ai Ssŭ. It is a very ancient temple dating
from the Southern Sungs (1127-1279). K'ang Hsi repaired the
temple and changed the name to *Hsiu Yü Ssŭ* (Cloud Cliff
Temple). But the common appellation for it at the present
day is *T'an Chou Ssŭ*, which is an old name for Ch'angsha, the
capital of Hunan, as it was founded by monks from that city.

The monks are said to have been recruited in former days
from escaped criminals who had taken monastic vows, and were
therefore, free from arrest. There is a vast area belonging to

the temple which they were obliged to cultivate for their livelihood.

In one of the halls is a large picture of a pagoda inscribed
with Chinese characters repeated again and again; it is called
Hsin Ching T'a T'u (Map of the Sacred Scriptures Pagoda).
K'ang Hsi and Ch'ien Lung, whenever they stayed at or visited
the temple burnt incense before the picture. Several scrolls
written by these two Emperors, of which the monks are very
proud, are still hanging on the walls of some of the halls.
In a hall at the back, dedicated to Kuan-yin, is a portrait
of the Princess Miao Yên, the daughter of Kublai Khan, a
devout disciple of Buddha, who cut off her hair and lived in
the temple. As she never ceased praying to Kuan-yin day
and night, her mortal remains—she died in this monastery—
were buried in the grounds, and her portrait hung on the walls,
where it is still to be seen at the present day. In the principal
hall are a couple of snakes in a box. The characters printed
on the outside read *Hu Fa Lung Wang* (Protectors of the Law,
Buddha-Dragon Kings). The faithful always burn incense
before them for good luck! At the back of this hall is a
pagoda about 50 feet high called *Yên Shou T'a* (Pagoda of
Extended Years), said to have been built by a Ming Prince
named Chan Yung, whose title was Yüeh Ching. The two
fine gingko trees here are worth noting.

Two springs, one coming from an easterly direction, and
the other from the south-west, meet together and feed the
Lung Ch'ih T'an (Dragon's Pool Altar), which is frequented
by thousands of pilgrims at festival time.

To visit both these temples in comfort, at least two days
are required, in which case it will be necessary to take bedding
and provisions along with one. Good accommodation, for
which there is a fixed tariff, can be obtained at both places.

CHINESE VIEW OF THE MING TOMBS

Chapter XXV.

THE MING TOMBS. THE GREAT WALL.

TONGSHAN HOT SPRINGS

THE MING TOMBS known in Chinese as *Shih San Ling* (Thirteen Tombs) are the burial-ground of thirteen Ming Emperors.

The tombs can be reached either by motor-car, by the road to the Summer Palace and turning north at Ch'ing L'ung Ch'iao ; or by train from Hsichihmen station to Nankow, from where it is a seven miles' ride (by donkey or chair) to the tomb of Yung Lo.

The gateway at the beginning of the approach attracts special attention. Ninety feet long by fifty feet high, composed of marble, and seemingly roofed with tiles, it is visible at a great distance. On nearer inspection, however, it is found that the roof is of carved marble. The whole structure is a remarkable piece of architecture. The *p'ai lou* in China takes the place of the triumphal arch of Europe and America, and this one at the Ming tombs is the finest in the whole country. It was erected three and a half centuries ago, at a time when the Chinese building art had reached its culminating point. The original red and green colours have long since weathered down to a sober grey.

About half a mile beyond we pass through the *Ta Hung Mên* (Great Red Gate) which was the real entrance to the cemetery ; originally it was closed by massive wooden doors which have long since disappeared. Proceeding through several avenues of trees—unfortunately now mostly cut down for fuel—and several gateways we reach the avenue of animals, a truly striking feature. Statesmen, lions, unicorns, camels and elephants stand and kneel in pairs. The four elephants are each cut from one block of stone and are thirteen feet high and fourteen feet long.

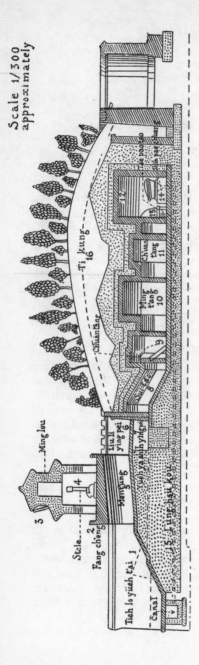

Scale 1/300 approximately

25. Cross Section of the Burial Chambers of an Imperial Tomb

From G. Bouillard's "Les Tombeaux Impériaux"

1 Tieh Lo Yüeh T'ai (Piled-up, or elevated Moon
   Terrace)
2 Fang Ch'êng (Square Ramparts)
3 Ming Lou (Brilliant Tower)
4 Pei (Stela mounted on Tortoise)
5 Mên Tung (Entrance to Tunnel)
6 Liu-li Ying P'i (Glazed Tiles Spirit Screen)
7 Yüeh Ya Shih Ying P'i (Crescent-shaped Stone Wall)
8 Sui Tao (Passage to the Vault)

9   Ch'uan T'ang (Open Passage)
10 Ming T'ang (Brilliant Hall)
11 Ch'uang T'ang (Entrance Hall leading to Gold
    Chamber of the Crypt)
12 Burial Chamber
13 Ts'ê Pao Tso (Precious Throne)
14 Shih Pao Ch'uang (Precious Stone Bed)
15 Lung Hsü Kou (Dragon Whiskers Drain)
16 Ti Kung (Subterranean Palace)

From here, in about a mile and a half, we come to the tomb of Yung Lo, the founder of modern Peking. The hall of sacrifice is another remarkable work of architecture. It is seventy yards long by thirty feet deep. The teak pillars, twelve feet round and thirty-two feet high, are thirty-two in number. The building is sixty-four feet high. It is reached by a marble ascent of eighteen steps, and is surrounded by beautifully-carved balustrades. The roof juts out ten feet beyond the walls on which it rests. The fourth great feature of the Ming tombs is the tomb itself. In front of it is a mass of solid stone-work which supports the stone tablet on which is inscribed in characters of enormous size the posthumous name of the Emperor Yung Lo who died in A.D. 1424. Beneath this is the coffin-passage, thirty-nine yards long, leading to the sealed tomb-door, from where the visitor ascends to the platform above by a long staircase. Here the tablet, three feet thick, six feet wide, and high in proportion, with the Emperor's name on it, may be observed. Then there is the mound, half a mile in circuit, containing a hemispherical chamber, in which the coffin is deposited. The chamber is said to be large enough to hold four hundred persons.

In the construction of the Ming tombs we see Chinese architectural skill at its best, so many remarkable features are combined which impart to these Imperial tombs an air of great dignity and solemnity. The remaining twelve tombs are on a much lesser scale, and need not be described.

The station on the Peking-Suiyuan line for the Great Wall is called *Ch'ing Lung Ch'iao* (Green Dragon Bridge), about two hours from Nankow. One can get a train up from the Hsichih-men Station in the morning, spend a few hours at the Wall, and return by the afternoon train. If this trip is combined with that to the Ming Tombs, then one can stay over at the hotel at Nankow Station.

THE GREAT WALL or *Wan Li Ch'ang Ch'êng* (Ten Thousand Li Long Wall), as it is called by the Chinese, stretches from Shanhaikuan on the Gulf of Chihli (lat. 40 degrees North; long. 119 degrees 44 minutes East) to Chia Yü Kuan in Kansu (long. 98 degrees, 14 minutes East). Starting from the sea coast, the Wall in its journey towards the highlands of Tibet traverses successively the breadths of four of the eighteen

KEY

1 Marble Pailou
2 *Ta Hung Mên* (Great Red Gate)
3 *Hsiao Hung Mên* (Small Red Gate)
4 Pavilion with Tablet
5 Avenue of Animals and Officials
6 *Ling Hsing Mên* (Starry Wicket Gate)
7 Tomb of Yung Lo   died 1424
8 „   „ Hung Hsi   „ 1425
9 „   „ Hsüan Tê   „ 1435
10 „   „ Chia Ching   „ 1566
11 „   „ T'ien Ch'i   „ 1627
12 „   „ T'ai Ch'ang „ 1620
13 „   „ Chêng T'ung „ 1449
14 „   „ Ch'êng Hua   „ 1487
15 „   „ Hung Chih   „ 1505
16 „   „ Chêng Tê   „ 1521
17 „   „ Wan Li   „ 1619
18 „   „ Lung Ch'ing „ 1572
19 „   „ Ch'ung Chêng „ 1644

Actually there were sixteen sovereigns of this dynasty. The three missing from the mausolea are: the founder, Hung Wu, buried at Nanking; the second, Chien Wen, who was not considered a lawful ruler by his successors; and the seventh, Ching T'ai, likewise so regarded, because he usurped the throne while his brother Cheng T'ung (later T'ien Shun) was a prisoner of the Tartars. Ching T'ai is buried near the Jade Fountain.

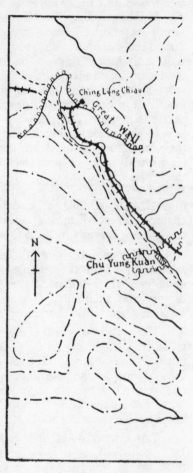

26. MING TOMBS

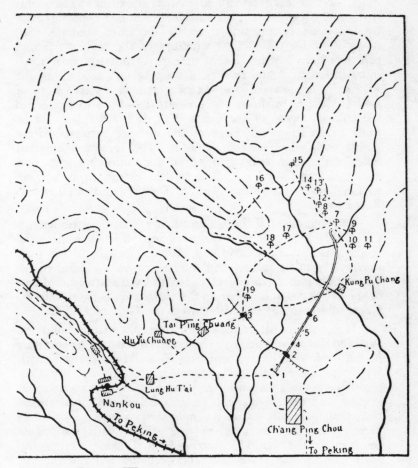

15

16

14 13

12

8

17 7

18 9

10 11

19 Kung Pu Chang

Tai Ping Chuang 3

Hu Yu Chuang 6

5

4

2

Lung Hu T'ai 1

Nankou

To Peking →

Ch'ang Ping Chou

↓
To Peking

AND GREAT WALL

provinces of China Proper, i.e. Chihli (the present Hopei), Shansi, Shensi and Kansu.

The distance between the two places in a straight line, is calculated by the Chinese to be roughly 4,440 li or 1,332 English miles. But as this great structure twists and turns and frequently doubles back on itself, it stands to reason that a measurement by longitude calculations must be far from accurate. So, if we allow for the various windings of the wall, we should probably have a main line of defence of not less than 1,700 miles in length. And further, if we take into account all the reinforcing arms and loops, we have at least a total length of no less than 2,500 miles. In order to enable us to appreciate the colossal extent of the Great Wall, it is helpful for us to think of its length in terms of the distance between certain points with which we are familiar. The seventeen hundred miles of the main wall (ignoring all the reinforcing loops and arms), if transported elsewhere, would extend from London to Leningrad, from New York to Denver, or from Paris to Bucharest.

The building of this extraordinary wall is attributed to Ch'in Shih Huang in 221 B.C.; but long before his time the feudal states of Yen, Chao and Ch'in built walls across their northern frontiers to keep out the Hsiung-nu and other tribes. Ch'in Shih Huang simply extended the walls after his defeat of the Six States and linked up the various walls from Chia Yü Kuan in Kansu to Shanhaikuan on the Gulf of Chihli.

It is stated that it took him twenty years to build the Wall and that, in addition to over 300,000 troops, all the criminals in the land were put to work on it, and even many literati. By the time the Wall was completed, probably no less than a million persons had been employed in its construction. It is even said that so many of these workers died in the hard task, that their corpses were simply thrown into the embankment. Hence the grim popular saying : " The Wall is the longest cemetery in the world." According to Chinese records the Wall was repaired seven times between the 2nd and the 7th centuries A.D., and once more under the Mings.

The dimensions of the Wall are : height varying from 20 to 30 feet ; width at base 25 feet to 15 feet on level of platform above ; the latter width would allow five or six horsemen to ride abreast. The mass of the Wall is heavily tamped earth faced on both sides with brick, and at the base with stone. The mortar used—its composition is now a lost art—is snowy white and binds the masonry firmly. By Chinese doctors it is considered to possess valuable medical properties. It is estimated that the cubic content of the Great Wall at the Nankow Pass is 422,400 cubic feet per mile, and that the cost of construction to-day would be at least $100,000 per mile.

Every 360 Chinese feet watch and defence towers were erected. These towers were mostly located at points of advantage on high peaks or at the head of valleys from which the sentries who defended them were able to watch for signs of the approaching enemy. Information was telegraphed to the defenders of the wall behind by means of smoke signals sent up from the platforms on the upper pavements of the towers.*

T'ang Shan (Hot Hills) lies twenty-one miles north of Peking. It can be reached by motor-car via the Summer Palace in two hours or less. If we take this route we cross the *Sha Ho* (Sand River) at the old highway leading to the Ming Tombs—seven miles to the east. On our right, behind old and crumpling walls, is the ancient city of *Sha Ch'êng* (Sand City) which takes its name from the river. Sha Ch'êng is also known as *P'ing An* (Peaceful temporary abode of the Emperor), because the T'ang Emperor Chêng Kuan is said to have put up here during a spell of sickness while on a campaign.

An alternative route is from the Anting Gate along the ancient dirt highway which leads direct north to the Springs. There is now a good bus service running daily taking about one hour either way. The charge is 80 cents per person.

The Chinese divide the Hot Hills into two—big and small. The Big Hot Hills have three peaks resembling three pen-racks ; the Small a curious conglomeration of piled-up rocks which are likened to fish scales. The Big and Small Hot Hills are only about two hundred yards apart. Between them lie two lakes, the *Pei Hu* (North Lake) and *Nan Hu* (South Lake). Officially the Hot Hills are called *Wên Ch'üan* (Warm Springs), and are famous for their curative qualities,

---

* For fuller details of this ancient bulwark the reader is referred to " The Great Wall of China, " by L. Newton Hayes, Shanghai.

especially in skin diseases. Although it is generally believed that there are TWO springs, there is really only one. The one on the east is a " dummy " fed by the one on the west from a conduit pipe laid into the tank at the bottom.

K'ang Hsi built a small palace here in 1650 and had the open air tanks enclosed by marble balustrades. Ch'ien Lung also took an interest in the Springs and as they had fallen into ruins, repaired them, setting up a stone slab inscribed with the characters *Chiu Hua Fên Hsiu* (Linked with the Beauties of Peking).

There is a foreign-style hotel with excellent baths, for which the charge is $6 per day inclusive. There are several pleasant walks about the grounds, and it is a convenient centre for excursions into the hills to view the numerous tombs there.

One of these is the tomb of Ch'êng Behlê, father of Prince Kung, the uncle of the ex-Emperor Hsüan T'ung. But the finest of all the tombs is that of Prince Kung, brother of the Emperor Hsien Fêng, who took charge of affairs during the British-French expedition in 1860-61. It stands some distance away to the north, at the foot of the hills, a magnificent mausoleum, well worth a visit while at the Springs.

NOTES

Page. 3.—TENT THEORY.—One striking feature of Chinese architecture are the curved ridges and corners of the roofs. This is generally explained as a throw back to the time when the Chinese were supposed to have lived in tents. There has been much disputation about this "Tent Theory" but no really satisfactory conclusion has been arrived at. Chinese books remain silent on the subject. If we are to assume— as some foreign authorities try to make out—that the shape of the tent was so familiar to the Chinese that they continued to preserve it even in their permanent structures of masonry, we must first of all be able to show that their dwellings were ever tents. In which period of the history of the Chinese people, complete as it is, do we find even a hint of their having lived in tents? If we go back as far as the mythical sovereigns Yu Ch'ao and the Yellow Emperor, we learn that they taught the people to build houses and cities. This is, of course, a myth; but would even myth abstain from mentioning the existence of tents, if they had been the first and usual form of dwellings?

In no Chinese works have we come across any reference pointing to their having used these portable structures as permanent habitations. Indeed, the Chinese were never nomads, but an always more or less settled people engaged in agriculture, a mode of life which excludes migratory habits. In actual fact they were cave and hut dwellers. That they used tents on their numerous warlike expeditions, even in remote antiquity, we must concede, as they would have learnt their usefulness in such cases from their northern nomadic neighbours.

Moreover it must be observed that the curve in Chinese roofs has scarcely anything resembling a tent. The outlines of the latter are necessarily straight, and it is only the space between the framework covered with cloth, skins and such material, that would sag and show a curve. The yurt of the

Tartars, Kalmuks, and Kirghiz is round and often hemi-spherical, bearing no resemblance whatever to a Chinese house.

In Chinese buildings it is the masonry or beams at both ends and sometimes the ridge of the roof that show the typical curve. The roof surface itself, on the contrary, is perfectly even and bears—more especially in South China—obvious traces of split bamboo roofing, alternately concave and convex. The convex portions swell upwards like ribs, a form that it has been found useful to follow even in the tile roofs. It is therefore probable that the Chinese house of the present day originated from caves and huts. And the puzzling flourish of corners and ridge of the roof can, if it must be derived from anything, be ascribed to the uneven forms of the rude material used to build the primeval hut.

Page 3.—The Eight Views of Peking.—Called in Chinese *Yen Ching Pa Ching* (Eight Views of Yenching). They are :—

(1) *T'ai I Ch'ing Po* (The rippling waves in fine weather on the T'ai I). That is the Three Seas : Pei, Chung and Nan Hai.

(2) *Yü Ch'uan Ch'ui Hung* (The reflection of the rainbow in the Jade Springs). At the Jade Fountain.

(3) *Hsi Shan Chi Hsüeh* (The clear snow on the Western Hills).

(4) *Chin T'ai Hsi Chao* (The reflection of the evening sun on the Golden Terrace). The Golden Terrace which lies about half a mile north-east of the Altar of Heaven was built by Prince Tan of the State of Yen. It is now nothing but a bare mound.

(5) *Chü Yung Tieh Ts'ui* (The Green Ranges of Chü Yung). This is the walled fortress of Chü Yung Kuan which lies about seven miles north-west of Nankow Station. It dates from the Sung dynasty (A.D. 960). It is not the Nankow Pass, as has been stated in some books, but is a gate in that pass, the name of which, *Nan K'ou* (South Mouth) refers to its whole length from Ch'ing Lung Ch'iao to the plains.

(6) *Chi Mên Yen Shu* (The density of the trees surrounding the Gate of Chi). (See Introduction).

(7) *Ch'iung Tao Ch'un Yin* (The Spring Warmth on Ch'iung Tao). The island in the Pei Hai.

(8) *Lu Kou Ch'iao Hsiao Yüeh* (The reflection of the moon at dawn on the bridge at Lu Kou Ch'iao i.e. the shadow cast by a pagoda on the bridge). This pagoda, the *Kuo Chieh T'a* (Crossing the Road Pagoda) was erected in 1346 by the Mongol Emperor Chih Chêng at the west end of the bridge.

Page. 29.—LIONS.—The question has often been asked: " Why is it that lions are placed at gateways of temples and palaces, when there are said to be no such animals in China ? " The reason probably is that the lion, indigenous to Persia and Syria, was first borrowed from that part of the world by the Buddhists of India as an ornament in their mythological conceptions, when they found, in their religious disputations with Persians, Greeks and others, that it was quoted as the king of beasts and the symbol of victory. From India it was carried to China. (In many parts of the Bible the lion is mentioned as a symbol of courage, power, and victory.)

The female is represented with a cub under her right paw beneath which is milk for the cub to suck. The male is represented as playing with a ball under his left foot. The ball is supposed to contain milk transferred from the female, not for the male to feed on, but to be squeezed out by sick people and used as a medicine.

Page 30.—YIN YANG.—Yin is the female or negative principle in nature, as opposed to Yang, which is the principle of light and life. North, for example, which is cold, is Yin, whereas, South is Yang, being warm. Cold water is Yin and hot water Yang. Anything concave, as, for instance, a tile, is Yin; the convex part is Yang. The bottom or inner side of a leaf is Yin, the top or outside, Yang. The sun is the concrete essence of the male principle, the moon the female principle. Hence darkness is Yin, and light Yang. As can be seen from the above, everything—animate or inanimate—has its Yin or Yang principle. Odd numbers are YANG, even numbers YIN.

Page 31.—LYTTON COMMISSION.—A Commission under the chairmanship of Lord Lytton was sent out to the Far East in

1932 by the League of Nations to report on the seizure of Manchuria by Japan.

Page 35.—THE TORTOISE.—Emblem of strength, endurance and longevity. It is mostly represented as supporting a pei or stela symbolizing the upholding of the world corresponding to the Greek legend of Atlas.

Page 49.—THE EIGHT BANNERS (*Pa Ch'i*).—These constituted the army of the Manchu Dynasty, corresponding roughly to divisions in a modern army. They were divided into two classes and distinguished by different colours as follows :—

The Three Superior Banners :
    (1) Bordered Yellow
    (2) Plain Yellow
    (3) Plain White

The Five Inferior Banners :
    (4) Bordered White
    (5) Plain Red
    (6) Bordered Red
    (7) Plain Blue
    (8) Bordered Blue

The nationalities composing the Banner troops were Manchu, Mongolian, Chinese. These last, known as *Han Chün*, were the descendants of those natives of North China who had joined the Manchu invaders during the period of their contest with the Ming dynasty in the early part of the seventeenth century.

Page 54.—THE " PEARL CONCUBINE."—All books refer to this lady as the " Pearl." This is incorrect. Her Manchu family name was T'at'ala Shih; her father whose Chinese name was Chang Hsü, was a gentleman-in-waiting at the Court. The daughters of Manchus were never given any special name, but were called *koko* or *ku niang* by friends and servants ; their "milk" or pet names being only used by members of the family.

When the " Pearl " and her sister entered the palace as Imperial Concubines of the Second Rank (*p'in fei*), she was given the courtesy title Chên Fei (The Precious Concubine) and her sister that of Chin Fei (The Brilliant Concubine). In 1886, on the occasion of the Empress-Dowager's sixtieth birthday, they were promoted to Imperial Concubines of the First Rank (*kuei fei*). Thereafter they were addressed as "Mistress," that is Chin Chu (Mistress Brilliant) and Chên Chu

(Mistress Precious). The mistake in calling the latter the
" Pearl " arose from the fact that *chu* (master or mistress) has
the same sound—but different tone—as *chu* (pearl).

Page 60.—LOHANS.—These Eighteen Lohans found along
the east and west walls of many temples are supposed to be the
images of Buddha's disciples who have not yet attained Nirvana.
Lohan is the Chinese for the Sanskrit word Arhan or Arhat.
Although incense is generally burnt before their images, they
are not worshipped or consulted, as are other temple deities.
Sixteen only are to be found in Korea and Japan ; the additional
two are of Chinese origin, called *Hsiang Lung* (Vanquishing the
Dragon) and *Fu Hu* (Subduing the Tiger), but it is not known
who they are.

Page 83.—HSI WANG MU.—The Western Royal Mother, a
Taoist divinity who dwelt on the legendary K'un Lun
Mountains on the banks of the Jasper Lake, the abode of the
Immortals.

Page 91.—THE LOTUS FLOWER.—There are two kinds of
lotus, the red and the white. The seeds of the former are eaten,
whereas the seed-cases of the latter being empty the Chinese
call them " blind " (*hsia*). The roots of both varieties are also
edible : those of the white, called *ou*, being succulent and tender
are preserved in sugar and eaten raw ; those of the red are tough
and stringy and have first to be cooked. A Chinese saying
distinguishes between the two kinds : " Hung hua chieh
lien p'êng, pai hua chieh ou " (The red flower bears the seed-case,
the white yields the root). As nothing is wasted in China, the
leaves of the lotus are also turned to practical use : for wrapping
up meats to keep them fresh, and for placing over a pot of steaming congee, to purify it and give it a greenish tint.

Apart from its food qualities, the lotus enters largely into
works of art. It is specially connected with Buddha who is
always represented sitting on a lotus throne. It also symbolizes
female beauty : the small feet of Chinese women were called
Chin lien hua (Golden Lotus Flowers).

On the 15th of the Seventh Moon the ceremony commonly
known as *Kuei Chieh* (Spirit Festival) is celebrated at night by
setting lotus leaves with lighted candles afloat on the lake.
This ceremony dates from A.D. 733 and was originally called
Yü Lan P'ên Hui (Festival of the Delivery of Hungry Souls).

Children join in the fun, going about the streets carrying lanterns of lotus leaf or other ingenious shapes. On this evening an official celebration in memory of those who had died in action is held. A large paper boat, sixty to a hundred feet in length, with a crew of paper men and rows of lighted candles, is set afloat to the accompaniment of martial music, to remind the dead that they are remembered by a grateful country for whom they have given their lives. After the ceremony the " ghost boat " is set on fire, so that its spirit passengers can return to their abode by the light of the countless lanterns floating on the water.

Page 95.—HSIANG FEI.—This is the translation of her maiden name in her own language, because from her childhood days a faint aroma was said to have exuded from her body.

According to some accounts, she did not commit suicide, but was strangled by two eunuchs with a white silken scarf, on the orders of Ch'ien Lung's mother, the Empress-Dowager.

Page 103.—THE AUDIENCE IN THE TZU KUANG KO.—(See illustration on p. 102) On June 29, 1873, the Emperor T'ung Chih received in audience the Ministers of Russia (Vlangaly), United States (Frederick F. Low), Great Britain (Thomas F. Wade), France (de Geofroy), and Netherlands (Ferguson). M. Vlangaly headed the Ministers, because he had been longest in Peking. The Japanese envoy does not appear in the picture, because as specially appointed plenipotentiary he was granted a special private audience prior to the arrival of the others.

The picture shows the Emperor seated on his throne facing south, with two Princes of the Blood on either side, and Prince Kung kneeling in front. Ranged on either side of the hall are the ministers of the Tsungli Yamen and other Boards. The Grand Secretary Wên Hsiang is seen standing to the left of the Dragon Table (Lung Shu An), a little in front of the foreign ministers.

The envoys entered the hall in their proper order, each carrying his Letter of Credence, and on reaching the centre aisle halted facing north, and bowed all together. Then advancing in line a few steps they bowed again, and when they had nearly reached the Dragon Table in the centre of the hall they bowed for the third time. After that they stood erect in the following order (from the right) : Russia, United States, Great

Britain, France, Netherlands. M. Bismarck, the Interpreter of the German Legation, is seen standing behind the Russian Minister. (The German Minister being ill was unable to attend).

M. Vlangaly then read aloud an address in French which was translated into Chinese by M. Bismarck. Its purport was as follows :—The Ministers on behalf of the Heads of their States had the honour to offer their congratulations to His Imperial Majesty on the attainment of His majority, and their best wishes for the future. They called to mind the achievements of his great ancestor, K'ang Hsi, who had raised the Empire to an unprecedented height of glory and power and who, at the same time, had always encouraged the arts and sciences of the West. They looked forward to a renewal of that same prosperity under His present Majesty, and especially to the establishment of friendly relations between China and the Treaty Powers which their governments ardently desired. They had the honour to lay before His Majesty their Letters of Credence.

The address having been read, the Foreign Ministers made another reverence and laid their Letters on the Dragon Table. The Emperor was pleased to make a slight inclination of the head in their direction and addressing Prince Kung in Manchu informed him that he acknowledged the receipt of the Letters of Credence. The Prince rising from his knees and with uplifted arms—following the rule of Confucius in the presence of his sovereign—came down the steps to the Foreign Envoys and gave them this message in Chinese. He then returned to his kneeling position in front of the throne. His Majesty then kindly asked after the health of the Chiefs of the States represented and expressed the hope that all foreign questions would be satisfactorily disposed of in discussion with the Tsungli Yamen. Prince Kung descended in the same way as before and passed on the Emperor's words.

The envoys made another obeisance and retired backwards, bowing repeatedly until they reached the entrance. From there they returned to the *Shih Ying Kung* (Palace of Prayer for Seasonable Weather), where they waited for the French envoy who had remained behind to dispose of some business connected with the Tientsin Massacre of 1870.

In the light of later knowledge, the following notes on this account of the audience may be of interest :—

(1) As we said in the text, the Tzŭ Kuang Ko was used for receiving tribute missions from the outer tribes, where for instance the chieftains from Formosa or the Liuchoo islands were given audience, when they visited the capital. The foreign ministers being too low in the scale of civilization to be admitted within the sacred precincts of a proper Throne Hall, this was apparently the only building that could be found for them.

(2) The Chinese account of this audience says " After an interval of some duration " the ministers were taken to the Hall of Audience. In other words " after being kept waiting a long time," a favourite method of Chinese officialdom for making their visitors feel small.

(3) Again it says : " . . . . . the representatives of the Foreign States were conducted to a matshed to await the arrival of His Majesty. . . . . ." Not exactly a very dignified kind of waiting-room !

(4) Moreover, the envoys were not allowed to enter the grounds of the Middle Sea by the main gate, but only through a side gate on the west, in the same way as a petty official enters through the side gate of a Yamen, the middle one being only opened for equals or superiors.

It must be assumed that in 1873 the foreign envoys were either ignorant of Chinese customs or so anxious to have an audience at last with an Emperor of China, that they gladly submitted to these pin-pricks.

Page 117.—THE FOUR RIVERS.—These are : Chiang (Yangtze), Huang (Yellow River), Huai (in Anhui), and Chi (in Hupeh—also called the Han).

THE FOUR SEAS.—This refers to the ocean which is supposed to surround China on the four points of the compass, hence sometimes used as a term for China.

THE FIVE SACRED MOUNTAINS.—These are : T'aishan in Shantung, Hêngshan in Hunan, Huashan in Shensi, Hêngshan in Hopei, and Sungshan in Honan.

Page 122.—FENG-SHUI.—Lit. " Wind and Water," or that which cannot be seen and cannot be grasped. It is a system

of dragonology, a " science " by which, from the configuration
of natural objects such as rivers, hills and trees, it is possible to
determine the desirability of sites for tombs, houses, and even
cities. It is also able to foretell the fortunes of any community,
family or individual according to the spot selected. The
Chinese believe, for example, that if a building is too high the
dragon cannot fly low enough to spout blessings on the people
living there. They also believe that a geomancer is able to
counteract evil influences by good ones and to save whole
districts from devastation by floods, pestilence and so forth.

Page 190.—THE FOUR DOOR GUARDIANS OR HEAVENLY
KINGS.—Ssu Ta T'ien Wang, or Ssu Ta Chin Kang (Four Great
Diamond Kings), are the protectors of Buddhist temples. They
also preside over the four quarters of the universe and the four
seasons. The king who watches over the North, is black ;
his symbol is a snake and a pearl ; he is the God of Autumn.
The one who presides over the South, is red ; he holds an
umbrella, the raising of which induces a violent thunder and
rain storm ; he is the God of Spring. The God of Summer,
who presides over the East is blue ; he touches with his right
hand the chords of a guitar held in his left. The God of Winter
presides over the West ; his colour is white ; he holds a sword
in his left hand and leads an army of serpent-gods.

THE EIGHT SYMBOLS OF BUDDHISM.—Wheel of the Law,
Conch-shell, Umbrella, Canopy, Lotus, Jar, Fish, and the
Mystic Knot. This last is a sign of longevity, because it
is endless, like a true lover's knot. The conch-shell is one
of the insignia of royalty : also the emblem of the voice of
Buddha preaching the laws of his doctrine. The umbrella is a
sign of dignity and high rank. The Canopy is one of the
auspicious signs on the sole of Buddha's foot and symbolical of
the lungs. The lotus is a symbol of purity and perfection
because it grows out of mud, but is not defiled thereby. The
jar is another one of the eight auspicious signs of Buddha's
foot : it often represents symbolically the sacred stomach of
Buddha. It is used as a receptacle for sacred relics of
Buddhist saints, or as a cinerary urn in which the ashes of
cremated priests are deposited. The fish is an emblem of
wealth and abundance, because yü (fish) has the same sound as
yü (abundance).

Appendix A

OLD SITES OF PEKING

(See map opposite)

1. CHI DYNASTY.—The first record of Peking is that of the city of Chi which was given in 1121 B.C. as an appanage to the descendants of the Emperor Yao by Wu Wang, the founder of the Chou Dynasty. In a village called Huang T'ing Tzŭ to the north-west of Peking is a stone tablet with an inscription by Ch'ien Lung in praise of the city of the Chi's.

2. T'ANG DYNASTY.—Under the T'angs there was a city called Yu-chou, to the south-west of the present Tartar City. The Fa Yüan Ssŭ (Chapter XV) is said to have lain in the south-east corner of this city. It was destroyed by the Liaos in A.D. 986.

3. LIAO DYNASTY.—The Liaos built a new city here and first called it *Nan Ching* (South Capital) to distinguish it from their old capital in Manchuria and in 1013 changed the name to Yen-ching. The Po Yün Kuan (Chapter XVIII) was close to its northern wall.

4. CHIN DYNASTY.—The Chins, a Tartar dynasty, overthrew the Liaos in 1135 and greatly enlarged the city, taking in the whole of what is now known as the " Chinese City," and called it *Chung Tu* (Central Capital).

5. YUAN (MONGOL) DYNASTY.—Kublai Khan after overthrowing the Chins in 1264 built a new capital to the north of the old Chin city and called it *Ta Tu* (Great Capital). The old earth mound running east and west about a mile outside the present north wall of the city was the north wall of the Yüan city ; its eastern limits are not definitely known, as is indicated on the map.

6. MING DYNASTY.—In 1368 the Mings under Hung Wu drove out the Mongols and established their capital at

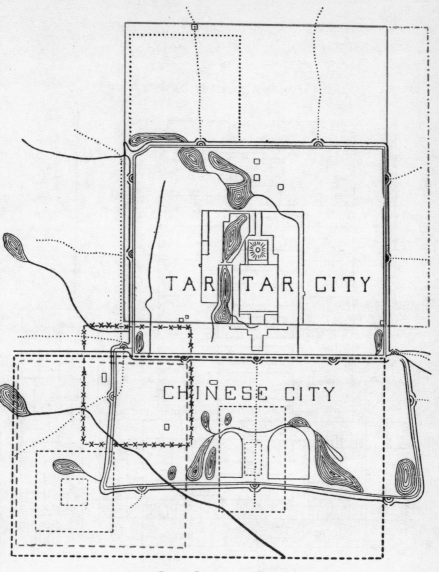

TAR TAR CITY

CHINESE CITY

27. Old Sites of Peking

(According to Favier's "Peking")

1	Chi Dynatsy	....	4	Chin Dynasty	-------------
2	T'ang Dynasty	-x-x-x-x-x-x-x	5	Yüan Dynasty	-----------
3	Liao Dynasty	-- -- -- --	6	Ming Dynasty	=========

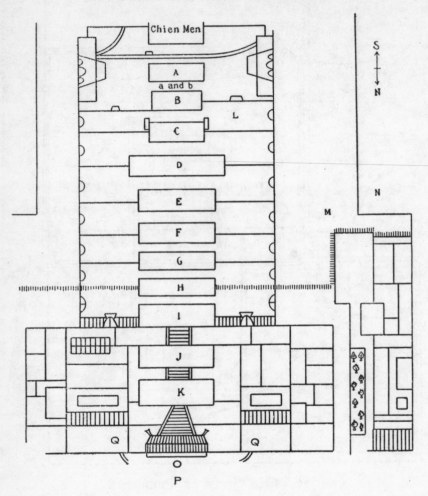

28. GEOMANTIC CHART OF PEKING

Nanking. The old capital of the Mongols became a prefectural city in 1409 under the name of Pei-p'ing Fu. Yung Lo moved the capital from Nanking to Peking which he extended to its present limits in 1421.

7. MANCHU DYNASTY.—The Manchus took over Peking from Mings in 1643, and it remained within the same limits.

8. REPUBLIC OF CHINA.—In 1928 the Nationalist Government moved the Capital back to Nanking, and Peking became Pei-p'ing again, as in the first Ming period.

KEY TO GEOMANTIC CHART

ILLUSTRATING THE INFLUENCES OF THE FIVE VISCERA AND THE FIVE ELEMENTS

A Mouth, influenced by earth and water elements

a & b Lungs, influenced by the element metal

B & C The pericardium, under the influence of fire

D The heart, under the influence of fire

E Peritoneum, influenced by the element fire

F A duct (said to connect the heart and liver) under the element wood

G Liver, under the influence of the element wood

H The gall, influenced by wood

I An anatomical point between the kidneys (said to be a danger spot).

J The left kidney, under the element water

K The right kidney, under the element fire

L The spleen, under the element earth

M The stomach, under the element earth

N The navel, under the element earth

O The end of the spine, under the element metal

P The membrum virile, under the influence of water

Q Large and small gutters. The large gutter comes under the element metal, and the small one under the influence of water

Appendix B.

·NO CHA'S BODY AS REPRESENTED BY THE CITY OF PEKING.

According to Liu Chi's* plan the various parts of No Cha's body were represented by the following sites in Peking :—

(1) No Cha's head is represented by the Ch'ien Mên
(2) His ears by the two side-gates of same
(3) His nose by the Ch'i P'an Chieh
(4) His mouth by the Chung Hua Mên
(5) His eyes by the two wells on the south side of the Ch'i P'an Chieh
(6) His right shoulder by the Hata Mên
(7) His left shoulder by the Shun Chih Mên
(8) His right hand by the Chao Yang Mên, holding the Tung Yüeh Miao, which represents No Cha's " Heaven and Earth " Diamond Bracelet
(9) His left hand by the P'ing Tsê Mên, holding the White Pagoda, which is symbolical of his " Precious Spear "
(10) His hips are represented by the Tung Hua Mên and Hsi Hua Mên
(11) His knee-pans by the Tung Chih Mên and Hsi Chih Mên
(12) His feet by the An Ting Mên and Tê Shêng Mên, treading on the " Yellow " and " Black " Temples which are symbolical of the " Wind and Fire " wheels.
(13) The red-painted walls of the Imperial City are symbolical of No Cha's red silk stomach-protector with which he subdued the third son of the Dragon King
(14) His wind-pipe is represented by the " Imperial Way " leading north from the Chung Hua Mên
(15) The ante-chambers on either side of the way represent his shoulder blades
(16) His breasts are represented by the Tung An Mên and Hsi An Mên
(17) His lungs by the space in front of the T'ien An Mên
(18) His pericardium by the T'ien An Mên and Tuan Mên

---

*Better known as Liu Po-wên, see page 28.

(19) His heart by the Wu Mên

(20) The fold of the peritoneum by the T'ai Ho Mên

(21) The T'ai Ho Tien represents a duct which according to Chinese physicians connects the heart and the liver

(22) His liver is represented by the Chung Ho Tien

(23) His gall by the Pao Ho Tien

(24) His stomach by the Three Seas

(25) His spleen by the Shê Chi T'an

(26) The open gutter in the West City (now covered-in) is his large intestine

(27) That in the East City his small intestine

(28) The Ch'ien Ch'ing Mên is an anatomical point between the kidneys, supposed to be a fatal spot

(29) The Ch'ien Ch'ing Kung and Yang Hsin Tien are his kidneys

(30) A well with a small aperture located in the western section of the Forbidden City represents the navel

(31) The Shih Ch'a Hai his bladder

(32) The bridge at the Hou Mên his membrum virile

(33) The Hou Mên the end of his spine.

Appendices C, D, E

(C) THE PRINCIPAL CHINESE DYNASTIES

Chou	1122—255 B.C.
Ch'in	255—207 B.C.
Han	206 B.C.—A.D. 264
Fourteen Minor Dynasties	A.D. 264—618
T'ang	A.D. 618—906
Five Minor Dynasties	A.D. 907—960
Sung	A.D. 960—1279
Yüan (Mongol)	A.D. 1260—1368
Ming	A.D. 1368—1644
Ch'ing (Manchu)	A.D. 1644—1912

(D) THE MONGOL (YUAN), MING, AND MANCHU EMPERORS

1.—THE ELEVEN YUAN (MONGOL) EMPERORS:

Reign Title

Chung T'ung	..	1260	Kublai Khan	A.D.	1260—1295
Chih Yüan	..	1264			
Yüan Chêng	..	1295	Timur	..	1295—1307
Ta Tê	..	1297			
Chih Ta	..	..	..	..	1307—1311
Huang Ch'ing	..	1312			1311—1320
Yen Yu	..	1314	..	..	
Chih Chih	..	..	..	..	1320—1323
T'ai Ting	..	1324	..	..	1323—1328
Chih Ho..	..	1328			
T'ien Shun	..	..	..	..	1328—1329
T'ien Li	..	..	..	..	1329
T'ien Li	..	1329	..	..	1329—1332
Chih Shun	..	1330			
Chih Shun	..	1332	..	..	1332—1335
Yüan T'ung	..	1333			
Chih Yüan	..	1335	..	..	1335—1367
Chih Chêng	..	1340			

2.—THE SIXTEEN MING (CHINESE) EMPERORS:

Reign Title

Hung Wu	..	1368—1398	
Chien Wên	..	1398—1402	
Yung Lo	..	1402—1424	(Capital moved to Peking
Hung Hsi	..	1424—1425	in 1421)
Hsüan Tê	..	1425—1435	
Chêng T'ung	..	1435—1449	
Ching T'ai	..	1449—1457	(Dethroned)
T'ien Shun	..	1457—1464	(Same Emperor as Chêng
Ch'êng Hua	..	1464—1487	T'ung, resumed
Hung Chih	..	1487—1505	government)
Chêng Tê	..	1505—1521	
Chia Ching	..	1521—1566	
Lung Ch'ing	..	1566—1572	

Reign Title

Wan Li	1572—1619
T'ai Ch'ang	1620—1620
T'ien Ch'i	1620—1627
Ch'ung Chêng	1627—1644

3.—THE TEN CH'ING (MANCHU) EMPERORS:

Reign Title

Shun Chih	1644—1662
K'ang Hsi	1662—1723
Yung Chêng	1723—1736
Ch'ien Lung	1736—1796
Chia Ch'ing	1796—1821
Tao Kuang	1821—1851
Hsien Fêng	1851—1862
T'ung Chih	1862—1875
Kuang Hsü	1875—1908
Hsüan T'ung	1908—1912 (Abdicated)

(E) PRESIDENTS OF THE CHINESE REPUBLIC

Sun Yat-sen	1912	(Provisional)
Yüan Shih-k'ai	1912—1916	
Li Yüan-hung	1916—1917	
Fêng Kuo-chang	1917—1918	
Hsü Shih-ch'ang	1918—1922	
Li Yüan-hung	1922—1923	(2nd time)
Ts'ao K'un	1923—1924	(Deposed)
Tuan Ch'i-jui	1924	("Provisional Chief Executive.")

GENEALOGICAL TABLE

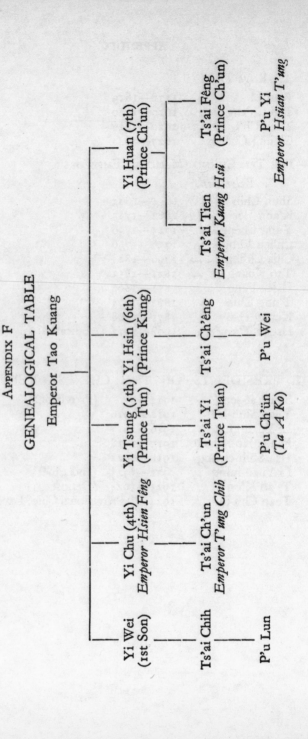

Emperor Tao Kuang

Yi Wei (1st Son)

Yi Chu (4th) *Emperor Hsien Fêng*

Yi Tsung (5th) (Prince Tun)

Yi Hsin (6th) (Prince Kung)

Yi Huan (7th) (Prince Ch'un)

Ts'ai Chih

Ts'ai Ch'un *Emperor T'ung Chih*

Ts'ai Yi (Prince Tuan)

Ts'ai Ch'êng

Ts'ai Tien *Emperor Kuang Hsü*

Ts'ai Fêng (Prince Ch'un)

P'u Lun

P'u Ch'ün (*Ta A Ko*)

P'u Wei

P'u Yi *Emperor Hsüan T'ung*

— G —

FOREIGN WORKS ON PEKING

1.—GENERAL, DESCRIPTIVE, AND TOPOGRAPHICAL :

J. R. BAYLIN, Visite aux Temples de Pékin (Translated from *Lin King*), 1921.

FATHER Hyacinth BITCHURIN, Description of Peking, 1829.

*JULIET BREDON, Peking, 3rd rev. ed., 1931.

JULIET BREDON, Le Roman d'une Ville Interdite, 1930.

BOY-ED und M. KRIEGER, Peking und Umgebung, 1910.

E. BRETSCHNEIDER, Recherches sur Pékin, 1879.

LOUIS CARPEAUX, Pékin qui s'en va, 1913.

C. GORDON CUMMINGS, Wanderings in China, Vol. 2, 1886.

*J. EDKINS, Description of Peking, 1898.

J. EDKINS, Recent Changes at Peking, 1902.

ALPH. FAVIER, Péking, 1897.

R. FORTUNE, Visits to Japan and China, 1863.

W. E. GEIL, The Eighteen Capitals of China, 1911.

PAUL GOLDMANN, Ein Sommer in China, Vol. 2, 1900.

A. E. GRANTHAM, Pencil Speakings from Peking, 1918.

DU HALDE, History of China, Vols. 1 and 2, 1735.

REV. A. P. HAPPER, A Visit to Peking, 1879.

ALPH. HUBRECHT, Grandeur et Suprématie de Pékin, 1928.

STANISLAS MILLOT, Pékin et ses Palais en Avril 1901.

*OSVALD SIREN, The Imperial Palaces of Peking, 3 vols., 1926.

OSVALD SIREN, The Gates and Walls of Peking, 1924.

2.—POLITICAL AND HISTORICAL :

BARROW, Travels in China, 1793.

*BACKHOUSE and BLAND, Annals and Memoirs of the Court of Peking, 1914.

*BLAND and BACKHOUSE, China under the Empress-Dowager, 1910.

*K. A. CARL, With the Dowager-Empress of China, 1906.

*PRINCESS DER LING, Two Years in the Forbidden City, 1912.

I. T. HEADLAND, Court Life in China, 1909.

*SIR R. F. JOHNSTON, Twilight in the Forbidden City, 1934.

STANLEY LANE-POOLE, The Life of Sir Harry Parkes, 1894.

*LOCH, Narrative of Events in China, 1863.

C. PETIT, La Femme qui commanda 500 millions d'hommes.

PAUL REINSCH, An American Diplomat in China, 1922.

*Father Ripa, Memoirs, 1855.
Sergeant, The Great Empress-Dowager of China, 1911.
Sir G. Staunton, Account of the Embassy to China, Vol. 2, 1797.
R. Swinhoe, Narrative of the North-China Campaign of 1860; 1861.
A. Thomas, Histoire de la Mission de Pékin, 2 vols., 1926.
Alfons Vath, s.j., John Adam Schall von Bell s.j., 1933.

3.—Life in Peking :

M. L. C. Bogan, Manchu Customs and Superstitions, 1928.
Henri Borel, The New China, 1912.
J. Bouchot, La Vie des Hutungs, 1922.
*J. Bredon and Mitrophanov, The Moon Year, 1927.
S. P. Conger, Letters from China, 1909.
A. Cormack, Chinese Birthday, Wedding, Funeral, and other Customs, 1927.
A. Duboscq, Sous le Ciel de Pékin, 1919.
*Wilhelm Grube, Zur Pekinger Volkskunde, 1901.
Mrs. A. Little, Round about my Peking Garden, 1905.
J. C. H. Lynn, Social Life of the Chinese in Peking, 1928.
*A. B. Freeman-Mitford, The Attaché at Peking, 1900.
*W. A. P. Martin, A Cycle of Cathay, 1897.
Dr. J. J. Matigon, Superstition, Crime et Misère en Chine, Paris 1902.
*D. F. Rennie, Peking and the Pekingese, 2 vols, 1865.
A. Resident of Peking, China as it really is, 1912.
*Student Interpreter, Where Chinese Drive, 1885.
R. W. Swallow, Sidelights on Peking Life, 1927.
Lady Susan Townley, My Chinese Note-Book, 1904.
La Vie Populaire à Pékin (Politique de Pékin), 7 Vols, 1922-1927.
E. T. C. Werner, Autumn Leaves, 1927.

4.—The Siege of the Legations :

*Rev. R. Allen, The Siege of the Legations, 1901.
Baron d'Anthouard, Les Boxeurs, 1902.
*Bland and Backhouse, China under the Empress-Dowager, 1910.
*Diary of H. E. Ching Shan (Transl. by J. J. L. Duyvendak), 1924.
R. Coltman, Beleaguered in Peking, 1901.

*E. DARCY, La Défense de la Légation de France, 1901.
LANCELOT GILES : Diary of the Boxer Riots and of the Siege of the Legations. (Christ College Magazine p.p. 4/125). 1900
W. HEINZE, Belagerung der Pekinger Gesandtschaften, 1901.
*MARY HOOKER, Behind the Scenes in Peking, 1911.
SAVAGE-LANDOR, China and the Allies, 2 vols, 1901.
F. LAUR, Le Siège de Pékin, 1904.
PIERRE LOTI, Les Derniers Jours de Pékin, 1902.
W. A. P. MARTIN, The Siege in Peking, 1900.
Dr. J. J. MATIGNON, Dix Ans au Pays du Dragon, 1910.
*H. B. MORSE, The International Relations of the Chinese Empire, 1918, Vol. III. Chaps. 8-10.
NIGEL OLIPHANT, The Siege of the Legations, 1901.
S. M. RUSSELL, The Story of the Siege of Peking, 1901.
*ARTHUR SMITH, China in Convulsion, 2 vols, 1901.
STANLEY P. SMITH, China From Within, 1901.
H. C. THOMSON, China and the Powers, 1902.
*PUTNAM WEALE, Indiscreet Letters from Peking, 1906.
WINTERHALDER, Kaempfe in China, Chap. 4, 1902.
(V. HEYKING), Briefe die ihn nicht erreichten, 1902.

5.—SPECIAL SUBJECTS :

*L. C. ARLINGTON, The Chinese Drama, 1930.
FLORENCE AYSCOUGH, A Chinese Mirror, 1925.
HENRI BERNARD, S.J., Aux Origines du Cimetière de Chala (1610-1611), Tientsin, 1934.
J. BOUCHOT, Le Temple des Lamas de Pékin, 1923.
*G. BOUILLARD, Le Temple du Ciel.
*G. BOUILLARD, Le Temple des Lamas, 1931.
DEVINE, The Four Churches at Peking, 1930.
PANKING, Livre de Cuisine d'un Gourmet Poète (Yüan Nei), 1924.
G. B. VITALE, Pekingese Rhymes, 1896.

6.—GUIDE BOOKS :

COOK's Guide to Peking, 1924.
CARL CROW : Handbook for China, 1933
ELLIS, Illustrated Guide to Peking (No date).
FEI SHI, Guide to Peking, rev. ed. 1924.
I. T. HEADLAND: Tourist Guide to Peking
Japanese Government Railways, Guide to China, 1924.

KIERUFF, Guide to Peking (Out of Print).
A. H. N. LITTLE, Guide to Peking, 1904.
MADROLLE, Northern China, Chap. 1, 1912.
" The Peiping Chronicle " Guide to Peking, 1933.

7.—PICTORIAL :
DONALD MENNIE, The Pageant of Peking, 1924.
HEINZ VON PERCKHAMMER, Peking, 1923.
OGAWA, The Imperial Palaces of Peking, 1906.

8.—ENVIRONS :
G. BOUILLARD, Les Tombeaux Impériaux, 1931.
G. BOUILLARD, Péking, et ses environs, Dixième Série,
Tsing Ming Yuan (La Fontaine de Jade), 1925.
G. BOUILLARD, Péking, et ses environs, Première Série,
Le Yang Shan et ses temples, 1922.
G. BOUILLARD, Péking, et ses environs, Septième Série,
Hsiang Shan ou Parc de Chasse, 1923.
G. BOUILLARD, Péking, et ses environs, Huitième Série,
Les Temples autour du Hsiang Shan, Tien t'ai sze,
Wo fo-sze, 1924.
CARROLL BROWN MALONE, History of the Peking Summer
Palaces under the Ch'ing Dynasty, 1934.
L. Newton HAYES, Great Wall of China, 1929.
G. E. HUBBARD, The Temples of the Western Hills, 1923.
C. T. HUTCHINS, Peking and the Surrounding Country, 1916.
J. M. PLANCHET, Le Cimetière at la paroisse de Tcheng-
Fou-sse 1732-1917, Pékin, 1918.

WORKS PARTICULARLY RECOMMENDED MARKED WITH *

APPENDIX H
DETAILS OF THE ASTRONOMICAL INSTRUMENTS CONSTRUCTED BY FATHER FERDINAND VERBIEST IN 1674

*(Capital letters refer to present position, as per sketch-map in text.
Small letters refer to original positions, as in illustration on page 157.)*

H (e) ZODIACAL ARMILLARY SPHERE.—Six feet in diameter.
Supported by the heads of four dragons whose bodies

after numerous folds rest on the ends of two brass cross-bars as support for the instrument. The ends of the brass bars are borne by four young lions whose heads work up and down by means of screws. The circles are marked on the inside and outside in divisions of 360 degrees ; each degree is divided into 60 minutes by transverse lines ; and the minutes divided at distances of ten seconds by means of sights.

E (c) ECLIPTIC ARMILLARY.—Six feet in diameter. Supported by a dragon, with back bent like a bow, his four paws, extended to four opposite points, clutch the extremities of the pedestal, which, like the preceding instrument, is formed of two cross-bars resting on four lions which serve to level it.

D (f) AZIMUTHAL HORIZON.—Six feet in diameter. Consists of a large horizontal circle. A double ruler equal to the diameter slides round the whole limb, for marking the degrees of the horizon, and carries along with it a triangle made by a string which passes through the head of an axle-tree erected perpendicularly to and in the centre of the horizon. Four twisted dragons bend their heads underneath the Great Circle to keep it steady. Two others winding round two small pillars raise themselves upwards almost in a semi-circle as far as the top of the axis to which they are rigidly attached as supports.

B (g) QUADRANT.—Six feet radius. Graduated at every tenth second. The lead for fixing it in a vertical position weighs a pound and hangs from the centre by very fine copper wires. The ruler is movable and slides readily along the limb. A twisted dragon with clouds carved about it holds the parts firmly together. Through the centre of the quadrant which is elevated in the air there passes an immovable axis round which it can be turned towards any point in the heavens. And lest its weight should cause it to shake or go out of its vertical position, two other axle-trees are set up at the sides firmly attached below to two dragons and to the middle axis by carved clouds which seem to descend from the sky.

G (h) SEXTANT.—Six feet radius. Represents the sixth part of the great circle. Supported by an axle-tree whose base is a kind of large empty basin which is held steady by dragons. In the middle is a brass pillar to the end of which is attached a machine with wheels on which the instrument revolves. To the middle of this machine a little copper bar is fixed, representing one of the radii of the sextant, and holds it immovable. The upper part terminates in a thick cylinder, the centre round which the ruler turns, whilst the lower part extends about a foot beyond the limb, to serve as a handle for raising and lowering it.

C (d) CELESTIAL GLOBE.—Six feet in diameter. The body of the globe is a perfect sphere and very smooth. The stars are well formed of tiny brass buttons and are placed in their correct positions in the skies, whilst all the circles are of a proportional breadth. The instrument is so perfectly balanced that the least touch will cause it to revolve, though it weighs more than 2,000 pounds. A large brass circular base with a channel round the edge is supported by four misshapen dragons placed at equal distances whose bristling manes support a horizon, magnificent on account of its width, the multitude of its ornaments, and the delicacy of its workmanship. The meridian which supports the axis of the globe is supported by clouds proceeding from the centre of the base on which the globe turns by means of concealed wheels. In addition the horizon, the dragons, and the crossbars at the centre, can each be moved separately, whereas the base remains stationary, thus enabling the horizon level to be so placed as to cut the globe exactly through the middle.

APPENDIX I

BIOGRAPHICAL SKETCH OF THE MING EMPEROR, YUNG LO

BORN, 1360 : DIED, A.D. 1424

Ch'êng Tsu was his dynastic title, his personal name was Ti. He was the fourth son of the first Ming Emperor, Hung Wu, by a lady-in-waiting named Wêng, who at his birth was raised to Secondary Empress, an act that caused great rivalry between her and the principal Empress Ma. When Ti had reached the age of fifteen, a conspiracy was hatched in the Palace between the Empress Wêng and several others of the Court to kill Yün-wên, the rightful heir to the throne, and elevate Ti to that position. The conspiracy leaked out, and he was arrested and imprisoned for about seven years. He was then pardoned and his conduct continuing satisfactory, the Emperor in 1390 gave him joint command with Prince Kang of Chin to lead an expedition against the North. After the capture of Peking, Hung Wu issued an edict in 1393 appointing him Prince of Yen (an old name for Peking), with full control of the armies of the North. In 1396 the Emperor ordered him to proceed to the frontier and quell a rising amongst the Mongols, and in the Fifth Moon of 1398 appointed him to the supreme command of all civil and military affairs of the North.

In the Sixth Moon of the same year, Hung Wu " departed to be a guest on high " and was succeeded by his grandson Yün-wên under the reign-title Chien Wên. The latter's tutor, Fang Hsiao-ju who had been appointed a Minister of State, persuaded the Emperor to relieve the Prince of Yen of his posts and send him to Nan-ch'ang in Kiangsi where he could be more easily watched. The Prince, however, refused to obey the summons and alarmed for the safety of his three sons, who were still in Nanking, sent for them to come to Peking. The President of the Board of War, Huang Tzǔ-chêng, and others then sent in a memorial that they be not allowed to quit Nanking but be kept there as hostages. The Emperor, however, refused to sanction their request and was taken completely by surprise when the Prince of Yen set up the standard of rebellion in the Seventh Moon of the first year of Chien Wên (1399). It seems that Chien Wên and his Minister Fang Hsiao-ju mismanaged the war, trusting to double-dealing, until, in 1402, the Prince of Yen crossed the Yangtze, and Nanking opened its gates to him.

" On his assumption of the Imperial dignity, under the now famous year-title of Yung Lo, the new Emperor showed that he could govern as well as he could fight. He brought immigrants from Shantung and Shansi to re-people the districts which had been laid waste. Peking was built, a Penal Code was drawn up, and missions under the charge of eunuchs were sent to Java, Sumatra, Siam, and even to Ceylon. Various military expeditions were dispatched against the Tartars, costing vast sums of money. In 1409, eunuchs were appointed to high official posts, and set to watch the doings of the regular staff."*

In 1419 the Japanese invaded Liao-tung, but their attempt proved a disastrous failure. In February 1421 the capital was moved to Peking. His Majesty was an ardent Buddhist, and the monks of that religion were raised to high positions and exerted great influence at Court. In 1421 there were loud complaints that some ten thousand monks were maintained in Peking, while millions of people in several provinces were reduced to eating bark and grass. Yung Lo patronized literature, and issued the huge encyclopædia known as *Yung Lo Ta Tien*, which occupied for over two years the energies of five chief directors, twenty sub-directors, and 2,629 subordinates. In addition, he is responsible for many of the beautiful palaces, parks, temples in and around Peking, as stated in various parts of this book. Yung Lo died at Yümu-ch'uan in Mongolia where he had gone to suppress an uprising, in the Seventh Moon of the 22nd year of his reign (1424).

APPENDIX J

TEMPLE WORSHIP DAYS IN PEKING

(*Fixed according to the lunar calendar*)

1.—First Moon, 2nd and 16th. At the *Wu Hsien Ts'ai Shên Miao* (Temple of the Five Gods of Riches), outside the Chang I Mên.

> Many different origins are ascribed to these deities, but the natives of Peking believe that they are five brothers, of the name of Wu, who lived in the early years of the Manchu dynasty and robbed the rich to give to the poor. In the end they were captured and executed; and their spirits roamed about the city so terrifying the natives that a petition was presented to the Throne to pacify them in some way. In the second year of K'ang Hsi (1663), therefore, this temple was built in honour of the five brothers and the rank of gods conferred upon them.

---

*Giles, Biog. Dict. No. 488.

2.—First Moon, 1st to 15th. At the *Huo Shên Miao* (Temple of the God of Fire), in the Liu Li Ch'ang (Chapter XV).

3.—First Moon, 1st to 15th. At the *Chüeh Shêng Ssŭ* (Temple of Awakening to a Sense of our former Existence), better known as the Ta Chung Ssŭ (Great Bell Temple), outside the Hsi Chih Mên. (Chapter XVII).

4.—First Moon, 1st to 19th. At the *Po Yün Kuan* (White Cloud Temple), outside the Hsi Pien Mên (Chapter XVIII).

5.—Third Moon, 1st to 5th. At the *P'an T'ao Kung*, inside the Tung Pien Mên. (Chapter XVI).

6.—Fourth Moon, 1st to 15th. At the *Hu Kuo Hung Tzŭ Kung* (Ancestral Hall of the Protectors of the State), commonly known as *Kuang Hsi T'ing* (Rambling at Hsi T'ing), outside the Hsi Chih Mên.

7.—Sixth Moon, 1st. At the *Pi Hsia Yüan Chün Miao* (Temple to the Princess of the Coloured Clouds). Generally known as *Kuang Chung T'ing* or *Ch'iao Hui* (Rambling or Seeing the sights at Chung T'ing). Outside the Yu An Mên.

> The fair formerly held at the temple of the same name outside the Yung Ting Mên, called Nan T'ing, on the 1st Day of the Fifth Moon, has been given up.

8.—Monthly. On the 2nd and 16th. At the *Ts'ai Shên Miao* (Temple of the God of Wealth).

> This deity has been ascribed to different persons. There are numerous shrines and temples dedicated to this god in Peking, the largest and most popular being that on the north side of the road just inside the Kuang Ch'ü Mên. According to legend the real God of Wealth is Pi Kan who lived during the 12th century B.C. He was the uncle and also Prime Minister of Chou Hsin, the notorious tyrant and last ruler of the Shang dynasty. When he remonstrated with the tyrant about his cruelties, the latter caused Pi Kan to be disembowelled in his presence, in order, as he said, to see whether, as was reported, the heart of a sage contained seven orifices. Pi Kan, not wanting to give the tyrant the pleasure of seeing him die, walked out of his presence, until he met an old woman who said "What! You are still going about with your heart cut out!", when he gave up the ghost. It is probably natural to suppose that a person without a heart would be the most perfect symbol to choose for a God of Riches!

9.—Monthly, 15th and 28th. At the Tung Yüeh Miao, outside the Ch'i Hua Mên (Chapter XIX).

10.—Dates variable. On the 15th of the Seventh Moon, 1st of the Tenth Moon, and the *Ch'ing Ming Chieh* (Festival of Worship at the Graves) in early spring. At the *Tu Ch'êng Huang Miao* (Temple of the City Gods).

Appendix K

DATES OF PEKING FAIRS

(The days refer to the foreign calendar)

T'u Ti Miao.—(Inside the Chang I Mên). On the 2nd, 3rd, 12th, 13th, 22nd and 23rd of each month.

Huo Shên Miao.—(At Hua Erh Shih, outside the Hata Mên). On the 4th, 14th and 24th of each month.

Pai T'a Ssŭ.—(Inside the P'ing Tsê Mên). On the 5th, 6th, 15th, 16th, 25th and 26th of each month.

Hu Kuo Ssŭ.—(Hsi Ssŭ P'ai Lou). On the 7th, 8th, 17th, 18th, 27th, and 28th of each month.

Lung Fu Ssŭ.—(Tung Ssŭ P'ai Lou). On the 1st, 2nd, 9th, 10th, 11th, 12th, 19th, 20th, 21st, 22nd, 29th and 30th of each month.

Appendix L

HOURS AND PRICE OF ADMISSION

Chapter	Hours	Price
II. Forbidden City (Entrance by the Tung Hua Mên or Hsi Hua Mên)		
South Section	9 a.m. to 4 p.m.	$0.10
II. T'ai Ho Tien, Chung Ho Tien, Pao Ho Tien		$0.50
Northern Part of Forbidden City (Entrance by the Shên Wu Mên)	10 a.m. to 3.30 p.m.	

III.	Central and Inner Sections (Wednesdays, Fridays, Sundays)		* $0.50
IV.	Inner and Outer Western Sections (Mondays, Thursdays, Saturdays)		* $0.50
V.	T'ai Miao	8.30 a.m. to 5 p.m.	$0.05
V.	Chung Shan (Central) Park		$0.05
VI.	Pei Hai		$0.05
VIII.	Altar of Heaven ..	9 a.m. to 5 p.m.	$0.30
VIII.	Altar of Agriculture ..	9 a.m. to 5 p.m.	$0.05
IX.	Coal Hill	8 a.m. to 4 p.m.	$0.05
X.	National Library ..	9 a.m. to 5 p.m.	free
XI.	Observatory	9 a.m. to 4 p.m.	$0.20
XIII.	Drum Tower	10 a.m. to 3 p.m.	$0.05
XIII.	Temple of Confucius ..	9 a.m. to 5 p.m.	$0.40
XIII.	Hall of Classics ..	9 a.m. to 5 p.m.	tip
XIII.	Lama Temple	9 a.m. to 5 p.m.	$0.45
XVII.	Yellow Temple ..	9 a.m. to 5 p.m.	$0.20
XVII.	Zoological Gardens ..	9 a.m. to 5 p.m.	$0.20
XVII.	Big Bell Temple ..		$0.20
XIX.	Tung Yüeh Miao ..		$0.50
XX.	Summer Palace	9 a.m. to 5 p.m.	
	Park and Lake ..		$1.00
	Through Ticket ..		$2.40
XXI.	Jade Fountain	9 a.m. to 5 p.m.	$0.50

(NOTE:—Above hours and prices are for rough guidance only, as they are subject to constant alteration).

*On first three days of month price of admission is $0.20

APPENDIX M.

SUGGESTED TOURS FOR EACH DAY

First Day

A.M. : Legation Quarter ; Forbidden City, South and Central Sections (Chaps 1 and 2).

P.M. : Altars of Heaven and Agriculture (Chap 8).

Second Day

A.M. : N-E Quarter of Tartar City, Lama and Confucian Temples, Hall of Classics (Chap 13).

P.M. : The Three Seas and the Coal Hill (Chaps 6, 7, and 9).

Third Day

Great Wall and Ming Tombs (Chap 25).

Fourth Day

A.M. : Northern Sections of Forbidden City (Chaps 3 and 4).

P.M. : Northern Suburbs, Yellow Temple and Altar of Earth (Chap 17).

Fifth Day

A.M. : Summer Palace and Jade Fountain (Chaps 21 and 22).

P.M. : Wo Fo Ssŭ, Pi Yün Ssŭ, Hunting Park (Chap 23).

Sixth Day

A.M. : T'ai Miao and Central Park (Chap 5).

P.M. : Eastern Suburbs, Tung Yüeh Miao, Altar of Sun (Chap 19).

Seventh Day

A.M. : S-E Quarter of Tartar City and Observatory (Chap 11).

P.M. : Chinese City, West Half (Chap 15).

Eighth Day

A.M. : West Suburbs, Marco Polo Bridge (Chap 18 and 24).

P.M. : Shih Ching Shan, Patachu, Palichuang (Chap 24).

Ninth Day

A.M. : Imperial City East Half, Mongol Temple (Chap 9).

P.M. : Chinese City, East Half (Chap 16).

Tenth Day

Hei Lung T'an, Wên Ch'uan, Ta Chüeh Ssŭ, T'angshan (Chap 23 and 25).

Eleventh Day
A.M. : N-W. Quarter of Tartar City (Chap 14).
P.M. : Imperial City, West Half (Chap 10).

Twelfth Day
Chieh T'ai Ssŭ and T'an Chê Ssŭ (Chap 24).

Thirteenth Day
S-W. Quarter of Tartar City (Chap 12).

NOTE :—The above list which is tabulated in order of suggested importance is a very compressed one and represents the maximum that could be done in one day. If more time is available, one day should be allotted to each of the chapters from 1 to 22 (excluding Chap 20), and several days to each of the chapters from 23 to 25.

INDEX

A

B

Liao dynasty, 3, 94, 185, 209, 300
Liaotung, Peninsula, 64
Liang, Manchu Duke, 15
Liang Kung Fu, *see* British Legation
Library, National (Kuo Li Pei P'ing Tu Shu Kuan), 34, 133
Lien Hua P'ao Tzŭ (Lotus Pond) 蓮花泡子, 202
Lien Hua Ssŭ (Lotus Flower Temple) 蓮花寺, 223
Lien Yüan, Manchu official, 23
Lin Hsi T'ing (Pavilion on the Brink of the Burn) 臨溪亭, 60
Ling Kuang Ssŭ (Temple of Spiritual Light) 靈光寺, 301
Lions, 327
  In front of Gates, 28
  On Roof ridges, 29
  Outside T'ien An Mên, 30
Liu Chi, 338, *see* Liu Po-Wên
Liu Chung, 221
Liu Kung-pei, 210
Liu Kuo Fan Tien, *see* Wagons-Lits
Liu Li Ch'ang, *see* " Streets "
Liu Po-wên, Astrologer, 28, 338
Liu T'ing, 143
Living Buddha, 197
Lo, River, in Honan, 72
Lo Shou T'ang (Hall of Pleasure and Longevity) 樂壽堂, 53
Loch, H. B., 202, 203, 249
Lockhart Mission Hospital, 15
Lohans, *see* Eighteen Lohans
Lohan T'ang, 羅漢堂, 288
Lots, Emperor Ch'ung Chêng, drawing lots, 182
Lotus, 91, Notes on p. 329
Louis XIV, 158
'Loyal to the Last,' *see* Yüeh Fei
Loyang, in Honan, 100
Lu, State of, 184
Lu Kou Ch'iao (Reed Ditch Bridge) 蘆溝橋, 312
Lu Pan (God of Carpenters, etc.), 29, 129, 131, 208, 232, 263
  In Ching Chung Miao, 232
  In Tung Yüeh Miao, 263
Lu Shan (Lu's Mountain) 廬山, 301

Lu Shih, the Founder of Pa Ta Chu, 盧師, 301, 303
Lu Shih An, Famous Scholar, 45
Lu Shih Ssŭ (Lu the Master's Temple), 301
Lü Tung-pin, Taoist Immortal, 154
Lucifer, 135
Lung Ch'ih T'an 龍池潭, (Dragon's Pool Altar), in Western Hills, 316
Lung Ch'ing, Ming Emperor, 221, 320
Lung Fu Ssŭ (Temple of Prosperity and Happiness) 隆福寺, 183
  Fair at, 183, 352
Lung Hua Miao (Temple of Civilizing Influences) 隆華廟, 198
Lung Wang Miao (Dragon King's Temple) 龍王廟, 295
Lung Wang T'ang (Dragon King's Hall) 龍王堂, 292, 302
Lytton Commission, 31, 327

M

Ma, Empress, 349
Ma Chia An (Ma Family Nunnery), *see* San Shan An
Ma Shên (God of Horses), 118
Ma Shên Miao (Temple of the God of Horses) 馬神廟, 123
Macdonald, Sir Claude, British Minister, 18
Mahakala Miao (or Mongol Temple) 瑪哈噶啦廟, 127
Maitreya Buddha, 194
Manchoukuo, 61
Manchu Dynasty, 6, 13, 61, 68, 111, 130, 170, 179, 184, 341
  Patron Saint of, 194
Manchuria, 3, 286
Mao Ch'i-ling, 229
'Maotzŭ' (Hairy Ones), 14
'Marble Boat,' 289
'Marble Pagoda,' The, 239, 299

Tzŭ Kuang Ko (Throne Hall of Purple Effulgence) 紫光閣, 81
Audience to Foreign Envoys in, 101-103, 330

Tz'ŭ Hsi 慈禧, "Western Empress," Late Empress-Dowager, also known as "The Old Buddha," (Lao Fo Yeh), 11, 23, 51, 52, 56, 58, 60, 61, 77, 88, 96, 100, 130, 135, 142, 150, 167, 170, 181, 201, 204, 206, 214, 240, 241, 243, 283-292, 286, 295
And Death of Aleutê, 149
And Death of Chên Fei, 55
And Death of Tz'ŭ An, 59
As Goddess of Mercy, 290
Assaults Aleutê, 47
Buries Treasure, 52
Flight in 1900, 54
Fond of Flowers, 52, 285
Death of, 80, 100
Imprisons Kuang Hsü, 96
Love of Summer Palace, 285
Overthrows Usurpers, 180
Photographed, 290
Responsibility for 1900, 22
Reviews Boxers, 131
Scolds Boxers, 53
Stops Bombardment, 137
Superstitious, 284

Tz'ŭ Ning Kung (Palace of Peace and Tranquillity) 慈寧宮, 59, 100

Tz'ŭ Shou Ssŭ (Temple of Compassionate Old Age) 慈壽寺, 308

Tz'ŭ T'ang, see Ancestral Temple

U

Unicorn 麒麟
On roof ridges, 29
Outside Palaces, 59
Tablet, 173
Evil Omen, 184

Universities, see Catholic, Peking, P.U.M.C., Yenching

U.S.A. Legation (Mei Kuo Fu) 美國府, 7, 8
Intervention against restoration, 122

V

Vassal kingdoms, 5
Vegetarianism, see Tsai Li Hui
Verbiest, Father Ferdinand, s.j., 158, 159, 346
Reforms Calendar, 159
His Tomb, 252
Versailles, Conference, 140
Treaty, 158
Veterinary, 148, 204
Victory Memorial, 70
See also Shih Shêng Szu, 300

W

Wagons-Lits Hotel (Liu Kuo Fan Tien) 六國飯店, 8
Wai Chiao Pu (Foreign Office) 外交部, 149
Wai Wu Pu (Board of Foreign Affairs) 外務部, 149
Walls, of Peking, 1
Wan Ch'un T'ing (Pavilion of Ten Thousand Springs) 萬春亭
In Forbidden City, 43
In Coal Hill, 126
Wan Li, Emperor, 134, 198, 209, 219, 240, 243, 251, 320
Wan Li Ch'ang Ch'êng (Ten Thousand Li Long Wall) 萬里長城, see Great Wall
Wan Liu T'ang (Hall of Ten Thousand Willows) 萬柳堂, 229
Wan Nien Pei (Tablet of Ten Thousand Destinies) 萬年碑, 221
Wan Shan Tien (Hall of Ten Thousand Virtues) 萬善殿, 103
Wan Shou Shan (Hill of Myriad Ages) 萬壽山, see Summer Palace, New
Wan Shou Ssŭ (Temple of Ten Thousand Ages) 萬壽寺, 243, 245
Wan Sung Lao Jên (Old Man of Ten Thousand Pines) 萬松老人, 313

Some other Oxford Paperbacks for readers interested in Central Asia,
China, Japan and South-east Asia, past and present

CAMBODIA

GEORGE COEDÈS
Angkor

MALCOLM
MacDONALD
Angkor and the Khmers*

CENTRAL ASIA

PETER FLEMING
Bayonets to Lhasa

ANDRÉ GUIBAUT
Tibetan Venture

LADY MACARTNEY
An English Lady in
Chinese Turkestan

DIANA SHIPTON
The Antique Land

C. P. SKRINE AND
PAMELA NIGHTINGALE
Macartney at Kashgar*

ERIC TEICHMAN
Journey to Turkistan

ALBERT VON LE COQ
Buried Treasures of
Chinese Turkestan

AITCHEN K. WU
Turkistan Tumult

CHINA

All About Shanghai: A
Standard Guide

HAROLD ACTON
Peonies and Ponies

VICKI BAUM
Shanghai '37

ERNEST BRAMAH
Kai Lung's Golden
Hours*

ERNEST BRAMAH
The Wallet of Kai Lung*

ANN BRIDGE
The Ginger Griffin

NIGEL CAMERON
The Chinese Smile

CHANG HSIN-HAI
The Fabulous Concubine*

CARL CROW
Handbook for China

PETER FLEMING
The Siege at Peking

ROBERT FORD
Captured in Tibet

MARY HOOKER
Behind the Scenes in
Peking

NEALE HUNTER
Shanghai Journal*

GEORGE N. KATES
The Years that Were
Fat

CORRINNE LAMB
The Chinese Festive
Board

G. E. MORRISON
An Australian in China

DESMOND NEILL
Elegant Flower

PETER QUENNELL
A Superficial Journey
through Tokyo and
Peking

OSBERT SITWELL
Escape with Me! An
Oriental Sketch-book

J. A. TURNER
Kwang Tung or Five Years
in South China

HONG KONG AND MACAU

AUSTIN COATES
City of Broken Promises

AUSTIN COATES
A Macao Narrative

AUSTIN COATES
Macao and the British

AUSTIN COATES
Myself a Mandarin

AUSTIN COATES
The Road

The Hong Kong Guide
1893

INDONESIA

S. TAKDIR ALISJAHBANA
Indonesia: Social and
Cultural Revolution

DAVID ATTENBOROUGH
Zoo Quest for a
Dragon*

VICKI BAUM
A Tale from Bali*

'BENGAL CIVILIAN'
Rambles in Java and the
Straits in 1852

MIGUEL COVARRUBIAS
Island of Bali*

BERYL DE ZOETE AND
WALTER SPIES
Dance and Drama in
Bali

AUGUSTA DE WIT
Java: Facts and Fancies

JACQUES DUMARÇAY
Borobudur

JACQUES DUMARÇAY
The Temples of Java

ANNA FORBES
Unbeaten Tracks in Islands
of the Far East

GEOFFREY GORER
Bali and Angkor

JENNIFER LINDSAY
Javanese Gamelan

EDWIN M. LOEB
Sumatra: Its History and
People

MOCHTAR LUBIS
The Outlaw and Other
Stories

MOCHTAR LUBIS
Twilight in Djakarta

MADELON H. LULOFS
Coolie*

MADELON H. LULOFS
Rubber

COLIN McPHEE
A House in Bali*

ERIC MJÖBERG
Forest Life and
Adventures in the
Malay Archipelago

HICKMAN POWELL
The Last Paradise

E. R. SCIDMORE
Java, Garden of the
East

MICHAEL SMITHIES
Yogyakarta:
Cultural Heart of
Indonesia

LADISLAO SZÉKELY
Tropic Fever: The
  Adventures of a Planter
  in Sumatra

EDWARD C. VAN NESS AND
SHITA PRAWIROHARDJO
Javanese Wayang Kulit

JAPAN

WILLIAM PLOMER
Sado

MALAYSIA

ISABELLA L. BIRD
The Golden Chersonese:
  Travels in Malaya in
  1879

MARGARET BROOKE
THE RANEE OF SARAWAK
My Life in Sarawak

HENRI FAUCONNIER
The Soul of Malaya

W. R. GEDDES
Nine Dayak Nights

A. G. GLENISTER
The Birds of the Malay
  Peninsula, Singapore and
  Penang

C. W. HARRISON
Illustrated Guide to the
  Federated Malay States
  (1923)

BARBARA HARRISSON
Orang-Utan

TOM HARRISSON
World Within: A Borneo
  Story

CHARLES HOSE
The Field-Book of a
  Jungle-Wallah

EMILY INNES
The Chersonese with the
  Gilding Off

W. SOMERSET MAUGHAM
Ah King and Other Stories*

W. SOMERSET MAUGHAM
The Casuarina Tree*

MARY McMINNIES
The Flying Fox*

ROBERT PAYNE
The White Rajahs of
  Sarawak

OWEN RUTTER
The Pirate Wind

ROBERT W. SHELFORD
A Naturalist in Borneo

CARVETH WELLS
Six Years in the Malay
  Jungle

SINGAPORE

RUSSELL GRENFELL
Main Fleet to Singapore

R. W. E. HARPER AND
HARRY MILLER
Singapore Mutiny

JANET LIM
Sold for Silver

G. M. REITH
Handbook to Singapore
  (1907)

C. E. WURTZBURG
Raffles of the Eastern
  Isles

THAILAND

CARL BOCK
Temples and Elephants

REGINALD CAMPBELL
Teak-Wallah

MALCOLM SMITH
A Physician at the Court
  of Siam

ERNEST YOUNG
The Kingdom of the
  Yellow Robe

Titles marked with an asterisk have restricted rights.